THE
LGBTQ+
COMICS
STUDIES
READER

THE LGBTQ+ COMICS STUDIES READER

CRITICAL OPENINGS, FUTURE DIRECTIONS

EDITED BY ALISON HALSALL AND JONATHAN WARREN

UNIVERSITY PRESS OF MISSISSIPPI / JACKSON

The University Press of Mississippi is the scholarly publishing agency of
the Mississippi Institutions of Higher Learning: Alcorn State University,
Delta State University, Jackson State University, Mississippi State University,
Mississippi University for Women, Mississippi Valley State University,
University of Mississippi, and University of Southern Mississippi.

www.upress.state.ms.us

The University Press of Mississippi is a member
of the Association of University Presses.

Library of Congress Cataloging-in-Publication Data

Names: Halsall, Alison, editor. | Warren, Jonathan, editor.
Title: The LGBTQ+ comics studies reader : critical openings, future
    directions / Alison Halsall, Jonathan Warren.
Description: Jackson : University Press of Mississippi, 2022. | Includes
    bibliographical references and index.
Identifiers: LCCN 2022023766 (print) | LCCN 2022023767 (ebook) | ISBN
    9781496841346 (hardback) | ISBN 9781496841353 (trade paperback) | ISBN
    9781496841360 (epub) | ISBN 9781496841377 (epub) | ISBN 9781496841384
    (pdf) | ISBN 9781496841391 (pdf)
Subjects: LCSH: Queer comic books, strips, etc. | Sexual minorities—Comic
    books, strips, etc. | Sexual minority culture. | Sexual minority
    community—Comic books, strips, etc. | Gays—Comic books, strips, etc. |
    Lesbians—Comic books, strips, etc. | Transgender people—Comic books,
    strips, etc.
Classification: LCC HQ73 .L425 2022 (print) | LCC HQ73 (ebook) | DDC
    306.76—dc23/eng/20220709
LC record available at https://lccn.loc.gov/2022023766
LC ebook record available at https://lccn.loc.gov/2022023767

British Library Cataloging-in-Publication Data available

CONTENTS

III. RESILIENCE: BECOMING QUEER

IV. SEEN/SCENE: DISCOVERY, VISIBILITY, COMMUNITY

THE
LGBTQ+
COMICS
STUDIES
READER

GENERAL INTRODUCTION

ALISON HALSALL AND JONATHAN WARREN

"Seeing ourselves reflected accurately in the world is crucial to a sense of well-being, to feeling whole and real."
—**Alison Bechdel,** foreword to Dylan Edwards's *Transposes*

Once upon a time, not terribly long ago, it might have been conceivable that an attendee at Toronto's annual Lesbian Gay Bisexual Trans* and Queer (LGBTQ+) Pride weekend could perceive the crush of celebrants for the climactic parade, emerging from a staging area down in one of the city's many miraculous green ravines, so near to and yet largely invisible from the vantage of the humdrum surface streets, as a momentary and transitory eruption of gayness into an otherwise utterly unqueer cityscape. Like a suddenly appearing tributary of dazzling lava, the LGBTQ+ revelry would flow through the central retail district, find its way to the gay village and, by Monday morning, leave little trace. Queerness in comics may have once struck a reader that way: as an exceptional disruption to a set of norms that its appearance left largely or superficially in place. But even when such "events"—the insinuation of non-standard gender expression, the whiff of same-sex inclination—occurred in comics history, there were also readers excited to discern them as a measure of the rising level of gay magma, roiling just beneath the surface. For them, the pride parade would never have been only the exception, but always the delicious promise of an endless proliferation of queerness bubbling up out of the city's underground, there year-round and more and more clear for those with eyes to notice. So, when in February 1939, Milton Caniff's *Terry and the Pirates* introduced Sanjak, the butch, genderqueer, and possibly lesbian-coded alter ego of the otherwise inconsequential Madame Sud, Caniff's fan mail preserves for us the recognition of and eagerness for this "most colorful personality" from women who frankly "wish she was a real person I could go for her myself" and who were attuned to relish the sapphic energy of "a jewel . . . single, unafraid, and cynically humorous" (McGurk and Robb). The women who were excited enough about Sanjak to write to her creator were reading comics queerly almost a century ago, noticing and relishing her as the visible hint of a vast subsurface sea amid which they lived lives that they might or might not self-identify as

LGBTQ+ but whose queerness is evident enough in their so particular and avid comics fandom.[1]

As in places like Toronto, where pride celebrations have come more and more to feel special not so much for their difference from the rest of the year but in their acknowledgment and affirmation of how queer the city's life has become generally, it now feels like a long time since LGBTQ+ comics achieved similar critical mass. Indeed, we are able to gauge the surfeit of LGBTQ+ comics by way of the profusion of excellent criticism about them. *The LGBTQ+ Comics Studies Reader* honors that under-celebrated category of comics scholarship, writing about LGBTQ+ comics that presaged, emerged from, and were influenced by the underground and alternative comics scenes of the mid-1960s and after, their critical openings, their provocative current iterations, and their future directions. This *Reader* provides a platform for sustained, theoretically rigorous thinking about the various social, economic, historical, cultural, ethical, affective, and pedagogical issues at work in LGBTQ+ comics from around the world. It takes up scholarship inspired by the work of self-identified LGBTQ+ comics creators as well as the queerness of other comics that have been meaningful to LGBTQ+ readers. Bringing together different ways of understanding comics' LGBTQ+-ness, among its other powerful modes of inquiry, the *Reader*'s chapters look at certain innovative and influential creators who self-identify as LGBTQ+, including Diane DiMassa, Gengoroh Tagame, Justin Hall, Howard Cruse, Jennifer Camper, and Edie Fake; explore work with meaningful queer content by creators who do not self-identify as LGBTQ+; examine familiar and not-so-familiar LGBTQ+ touchstone characterizations, including the lesbian activist, the bondage/domination sadomasochist (BDSM) trainer and initiate, the sexual health advocate, the queer detective figure, the gay superhero, the teen outsider, and the butch mother; track the reception of LGBTQ+ comics in print, online, and in different media; reflect on the political and activist work represented in and performed by LGBTQ+ comics; situate the historical emergence and flourishing of LGBTQ+ comics in varied regional publication, commercial, and sexual cultures; address how LGBTQ+ comics posit specifically queer modes of knowing oneself and one's world; and consider LGBTQ+ comics' visualizations of desire, sexuality, and gender expression across time and place. "In order to capture the capaciousness of queer gender and sexuality we cannot presume a stable ground of 'gay' or 'lesbian' or 'bisexual' or 'transgender' identity," Ramzi Fawaz reminds us in the interview included in this collection. "All of those terms have multiple meanings in different contexts" (Fawaz, see page 102). Remembering Eve Kosofsky Sedgwick's understanding of queer as an "open mesh of possibilities, gaps, overlaps, dissonances and resonances, lapses and excesses of meaning" (1993, 8), *The LGBTQ+ Comics Studies Reader*'s multiple voices engage, address, and question the possibilities of LGBTQ+ comics from various scholarly and critical positions, multiple geographical vantages, and across a range of queer lived experience. With that in mind, the *Reader* makes room for long-form critical engagements and shorter focused readings of specific comics by scholars at different stages of their careers.

• • •

If you go looking for a tipping-point moment or placeable ur spot, a when or a where at which LGBTQ+ comics' proliferation originated, their everywhere-at-once-ness today makes fun of the tantalizing premise. Is there a particular rocket launch of an artistic career that recast the world? No doubt the popular and critical achievement of Alison Bechdel's syndicated comic strip *Dykes to Watch Out For* (1983–2008) and her graphic memoir *Fun Home: A Family Tragicomic* (2006) stand out not just for the impact of Bechdel's multi-decade cultivation and consolidation of an enthusiastic queer comic strip readership but as an astonishing instance of a queer comics artist finding sweeping mainstream success. Not since Art Spiegelman's *Maus* (1980–1991, 1991) made major commercial presses receptive to ambitious comics, especially when the complexity, maturity, or gravitas of their subjects resonated with the prestige-asserting "graphic novel" label, has there been anything to rival what Bechdel has done. Indeed, Bechdel has set the new standard for triumph. Now translated into French, Italian, Spanish, Portuguese, German, Hungarian, Korean, Polish, and Chinese, *Fun Home* is an increasingly global phenomenon. Her career links the LGBTQ+ comics' underground to the ambit of prestige publishing and Broadway, where the stage adaptation of *Fun Home* won the 2015 Tony Award for Best Musical, ranges in genre from the soap opera seriality of her episodic comic strip to her long-form comic memoirs, generates diverse fandoms that include teachers, critics, and scholars, and attests to the protean energy of LGBTQ+ comics and the interest and curiosity contemporary audiences have for queer narratives.

Might that audience readiness be traceable to foregoing developments in the world of comic book publishing? The 1989 revision of the Comics Code relaxed rules governing the representation of queer characters and content in comic books.[2] Since then, the major American publishers, DC, Marvel, and Archie Comics have incorporated LGBTQ+ characters into their storylines with increasing frequency. The innuendo and implication in which Golden and Silver Age comic books and contemporaneous comic strips trafficked, the villainizing of effeminate masculinity (as with *Flash Gordon*'s race-baiting Ming the Merciless) or masculine femininity (cue early *Wonder Woman*'s cast of cold-hearted Nazis), the pathologizing of same-sex orientations as criminal fixations or obsessions, and the all but total invisibility of trans* lives gradually ebbed as comic books in the late 1980s and early 1990s found ways to include LGBTQ+ minor characters and small opportunities to begin to humanize self-identified queer people. Initially, this mostly meant that LGBTQ+ characters were present to do little but allow others soberly to accept them, their "choice" or "sexual preference," or, as in the earliest 1990s DC comics representation of trans* life to shrink their whole personhood to a matter of what gendered name would end up on their tombstone. Like such lingering exoticizing of queer lives and their exclusive use as abbreviations for kinds of non-queer anxiety and awkward virtue signaling more generally, Marvel's specific aversion to gay content in the 1980s and its 1990s practice of relegating gay representation to an "Adults Only" label has also not survived.

As with a proliferation of LGBTQ+ characters at DC comics, including a lesbian Batwoman, a bisexual Pied Piper, and Midnighter and Apollo, super-hero comics' "most iconic queer couple" (Avery 2016), Marvel's retinue now includes numerous self-identified LGBTQ+ superheroes and villains whose more fully realized queer identities are integrated organically and plausibly into characterization and plotting. Marvel's series *The Young Avengers*, the recipient of multiple Gay and Lesbian Alliance Against Defamation (GLAAD) awards, debuted with two gay teenagers featured as major characters and eventually revealed that most of the other Avengers are also LGBTQ+. The Young Avenger, America Chavez, recently starred in her own comics series (Garcia 2017), marking the culmination of over fifty Latinx Marvel and DC superheroes and supervillains that precede her (Aldama and González 2016, 10). A far cry from the stereotypically fey Gregario de la Vega, otherwise known as Extraño, and Hero Cruz, the Afro-Puerto Rican superhero from Metropolis whose exaggerated masculinity belied a presumed need to compensate for his sexuality, America Chavez's strength is inseparable from her lesbian swagger and queer intersectionality. With iconic brown skin, dark hair, and gold hoop earrings complementing her uniform's American red, white, and blue, Chavez embodies bicultural and bilingual power through a character as deeply intersectional as her United States, where multiple chosen families provide her a refuge, a home, and a complex "in-between space" (Aldama 2017, 103) for stories featuring the interrelated resilience and precarity of American women, and LGBTQ+ and Latinx communities. Chavez is a "powerful and confident strong brown girl, [with] every right to be front and center in her own comics series. . . . Even with all the haters shouting and doubting, you believe in her" (Rivera 2018, n.p.). It is remarkable that, in today's comics world, we would be unsurprised that even Archie Comics, the traditional redoubt of "wholesome" formulaic heterosexlessness, introduced a gay character who has gone on to star in two of his own comic digest series and to marry his boyfriend.

While such mainstream, profit-driven American comics enterprises spent a generation's time figuring out how to acknowledge the existence of LGBTQ+ lives, queer and queer-positive creators continued to abound, mostly unrestricted by the Code or the dictates of company style books or the obligation to satisfy corporate sales margins. Without apparent torturous effort, American alternative comics could more easily channel the liberated spirit of the norm-breaking underground. In the 1980s, queer-positive, alternative comics artists gave readers the intricate tenderness of queer lives in *Love and Rockets* (Gilbert, Jaime, and Mario Hernandez) and the epic, serialized story of love, sexual fluidity, and polyamory, *Strangers in Paradise* (Terry Moore). In the early 1990s, in *Ernie Pook's Comeek*, Lynda Barry's right-on child heroine, Marlys Mullen, was already saying, "Excuse me but right on and welcome to the queers," calling out a homophobic assault on her uncle and his boyfriend and defying her friends' bigoted parents:

> Personally I like queers!!! So far I only know two queers and I am looking for more queers!!! So if you see me please say hi don't be all snobbish!!! Also if you know other queers tell them "Marlys says hi." Say "right on from Marlys" and do the power sign. And if you see my uncle John and Bill please say I miss them and come back soon. (2016, n.p.)

Certainly, by the late 2010s, there was no disputing comics scholar Hillary Chute: "Queer comics are one of the most vibrant areas of contemporary comics" (2017, 349). In 2012, Justin Hall's trail-blazing anthology *No Straight Lines: Four Decades of Queer Comics* looked toward the vibrant productivity of the underground and alternative comics scenes to celebrate an already deep history by way of assembling a dazzling showcase of stylistically and emotionally diverse works by queer comics powerhouses, legends, forebears, and innovators, many of whom continue to produce new work. Hall's book spurred Peabody Award-winning and Emmy-nominated filmmaker Vivian Kleiman to begin shooting her documentary *No Straight Lines: The Rise of Queer Comics*, which profiled the work of artists whom Chute dubs "pioneers": Bechdel, Camper, Cruse, Rupert Kinnard, and Mary Wings.

The first decades of the twenty-first century have enjoyed a further surge in all kinds of queer comics, from work that moves past realist, memoir-driven stories to speculative fiction or magic realism, among many other comics sub-genres. The explosion in generic and topical diversification of LGBTQ+ comics correlates with a transformation in how queer comics circulate. The availability and range of queer comics (online and in print) has increased dramatically since 2010, and that greater variety reflects the "evolving nature and politics of queer identities" (Hall 2018, 299). Along with stories that feature

Figure I.1. "Marlys' Guide to Queers," Lynda Barry, in *The! Greatest! Of! Marlys!* (Fantagraphics, 2016), n.p.

gay, lesbian, and bisexual lives and characters are more comics featuring trans* and nonbinary ones. A now well-established cadre of LGBTQ+ creative, media, publishing, and political advocacy groups regularly acknowledges, promotes, and celebrates these developments. Prism Comics, a nonprofit, all-volunteer organization that formed in 2003 to support LGBTQ+ and LGBTQ+-friendly comics, comics professionals, readers, and educators with an organization and internet presence where LGBTQ+ and LGBTQ+-friendly comics creators could network and share their comics and readers could find works that spoke directly to their experiences and lives, presents annual awards to recognize, promote, and celebrate diversity and excellence in the field of queer comics. Likewise, GLAAD, the American Library Association, and the Human

Rights Campaign Foundation (the educational arm of America's largest civil rights organization working to achieve lesbian, gay, bisexual, and transgender equality) all regularly acknowledge and find common cause by supporting LGBTQ+ comics.

From comics' earliest days, their queerness was emergent, incipient, and implicit. Now, in sequential art the world over, LGBTQ+ comics proliferate across every genre and type. LGBTQ+ characters and ways of being are apt to feature organically in the worlds of mainstream, commercial comics, to anchor narratives of their own, and to propel a multitude of alternative press comics. Protean, widespread, and powerful, LGBTQ+ comics assert an unstoppable, enduring, and transformational affect: revealing comics' queer implications and subtending energy, and insisting on the value of LGBTQ+ art, artists, and lives.

• • •

From their humble beginnings in newsprint culture, comics have always accrued readership in part as a mark of their functionality and service as a gateway to various kinds of literacy, as specifically concerned with the relationship between cultural outsiders and insiders. If we think of literacy most broadly as the ability to read not just written language but all sorts of signs and social codes, for example, we will recall that a familiar feature of the economic history of the American newspaper strips that emerged and competed for influence at the end of the nineteenth century is that they leveraged comics' pictographic appeal to expand sales of English-language print journalism to inexpert readers of English (especially urban immigrants and the poor), and served as a means of entry for new Americans to the proclivities and oddities of newspaper discourse, American political rhetoric, sensational culture, urban multiplicity, and capitalistic valuation, along with English-language literacy. Similarly, young readers have become accustomed and inured to the expectations of subgenre and the pleasures of intertextuality via the primer-like regularity of such attributes in superhero comics, and they do so in sync with learning to navigate comics' useful and powerful abbreviation, simplification, or distortion of notions of identity at the level of the individual (self, body, mind) and the collective (tribe, people, culture, nation) as comics inscribe habits of outlook and understanding. Comics carve deep grooves of readerly normativity while their familiar patterns also activate and designate overdetermined and multifaceted crossings and intersections. Increasingly, as the twentieth century wore on, queer tendencies and possibilities in comics and newspaper strips provided a literacy of another sort: the ability to read and recognize social and identity cues that affirmed ways of being for readers attuned to the non-normative. Wonderfully resonant and quietly subversive character

Figure I.2. *Terry and the Pirates*, Milton Caniff, February 12, 1939.

types like Batman and Robin, Sanjak, Wonder Woman, Peppermint Patty and Marcie, and many others broadened the representational scope of comics, even though these figures were frequently influenced by negative social stereotypes or homophobic medico-scientific opinions about queer ways of being (Abate 2018). Part of the eventual purpose of more open and explicit LGBTQ+ comics was therefore to teach another kind of legibility: one of pride, empowerment, representational affirmation, and social activism.

Contending with that diversity of implicit and explicit representation is a tremendous appeal of and important challenge for comics scholarship. The elegant simplicity of comics—key to their accessibility to novice readers—has supported valuable critical attention to correlatively straightforward notions of national affiliations, historical periodicity, taxonomies of narrative style, and species of subgenre and theme. We have treatments of American comics, comics of the Golden Age, gag strips and episodic storylines, detective comics, the underground and the mainstream, and more. And within such stabilizing heuristic categories, exceptional, norm-busting oddities often prove the rules. *Krazy Kat*'s aesthetico-erotic logical whirligig in George Herriman's Coconino County runs up against Harold Gray's right-wing fantasia in *Little Orphan Annie*, but both are explicable as creations of the American 1920s and '30s. Another approach to such comics respects their referential sprawl and intersections as a mark of their particularly queer vitality and instructiveness. *MAD* magazine's eruption in the midst of an oppressive culture of hyper-conformity helped readers to acknowledge what was already worth asking. What if the sado-masochistic perpetual motion machine of Krazy and Ignatz's cockamamie desert romance—with its joyful free play of identity, role, desire, control, sex, gender, feeling, and knowing—were a primer for, and not an exception to, the age of heroic procedurals, obsessions with law and order, displays of muscle and force, and paeans to reason and morality? Seen that way, the bright

Figure I.3. *Krazy Kat*, George Herriman, 1939.

sunlight of Metropolis, the contentment of Little Orphan Annie in the arms of Daddy Warbucks, and the teen rituals of *Archie*'s Riverdale inevitably prompt their own satirical dismantlement. The brightly lit normality of comics is not a countermeasure to their subversiveness; it is a measure of its implicit depth.

Gradually, out of early American comics' murky innuendo began to emerge numerous comics featuring openly gay and lesbian characters and themes, though such comics sometimes struggled to find a place in the mainstream or to survive by its side. Considering that comics' readers have themselves often been queer subjects, identified as sexual deviants, juvenile delinquents, dropouts, the working class, and/or minorities (Scott and Fawaz 2018, 197), it isn't surprising that at almost every stage of their cultural history, "comic books have been linked to queerness or to broader questions of sexuality and sexual identity in U.S. society" (Scott and Fawaz 2018, 198).[3] Three daily strips in the United States featured characters who could be read as lesbian, well before 1950: *Lucy and Sophie Say Goodbye* (1905), *Terry and the Pirates* (1934), and *Brenda Starr, Reporter* (1940) (McGurk 2018). Even so, early comics relied predominantly on negative stereotypes. Fredric Wertham's anti-comics crusade, partly fueled by his fretting over possible homosexual subtexts in comic book depictions of Batman and Robin, and ostensibly hinted-at glorifications of BDSM and lesbianism in early Wonder Woman comics, had the ironic consequence of crediting works of disposable pop culture with profound significance and encouraging other less panicked readers to look at comics anew and more deeply, enriching the sophistication and range of their appreciation. The kind of subversive literacy and legibility that were encouraged—about gender and sexual nonconformity, about public and private identities, about varied modes of affective attachment and affinity, for example—linked comics readership to queerness and to the activism of the nascent gay liberation movement in the years before the Stonewall riots of late June 1969. Fawaz contends that the revitalized Marvel comic books of the 1960s and '70s, particularly *The Fantastic Four* and *X-Men*, repaid such queer attention with stories and visualizations that were infused with the political ideals of gay and women's liberation, and superheroes dramatizing the politics of inequality, exclusion, and difference (2016, 144).

In the United States, LGBTQ+ comics also emerged from and were influenced by the underground and alternative comics scenes of the mid-1960s and after. One of the first female artists of the underground, Trina Robbins founded *It Ain't Me, Babe Comix* in San Francisco in 1970, and formed a collective of other women to produce the *Wimmen's Comix* anthology with which she was involved for twenty years. Beyond offering a powerful corrective to that era's comics misogyny, *Wimmen's Comix* no. 1 featured Robbins's *Sandy Comes Out*, the first comic strip about an "out" lesbian that was not derogatory or erotic. The "Sandy" in Robbins's title was based on and received creative input from the sister of the underground comics star, R. Crumb, himself well-known for introducing an ethos of unblushing and sometimes uncomfortable sexual candor to comics. The crosscurrents, personal connections, and artistic influences within the underground scene suggest that the origins of the underground's penchant for bracing sexual frankness are just as attributable to Robbins as to Crumb. Another of the founders of *Wimmen's Comix*, Lee Marrs created comics parodies of mainstream culture featuring lesbians in the place of heterosexual characters and a three-part comic book series *The Further Fattening Adventures of Pudge, Girl Blimp* (1973) that was an early exemplar of bisexual representation before bringing her powerful, queer, feminist sensibility to bear on the mainstream comics to which she contributed for DC, Marvel, Dark Horse, and others.

For American queer comics artists especially, the counter-cultural impulses of the underground were turbocharged during the immediate, post-Stonewall 1970s, as the emerging precepts of gay liberation found expression throughout the era's LGBTQ+ cultural forms:

> Unlike traditional gay culture, the new culture publicly affirms rather than conceals our identity and confronts society with gay sexuality and demands equal rights rather than seeking to win tolerance by "neutralizing moral indignation." The new gay culture is concerned not just with affirming the rights and legitimacy of being homosexual; it is also, and

equally, concerned with working out ways of living as a homosexual in a society that assumed happiness is predicated on the heterosexual family. . . . Thus gay culture addresses itself to questions of who we are and how we should live. . . . Having so recognized ourselves, we rely on cultural forms, both social and aesthetic, to help show us how to live. (Altman 1982, 155–56)

Writing at the time, Dennis Altman noted a penchant for realism in lieu of the closet's legacy of "disguise and evasions" (158), authenticity, political consciousness, the assertion of the validity of LGBTQ+ sex and emotions, the open and legitimating use of gay terminology and references, and an abiding ethos of self-affirmation. Reflecting on the scope and impact of gay liberation, Karla Jay attests to the superlative importance of LGBTQ+ culture:

The culture that has grown since the Stonewall rebellion has been an important contribution (perhaps the most important) of the current gay and lesbian movements. Legislative gains have been minimal. We have merely chipped away at silences and at social prejudice; we have gained but a few token open representatives in prestigious positions (although thousands more lurk in the closets!). But in the almost ten years since the Stonewall uprising we have created a culture and put fruitful energy into unearthing our heritage. That's a major achievement. Even if all the laws turn against us, if the so-called backlash of heterosexuals against "permissiveness" increases . . . we will still have our songs to sing, our books to keep with us, our herstory to treasure in our hearts, and the knowledge that there is a common core uniting us as a people. (1979, 50–51)

It is in that light, that we should appreciate the significance of Howard Cruse's pivotal contributions to LGBTQ+ comics publishing. Appreciating the abundance of queer creativity at play among the era's comics artists and others, at the end of the 1970s, the underground comics publisher, Denis Kitchen encouraged Cruse to edit an anthology of gay comics. The result, *Gay Comix*, became the principal venue for gay-themed comics throughout the 1980s. It included work by emerging artists like Bechdel, Wings, Marrs, Roberta Gregory, Jerry Mills, Tim Barela, as well as Cruse himself, and, in a first for comics history, featured depictions of actual gay and lesbian lives. *Gay Comix* was one of the longest running underground comics anthologies, publishing twenty-five issues over eighteen years, and it was groundbreaking in its encouragement of gender equity among its contributors. Alison Bechdel frequently attributes the discovery of a first issue of *Gay Comix* in a local gay and lesbian bookstore as a galvanizing moment for her sense of queer creative purpose (2020, n.p.).

Embracing and asserting LGBTQ+ sexuality, Cruse's anthologies did not shy away from comic depictions of erotic queerness, but the roughly contemporaneous anthology of gay erotic comics edited by Winston Leyland, the founder of Gay Sunshine Press, the oldest LGBTQ+ publishing house in the United States: *Meatmen*. The anthology, which appeared in twenty-six paperback volumes between 1986 and 2004, featured Cruse's more sexually explicit work as well as that of such titans of gay beefcake illustration, erotic art, and sexually explicit comics as Tom of Finland (Touko Laaksonen), (Gerard P.) Donelan, Patrick Fillion, and many others. The enduring popularity of queer erotica connects modern, post-Stonewall LGBTQ+ history to its antecedents when the secretive circulation of such images was more fraught and dangerous, and by the late 1970s and '80s the proliferation of sexually explicit comics was an index of gay liberation. The anthologizing impulse was taken up with respect to what many consider the early 1990s golden age of "dyke" comics. Two of the longest-running lesbian strips characterize the period's lesbian comics creative energy: Bechdel's *Dykes to Watch Out For* and Diane DiMassa's *Hothead Paisan* (which debuted in 1991). Many of the best English-language lesbian comics are collected in *Dyke Strippers: Lesbian Cartoonists A to Z* (1995), edited by Roz Warren, including work by Paige Braddock, Jennifer Camper, Leanne Franson, and Roberta Gregory.

By the close of the 1980s, LGBTQ+ artists were transforming how queer lives appeared in comics. Within the imagined worlds of LGBTQ+ comics, the underground comics collectives that LGBTQ+ comics creators formed, and the pages of LGBTQ+ comics anthologies, an ethos of LGBTQ+ identity, community, and togetherness flourished as the best means of survival in response to the real precarity of queer lives, especially in the face of anti-LGBTQ+ bigotry and the existential threat of the HIV/AIDS crisis. Comics that featured collectives—whether a lesbian "cohort" of comics creators united against homophobia or creators of graphic memoirs about HIV/AIDS, like David Wojnarowicz, James Romberger, and Marguerite Van Cook's collaboration in *7 Miles a Second* (1996), *Strip AIDS* (1987), and *Strip AIDS U.S.A.: A Collection of Cartoon Art to Benefit People with AIDS* (1988)—acknowledged, respected, and appreciated the particularity of individual LGBTQ+ lives on both sides of the Atlantic while projecting common purpose and solidarity in their defense. Moreover, they elicited solidarity from their readers, whether visualizing the different regionally inflected experiences of people living with HIV/AIDS or weathering homophobic violence, LGBTQ+ comics encourage readers' sympathetic identification and invite their audience to share their characters' emotional and affective states. Often they evoke rage: rage against disease, against homophobia, against the dehumanizing American political machine, against the intransigence of government officials, against the glorification of the nation's military-industrial complex, against neo-liberalism, and so on. In their own very different ways, Wojnarowicz's fury and the evergreen ire of DiMassa's spectacularly irreverent *Hothead Paisan* each exemplify LGBTQ+ comics impelled to provoke readers' political response, to seek action, and to propel social transformation.

To J. Jack Halberstam, the transgender body is understandable as "futurity itself, a kind of heroic fulfillment of postmodern promises of gender flexibility" (2005, 18). The recent exciting onrush of trans* and gender-queer comics certainly suggests that LGBTQ+ comics now and to come will be an extension of such futurity. The commensurability of comics' aptitudes for abstraction, plasticity, seriality, and open potentiality with trans* comics' aesthetic and narrative investments in the protean possibilities of embodiment, pliability, and metamorphosis are tested with great imaginative adventurousness and visual experimentalism in Edie Fake's *Gaylord Phoenix* (2010) and Jeremy Sorese's *Curveball* (2015). David Kottler's story "I'm Me" in *Gay Comix*, issue 3 (1983), and Diana Green's *Tranny Towers* in *Gay Comics*, issue 19, are two landmarks from the earliest self-identified trans* comics creators (Hall 2018, 299). Gina Kamentsky's *T-Gina: A Transgendered Gal's Search for Validation and a Decent Cup of Coffee* and Dylan Edwards's *Tranny Toons* both appeared in 2001, and Edwards followed these comics up with *Transposes* (2012), a graphic novel about six queer-identified trans men. *Transposes* begins with an etymological breakdown of the title that emphasizes movement, change, alteration, transformation, and the continuous process of transition that eludes a fixed state of gender identity, marking a significant departure from early trans* autobiographies with their focus on closure as providing affirmation of the creator's new gender identity. For example, Higu Rose's *Tittychop Boobslash* (2017) and Victor Martins's *You Don't Have to Be Afraid of Me* (2018) make use of the comics form to elude any fixed sense of gender identity. Likewise, trans* storyteller and graphic novelist Elisha Lim's *100 Crushes* (2014) catalogues 100 single-page illustrated biographies of the artist's former crushes or infatuations that in turn affirm the creator's continuous and life-long explorations of gender and sexual experience.

• • •

LGBTQ+ self-knowing and representation—what David M. Halperin calls "how to be gay"—depends upon traceable and variously inflected kinds of noticing, appreciating, and making use of overdetermined, queer-ready cultural instruments. This happened among readers and creators of American comics who knew how to make use of comics' ability to fracture and problematize notions of American hegemonic normality. Of course, queer subversion in comics is hardly exclusive to the United States, but LGBTQ+ comics' functionality as disruptions of the normative varies by locality in ways that can indicate the exceptional fervency of homophobia in the American context and the value of considering the other specific local textures of LGBTQ+ liberation. Just a few examples hint at the variety of ways in which LGBTQ+ work speaks to its particular locale in ways that differ from an American framing. In France in the 1970s, underground writers and artists refocused comics as adult entertainment, social commentary, and theoretically inflected artistic provocation. Emerging from her participation with the creatively revolutionary Bazooka Group in the 1970s—which had differentiated itself stylistically from other comics innovators who were ironically emulating the so-called *ligne claire* style, most famously associated with Hergé's *Tintin*, so as to underscore the artifice and constructedness of traditional comics' fictional worlds, and instead favoring collage to defamiliarize the reality effect of authoritative images—Olivia Clavel used traditional comic book style in her sexually explicit adventure comic, *Matcho Girl* (1980) to resist heterocentrism by means of its radical queer feminist themes. In Germany, Ralf König's astonishingly successful career has been largely unimpeded by his coming out in the 1970s or by the fact that his comics are often set in a gay milieu. König's early work was collected as *SchwulComix* (Gay Comics) and published in multiple volumes beginning in 1981. They have spawned several film adaptations, and König was the subject of a 2012 Rosa von Praunheim documentary film tribute, *König des Comics*. In Spain in the 1970s and '80s, Nazario, "the god-father of Spanish underground comics" (Hall 2018, 293), connected with other comics creators to form the collective, El Rollo Enmascarado, to produce underground comics that spoke out against the police and Francoist censors. In *Anarcoma*, which first appeared as a comic strip in a pornographic magazine and, by 1979, was a recurring feature in *El Víbora*, the now-defunct Spanish alternative comics monthly, Nazario uses the transsexual titular detective to challenge oppressive cultural and sexual expectations in post-Franco Spain.[4] Although it is not an LGBTQ+ comics memoir per se, even Marjane Satrapi's depiction of bicultural translocation, marginalization, closeting, and self-discovery in *Persepolis* (2000, 2004) affords a queer reading for its resonances with the corollary LGBTQ+ tropes like discomfiture with normative power, pleasure found in liberating cultural expression, and self-affirmation. We could go on.

To be sure, American comics wield outsized influence, yoked as they are to the juggernaut of global capitalism. Yet the most evocative recent American comics complicate the premise of American hegemonic coherence. Gilbert Hernandez's *Julio's Day*—serialized from 2001 to 2007 in *Love and Rockets*, and published as an expanded, stand-alone graphic novel in 2013—personalizes 100 years of experience via a protagonist whose life span may match that of the so-called American century but whose story is largely divorced from ostensibly explanatory landmarks of that history and whose adumbrated sexuality becomes legible through surprising and mostly unacknowledged attachments to his extended biological family's idiosyncratic experiences of desire. Even *Superman*, after all, distributes a story about consolidated American power within which we find subtended stories of cultural, racial, and planetary dislocation and dispossession, secret identity, public and private gender performance, and solitude and sociality. LGBTQ+ comics around the world do not simply speak back to Americanness, but they speak through and within a global web of interrelated queer topicality the primers for which have been comics' representations of bearding, fronting, concealment, fear of being outed, migration, chosen families, displacement, protean identity, heterosocial panic, bodily difference, erotic physicality, risqué situations, and more. The infinite earths and rhizomatic universes of potential queer pleasure in and of comics are dizzyingly diverse, and one way to make their contours legible has been to parse the world by national tradition or geographic region, foregrounding American works and devoting subsequent chapters to other regions. This *Reader*'s contributors favor a different approach, examining the crossings and intersections between and among traditions, regions, and temporal periods with an eye towards moving past single-author analyses to explore the complex translocal web that shapes queer sequential art on a global scale.

Tracking the emergence of an LGBTQ+ comics globality of distinct and interconnected resonances, traditions, movements, and intertextual dependencies and connections, this *Reader* charts ways in which LGBTQ+ comics from around the world (the United States, Canada, France, the United Kingdom, Germany, and Japan) emerge in relation to and influence one another. Chapters theorize new ways to think about and represent global comics, in different temporal periods and in varied international and transcultural contexts. Topics include an exposé of the precarity of the German lesbian and gay liberation movement after World War II and the rise of the German queer comics scene in the 1970s; gay fanzines as contact zones, specifically the French fanzine *Dokkun*'s creative investment in gay Japanese manga; interpretations of American queer comics in India; Gengoroh Tagame's Japanese manga as *bildungsroman* of BDSM play; Hagio Moto's exploration of nonbinary and trans* subjects in science fiction manga; and visualizations of queer-questioning and trans* identities and ethnicities (Indigenous, Japanese, and South Asian) in Canadian graphic texts.

Such influencing and mixing of artistic traditions and intertextual dependencies is even more common and powerful with the emergence of dynamic electronic channels of publication. The speed and proliferation of online creativity outpaces the relative slowness of printed comics' production and distribution. The *Reader* addresses the ways in which transmediality contributes to developments in LGBTQ+ comics, specifically queer webcomics. What kinds of productive synergies are generated by the diffusion and interplay of LGBTQ+ comics characters and content across media? Digital comics and fanzines, with their free or low-cost comics distribution, have enabled queer and trans* comics creators to move past the need for publishing contracts and to engage directly with their readership, often offering particular and specific representations of queerness. Two quite different web-based comics creations hint at the possibilities. *ArtQueerHabibi*, an Instagram account with more than 50,000 followers around the world, showcases work by an anonymous comics artist that foregrounds diverse representations of queer Arab love specifically to address the lack of representation of LGBTQ+ people of Middle Eastern origin in mainstream media. Many of the single-panel comics and portraits on this account feature romantic couples, drag queens, muscled gay men in Middle Eastern locales, from Damascus, Amman, Dubai, Riyadh, Palestine, and Beirut, that visualize and value the manifold lived experiences of Middle Eastern queers. *Theelsalomons*, another Instagram account that showcases single-panel comics by Jesse Brown about the lives of comedians Jess Salomon and Eman El-Husseini, a Jewish-Palestinian lesbian couple living in New York City, also uses the digital medium to reach followers to characterize the opportunities for cultural humor that this intersectional couple experiences. COVID-19, immigration, interfaith marriage, cooking, even pets offer almost daily comics insights into the relationship dynamic of these two quick-witted lesbian women. Such contemporary work heralds the emergence of transcultural, translocal, and diasporically inflected LGBTQ+ comics that take up the question of how queerness resonates for LGBTQ+ creators and characters who transit beyond homelands, transporting and relocating various local modalities of queerness, sexual liberation, and gender.

The *Reader* is organized into four broad sections suggested by the analytical focuses and critical resonances of the chapters included in them, but our unavoidable need to locate chapters physically should not preclude readers' imagining or discerning potential alternative arrangements. Indeed, "Queer in Common," the *Reader*'s first section, might well suit more than the chapters collected there; in one way or another, all of the *Reader*'s contributors acknowledge the power of LGBTQ+ comics as a kind of common ground for LGBTQ+ creators and readers, a notional shared space of connection to one another. In this first section, we have grouped chapters that take up the ways in which LGBTQ+ comics represent and manifest the collective urgency of queer togetherness. To affirm a collective sense of strength in the face of threat, to validate one another's experiences, to pay tribute to those who came before us, to rally in our own defense, and to take pleasure in our own company, these

Figure I.4. "Lebanese Drag Queens," *ArtQueerHabibi*. @artqueerhabibi.

chapters explore and celebrate LGBTQ+ comics' abiding evocation of queer commonality. The chapters grouped in the second section, "Global Crossings and Intersections," question how regional specificity and LGBTQ+ history inflect the possibility and recognizability of such shared queerness. The third section, "Resilience: Becoming Queer," brings together chapters that take up touchstone ideas about expansive registers of LGBTQ+ selfhood—including defiance of oppressive norms, openness to diverse modes of love and affection, sensitivity to intersectional awareness, and more—as we see them in comics. Relishing the visual splendiferousness of LGBTQ+ comics, the *Reader*'s fourth and final section, "Seen/Scene: Discovery, Visibility, Community," brings together chapters that take up the urgency and pleasure of showing queerness, from seeing oneself to discerning LGBTQ+ community. Each of these sections is introduced by its own individual overview, offering capsules of each chapter as well as context and points of contact.

• • •

We agree with the *Reader*'s contributors: LGBTQ+ pride and power are inextricable from cooperation and community. The experience of assembling the *Reader* itself has allowed us to know and to feel that queer "commons," and it has been a pleasure to discover and depend upon it. From the *Reader*'s inception, we have delighted in the good will and collegiality that the project has inspired. We are grateful to Vijay Shah at the University Press of Mississippi, who responded to our proposal with such alacrity and enthusiasm for recognizing the *Reader*'s timeliness and necessity and for his support and guidance along the way. The *Reader* represents the best work from a really dazzling range of proposals that arrived in response to our call for papers. Knowing that there was so much more out there than we could ever hope to include in a single volume further assured us of the field's enormous range and depth. We were bowled over, and, once we got up, sustained by the enthusiasm, creativity, and commitment of every last one of those proposals. They assured us of the vitality of the field now and to come. We thank our contributors for such excellent writing. Reading, learning from, and editing their thought-provoking work has been a consistent pleasure in the years since the *Reader* began. We regularly marveled at our contributors' good will and generosity with their wisdom and effort at all stages of the editorial process and in the midst of a global pandemic. For their help with finalizing the manuscript, we are grateful to project editor Laura Strong, copyeditor Peter Tonguette, and indexer Matthew MacLellan. In addition, we thank Marco Del Din, Misha Grifka, Marcus Haynes, Julie Jolo, and Ana Micaela Manansala.

As the *Reader* came together, we were also happily boosted by the support it received from central figures in the LGBTQ+ comics community. Creators like Alison Bechdel, Jennifer Camper, and Justin Hall generously permitted us to reproduce their comics and to include previously unpublished work. Creators and scholars coordinated with one another, allowing us to add conversational dynamism to the *Reader* with interviews featuring Hillary Chute, Jennifer Camper, Ramzi Fawaz, and Justin Hall. Thanks are due to the Stanford Humanities Center for their warm welcome and hospitality when we interviewed Fawaz and to York University's Faculty of Liberal Arts and Professional Studies for its research grant support to make it possible.

Secret heroes of the *Reader*'s success include Beth Callaghan, whose LGBTQ+ networking prowess is a measure of her coolness and her kindness, Joel Baetz, who provided early inspiration, Nan Buzard and the Oscar Wilde Memorial Bookshop, who gave even earlier inspiration, Professors Lesley Higgins, Marie-Christine Leps, Elicia Clements, and Natalie Neill, for their collegiality and guidance, as well as Mary Lou, Colin, Angela and Bob, for their positive vibes and good faith. For their love, support, and enthusiasm, we give our final heartfelt thanks to Alison's wife, Anne, and their kids, Alex and Claire, and to Louise and Ben Warren, the best gay-positive parents you could ask for, to Jonathan's friends, Joseph Flessa and Logan MacDonald, and to his boyfriend, Hao Wu.

Notes

1. A note on terminology. Unless a contributor has specified otherwise in their own work, the *Reader* regularly uses the acronym "LGBTQ+" (lesbian, gay, bisexual, trans*, and queer) and occasionally defaults to "lesbian," "queer," or "gay" when contextually appropriate. Similarly, except as contributors have specified otherwise in their work, the *Reader* uses the capacious umbrella term "trans*." The *Reader* uses pronouns in accordance with contributors' preferences. LGBTQ+ nomenclature and usage are alive and evolving. Our choices in the *Reader* strive to reflect an affirming and respectful spirit of inclusivity and solidarity.

2. The Comics Magazine Association of America's Comics Code Revision of 1989 includes a section focused on appropriate representations of "institutions" which directs publishers to respect the following provisions:

> In general recognizable national, social, political, cultural, ethnic and racial groups, religious institutions, law enforcement authorities will be portrayed in a positive light. These include the government on the national, state, and municipal levels, including all of its numerous departments, agencies and services; law enforcement agencies such as the FBI, the Secret Service, the CIA, etc.; the military, both United States and foreign; known religious organizations; ethnic advancement agencies; foreign leaders and representatives of other governments and national groups; and social groups identifiable by lifestyle, such as homosexuals, the economically disadvantaged, the economically privileged, the homeless, senior citizens, minors, etc.

The updated guidelines for comic books specified that "[c]haracter portrayals will be carefully crafted and show sensitivity to national, ethnic, religious, sexual, political and socioeconomic orientations."

3. Despite such varied queer affinities between comics and their readers, Fawaz and Scott marvel that "[c]omics studies and queer theory have remained surprisingly alienated from each other" (2018, 197).

4. Pablo Dopico proposes that Anarcoma's gender fluidity reflected ideas about gay identity in post-Franco Barcelona, noting that Nazario's protagonist—"un famoso travesti" ("a famous transvestite")—epitomizes the importance of celebratory displays of transvestism associated

with Spain's emergence from dictatorship and the country's cultural liberation during its transition to democracy (Dopico 2005, 393; Vernon and Morris 1995, 7). Heralding that historic transformation, a vogue for trans* visuality, especially in the cultural prominence of simultaneously masculine and feminine presentation and embodiment, evokes the dynamism of the new Spanish future, encouraging readers to step beyond gender binaries and to question customary markers of gender and sexuality. Nazario's character "is neither completely male nor female, nor even traditionally transsexual. Anarcoma is truly queer, questioning identity and sexuality at a new level" (Harrison 2009).

Works Cited

Abate, Michelle Ann. "Introduction: 'Suffering Sappho!': Lesbian Content and Queer Female Characters in Comics." *Journal of Lesbian Studies* 22, no. 4 (October 2018): 329–35.

Aldama, Frederick Luis. *Latinx Superheroes in Mainstream Comics*. University of Arizona Press, 2017.

Aldama, Frederick Luis, and Christopher González, eds. *Graphic Borders: Latino Comic Books Past, Present & Future*. University of Texas Press, 2016.

Altman, Dennis. *The Homosexualization of America*. Beacon Press, 1982.

Avery, Dan. "DC Comics Launches 'Midnighter and Apollo,' First Comic Book Featuring Gay Superhero Couple." *NewNowNext.com*, September 22, 2016. http://www.newnownext.com/midnighter-and-apollo-miniseries/09/2016/

Barry, Lynda. "Marlys' Guide to Queers." 1991. *The! Greatest! Of! Marlys!* Fantagraphics, 2016.

Bechdel, Alison. "Introduction." *Stuck Rubber Baby: 25th Anniversary Edition*. 1995. First Second, 2020.

Chute, Hillary. *Why Comics? From Underground to Everywhere*. HarperCollins, 2017.

Comics Magazine Association of America. "Comics Code Revision of 1989." http://cbldf.org/comics-code-revision-of-1989/

Dopico, Pablo. *El cómic underground español, 1970–1980*. Cátedra, 2005.

Edwards, Dylan. *Transposes*. Foreword by Alison Bechdel. Northwest Press, 2012.

Fawaz, Ramzi. *The New Mutants: Superheroes and the Radical Imagination of American Comics*. New York University Press, 2016.

Fawaz, Ramzi. "A Queer Sequence: Comics as a Disruptive Medium." *PMLA* 134, no. 3 (2019): 588–94.

Garcia, Patricia. "Marvel is Introducing a Queer Latina Superhero." *Vogue*, April 6, 2017. https://www.vogue.com/article/america-chavez-marvel-queer-latina-comic.

Halberstam, J. Jack. *In a Queer Time & Place: Transgender Bodies, Subcultural Lives*. New York University Press, 2005.

Hall, Justin. "The Secret Origins of LBGTQ Graphic Novels." *The Cambridge History of the Graphic Novel*, edited by Jan Baetens, Hugo Frey, and Stephen E. Tabachnick, 286–302. Cambridge University Press, 2018.

Hall, Justin, ed. *No Straight Lines: Four Decades of Queer Comics*. 2012. Fantagraphics, 2015.

Halperin, David M. *How to Be Gay*. The Belknap Press of Harvard University Press, 2012.

Harrison, Michael. "The Queer Spaces and Fluid Bodies of Nazario's *Anarcoma*." *Postmodern Culture: Journal of Interdisciplinary Thought on Contemporary Cultures* 19, no. 3 (May 2009). http://www.pomoculture.org/2013/09/05/the-queer-spaces-and-fluid-bodies-of-nazarios-anarcoma/.

Hernandez, Gilbert. *Julio's Day*. Fantagraphics, 2013.

Jay, Karla. *Lavender Culture*. Jove/Harcourt Brace Jovanovich, 1979.

Lim, Elisha. *100 Crushes*. Koyama Press, 2014.

McGurk, Caitlin. "Lovers, Enemies, and Friends: The Complex and Coded Early History of Lesbian Comic Strip Characters." *Journal of Lesbian Studies* 22, no. 4 (October 2018): 336–53.

McGurk, Caitlin, and Jenny Robb. *Tales from the Vault: 40 Years/40 Stories.* "Sanjak and Sexuality." https://library.osu.edu/site/40stories/2020/01/31/sanjak-and-sexuality/

Rivera, Gabby. *America: The Life and Times of America Chavez*. Marvel, 2018.

Scott, Darieck, and Ramzi Fawaz. "Introduction: Queer about Comics." *American Literature* 90, no. 2 (June 2018): 197–219.

Sedgwick, Eve Kosofsky. *Tendencies*. Duke University Press, 1993.

Vernon, Kathleen M., and Barbara Morris, eds. *Post-Franco, Postmodern: The Films of Pedro Almodóvar*. Greenwood Press, 1995.

I.
QUEER IN COMMON

Chapter 1

QUEER IN COMMON
SECTION INTRODUCTION

ALISON HALSALL AND JONATHAN WARREN

As social media and the internet transform LGBTQ+ life, the central importance of recognizably gay bars, clubs, parties, gyms, cafés, bookstores, balls,
theatres, places of worship, and other physical places where queer people can
find one another and, however temporarily, constitute a majority has increasingly been supplemented by and, in some cases, given way to virtual kinds of
interaction. In noteworthy respects, the advent of internet meeting grounds
has had the advantage of making queer spaces more accessible, across distance and kinds of ability, for example. Yet, as the growth of electronic culture
has also witnessed some decline in the availability of brick-and-mortar queer
spaces, the transformation has provoked a poignant reckoning with the value
of physically being together en masse. The pre-cognitive thrill brought on by
an immense Pride celebration, the consoling safety when homophobic scrutiny
is not a threat, the restorative dynamism that comes from being in the actual
company of LGBTQ+ diversity, the spontaneity of unmediated sensual possibility, the serendipity of electronically unfiltered queer discovery, such powerful, emotional, and embodied registers of queerness are not easily replicated
anywhere but in person.

 That's why attacks on gay venues are so existentially shocking; they highlight the relative rarity, value, and fragility of our common spaces even as
they underscore our need for them. To date, the Pulse nightclub shooting, in
Orlando, Florida, on June 12, 2016, remains the deadliest incident of violence
against LGBTQ+ people in the United States, an incident that exemplifies the
continued vulnerability of queer communities in North America and around
the world. Despite its exceptional lethality, the Pulse shooting exemplifies
LGBTQ+ precarity that long predates the 1969 Stonewall riots, a sense of which
all queer people share. Tracking by the Human Rights Campaign Foundation
shows that "sexual orientation consistently ranks as the third-highest motiva-
tor for hate crime" in the United States after race and religion (Marzullo and
Libman 2009, 2) and the most likely to correlate with violence against persons
(e.g., assault, intimidation) rather than against property (e.g., theft) (6). FBI
statistics chart an increase in such incidents (Hauck 2019). "Transgender" or

"gender nonconforming" people face "shocking amounts" of violence and dis-crimination (*VAWnet*), with the violence against transgender women who are Black, Indigenous, and people of color being especially prevalent ("Pride and Pain" 2019, 2).

For reasons affirmative, celebratory, defensive, and reactive, LGBTQ+ com-munity togetherness has proven the resilience of queer solidarity and the power of collective action in response to threats to our security. Whether in the face of the epoch-defining AIDS crisis, the fight for same-sex marriage, myriad daily aggressions of homophobia and transphobia, violent hate crimes, familial estrangement, or state-sponsored oppression, LGBTQ+ commons-forming initiatives discover the promise of a more secure queer future in social, com-munity, and collective activism. The potential of such a "queer commons" to "unleash power," as ACT UP's name, credo, and accomplishments attest, manifests in forms of social and political resistance to racial, national, and gendered forms of violence directed at LGBTQ+ communities and individuals (Millner-Larsen and Butt 2018, 400). Recognizing that the might of the queer individual multiplies exponentially when connected to others, the ideal of the "queer commons" is to transcend limiting boundaries so as to mobilize broad, horizontal commonalities among queer people.

The essays in this section consider how LGBTQ+ comics help to visualize and motivate such an effective queer force. We should not forget to acknowl-edge the affirmative and rallying effect of queer comics simply greeting their readers as queer citizens together. By addressing and thereby helping to assemble their implied audience, LGBTQ+ comics establish a sense of read-ers' shared affinity. Their community-promoting function, moreover, derives considerable energy through the comics' propensity to position their readers as, and teach them how better to be, critics of heteronormative social relations. By visualizing LGBTQ+ antagonists, by naming and validating LGBTQ+ lived experiences—of desire, oppression, alienation, transformation, and so on—and by presenting queer readers' fraught, vital, and pivotal status as a coherent force, queer comics valorize and elevate comics fandom—what Ramzi Fawaz and Darieck Scott describe as "their solicitation of nonnormative counter-publics" (2018, 200)—to stir a sense of queerness in common and to inspire activism. In the comics considered in this section, including those taken up in our wide-ranging interview with Fawaz that concludes it, intense critiques of heteronormative social and political conditions, circumscriptions of sexual possibility, and their consequences work to fuel fan cultures' affective responses, to inspire the emergence of activist networks, and to make available new and surprising conceptualizations of sex, sexuality, and gender expression as well as new social relations and publics.

Connecting all LGBTQ+ comics' development of a "queer commons" is the visualization of the protean energy and dynamism of LGBTQ+ people, our rootedness in shared experiences of precarity. The representation of systemic oppression or of individual or collective experiences of injustice serve as occasions to acknowledge and affirm the consequential resentment and anger and to demonstrate the importance of LGBTQ+ memory, history, and archiving. True to the ethos of the underground and alternative comix scenes from which they emerged, LGBTQ+ comics look at heteronormativity as its would-be outsider, its impatient target, and its crafty subversive. Visualizing and remembering the ravaging AIDS epidemic of the 1980s and 1990s, tracking and endorsing the complex variations of dyke rage in the 1990s, depicting and enjoying queer eros and kink, these LGBTQ+ comics ground queer collective action in our lived experiences. Thematically, these comics are *about* what LGBTQ+ readers have in common. Effectively, they work to build and strengthen a readership that believes in such solidarity, inviting affective responses, "meant to address a sense of being-in-common as it is transmitted, across people, place, and spaces" (Muñoz 2018, 396).

The chapters in this section focus on LGBTQ+ comics' evocation of organic queer togetherness, texts that are political acts in and of themselves. In seeing and remembering lived experiences and experiential and affective rootedness of the queer commons—in gay villages, baths, bars, discos, parades, and demonstrations—they extend our sense of LGBTQ+ identity and LGBTQ+ people's claim not only to our selfhood and our bodies but to the world. The queer commons comprise more than queer people. As Muñoz explains in relation to the Brown commons that he was writing about before his death, it includes the "feelings, sounds, buildings, neighborhoods, environments, and the nonhuman organic life that might circulate in such an environment alongside humans" (2018, 396). As Batman is inextricable from Gotham, Superman from Metropolis, or Wonder Woman from Paradise Island, queerness extends itself and receives power back from the settings within and through which it comes to know itself and to flourish.

The world of the American 1990s was ideal as a catalyst for stirring and a screen for projecting dyke rage, as Michelle Ann Abate's exploration of a cohort of lesbian creators from the United States whose common experiences of queerness—often in the accumulated friction of daily homophobic and misogynistic hostility, disrespect, and indignity—burst forth in comic depictions of shared anger, funny disgruntlement, and determined resistance to injustice. She shows how rage works within these comics as a wholly appropriate response to injustice and oppression, emerging from a desire to inspire political action and to propel social and intersectional transformation. Moreover, the rage of characters in the 1990s lesbian comics that Abate discusses exemplifies what the comics believe could and should be the political power of readers' queer anger. Iconic lesbian heroines like Diane DiMassa's Hothead Paisan and Roberta Gregory's Bitchy Butch frequently look out to speak directly to their readers, implicating us in their affective experience, and urging that we feel their visceral fury with them and know that they and other readers share our anger so that we might make good use of it in our queer lives beyond the comics. When we are enraged, we burn with the heat of Hothead and Butch. Their fury, our flag.

In *Dykes to Watch Out For*, Alison Bechdel shows that a diverse group of lesbians can flourish under that kind of pressure. One of the earliest LGBTQ+ comics to focus exclusively on the lives and loves of queer people (mainly lesbians), Bechdel's strip fashions an archive of lesbian social history narrated against its searing indictment of contemporaneous American politics. The individual lives of Bechdel's characters evoke the in-common nature of weathering homophobia, racial bias, and depression without sacrificing their human specificity. Bechdel's taxonomy of the complexity of lesbian lives—set against presidential elections, the war in Iraq, the O. J. Simpson trial, increasing trans* visibility, and more—recognizes the full personhood of characters that are as inextricable from their queer community as, the strip suggests or teaches, readers might be from our own. Their queerness in common is a solace for the stresses of the everyday as well as for the institutionalized social and political injustices that they and all LGBTQ+ people endure.

The value of leaning on one another is especially poignant and pertinent in the comics and graphic memoirs written at the height of the AIDS crisis as Tesla Cariani's chapter makes clear by attending to how they foster and serve as a repository for collective memory, evoke absence, materialize affect, and mobilize action. These comics visualize illness, trauma, social and political marginalization, and collective memorialization as further features of the "queer commons." As with 1990s lesbian comics, these often speak directly to their readers to invite us to feel along with the helplessness, fear, impatience, and rage of people living with HIV/AIDS and caregivers. *Strip AIDS* (1987) and *Strip AIDS U.S.A.* (1988) use the tools of the comics collection or anthology to evoke queer commonality as it assembles different comics to feature the range of experiences of HIV/AIDS, including ways of seeing other than those of white gay men. For Margaret Galvan, these collections were instrumental in educating readers about the crisis, fostering communities of artistic creation and collaboration, and foregrounding "affective activism" by acknowledging loss and isolation, emotional care work, and the toll of commemoration as integral to their comics work on behalf of social justice in the United Kingdom and the United States. Like the NAMES Project, which commemorated the lives of people who had died of AIDS by assembling individual textile memorial panels into the massive AIDS Memorial Quilt, in its very form *Strip AIDS* evokes queer solidarity as a piece-by-piece assemblage in response to a shared crisis and as a memorial to it that can persist after death.

To read an LGBTQ+ comic might not, of course, inevitably activate an electric circuit connecting oneself to all others' queerness. The utopian ideal of the "queer commons" that informs these works is as aspirational an ethic as the motive force for the Quilt, one that derives its great faith in the LGBTQ+ future by trying to realize our connection to one another today. Making those connections tangible and felt allows them to emulate the affect of empowering togetherness that we enjoy in queer spaces. Taking their cue from Muñoz, Millner-Larsen and Butt rightly regard the commons "as an ideality 'not yet here'" (2018, 402), whose power is oriented towards the potentiality of the future that could be enjoyed by the many rather than the few.

Works Cited

Hauck, Grace. "Anti-LGBT Hate Crimes are Rising, the FBI Says. But it Gets Worse." *USA Today*, June 28, 2019.

Marzullo, Michelle A., and Alyn J. Libman. *Research Overview: Hate Crimes and Violence Against Lesbian, Gay, Bisexual, and Transgender People*. Human Rights Campaign Foundation, 2009.

Millner-Larsen, Nadja, and Gavin Butt. "Introduction: The Queer Commons." *GLQ: A Journal of Lesbian and Gay Studies* 24, no. 4 (October 2018): 399–419.

Muñoz, José Esteban. "Preface: Fragment from the *Sense of Brown* Manuscript." *GLQ: A Journal of Lesbian and Gay Studies* 24, no. 4 (October 2018): 395–97.

"Pride and Pain: A Snapshot of Anti-LGBTQ Hate and Violence during Pride Season 2019." *National Coalition of Anti-Violence Programs (NCAVP)*. 2019. http://avp.org/wp-content/uploads/2019/08/AVP_Pride2019_HV_infographic.pdf.

Scott, Darieck, and Ramzi Fawaz. "Introduction: Queer about Comics." *American Literature* 90, no. 2 (June 2018): 197–219.

"Violence Against Trans and Non-Binary People." *VAWnet: An Online Resource Library on Gender-Based Violence*. 2020. https://vawnet.org/sc/serving-trans-and-non-binary-survivors-domestic-and-sexual-violence/violence-against-trans-and.

Chapter 2

"RUDE GIRLS AND DANGEROUS WOMEN"

LESBIAN COMICS FROM THE 1990s

MICHELLE ANN ABATE

The final decade of the twentieth century witnessed a surge in lesbian-themed comics in the United States. Although Alison Bechdel's *Dykes to Watch Out For* series began appearing in newspapers in 1983, it reached the height of its creative powers and public popularity during the 1990s. This ten-year span saw the release of no fewer than six collections of the weekly strip: *New, Improved! Dykes to Watch Out For* (1990), *Dykes to Watch Out For: The Sequel* (1992), *Spawn of Dykes to Watch Out For* (1993), *Unnatural Dykes to Watch Out For* (1995), *Hot, Throbbing Dykes to Watch Out For* (1997), and *Split-Level Dykes to Watch Out For* (1998). By the dawn of the new millennium, Bechdel's series established itself as not only the longest running lesbian comic in US history, but also the most successful (Garner 2008).

Dykes to Watch Out For was not the only popular comic featuring queer women during this decade. In 1991, Diane DiMassa released the first issue of *Hothead Paisan*. Appearing as a zine in the burgeoning underground comix scene, *Hothead* quickly amassed a loyal cult following. Twenty more issues would follow before the series ceased with the close of the decade in 1999. Akin to Bechdel's comic, DiMassa's strips were collected and released in several volumes: *Hothead Paisan* (1993), *The Revenge of Hothead Paisan* (1995), and *The Complete Hothead Paisan* (1999). In a telling indicator of how prolific the series had been, *The Complete Hothead Paisan* spanned over 400 pages. Meanwhile, what began as an alternative zine ended with DiMassa selling an array of *Hothead*-themed merchandise: hats, mugs, T-shirts, stickers, etc.

DiMassa's work in the underground comix scene was accompanied by another lesbian cartoonist: Jennifer Camper. A mainstay in the queer cartooning landscape since the early 1980s when her comics appeared in publications ranging from *Gay Community News*, *On Our Backs*, and *Gay Comix*, Camper released two book-length volumes in the 1990s: *Rude Girls and Dangerous Women* (1994) and *SubGURLZ* (1999). The first volume collected the strips that Camper had created for various print venues over the years. By contrast, the latter book was an episodic narrative that followed the exploits of three queer female protagonists. Both titles affirmed Camper's status as one of the most influential voices in lesbian cartooning.

During this same time, Ariel Schrag was writing and releasing her series of autobiographical comics: *Awkward* (1995), *Definition* (1996), *Potential* (1997), and *Likewise* (1998). Each volume documented a different year of her experiences at Berkeley High School in California. Moreover, they were created while Schrag was still a student, initially appearing as self-published books that she sold to friends and classmates. Near the end of *Definition*, Schrag comes out as bisexual. Then, in the opening pages of *Potential*, she begins identifying as a lesbian, announcing in what quickly became an oft-repeated mantra: "DYKE-DOM Here I come!" (Schrag 1997, 9).

Finally, but far from insignificantly, Roberta Gregory's *Bitchy Butch* also populated the decade. The title character made her debut in 1991 as a secondary figure in Gregory's series *Bitchy Bitch*, about heterosexual malcontent Midge McCracken. Gregory, who is herself a lesbian, introduced Bitchy Butch as her queer female counterpart. The figure would become a recurring one in the series, appearing in comics throughout the remainder of the decade. In 1999, the strips featuring Bitchy Butch—along with ten pages of new content—were collected and released as their own stand-alone book. The volume quickly became a cult classic.

As even this brief overview indicates, the 1990s gave rise to a bevy of titles that were by, about, and for queer women. The final decade of the twentieth century has been known as "The Dot-Com Decade"—given that it witnessed the rise of the internet—as well as "The Good Decade" or even "The Best Decade Ever," after the fact that the 1990s was a period of relative peace and prosperity (Cohen 2008; Coupland 2017; Anderson 2015). In light of the number of lesbian-themed comics that appeared during this era, this era could also be termed—in a nod to Ariel Schrag's now-iconic coming-out declaration—"The Decade for Drawing Dykedom."

In spite of the strong cultural presence of lesbian comics during the 1990s, they have received scant critical attention to date. Diane DiMassa's *Hothead Paisan* has been discussed in only a few journal articles and book chapters. Meanwhile, the cartooning of Jennifer Camper as well as that of Roberta Gregory have been the subject of just a couple of essays apiece. Even more surprising (as well as disappointing), Ariel Schrag's influential work has been wholly overlooked by scholars. Finally, Alison Bechdel's *Dykes to Watch Out For* series, which is arguably the most popular of these strips, has only been the subject of a handful of essays to date.

This chapter gives much-needed critical consideration to this cadre of lesbian comics from the 1990s. I bring the work of Bechdel, DiMassa, Schrag,

Gregory, and Camper together for the first time, viewing them as part of a creative and cultural cohort. More specifically, I argue that while these strips present original characters, distinct aesthetics, and unique storylines, they are united by a powerful common element: the expression of queer female anger. From fury over sexism, homophobia, and ableism to rage over classism, racism, and xenophobia, these strips articulate ire about a wide range of social ills and political injustices. Moreover, they do so candidly, openly, and fearlessly. In so doing, these comics collectively offer an illuminating survey of the multitudinous forms of queer anger during the 1990s as well as their sociocultural functions. Ultimately, titles like *Bitchy Butch*, *Hothead Paisan*, and *SubGURLZ* do more than simply serve as a mouthpiece for disgruntled characters or a steam valve for agitated readers; they also function as a rallying cry for the queer female community: raising individual awareness, urging community organizing, and calling for social action. Written and released during a decade that saw the LGBTQ+ movement increasingly move toward strategies of polite, palatable assimilationism, these comics provide a poignant testament—to readers then as well as now—to the ideological importance as well as political power of queer anger.

"WORLD'S ANGRIEST DYKE": FRAMING QUEER FEMALE FURY

Given their longtime home in the "funny papers," comics have commonly been associated with humor. Indeed, the name by which sequential art is most widely known—as "comics"—reveals the centrality of levity in and to the genre.

The lesbian-themed comics that appeared during the 1990s, however, became a platform for a far different affective register: rage. One of the first lesbian characters to appear in a strip from the 1990s was also one of the most powerful examples of this phenomenon: Roberta Gregory's Bitchy Butch. Making her appearance in a 1991 issue of *Gay Comics*, the subtitle that Gregory chose for the strip aptly encapsulated her character: "World's Angriest Dyke." Far from hyperbole, Bitchy Butch is, indeed, filled with rage. It takes only the second panel of the inaugural strip for her to erupt in anger. After the male clerk at a convenience store mistakenly calls her sir, she explodes: "I am a WOMAN, you stupid jerk!!" (Gregory 1999, 3). Bitchy Butch transforms from a relatively unremarkable white woman with a crew cut to a towering beast who is serpent-tongued and has long, spikey fangs and a heavily furrowed brow (Gregory 1999, 3). Exploding in the convenience store does not sate Bitchy Butch's rage, however. As she walks home, Gregory's eponymous character continues to seethe. In thought balloons that appear above her head, she ruminates about a panoply of ills: heteronormativity, sexism, misogyny, sexual

Figure 2.1. Panels from the debut comic of *Bitchy Butch*. Reprinted in *Bitchy Butch: World's Angriest Dyke!*, Roberta Gregory (Fantagraphics, 1999), 6.

assault, domestic violence, incest, traditional standards of feminine beauty, and conservative family values. In an attempt to pacify her anger, Bitchy opens the queer newspaper that she just purchased and excitedly browses the "Women Seeking Women" personals section. After seeing multiple listings requesting "feminine" women only, she yells in disgust and then angrily rips the newspaper into shreds (Gregory 1999, 4). Bitchy then bumps into a former girlfriend. The two begin reminiscing when Bitchy learns that the woman is now dating a man. "You mean you're SCREWING this . . . this . . . TESTOSTERONE-SOAKED PENIS-MUTANT?" she explodes, her teeth turning to fangs and her brow furrowing deeply like a werewolf (Gregory 1999, 5). Over the following few panels, Bitchy completely loses control, not just verbally but also physically: she smacks the woman, then she roars at and pummels the man.

Figure 2.2. Opening panel from "Bitchy Butch Returns" (1993). Reprinted in *Bitchy Butch: World's Angriest Dyke!*, Roberta Gregory (Fantagraphics, 1999), 8.

Far from an anomalous strip, this debut of *Bitchy Butch* is an apt representation of this character. If anything, in fact, the initial sequence is understated. In "Bitchy Butch Returns" (1993), the title character goes beyond being the "World's Angriest Dyke" to one who teems with incessant rage. The opening panel depicts Bitchy stomping angrily down the street. A balloon above her head conveys her thoughts: "LIFE SUCKS THIS WORLD SUCKS PEOPLE SUCK HETEROS SUCK EVERYTHING SUCKS THIS CITY SUCKS THAT DOG SUCKS THAT KID SUCKS THIS STREET SUCKS" (Gregory 1999, 8). The bulk of the rest of the strip—and the series as a whole—follows a similar tactic. It depicts Bitchy Butch either silently stewing or verbally exploding about a wide array of social ills and political injustices: heterosexual privilege, ageism, homophobia, and dyke-phobia within the lesbian community, etc. That said, the main source of Bitchy's ire is the straight world. One thought balloon from "Bitchy Bitch Returns," in fact, depicts her muttering "FUCKING HETEROS FUCKING HETEROS FUCKING HETEROS" over and over and over (Gregory 1999, 9).

Diane DiMassa's *Hothead Paisan* amplifies the affective state of *Bitchy Butch*. While the subtitle that Gregory chose to summarize her character was the "World's Angriest Dyke," the one that DiMassa selected was a "Homicidal Lesbian Terrorist." This description was not attention-grabbing sensationalism. As Cynthia Barounis has said about the strip: "Balancing wicked camp humor with violent revenge fantasies, the comic's 20 issues follow the adventures of its unhinged lesbian heroine as she wreaks havoc on the straight White male

Figure 2.3. Panel from "Bitchy Butch Returns" (1993). Reprinted in *Bitchy Butch: World's Angriest Dyke!*, Roberta Gregory (Fantagraphics, 1999), 9.

world" (2018, 1). The panel that prefaces the complete collected series—and which is taken from the comic sequence titled "When Hothead Was Born" (1993)—shows the eponymous character looking directly at the reader, pointing the barrel of a gun at them from her car window, and saying "I'm not your fuckin' spritz-head girlfriend, I'm Hothead Paisan!" (DiMassa 1993). This tactic of breaking the fourth wall and addressing the reader directly happens repeatedly in DiMassa's strip—and it is also a recurring feature in the work of Gregory, Camper, and Bechdel. Direct address, of course, has a long history in sequential art from the United States (Groensteen 2015). The first popular newspaper comic strip, Richard Outcault's *Hogan's Alley* (1895), frequently had its central character, known as the Yellow Kid, speak directly with readers. In the decades since, this tactic has been a common facet in many of the most commercially successful as well as critically acclaimed strips, ranging from *Nancy, She-Hulk*, and *Squirrel Girl* to *Doonesbury, Calvin and Hobbes*, and *Deadpool* (Jensen 2018; Voutiritsas 2018). That said, the direct address that permeates *Hothead Paisan*—along with the work of other lesbian cartoonists during the 1990s—operates in a specific way and serves a particular function. As Thea Voutiritsas has written about this general phenomenon in US comics, "When characters interact with the audience, it makes us feel like we're part of an inside joke. And participating (rather than observing) is a lot more fun" (2018). The official fandom for DC Comics echoes this observation, defining a breach of the fourth wall as a moment "wherein fictitious characters become aware of their own false existence" ("Fourth Wall"). Direct address in lesbian comics from the 1990s operates differently. Rather than calling attention to their

Figure 2.4. Prefatory panel to *The Complete Hothead Paisan*, by Diane DiMassa (Cleis, 1993).

own inner artificiality, transgressions across the fourth wall in *Hothead Paisan* and other titles call attention to their outer authenticity. Instead of pulling the reader out of the fictitious world of the comic, direct address pulls them into their shared factual reality.

DiMassa's protagonist specializes in identifying, confronting, and—in her view, at least—rectifying forms of injustice. In the first issue alone, she shoots a man who refuses to cede space on the sidewalk, smashes the groin of another who is urinating in the street, and chops off the penis of a guy who exposes himself to her in an alley (DiMassa 1999, 21, 24). Hothead does not perform these acts with the cool detachment or emotional reserve of a Hollywood action star or Golden Age superhero. On the contrary, she is filled with unbridled rage. "Hey! Wake up, you rude, dead, lyin' motherfucker!!" she shouts at the man whose penis she has chopped off (22). Hothead's wrath, however, is directed at more than simply men. It also includes a plethora of other social problems, political injustices, and forms of systemic oppression. Hothead frequently watches television in her apartment, and she is commonly incensed by what she sees on the news, in commercials, or via television shows. From the reinforcement of traditional gender roles, the glorification of the nation's military-industrial complex, and the perpetuation of rape culture to the harmful messages disseminated by the feminine beauty industry, the looming threat of nuclear war, and the insidiousness of consumer capitalism, DiMassa's

Figure 2.5. Views of the television screens, in a panel from the debut issue of *Hothead Paisan*, Diane DiMassa. Reprinted in *The Complete Hothead Paisan* (Cleis, 1993), 27.

character is bombarded by infuriating media messages and is usually pushed over the edge by them. Hothead, in fact, engages in many of her most rage-filled verbal harangues as well as violent physical actions after she has been watching television.

Hothead's most common cultural touchstone—for her actions, her attitude, and even her appearance—is the punk movement from the 1970s and 1980s. However, given both the common causes for her ire and the actions that she takes in response to these emotions, DiMassa's protagonist can be placed in dialogue with a far different set of figures: the Erinyes or Furies, from Greco-Roman mythology. Created from the blood of Ouranus when he was castrated by his son Kronos, these individuals "were the goddesses of retribution and vengeance whose job it was to punish men who committed heinous crimes" ("Erinyes"). As Aaron J. Atsma has commented, "They were particularly concerned with homicide, unfilial conduct, offenses against the gods, and perjury. A victim seeking justice could call down the curse of the Erinyes upon the criminal." After doing so, "the wrath of the Erinyes could only be placated with the rite ritual purification and the completion of some task assigned for atonement" (Atsma 2019). While Hothead usually acts on her own accord rather than by being summoned by another person, she operates in much the same way: punishing individuals and men especially who commit heinous crimes. Finally, and far from insignificantly, even the protagonist's physical presentation—with her wild, wiry hair and facial expressions that are so exaggerated that they can be regarded as distorted—can be placed in dialogue with the Furies. In various poems and plays, the Erinyes "were depicted as ugly, winged women with hair, arms and waists entwined with poisonous serpents" (Atsma 2019).

Unlike Bitchy Butch, who largely does not contemplate her whiteness nor the discrimination that arises from race and ethnicity in addition to gender and sexuality, Hothead is concerned with issues of racism and xenophobia. In a series of panels near the middle of the first issue, she imagines the terrible impression that aliens from outer space would get about white people if they ever visited Earth. Not only do "white men in glasses and ties" control everything, but—as she elaborates in a subsequent panel—"look what they do": the image above her head shows a man dressed in a Klansman's robe (DiMassa 1999, 29). Meanwhile, in the panel beside it, she wonders "How is it that they get away with this kind of shit?": the image above her now shows a neo-Nazi skinhead. Hothead initially despairs at this situation, wishing that she could either leave planet Earth with the aliens or, even more futilely as well as problematically, renounce her affiliation with white people rather than contemplating ways in which she can engage in the work of antiracism. Unsurprisingly, though, DiMassa's protagonist quickly regains her ire. "One of us has to go!! An' it ain't me!" she vows (DiMassa 1999, 29). In a three-panel sequence that aptly summarizes not only the remainder of this first issue but the entire series, Hothead opens her trunk labeled "Ammo 'n' Shit," gets out her military-style rifle and tells her beloved cat Chicken: "I'm going out to clear a space in society for you an' me!" (DiMassa 1999, 30). In the third panel, she turns to the reader and says to them directly: "You an' me, me an' you!!" Through these and other comments, DiMassa makes clear that her title character is not a rogue agent acting in service of her own agenda; rather, she is a representative activist who is working on behalf of a larger community. This reading of Hothead gives new meaning or, at least added significance to her surname: "Paisan." While this Italian appellation is commonly seen as signaling a character's ethnic heritage, it can also be seen as indicating that—in spite of her seemingly loner tendencies and even antisocial behavior—she is a "friend," "compatriot," or even "country(wo)man" to the comic's queer female audience and broader community.

The work of Alison Bechdel, as Kathleen Martindale has observed, "looks pretty tame compared to DiMassa" (1997, 62). Indeed, none of the members of the ensemble cast that constitute her *Dykes to Watch Out For* (*DTWOF*) series ever engage in the physical violence that permeates *Hothead* nor do they display the verbal explosions that typify *Bitchy Butch*. That said, they certainly do get frustrated, annoyed, and upset. This quality is especially true of the strip's protagonist, Mo Testa. While this character is most commonly characterized as anxious and neurotic, she can also just as accurately be regarded as aggravated and even angry. The second book-length collection of the series, *Dykes to Watch Out For: The Sequel*, which was released in 1992 and contains strips that

Figure 2.6. Panel sequence from the debut issue of *Hothead Paisan*, Diane DiMassa. Reprinted in *The Complete Hothead Paisan* (Cleis, 1993), 30.

originally appeared over the previous two years, is replete with examples. One of the first comics in the collection, "Free Lunch," provides a vivid illustration. While pals Lois and Clarice try to have a pleasant meal at their favorite lesbian-owned café, Mo is stewing about current events. "Well whaddya call **Oliver North** and company walking off with slaps on the wrist for **arms-smuggling**, **drug-running**, and **murder?**" she asks at one point in a comment that is meant as a rebuke to her friends' perceived political naivete (Bechdel 1992, 11; bold in the original). Mo's ire is frequently a response to national politics and especially to reading the newspaper. "I don't know what this country is coming to!" she says to Lois immediately upon walking through her front door. "Did you see the paper? The cofounder of the **National Review** just came out!" (Bechdel 1992, 30; bold in the original). Rather than seeing this event as a positive testament to the progress that the LGBTQ+ community has made, she views it as depressing proof of how conservativism is taking over queer politics. "What'll it be next? Gay C.I.A. agents? Lesbian corporate raiders? Queer fundamentalist preachers?! It's . . . It's **immoral!**" Mo remarks in an increasingly impassioned tirade (Bechdel 1992, 31; bold in the original). When her friends attempt to dissuade her, their efforts backfire. "**Face it! The worst is already happening! LIFE ON THIS PLANET SUCKS!!!**" she erupts near the end of the comic, her brow furrowed, her eyes clenched tight, and fists shaking (Bechdel 1992, 31; bold in the original). That said, nothing makes Bechdel's protagonist angrier than when Harriet calls her the "L" word: liberal. Occurring during the middle of a fight about problems in their relationship, the label absolutely incenses Mo, not because she is conservative but because she sees herself as more progressive and more enlightened. Not only does she yell at Harriet—"Take it **back!** I am **not** a liberal, you . . . you **burger-licking bonehead!**" (Bechdel 1992, 40; bold

Figure 2.7. One of Mo's most pronounced verbal and physical expressions of anger. In *Dykes to Watch Out For: The Sequel*, Alison Bechdel (Firebrand Books, 1992), 40.

in the original)—but she also becomes uncharacteristically physical, picking up a tomato and throwing it against the refrigerator.

Acts of violence that are prompted by frustration over politics are a common occurrence in Jennifer Camper's comics. Her first book-length collection, *Rude Girls and Dangerous Women* (1994), reprinted strips that had appeared in various LGBTQ+ newspapers, zines, and underground publications. While these comics do not contain a recurring cast of characters, they do contain a recurring theme: the verbal as well as physical expression of female anger. In one early strip titled "Identity Crisis," a woman stands between two men who are engaged in a heated argument over identity labels. The two men shout back and forth at each other, "Gay!" and "Queer!" (Camper 1994, 13). The woman's solution to this situation is simple: she grabs both men by the neck, smashes their faces together, and knocks them out cold. The final panel shows her standing with a smile on her face, looking directly at readers, and proudly as well as matter-of-factly stating her identity: "Dyke" (Camper 1994, 13). Another comic offers an overview of "How Today's Woman Combats Stress" (Camper 1994, 24). After panels that depict a soothing bubble bath and a relaxing motorcycle ride through the country, Camper reminds readers that it is not enough to simply treat feelings of anxiety; they must also "be sure to identify stressful elements in your life and remove them" (Camper 1994, 24). The image that appears below this remark shows a woman bursting into an executive men's washroom and opening fire with a machine gun (Camper 1994, 24).

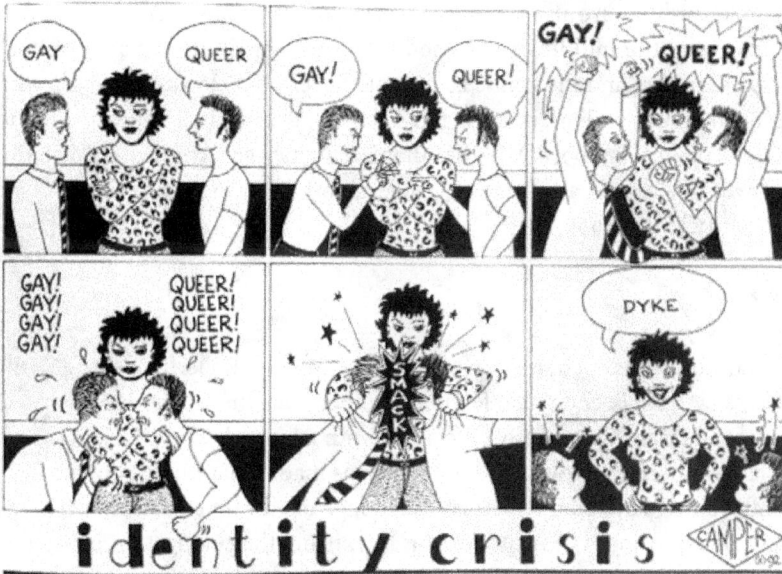

Figure 2.8. "Identity Crisis" from *Rude Girls and Dangerous Women*, Jennifer Camper (Laugh Lines Press, 1994), 13.

Figure 2.9. Panel from "How Today's Woman Combats Stress" from *Rude Girls and Dangerous Women*, Jennifer Camper (Laugh Lines Press, 1994), 24.

Portrayals of women's anger sparking powerful verbal stances as well as violent physical action permeate Camper's next collection, *SubGURLZ* (1999). The comic follows the adventures of three female protagonists—Swizzle, Byte, and Liver—who live in the tunnels of the New York City subway system. Each character has a day job (as a bartender, custodian, and nurse, respectively), but what they really do is battle injustice. From police brutality and street harassment to political corruption and economic inequality, the trio specializes in righting social wrongs. In so doing, these characters likewise evoke the Erinyes or Furies. Moreover, Camper's characters arguably possess an even greater kinship to them than Hothead Paisan, since—akin to these figures from Greco-Roman mythology—they are also a trio. An exchange that occurs between Liver and Swizzle near the middle of the book offers a compelling snapshot of both these characters and the comic as a whole. Liver offers to assist Swizzle with a problem, but she demurs, saying "Aw, thanks. But I'm in a really bad mood tonight" (Camper 1999, 85). Rather than seeing her grouchiness as a liability, Liver regards it as an asset. "Good, you're at your best when you're angry!" she tells her (Camper 1999, 85).[1]

• • •

The various forms of anger expressed in the comics of Roberta Gregory, Diane DiMassa, Alison Bechdel, and Jennifer Camper unite these otherwise disparate titles, while it simultaneously links them with a larger history. Back in 1970, a leaflet produced by the group Radicalesbians made what would soon become an oft-quoted statement: "A lesbian is the rage of all women condensed to the point of explosion" (3). As it went on to explain, the subjugation of women "bring[s] her into painful conflict with people, situations, the accepted ways of thinking, feeling and behaving, until she is in a state of continual war with everything around her, and usually with her self" (Radicalesbians 1970, 3). Although these comments were uttered about lesbians in the 1970s, they certainly apply to the queer female characters who populated comics two decades later. If queer women were engaged in a continual war, then titles like *Hothead Paisan*, *Bitchy Butch*, and *SubGURLZ* were dispatches from the front lines.

"NOT GAY AS IN HAPPY, BUT QUEER AS IN FUCK YOU": THE ROLE OF ANGER IN LGBTQ+ POLITICS DURING THE 1990s

The modern LGBTQ+ movement in the United States, of course, also has its roots or origins in anger. For decades, nonheteronormative individuals faced both de facto and de jure forms of discrimination. From being fired from their jobs, involuntarily committed to mental institutions, and ostracized by their families to being arrested for violating sodomy laws, harassed or even beaten on the street, and losing custody of their children, they were subjected to legal criminalization, medical pathologization, and social stigma.

On June 28, 1969, this longstanding situation changed. That night at the Stonewall Bar in New York City, police staged what they imagined would be another routine raid. When officers entered the establishment to round up and arrest homosexuals, however, some patrons refused to resign themselves to the situation. Instead of acquiescing to the humiliation of being handcuffed and brought down to the station for booking, they resisted and fought back. The unrest that erupted at the bar soon spread to the surrounding neighborhood of Greenwich Village. Over the next several days and nights, members of the LGBTQ+ community took to the streets, protesting homophobia, police brutality, and the criminalization of same-sex individuals and identity. The event became known as the Stonewall Rebellion, or even the Stonewall Riot. As both Martin B. Duberman and David Carter have discussed, it "signaled the end of the largely accommodationist homophile movement" of the 1950s led by groups like the Mattachine Society and Daughters of Bilitis "and the commencement of the more activistic fight for gay and lesbian liberation" (Abate 228). Indeed, Darren Stehle offered the following comment about both the significance of Stonewall and centrality that anger played in it: "We stood up, faced the police, and the establishment and said 'Fuck you! No more!'" (2018).

Anger would play a central role in the fight for LGBTQ+ rights during the 1990s as well. Throughout the previous decade, the AIDS crisis had decimated the queer community, especially gay men. The tragedy gave rise to a level of organization and activism that was unprecedented in the history of the queer community in the United States. As I have written elsewhere on this topic, "Advocacy groups like ACT-UP (AIDS Coalition to Unleash Power), GLAAD (Gay and Lesbian Alliance Against Defamation), the Lesbian Avengers, and Queer Nation were either founded during this decade or gained increased prominence during it" (Abate 2008, 228). That said, these "organizations did not make a polite case for homosexual rights" (Abate 2008, 228). Instead, as Lauren Berlant and Elizabeth Freeman have written, they went "for the broadest and most explicit assertion of presence" (1994, 156). Employing tactics "like public kiss-ins, the forced outings of closeted officials and—in a self-conscious inversion of the 1950s paradigm—queer invasions of straight bars, gay men and lesbians were no longer willing to quietly wait for recognition" (Abate 2008, 228). Given the immediacy of the AIDS crisis, they no longer had the luxury of doing so. The "decimation of the LGBTQ community by HIV while the Reagan Administration largely stood by, many realized—as one popular slogan of the era put it—that their silence would equal their death" (Abate 2008, 228–29).

The sense of urgency in the face of AIDS was matched only by feelings of anger. A popular lapel button during the 1990s, for example, declared "Not Gay as in Happy, but Queer as in Fuck You." Frustration with, and even outright hostility for, heteronormative society were widely held sentiments, arising not simply from the epidemic but from decades of discrimination. A manifesto titled "Queers Read This"—which was published anonymously, distributed at the 1990 Pride March in New York City, and became the founding document for Queer Nation—began with the proclamation: "Until I can enjoy the same freedom of movement and sexuality, as straights, their privilege must stop. . . . Straight people will not do this voluntarily and so they must be forced into it. Straights must be frightened into it. Terrorized into it. Fear is the most powerful motivation" ("Queers Read This" 1990, 1). Over the next eleven pages, the manifesto outlined the hardships that nonheteronormative individuals face. "Being queer is not about a right to privacy," it explained, "it is about the freedom to be public, to just be who we are. It means everyday fighting oppression; homophobia, racism, misogyny, the bigotry of religious hypocrites and our own self-hatred" ("Queers Read This" 1990, 1). Accordingly, at numerous points the manifesto urged its readers in strident language: "BE OUTRAGED! . . . DO SOMETHING," "LET YOURSELF BE ANGRY" ("Queers Read This" 1990, 9, 12).

Lesbian comics from the 1990s constitute a poignant reminder of both the personal necessity and the ideological utility of anger. As J. Jack Halberstam reminds us, "rage is a political space" (1993, 187). Anger is not only an understandable but even wholly appropriate response to injustice and oppression. Moreover, it is also one that can be personally empowering as well as politically efficacious. Audre Lorde pointed out in her landmark address "The Uses of Anger," for example, "anger is loaded with information and energy" (1997, 280). Although it is an emotion that many women, both queer and straight, have been taught to resist, repress, and even fear in themselves, it can be exceedingly productive. "The angers of women can transform differences through insight into power," Lorde observes (283). Speaking more personally, she goes on to reveal, "I have suckled the wolf's lip of anger and I have used it for illumination, laughter, protection" (Lorde 1997, 285). Halberstam echoes these beliefs, asserting "rage is ground for resistance" (188). It is a means both to mobilize and to disrupt. When individuals from marginalized communities—to paraphrase Darren Stehle's remark about Stonewall once again—get angry, stand up, and say "Fuck you! No more!" they are challenging the status quo. Their anger represents a firm refusal to accept systemic modes of discrimination and instead advocate for, and even insist upon, change. In this way, anger helps to engender political action and precipitate social transformation.

A key facet to the personal power and political efficacy that can be harnessed through anger lies in the distinction between it and hatred. As Audre Lorde articulates, these emotions "are very different. Hatred is the fury of those who do not share our goal, and its object is death and destruction. Anger is the grief of distortions between peers, and its object is change" (Lorde 1997, 282). These two modes of affect are often seen as synonymous and even interchangeable, but their origins as well as their outcomes are vastly different. Anger, as the *Oxford English Dictionary* notes, is the byproduct of a "distress, trouble, vex, hurt, wound." By contrast, hatred is framed as "loathing, hostility, malevolence." While the former sentiment—if left unexpressed and especially unresolved— can turn into the latter one, they do not start in the same way. Anger arises from a personal wrong and even a sociopolitical injustice, and it seeks to correct or at least confront this problem. Conversely, hatred is more toxic, more personal, and far more destructive.

Of course, the comics of Roberta Gregory, Diane DiMassa, Alison Bechdel, and Jennifer Camper all serve as a platform for expressions of anger, but they do not articulate the exact form. From the verbal fury of Bitchy Butch to the homicidal rage of Hothead Paisan to the political harangues of Mo Testa and the righteous indignation of the SubGURLZ, these titles map the rich and diverse topography of queer female anger. Even more importantly, they offer illuminating and even instructive examples of not only how anger can be harnessed for social change, but also why it could and even should be. As Brittany Cooper remarks in a recent book about the power and importance of Black women's anger, "The clarity that comes from rage should also tell us what kind of world we want to see, not just what kind of things we want to get rid of" (2018, 273). A similar observation applies to the queer female anger in lesbian comics from the 1990s. Whether targeting sexism, racism, homophobia, classism, ableism, or xenophobia, the works of Gregory, Bechdel, DiMassa, Camper, and Schrag are not advocating the annihilation associated with hatred. Instead, the anger expressed in their comics is meant to be instructive and, ultimately, productive: to tear down existing systems of oppression so that we can rebuild a more just and equitable world.

David Wojnarowicz, in *Close to the Knives: A Memoir of Disintegration*, offered the following observation about the LGBTQ+ community in the midst of AIDS: "We're supposed to quietly and politely make house in this killing machine called america [*sic*] and pay taxes to support our own slow murder *and I am amazed that we're not running amok in the streets*" (108; my emphasis). The queer community during the 1990s may not have been collectively running amok in the streets, but figures like Hothead Paisan, Bitchy Butch, and SubGURLZ certainly were. Moreover, the fury that they expressed was not limited to the epidemic. Instead, it extended to a panoply of socioeconomic ills, cultural injustices, and political problems. From racism, classism, sexism, and xenophobia to colonialism, imperialism, ableism, and internalized homophobia, these strips engage with a wide range of obstacles that women face as well as the ways in which these forms of oppression overlap, interlock, and—most importantly of all—compound.

Susie Bright once observed: "Lesbians are known for noble anger—you know, the righteous, unimpeachable kind that shows the rest of the world just what it takes to fight for social justice" (Bright 1999). Comics characters like Bitchy Butch, Hothead Paisan, and the SubGURLZ can certainly be seen in this way. Jennifer Camper titled her 1994 collection, *Rude Girls and Dangerous Women*. Comics by, about, and for queer women from the 1990s, however, offer a slight variation on this appellation. The expressions of anger that permeate Camper's work, along with that of DiMassa, Gregory, Bechdel, and Schrag, demonstrate that rude girls *are* dangerous women.

Note

1. Admittedly, Ariel Schrag's autobiographical comics are not as infused with expressions of ire. However, they are also not entirely devoid of such sentiments. Her high-school-aged avatar may get upset only occasionally, but when she does, it is noteworthy. For example, in *Potential* (1997)—the volume in which Schrag begins identifying as a lesbian—she becomes incensed when some boys at her school steal a goat from a local petting farm and then cruelly leave it up on the roof as a prank (214). She confronts one of them about this action and verbally explodes on them.

Works Cited

Abate, Michelle Ann. *Tomboys: A Literary and Cultural History.* Temple University Press, 2008.

Anderson, Kurt. "The Best Decade Ever? The 1990s, Obviously!" *New York Times*, February 7, 2015.

"anger, v." *OED Online*, Oxford University Press, March 2019. www.oed.com/view/Entry/7499. Accessed April 4, 2019.

Atsma, Aaron J. "ERINYES." Theoi Project. https://www.theoi.com/Khthonios/Erinyes.html. Accessed April 1, 2019.

Barounis, Cynthia. "Survival Angst: Rereading Hothead Paisan in the Trump Era." *Journal of Lesbian Studies* 22, no. 4 (2018): 1–9.

Bechdel, Alison. *Dykes to Watch Out For: The Sequel.* Firebrand, 1992.

Bechdel, Alison. *Hot, Throbbing Dykes to Watch Out For.* Firebrand, 1997.

Bechdel, Alison. *New, Improved! Dykes to Watch Out For.* Firebrand, 1990.

Bechdel, Alison. *Spawn of Dykes to Watch Out For.* Firebrand, 1993.

Bechdel, Alison. *Split-Level Dykes to Watch Out For.* Firebrand, 1998.

Bechdel, Alison. *Unnatural Dykes to Watch Out For.* Firebrand, 1995.

Berlant, Lauren, and Elizabeth Freeman. "Queer Nationality." *Fear of a Queer Planet: Queer Politics and Social Theory*, edited by Michael Warner, 193–229. University of Minnesota Press, 1993.

Bright, Susie. "Anger." *The Stranger*, June 17, 1999.

Camper, Jennifer. *Rude Girls and Dangerous Women.* Laugh Lines Press, 1994.

Camper, Jennifer. *SubGURLZ.* Cleis, 1999.

Cohen, Benjamin. "The Dot-Com Decade." Channel 4 News, March 25, 2008. http://www.channel4 .com/news/articles/science_technology/the+dotcom+decade/1864247.html. Accessed January 9, 2019.

Cooper, Brittany. *Eloquent Rage: A Black Feminist Discovers Her Superpower.* St. Martin's Press, 2018.

Coupland, Douglas. "1990s: The Good Decade." History.com, March 17, 2017. https://www.his tory.com/news/1990s-the-good-decade. Accessed January 9, 2019.

DiMassa, Diane. *The Complete Hothead Paisan.* Cleis, 1999.

DiMassa, Diane. *Hothead Paisan.* Cleis, 1993.

DiMassa, Diane. *The Revenge of Hothead Paisan*. Cleis, 1995.

"The Erinyes." Greek Gods & Goddesses. June 10, 2018. https://greekgodsandgoddesses.net/goddesses/the-erinyes/. Accessed April 1, 2019.

"Fourth Wall." DC Fandom. https://dc.fandom.com/wiki/Fourth_Wall. Accessed April 1, 2019.

Garner, Dwight. "The Days of their Lives: Lesbians Star in Funny Pages." *New York Times*, December 2, 2008. https://www.nytimes.com/2008/12/03/books/03garner.html. Accessed January 9, 2019.

Gregory, Roberta. *Bitchy Butch: World's Angriest Dyke*. Fantagraphics, 1999.

Groensteen, Thierry. *The Expanding Art of Comics: Ten Modern Masterpieces*. Translated by Ann Miller. University Press of Mississippi, 2015.

Halberstam, Judith [Now J. Jack]. "Imagined Violence/Queer Violence: Representation, Rage, and Resistance." *Social Text* 37 (Winter 1993): 187–201.

"hatred, n." *OED Online*, Oxford University Press, March 2019. www.oed.com/view/Entry/84584. Accessed April 4, 2019.

Jensen, K. Thor. "A History of Comic Book Characters Breaking the Fourth Wall." Geek.com, May 22, 2018. https://www.geek.com/comics/a-history-of-comic-book-characters-breaking-the-fourth-wall-1740639/. Accessed April 1, 2019.

Jordan, June. "Poem about My Rights." https://www.poetryfoundation.org/poems/48762/poem-about-my-rights.

Lorde, Audre. "The Uses of Anger." *Women's Studies Quarterly* 25, nos. 1–2 (Spring/Summer 1997): 278–85.

Martindale, Kathleen. *Un/Popular Culture: Lesbian Writing after the Sex Wars*. SUNY, 1997.

Parmar, Pratibha, dir. *A Place of Rage*. 1991. Perfs. Angela Davis, June Jordan, Alice Walker.

"Queers Read This." Leaflet distributed at Pride March in New York, June 1990. Published anonymously by Queers. http://www.qrd.org/qrd/misc/text/queers.read.this.

Radicalesbians. 1970. "The Woman-Identified-Woman." Available full text here: https://www.historyisaweapon.com/defcon1/radicalesbianswoman.html.

Schrag, Ariel. *Awkward*. Touchstone, 1995, 2008.

Schrag, Ariel. *Definition*. Touchstone, 1996.

Schrag, Ariel. *Likewise*. Touchstone, 1998.

Schrag, Ariel. *Potential*. Touchstone, 1997, 2008.

Stehle, Darren. "Why Do Queers Get So Fucking Angry?" *Medium*, March 5, 2018. https://medium.com/th-ink/why-do-queers-get-so-fucking-angry-68f920525f41. Accessed January 10, 2019.

Voutiritsas, Thea. "Why Do Comics Break the Fourth Wall?" Go Comics, October 22, 2018. https://www.gocomics.com/blog/4703/why-do-comics-break-the-fourth-wall. Accessed April 1, 2019.

Wojnarowicz, David. *Close to the Knives: A Memoir of Disintegration*. Vintage, 1991.

Chapter 3

CONDOMS NOT COFFINS
1980S–1990s AMERICAN AIDS COMICS AS COLLECTIVE MEMORY

TESLA CARIANI

David wakes, nauseous and sweaty, in the middle of the night. His lower body is bathed in a red light, which only underscores how pale he has become. Sick of being sick, and sick of fighting to stay alive in a world that views him as disposable, David clasps the TV remote in an attempt to focus on something beyond his illness. But the TV provides no respite, projecting the soundbite: "If I had a dollar to spend for health care I'd rather spend it on a baby or innocent person with some defect or illness not of their own responsibility, not some person with AIDS" (Wojnarowicz, Romberger, and Van Cook 2012, 46). The callousness of this statement made by a healthcare official is reflected in the sharp edges of the speech bubble emanating from the TV. Intruding into David's bedroom, these words hover in the middle of the frame, uneasily inhabiting the same space as David, his pill bottles, and the skeleton of a baby elephant.

This scene from David Wojnarowicz's graphic memoir, *7 Miles a Second* (1996),[1] vividly encapsulates the glaring disconnect between an uninformed, fearful public and individuals living with HIV/AIDS in America from the mid 1980s to the early 1990s, especially in major cities. As the number of people with HIV continued to rise, comics circulated within queer networks to educate, share stories, provide political commentary, and document lives on the brink of death. Though the history of comics as a public health tool is well documented from warnings about STIs targeted at soldiers to anti-smoking campaigns, the comics and graphic memoirs that emerged during the AIDS epidemic would greatly expand visual representations of illness, of queer lives, and of attendant social, cultural, and political effects.

Focusing on works primarily from San Francisco and New York City, this chapter examines the graphic memoir *7 Miles a Second* alongside comics from the collection *Strip AIDS U.S.A.: A Collection of Cartoon Art to Benefit People with AIDS* (1988). Divided into three parts, *7 Miles a Second* vividly chronicles scenes and impressions from David Wojnarowicz's life as a young hustler, artist, and activist in New York City, and his eventual death from AIDS-induced illness. Predominantly compiled before Wojnarowicz's AIDS-related death in

1992, *7 Miles a Second* was drawn and colored respectively by his friends and fellow artists, James Romberger and Marguerite Van Cook. Instead of focusing on a single person's story, *Strip AIDS U.S.A.* collects comics from a variety of artists and was published to raise money for the Shanti Project, a San Francisco-based volunteer organization that provides support for individuals with life-threatening illnesses (Shanti Project 2019), and to push back against a climate of misinformation and fear. Through a close engagement with both texts, this chapter argues that these queer comics come to function as collective memory for the HIV/AIDS epidemic by visually representing changing conceptions of absence, affect, activism, and sociality in urban life. By examining these texts through the lens of collective memory, this chapter further contends that these comics characterize the process of collective remembering as a political act, an aspect of queer identity, and as an impossibility. These comics can be considered queer on a number of intersecting and diverging levels: they are queer in that they are largely created by and about queer people; they are largely created from and for queer communities; and they are queer in the Sedgwickian sense that they travel cross-wise. Theorizing about the etymology of "queer," Sedgwick writes, "Queer is a continuing moment, movement, motive—recurrent, eddying, *troublant*. The word 'queer' itself means *across*" (Sedgwick 1993, xii). She goes on: "The immemorial current that queer represents is antiseparatist as it is antiassimilationist" (Sedgwick 1993, xii). Likewise, these comics try at once to resist a fatal call for queer separatism and also to maintain difference. Taken together, they move across divisions—between and among the signs L/G/B/T/Q, between fear and anger, between temporalities, and between those who are sick, not yet sick, or well.

Back in David's room with the TV and the pill bottles and the skeleton of a baby elephant, the affective cost of refusing to be isolated and also refusing to assimilate play out in his fantasy. After listening to the callous opinion from a healthcare official who believes those with AIDS are responsible for their own illness, David reacts. Half-awake, he "[reaches] in through the TV screen and [rips] [the official's] face in half" (Wojnarowicz, Romberger, and Van Cook 2012, 46). David's elongated arm glows and crackles with electricity, suspended while pushing back through the screen and reversing the unidirectional transmission that had transported this health official's unwanted presence into his bedroom. David's angry, agential response appears as a fantasy of exceptional embodiment. The entire graphic memoir might be understood as replicating this forceful movement of David's arm—as a way of reaching *across* time and space to offer up testimony and display enduring anger. Not only aimed at the "replaceable head" (Wojnarowicz, Romberger, and Van Cook 2012, 46) on the TV screen, the move to shatter the fourth wall reaches towards the audience as well. We become part of his memory.

I WAKE UP WITH INTENSE NAUSEA, FEELING WET LIKE SOMETHING FROM MY SOUL, MY MEMORY IS SEEPING OUT THE BACK OF MY HEAD INTO THE PILLOW. NIGHT SWEATS. I TURN ON THE TV TO TRY TO GET SOME FOCUS OUTSIDE MY ILLNESS.

IF I HAD A DOLLAR TO SPEND FOR HEALTH CARE I'D RATHER SPEND IT ON A BABY OR INNOCENT PERSON WITH SOME DEFECT OR ILLNESS NOT OF THEIR OWN RESPONSIBILITY, NOT SOME PERSON WITH AIDS

SAYS THE HEALTH CARE OFFICIAL IN THE MIDDLE OF AN HOUR-LONG VIDEO OF PEOPLE DYING ON CAMERA BECAUSE THEY CAN'T AFFORD THE LIMITED DRUGS AVAILABLE THAT MIGHT EXTEND THEIR LIVES AND I DON'T EVEN KNOW WHAT THIS OFFICIAL LOOKS LIKE BECAUSE I REACH IN THROUGH THE TV SCREEN AND RIP HIS FACE IN HALF

SZKKRRZZT

THE MAN ON THE TV HAS A REPLACEABLE HEAD. HE CAN HAVE THE FACE OF A DOCTOR OR A POLITICIAN, OF A RESEARCH SCIENTIST OR A PRIEST WITH A SWASTIKA TATTOOED ON HIS HEART CLAIMING THIS IS GOD'S PUNISHMENT AND HE TALKS ABOUT ME IN WORDS THAT MAKE ME SOUND LIKE AN INSECT: "CARRIER" AND "INFECTED" AND WHENEVER HE SHOWS PICTURES OF ME I AM ALWAYS BEDRIDDEN AND ALONE AND ON THE EDGE OF DEATH AND HE SAYS I MUST SUPPRESS MY SEXUALITY WHETHER I AM A MAN OR A WOMAN, WHETHER I AM HOMOSEXUAL OR HETEROSEXUAL, WHETHER I HAVE AIDS OR NOT, AND HE SAYS I MUST NOT FUCK AND I MUST NOT SUCK AND I CAN'T HAVE DESIRES... AND IT IS IRONIC WHEN HE TAKES ON THE FACE OF A FAMILY MAN WHO WANTS TO PROTECT HIS CHILDREN BECAUSE I AM HIS CHILD AND I HAVE AIDS AND AIDS IS USED AS A WEAPON TO ENFORCE THE CONSERVATIVE AGENDA.

Figure 3.1. "I wake up with intense nausea," David Wojnarowicz (w), James Romberger (p), Marguerite Van Cook (c), in *7 Miles a Second*. Copyright 2019 by James Romberger, Marguerite Van Cook, and the estate of David Wojnarowicz. Courtesy of Ground Zero Books.

In this scene, the growing disconnect between David's mental and physical capacity reflects his subjectivity as he experiences a low point in his illness. Aesthetically rendered in panels where the narration relocates from boxes of text inside frames (as is the case in other parts of this graphic memoir) to unbounded text in the gutters, there is a visual untethering of David's thoughts from his present. With no information about his precise symptoms, these panels focus instead on the affective, social, and political qualities of illness. These broader qualities more widely resonate across people who have experience with HIV/AIDS, helping to render visually collective experiences of HIV/AIDS. In place of a particularizing litany of symptoms, the text portrays isolation in illness, fear of dying, and rage against a dehumanizing and apathetic political system. Since the words and images separate from each other, the gutters (the spaces between panels) function as a void of swirling thoughts that exceed David's present embodiment. In just these few panels, *7 Miles a Second* covers bodily and emotional exhaustion, night sweats, hallucinatory imaginings, violent desires, and a bleak political landscape, and serves to foreshadow David's future. The text is associative, forming a series of ideas that connect different geographic locations to conservative and white supremacist views to pervasive institutional violence. While the graphic memoir focuses inward through auto- and collective biography, the text remains outwardly committed to highlighting the web of relations between individuals and society.

COLLECTIVE MEMORY

Theoretical work about collective memory and queer archives offers up a window into the ways in which cultural objects like comics participate in the making of group identities, histories, and practices. As Maaheen Ahmed and Benoît Crucifix (2018) describe, comics are usually left out of archives: "Situated at the lower end of the economies of cultural memory, comics have more often ended up in the waste bins . . . than in the closely monitored storage of archives" (6). Rather than focusing on what gets placed in archives, this chapter recovers comics from waste bins to consider how comics and graphic memoirs themselves are rich repositories of, and constitutive of, cultural information. In the absence of officially documented histories, "memory," Ann Cvetkovich (2003) notes, "becomes a valuable historical resource, and ephemeral and personal collections of objects stand alongside the documents of the dominant culture in order to offer alternative modes of knowledge" (8). Largely overlooked in past scholarly work, queer comics and graphic memoirs are arguably more at risk of becoming ephemeral objects that contain almost-forgotten memories of queer lives and experiences than other cultural objects. Comics as medium

incorporate graphic and textual elements that capture a wide range of affective, linguistic, symbolic, optic, and expressive cues, which in turn visually
animate distinct subcultures and experiences of trauma. Since both *7 Miles a
Second* and *Strip AIDS U.S.A.* seek to intervene into the silence, ignorance, and
fear surrounding AIDS, these texts incorporate a myriad of visual strategies
to document and depict how the American AIDS epidemic in the late 1980s
and early 1990s permeates representations of daily life. Read together, these
texts function as collective memory, representing both the impossibility of
ever completely recovering this time period and also sketching in some of the
contours and textures of a rapidly changing culture.

Though Laura Doan (2017) argues that collective memory is able to "capture the tactile immediacy of a past event that binds the political identity of
a group '*already well established*'" (114), queer responses to AIDS through art
and activism also served as binding agents for a conception of queer that
would, albeit unevenly, bring together multiple identities on the sexuality and
gender spectrum in the fight for survival. As the epidemic persisted, queer
political identity would become inextricably bound up with a set of investments in visibility ("we're here, we're queer"), healthcare ("drugs into bodies"),
and remembering the dead (political funerals, die-ins). Ahmed and Crucifix
describe the process of collective memory as the place where "different kinds of
memories are in constant interaction, for instance, through the confluence of
an individual reader's memory, historical context, and the collective memories
of comics, including the intertwined memories of the genres, styles, and series
populating them" (2018, 2). In the wake of high rates of death and significant
losses to communities, *Strip AIDS U.S.A.* and *7 Miles a Second* arguably stand
in as collective memory, raising questions not only about memory but also
about memorialization amidst erasure.

ABSENCE

First published in 1988, *Strip AIDS U.S.A.* embodies a commitment to col-
lectivity in both the range of materials and in its very assemblage. Inspired by
Strip AIDS U.K. (1987), Trina Robbins approached Robert Triptow about editing a collection of American comics about AIDS. Both living and working in
San Francisco, Robbins and Triptow connected with Bill Sienkiewicz, an East
Coast native, who had expressed interest in compiling a similar volume. With
Sienkiewicz on board as a third editor, the team of influential comics artists
worked quickly to assemble *Strip AIDS U.S.A.* to begin raising funds and raising consciousness as fast as possible. Collected from both coasts, these comics
represent a diversity of experiences, artistic styles, and perspectives. As Triptow

Figure 3.2. "The Glitter Winks Out!" Ned Sonntag, in *Strip AIDS U.S.A.: A Collection of Cartoon Art to Benefit People with AIDS* (Last Gasp, 1988), n.p.

writes in an introductory blurb, "Fear and hatred are unfortunately nothing new to gay men and women, but such prejudices are even more misplaced when confronting a medical epidemic. That the tragedy of AIDS transcends bias and politics—it transcends all personal differences—is a message I hoped for in *Strip AIDS U.S.A.*" (1988). By curating a collection that sought to encompass an array of narratives, these comics tackle a breadth and range of experiences and information related to HIV/AIDS that one comics artist alone could not.

Though *Strip AIDS U.S.A.* contains many narratives of individuals impacted by AIDS, some of the most powerful strips represent uncanny scenes of absence in daily life juxtaposed against urban backdrops. In Ned Sonntag's "The Glitter Winks Out!" the main character narrates walking through Greenwich Village in New York City: "As I'd left the Grocery after seeing Charles, I'd looked West on Bleecker to Christopher and had a strange memory overlay of some summer five or six years earlier" (Robbins, Sienkiewicz, and Triptow 1988). The narrator's

Figure 3.3. "Help Fight the AIDS Monster!" Thomas Yeates, in *Strip AIDS U.S.A.: A Collection of Cartoon Art to Benefit People with AIDS* (Last Gasp, 1988), n.p. Courtesy of Thomas Yeates.

stream of consciousness runs parallel to the image of an overexposed, ghostly sea of people. But it is not until the second tier on this page that the narrator describes exactly what she remembers: "The corner impassable, a casual riot of milling blonde men in tight 501's a pilgrimage Saturday for all clones of this gay archetype, a grapevine a mass mind . . . sexual socialism on parade!" (Robbins, Sienkiewicz, and Triptow 1988). Next to this description, the corner of Bleecker and Christopher is empty of all figures. The sky appears overcast, shadowing the entire scene. The decision to invert descriptions from adjacent images visually represents the narrator's memory overlay, crossing between a mismatched past and present. The uniformity of panels, positioned with their gutters, forms a kind of street corner, which in turn underscores interchangeability and invites comparison.

In the movement between one panel and the next, comics require a high level of participation by readers to fill in the gaps, and Sonntag relies on the imaginative space created between panels to represent resurfacing memories and point towards unrecorded history. In early spirit photography, overlaying images, known as double exposure, were used to create portraits of ghosts. Here, the figures moving through the street are similarly haunting. Unlike the process of double exposure that blends two images from different spatial and/or temporal moments into one image, the gutter between these panels calls on the reader to imagine a disjunctive temporal distance between the two moments on the corner of Bleecker and Christopher just as it textually connects them. By the time the narrator poses the question, "Where were they all now?" (Robbins, Sienkiewicz, and Triptow 1988), the visuals have already communicated the answer. Evoking the photographic technologies of double exposure allows Sonntag to place this illustrated comic in conversation with photography—a temporary conflation with a medium that is strongly associated with documenting and displaying evidence. As Hillary Chute (2016) observes, "Comics makes a reader access the unfolding of evidence in the movement of its basic grammar, by aggregating and accumulating frames of information" (2). These panels participate in displaying evidence for a mounting case against the sorely inadequate governmental and public responses to the epidemic. Relying on documentary aesthetics positions the viewer as a witness to the everyday horror that is constituted in the absence of so many people who no longer exist, except to haunt our collective memory. These panels become a monument to the dead.

AFFECT

Though there is horror to be found in representations of empty streets in queer neighborhoods, Strip AIDS U.S.A. demonstrates how the deadlier monster arises from a contagious climate of panic and terror. In a splash page by Thomas Yeates titled "Help Fight the AIDS Monster!" (3/13/1988), the monster that AIDS has created is a looming, hairy beast with at least three arms. "Fear" and "Ignorance" are inscribed on two of its taloned limbs. A single figure stands outside the monster's cave, armed with a wooden "sword," bearing a condom on its tip. He wears a robe reminiscent of the AIDS quilt that appears adorned with a patchwork of deceased faces from a variety of different ages, races, cultures, religious backgrounds, and genders. Similar to these collected comics, the AIDS

Figure 3.4. "A Coupla Dykes Sittin' Around Talkin' About AIDS," Alison Bechdel, in *Strip AIDS U.S.A.: A Collection of Cartoon Art to Benefit People with AIDS* (Last Gasp, 1988), n.p.

Memorial Quilt is another public memorial assembled as collective memory. In terms of formal qualities, patchwork quilts share some similarities with comics. Looking at images of the AIDS Memorial Quilt laid out on the National Mall in Washington, DC, the square pieces of fabric are akin to panels, and the stitching or physical spaces between mirror gutters. It seems no accident that these complementary media, comprised of separate and connected squares, afford an especially powerful way to visualize the relationship between individuals and a collective. In this splash page, Yeates fuses the identity of the figure with those of the dead by adorning him with their faces.

Though the monster is called the "AIDS Monster," the monster's first means of "attack" spreads fear and creates barriers to knowledge. Fear and ignorance go hand in hand (or claw in claw), existing as part of the same creature. Evoking wood-cut aesthetics and a scene reminiscent of Arthurian legends, the Chucks on the young man's feet signal how ordinary and unprepared he is to face off against the salivating monster. Condoms seem no match for such a beast. Practicing safe sex may be a barrier against HIV, but it does not stop fear. As Cathy Cohen (1999) has demonstrated, fear of AIDS not only contributed to a lack of public and governmental support, but fear also stymied efforts to deconstruct the prevailing notion that AIDS only affected white gay men, effectively hindering large-scale activism that linked the AIDS epidemic with racial injustice. This comic reveals a desperate and pertinent anxiety about the failure to stop the spread of fear and ignorance from consuming everyone. The ramifications are high, yet the figure seems outmatched. Wizard robes and a hat with a drooping star hint at the hope that magic might save him. A clear commentary on the inadequate and uneven fight ahead, this splash page ultimately calls for others to join. But who else is there to fight for? The landscape behind the figure is both sunny and barren. When looking at this page, one wonders if there are any people left or if they have all fallen. The past and future are both indecipherable in this scene. The AIDS epidemic has reached a crossroads. This page visualizes both the insufficiency of an individual hero and suggests a deep attachment to continuing to remember and fight for the dead.

ACTIVISM

Taking up the question of who fights and how, *Strip AIDS U.S.A.* also documents narratives of political activism. Alison Bechdel's strip from her series *Dykes to Watch Out For* called "A Coupla Dykes Sittin' Around Talkin' About AIDS" (1988) chronicles a conversation between Mo, a lesbian who possesses a "rhetorical, if not action-based, dedication to social justice" (Bechdel 2019a) and Ginger, an English graduate student (Bechdel 2019b) who regularly participates in social justice. The prominent coverage of AIDS in the newspaper shown in this strip acts as visual testament to the processes by which the epidemic seeps into seemingly unconnected domestic space. After reading the latest obituaries in the *Fag & Dyke Gazette*, Mo exclaims, "Maybe I otta **do** something! Volunteer at the **AIDS Hotline** or be a **buddy** to a **P.W.A!**" (Robbins, Sienkiewicz, and Triptow 1988). Ginger responds by reminding Mo that gay men probably would not lend a hand if lesbians were infected and Mo should not act solely because she feels guilty. After accusing Ginger of being "petty," Ginger responds by reminding Mo that there are still other issues to fight for. Ginger's response, which implies that AIDS activism will not fix everything, resonates with the work of many Black feminists and activists like Barbara Smith, cofounder of the Combahee River Collective, who were involved in AIDS organizing in the late 1980s and early 1990s. Smith (2019) continues to remain critical of the hierarchies of power and priorities within mainstream queer activism that replicate intersectional oppression along the lines of economic status, race, gender, and age.

Disregarding Ginger's response, Mo continues to rant, while Ginger's body language—her crossed arms and rolling eyes—indicates Ginger neither wants nor needs a lesson in public health. Ginger finally gets a word in to respond sarcastically, "I **love** it when white women quote statistics about people of color!" (Robbins, Sienkiewicz, and Triptow 1988). As Mo self-righteously storms out presumably to go volunteer immediately, it becomes clear that Ginger has been volunteering for two weeks already. By including a comic about lesbian activism in *Strip AIDS U.S.A.*, the collection not only documents the biopolitical realities of those living with AIDS, but it also resists the problem Cvetkovich identifies in relation to AIDS activism whereby "lesbians, many of whom came to ACT

Figure 3.5. "A Coupla Dykes Sittin' Around Talkin' About AIDS," Alison Bechdel, in *Strip AIDS U.S.A.: A Collection of Cartoon Art to Benefit People with AIDS* (Last Gasp, 1988), n.p.

UP with considerable political experience, seem to be the first to disappear from ACT UP's history" (2003, 144). Black women, especially, have been some of the first to disappear from narratives of political struggle, which Bechdel highlights in this strip.

For Mo, interior, domestic space is one of disconnection from the outside world, whereas Ginger dismantles this indoor-outdoor binary by demonstrating the necessity of both to sustain long-term activism. Bechdel's strip depicts the widespread impact of AIDS beyond circles of white, gay men, its commonly assumed sole focus. Treating *Strip AIDS U.S.A.* as an archive provides a way to glimpse how issues of race, gender, and sexuality complicate dominant narratives of AIDS care, illness, and activism. Cvetkovich describes how "cultural artifacts become the archive of something more ephemeral: culture as a 'way of life'" (2003, 9). In this strip, Bechdel demonstrates how activism as a cultural value comes to define a queer "way of life" or orientation towards the world. At the same time, this strip uses an ironic moment between Mo and Ginger to show the mechanisms of erasure in action when Mo assumes Ginger is not involved. The ideals and promise of queer collectivity as a liberating force come under scrutiny in Bechdel's strip, but ultimately this comic ends with the promise that both Mo and Ginger will volunteer together.

SOCIALITY

While Bechdel's strip illustrates how activism permeates daily life, Jerry Mills's contribution from his series *Poppers* explores changing social and domestic landscapes. *Poppers* follows three friends: Billy, a sometimes frivolous and conspicuously muscled blond; Andre, a well-muscled, flamboyant Black man; and Yves, a socially awkward, good-natured Jewish guy. In this strip, Yves and Andre arrive at Billy's house to pick him up only to find Billy silhouetted and sitting alone in the dark. What follows is a conversational inventory of those who have died, of bath houses that have closed, and of their fears about whether they, too, will become sick. Without reading the words, the solid, high-contrast black of these panels imparts a gloomier mood than one might expect from a pre-party scene.

The shadows cast by the window blinds evoke prison bars, which are repeated in the even lines of the gutters that crisscross this page. The characters themselves become obscured in impenetrable darkness. Of the sixteen panels, only half have any discernable human figures at all, so dialogue echoes from the margins. In the middle tier, the only way to follow who is speaking is to track which side speech bubbles are anchored to, suggesting that these worries and doubts could attach to anyone. A single black panel stands out,

Figure 3.6. *Poppers*, Jerry Mills, in *Strip AIDS U.S.A.: A Collection of Cartoon Art to Benefit People with AIDS* (Last Gasp, 1988), n.p.

allowing the reader a pause to imagine the swirling thoughts of characters or perhaps their own before the tone shifts, signaled visually by the introduction of a match and Andre's pronouncement: "Lissen, children. I knows one thing! You can't stop human natchuh . . . come hell or high watuh, people will always need to dance and party and laugh!" (Robbins, Sienkiewicz, and Triptow 1988).

Throughout, Andre's speech is characterized as "dialect" with contractions, phonetic misspellings, and pluralization. Just as a visual sense of community takes shape among their disembodied thoughts, racialized traces of difference unsettle this representation of unity by bringing into the foreground questions about how the AIDS epidemic differently affected gay men of color in San Francisco, so much so that Mills represents Andre as the character who has the emotional experience necessary to show them how to carry on. Andre performs affective labor to shift Billy and Yves away from their spiraling thoughts, and this strip serves as another testament to the ways in which caretaking is often performed by more marginalized subjects. Andre offers Billy and Yves a way to cope—a way out of Billy's dark home and therefore his mind. Through the formal qualities of this strip, Mills evokes an inert, lonely interior in contrast to the luminous city full of the possibility of connection. The reversal of spaces that seem safe and nurturing subverts ideas of home. In this strip, the bars, baths, and other social spaces of the city forge queer collectivity and kinship. Remembering and evoking these places become synonymous with remembering and evoking the people who inhabit them.

MEMORIALIZATION

Returning to David's room, the skeletal proboscidean stalks ever closer to David's bed. Its upright appearance conjures images of extinction—bones long since stripped of flesh that have been reassembled as a monument to the dead. David and the baby elephant are doubles of each other. As the elephant draws nearer, staring with eyeless sockets, David's body faces away from the TV. Like the elephant before him, David's body is skeletal. Rotting flesh gives way to bones. David has become a corpse like those from *Tales from the Crypt* (James Romberger, email to author, June 4, 2019). Perhaps foreshadowing the undying force of this graphic memoir and the bodies that have not been laid to rest, the panel raises questions about how communities mourn their dead when state and governmental harm remains unacknowledged. As the specter of extinction draws closer, David's own remains seem more inert, even, than the skeleton of the baby elephant. There is no one present to mourn David as he rots, except those who have already become extinct. The TV flickers beside his bed, caught between faces. It does not matter which face the media presents.

AFTER THE LAST FEW YEARS OF LOSING COUNT OF THE FRIENDS AND NEIGHBORS WHO HAVE BEEN DYING SLOW VICIOUS AND UNNECESSARY DEATHS BECAUSE FAGS AND DYKES AND JUNKIES AND THE POOR ARE EXPENDABLE IN THIS KILLING MACHINE CALLED AMERICA. "IF YOU WANT TO STOP AIDS SHOOT THE QUEERS" SAYS THE GOVERNOR OF TEXAS AND HIS PRESS SECRETARY LATER CLAIMS HE WAS ONLY JOKING AND DIDN'T KNOW THE MICROPHONE WAS ON AND BESIDES THEY DIDN'T THINK IT WOULD HURT HIS CHANCES FOR RE-ELEC-TION ANYWAY AND I'VE BEEN LOOKING ALL MY LIFE AT THE SIGNS SURROUNDING US IN THE MEDIA OR ON PEOPLE'S LIPS; THE RELIGIOUS TYPES OUTSIDE ST. PATRICK'S CATHEDRAL SHOUTING TO MEN AND WOMEN IN THE GAY PARADE "YOU WON'T BE HERE NEXT YEAR YOU'LL GET AIDS AND DIE HA HA."

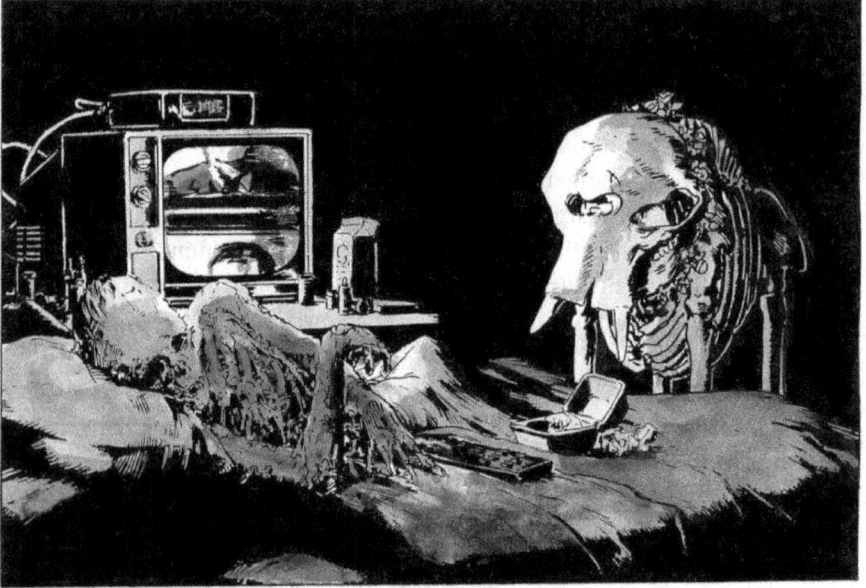

AND THE AREAS OF THE USA WHERE IT IS POSSIBLE TO MURDER A MAN AND WHEN BROUGHT TO TRIAL ONE ONLY HAS TO SAY THE VICTIM WAS A QUEER AND HE TRIED TO TOUCH YOU AND THE COURTS WILL SET YOU FREE AND THE FACT THAT AIDS DRUG TRIALS ARE NOT OPEN TO PEOPLE OF COLOR OR THE POOR UNLESS THEY HAVE A PRIVATE PHYSICIAN WHO CAN MONITOR THE EXPERIMENTAL DRUGS THEY NEED BECAUSE DOCTORS IN CLINICS ARE CON-STANTLY ROTATED AND INTRAVENOUS DRUG USERS HAVE TO BE CLEAN OF DRUGS FOR SEVEN YEARS BEFORE THEY'LL BE CONSIDERED FOR THESE TRIALS AND THERE ARE THREE HUNDRED AND FIFTY OPPORTUNISTIC INFECTIONS THE DISEASES OF BIRDS AND SMALL MAMMALS AND AS OF THIS YEAR NYC ALONE WILL HAVE THIRTY-THREE THOUSAND PEOPLE HOMELESS AND DYING OF AIDS ON THE STREET. A HANDFUL OF SENATORS BREEZED THROUGH HERE LAST YEAR AND WERE ASSURED THAT THESE PEOPLE WERE DYING SO QUICKLY FROM LACK OF HEALTH CARE THAT THERE WOULDN'T BE A NOTICE-ABLE INCREASE IN VISIBILITY. THE ONES WHO DIED WOULD MAKE ROOM FOR THOSE COMING UP BEHIND.

Figure 3.7. "Losing count of the friends and neighbors who have been dying," David Wojnarowicz (w), James Romberger (p), Marguerite Van Cook (c), in *7 Miles a Second*. Copyright 2019 by James Romberger, Marguerite Van Cook, and the estate of David Wojnarowicz. Courtesy of Ground Zero Books.

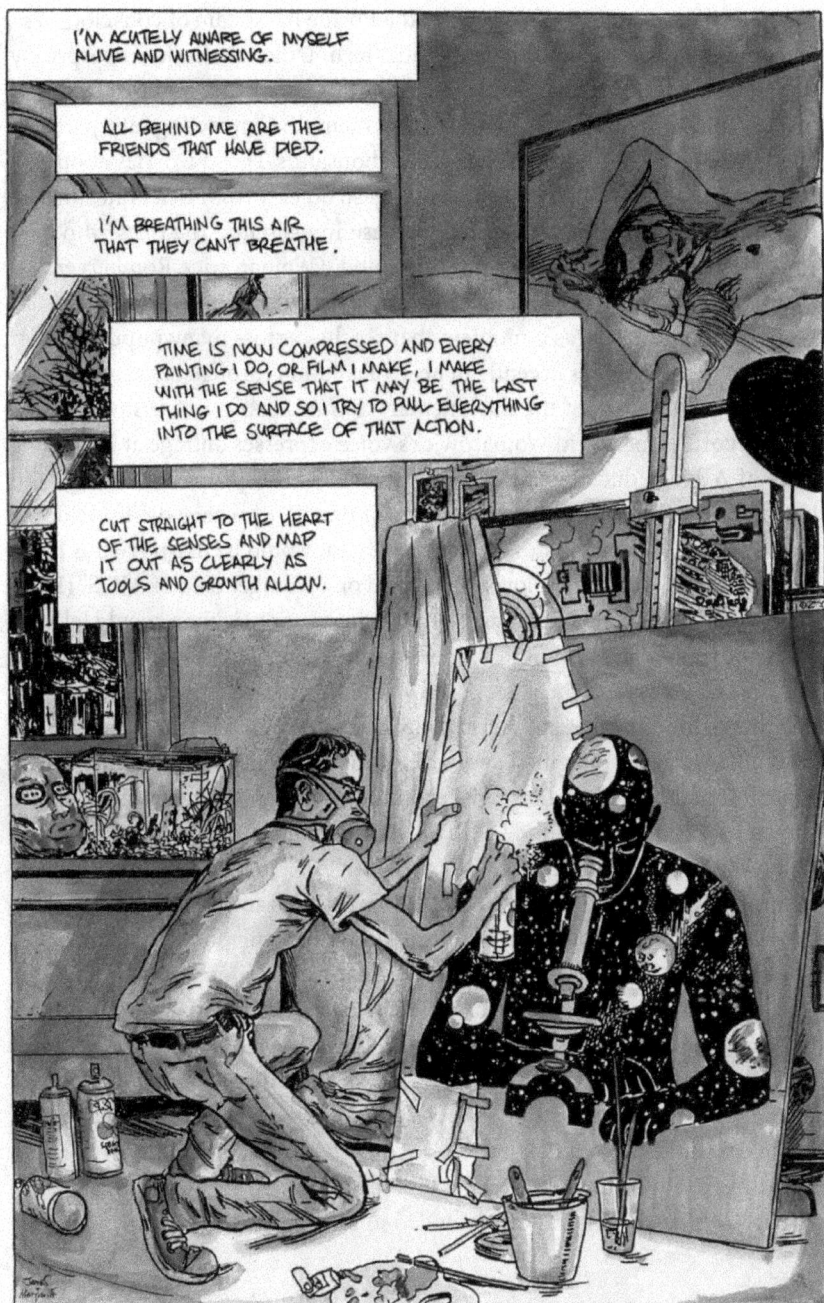

Figure 3.8. "I'm acutely aware of myself alive and witnessing," David Wojnarowicz (w), James Romberger (p), Marguerite Van Cook (c), in *7 Miles a Second*. Copyright 2019 by James Romberger, Marguerite Van Cook, and the estate of David Wojnarowicz. Courtesy of Ground Zero Books.

They are all static. Quotes from the media invade his stream of consciousness, and even though the visuals suggest death, the untethered text shows surprising life. David's anger persists even when his body cannot. The intense current of his emotions provides the lifeblood of this memoir. Connecting interpersonal and institutional failings to the death of thousands, David worries about the problem of visible dead: "People were dying so quickly from lack of health care that there wouldn't be a noticeable increase in visibility. The ones who died would make room for those coming up behind" (Wojnarowicz, Romberger, and Van Cook 2012, 47). The problem of what constitutes visible, grievable death is conceptualized here as a problem that reaches across many populations of people and is one that is urgently in need of solution through collective action.

During the climax of the documentary *United in Anger: A History of ACT UP*, a recording of David Wojnarowicz's voice expresses outrage at increasing rates of AIDS-induced death. Overlaying footage of people marching with banners that broadcast name after name of people who have died (including David's own), his voice states, "I imagine what it would be like if friends had a demonstration each time a lover or a friend or a stranger died of AIDS" (Hubbard 2012). He goes on to fantasize, "Friends, lovers, or neighbors would take the dead body and drive with it in a car a hundred miles an hour to Washington, DC, and blast through the gates of the White House and come to a screeching halt before the entrance and dump their lifeless form on the front steps" (Hubbard 2012). David's imagined spectacle of mourning is literalized in a public funeral for activist Mark Lowe Fisher. In the documentary, fellow activists are shown covering Fisher's body with a list of demands and carrying his coffin to the White House. As Cvetkovich (2003) writes, "Queer activism . . . remade mourning in the form of new kinds of public funerals and queer intimacies" (5). By making funerals public and political, rituals of remembrance become part of a queer culture that is not predicated on a direct relationship with the dead. Memory becomes distributed *across* friends, lovers, neighbors, and strangers. By tracing absences, affects, activism, and sociality in *Strip AIDS U.S.A.* and *7 Miles a Second*, it is possible to see how these texts embody processes of collective memory. These processes move across temporalities and experiences to bear witness to the AIDS epidemic and also foreground impossibilities embedded at the heart of representation. Like Fisher's body, *7 Miles a Second* and *Strip AIDS U.S.A.* are collaborations intended to be carried.

Note

1. James Romberger and David Wojnarowicz began discussions of the project in 1986 when Wojnarowicz was working on a show at Ground Zero, a gallery in the East Village run by Romberger and Marguerite Van Cook. Romberger and Wojnarowicz worked on the first

section, "Thirst," together. Romberger finished inking those pages when he was abroad and sent them to the magazine *El Víbora* in Spain. In 1988, a Spanish translation of the first section was published in black-and-white by *El Víbora*; the English version was published by *World War 3 Illustrated* in the US. An excerpt from the second part "Stray Dogs" was published in *Red Tape* magazine around 1989. Though they met a few times, Wojnarowicz did not live to see the finalized version of part three. Romberger completed the third section in the year following Wojnarowicz's passing, partly with the help of Wojnarowicz's journals. Van Cook joined the collaboration as a colorist after *7 Miles a Second* was accepted for publication by Vertigo Comics and published as a complete graphic memoir in 1996. Romberger remastered the color for the Fantagraphics publication in 2013 (the version included in the figures) to make it "more like a French album format" (James Romberger, email to author, June 4, 2019).

Works Cited

Ahmed, Maaheen, and Benoît Crucifix. *Comics Memory: Archives and Styles.* Palgrave Macmillan, 2018.

Bechdel, Alison. 2019a. "Cast Biographies." http://dykestowatchoutfor.com/cast-biographies.

Bechdel, Alison. 2019b. "DTWOF Trivia Answers." http://dykestowatchoutfor.com/dtwof-trivia.

Chute, Hillary L. *Disaster Drawn: Visual Witness, Comics, and Documentary Form.* Belknap Press of Harvard University Press, 2016.

Cohen, Cathy. *The Boundaries of Blackness.* University of Chicago Press, 1999.

Cvetkovich, Ann. *An Archive of Feelings: Trauma, Sexuality, and Lesbian Public Cultures.* Duke University Press, 2003.

Doan, Laura. "Queer History / Queer Memory." *GLQ: A Journal of Lesbian and Gay Studies* 23, no. 1 (January 2017): 113–36. doi:10.1215/10642684-3672321.

Hubbard, Jim, dir. 2012. *United in Anger: A History of ACT UP.*

Robbins, Trina, Bill Sienkiewicz, and Robert Triptow, eds. *Strip AIDS U.S.A.: A Collection of Cartoon Art to Benefit People with AIDS.* Last Gasp, 1988.

Sedgwick, Eve Kosofsky. *Tendencies.* Duke University Press, 1993.

Shanti Project. 2019. "Our Story." https://www.shanti.org/about-us/our-story/.

Smith, Barbara. "Barbara Smith: Why I Left the Mainstream Queer Rights Movement." *New York Times*, June 19, 2019. https://www.nytimes.com/2019/06/19/us/barbara-smith-black -queer-rights.html

Villarosa, Linda. "America's Hidden H.I.V. Epidemic." *New York Times*, June 6, 2017. https://www .nytimes.com/2017/06/06/magazine/americas-hidden-hiv-epidemic.html

Wojnarowicz, David, James Romberger, and Marguerite Van Cook. *7 Miles a Second.* Fantagraphics Books, 2012.

Chapter 4

OF ANTHOLOGIES AND ACTIVISM
BUILDING AN LGBTQ+ COMICS COMMUNITY

MARGARET GALVAN

Don Melia and Lionel Gracey-Whitman's gay superhero comic *Matt Black: Charcoal* no. 6 (1987) includes a moment that connects readers to the contemporary worries of gay men: a man showering alone following an intimate encounter with his male partner worries over "some lumps under [his] arm . . . and in [his] groin" and heads to the doctor's office where he says that he would like to be tested for HIV/AIDS, recounting his symptoms, including the lumps. His exchange with the doctor highlights how isolating the experience can be. As they discuss his health, the bodies of doctor and patient disappear from view, and we see only their words hanging in the space between them. Within the confines of the scene, we find no resolution of the character's quandary, but we come to empathize with him in these tense moments.

And, yet, just beyond the boundaries of the scene, we learn how embedded this character, Russell, is in a community of caring individuals, despite how alone he may feel. His experience, shaped as a series of three-panel strips, plays out across the bottom quarter of several pages of the comic and is separated from the rest of the action by a gray border. In the top three rows of panels on the same pages, the main plot advances: the character's boyfriend, superhero Matt Black, worries about him and his abrupt departure while having to deal with a band of bad guys. The parallel plots unite at the moment that Russell receives the news that Matt has been kidnapped and is devastated both by this news and an earlier revelation that we understand to be his diagnosis. At this moment, however, he is no longer physically alone, and he is more aware of the communities of care that might help him. This scene ends the issue, and no further issues of *Matt Black: Charcoal* followed. But this exchange shows how deft Melia and Gracey-Whitman are at embedding pressing social issues within the superhero framework.[1] The two men were partners in both life and work, and this comic is an early collaboration. Released under their own small UK press imprint in the late 1980s, it allowed them to explore and repurpose familiar comics environments and tropes for the examination of gay experiences, including HIV/AIDS, which they continued in their next project, the anthology comic, *Strip AIDS* (1987).

The community of support that Russell feels within the comic echoes the growing support in the real world at this time. At the time, LGBTQ+ individuals were responding to HIV/AIDS, rapidly forming organizations to support those affected more than medical and governmental support systems could or would. In lieu of government support, individuals worldwide created hundreds of organizations to provide medical, social, financial, and other forms of support and to advocate on behalf of persons living with HIV/AIDS (PWAs) and its associated stigma. When discussing how activists mobilized art as part of the fight, scholars often focus on the mass media work of ACT UP and the Gran Fury artist collective that arose out of it, which included posters, fliers, and other public art projects (Burk 2015; Campbell 2019; Crimp 2004; Cvetkovich 2003; Finkelstein 2017; Gould 2009; Reed 2005). Alongside all of these forms of visual media, comics were also part of the artistic response used to spread information, empathy, and support. They were used to visualize and to build community. Since the 1980s, many HIV/AIDS organizations like the San Francisco AIDS Foundation and Gay Men's Health Crisis have created educational comics to raise awareness about HIV/AIDS in various targeted populations, but this essay looks to other contemporaneous comics, like *Matt Black* (1986–87), that were created by cartoonists to raise awareness about HIV/AIDS (*Safer Sex Comix* nos. 1–8, 1986–87; *Risky Business*, 1988). Specifically, this essay looks to *Strip AIDS* (1987) and *Strip AIDS USA* (1988) that LGBTQ+ comics artists made in collaboration with straight cartoonists from across comics communities in the United Kingdom and then in the United States. These affinity-building projects are part of a history of LGBTQ+ individuals making space within comics communities for their concerns and involving straight artists in that effort. While educational comics about HIV/AIDS have played an important role in raising public awareness, these two comics anthologies were specifically created to fundraise for HIV/AIDS organizations, so this essay also allows us to think through the different ways that comics operate as instruments of social justice.

This history will show how American LGBTQ+ cartoonists formed community through anthologies and foregrounded activism as integral to their comics work. In the HIV/AIDS anthologies in particular, LGBTQ+ artists viscerally represent their community under threat and the different tactics they undertake for survival. Their contextual history and close readings of selected comics will establish how activist discourses were foundational to the development of LGBTQ+ comics communities and, in turn, how cartoonists visualized their engagement with such discourses. More generally, this chapter is a corrective to comics studies' narrow focus on alternative and mainstream comics industries and output, and neglect of other important histories and spaces of production.[2]

ANTHOLOGIES WITHIN LGBTQ+ COMICS HISTORY:
GAY COMIX (1980–98) AND *STRIP AIDS* (1987)

Local American grassroots periodicals fostered LGBTQ+ cartoonists from the 1970s to the 1990s, but many artists were disconnected from each other. They started to address this by building networks of self-syndication (Galvan 2015, 2018a, 2018b). Such comics existed in "a parallel universe" of grassroots LGBTQ+ media networks as Justin Hall puts it, and specific artists like Alison Bechdel and Jennifer Camper built careers, deftly negotiating and seeking out multiple venues in which to publish (Sammond 2018; Shamsavari 2017a, 2017b; Hall 2013; Galvan 2018a, 2018b). Anthology series helped to knit artists together. One of the longest running series, *Gay Comix* (1980–98), curated a diverse group of creators, allowing them to share their local experiences and to come together in common cause. In turn, as we shall see, the *Gay Comix* series and the *Strip AIDS* (1987) British comics anthology set the stage for another anthology, *Strip AIDS USA* (1988), which was directly inspired by *Strip AIDS* and featured many *Gay Comix* contributors. Because there was no analog to *Gay Comix* in the British scene, *Strip AIDS* served as the watershed title in starting to connect local queer artists together who had published their comics in various newspapers and periodicals and would use this title as inspiration to publish together in future anthologies and assorted publications.

Running for twenty-five issues and nearly two decades from 1980 to 1998, the American-produced *Gay Comix* stood out for its longevity and range, supporting multiple generations of LGBTQ+ artists as the publication landscape changed around it and as artists were able to create other publications and networks from this launching pad. While the comic was originally created within the underground comix scene and published by Kitchen Sink Press, it shifted to a gay publisher, Bob Ross, by its sixth issue, continuing with Ross for its duration.[3] Three cartoonist-editors—Howard Cruse, Robert Triptow, and Andy Mangels—helmed the series and each responded to the changing era with their editorship.

Underground cartoonist Cruse came out when he launched the series with Kitchen Sink Press in 1980, and other underground veterans like Mary Wings, Roberta Gregory, and Lee Marrs joined him in the first few issues, but the series welcomed artists from beyond the underground publishing scene from its outset. Cruse actively mentored new artists, such that each issue contained a new array of artists rather than a set group. Over the course of an editorship that spanned the first four issues (1980–83), Cruse established the voice of the publication. He insisted that it include a range of LGBTQ+ perspectives, which distinguished it from other contemporaneous comics publications that focused on only one letter of the alphabet soup; for example, *Gay Heart Throbs*

(1976–81), another important early title, included only gay men. He expressed the rationale for this approach inside the front cover of *Gay Comix* no. 1 (1980): "In drawing this book, we gay cartoonists would like to affirm that we are here, and that we live lives as strewn with India-inked pratfalls, flawed heroics, quizzical word balloons and surreptitious truths as the rest of the human race and even a few talking animals." In expressing unity between gay, lesbian, and bisexual cartoonists, and connecting them to "the rest of the human race" through a cartoonist-specific catalog, Cruse articulates the need for this kind of experience to be expressed on the comics page. He is likely responding to having felt closeted by the underground comics community, as he told publisher Denis Kitchen in correspondence as they planned the series, and he worried whether outing himself with this comic would kill his career.[4] The success of his approach can be seen in letters in which readers respond affirmatively to work by creators unlike themselves. As a gay man writes in *Gay Comix* no. 4 (1983): "Relations between lesbians and gay men in this country are 'difficult,' but these comix make one believe there might be close similarities in experience—something I forget, living in a gay male world." This letter identifies the distance between the "world" of gay men and lesbians that Cruse worked to bridge, creating a space for exchange that subsequent editors would continue and which would become increasingly important in the latter half of the 1980s with the rise in HIV/AIDS diagnoses and deaths.

Triptow oversaw *Gay Comix* from its fifth through thirteenth issues (1984–88), producing both the comic and some affiliated publications—*Strip AIDS USA* (1988) and *Gay Comics* (1989)—that situated the artists and their work within new critical conversations. In *Gay Comics*, Triptow wrote a contemporary textual history of LGBTQ+ cartooning in the United States, locating the beginning of his history in the 1940s with Tom of Finland's work, which is decades earlier than the development of the underground scene in the 1960s and 1970s, the groundswell of the Stonewall uprising and gay liberation in the 1970s, and the continued growth of the gay and grassroots press across the 1980s which further supported the development of LGBTQ+ cartoonists (Triptow, 6). This volume prominently features artists that published in *Gay Comix*, but it traces the larger publication landscape they operated within and other key artists who worked in earlier eras or with different publications. Triptow relies on artist interviews, allowing them to construct their own histories and to position the artists themselves within the history of gay comics.

This book coincided with a benefit project released a year earlier, *Strip AIDS USA* (1988). Triptow served as one of three editors of this volume published to fundraise for the Shanti Project, a San Francisco-based organization started in 1974 and still operating today. The volume will be discussed later at length, but it is important to note here that Triptow, in his role as editor of *Gay Comix*, was responsible for rounding up LGBTQ+ contributors for it. *Gay Comix* artists had reflected on HIV/AIDS and sexual health more broadly both within the comics series itself as well as in other publications, particularly in the pages of the LGBTQ+ press. Triptow's additional publications demonstrated the relevance of the *Gay Comix* series in fostering artists who were historically important (as *Gay Comics* detailed) and continuing to work for social change, as exemplified by their contributions to *Strip AIDS USA*.

Mangels served as editor for issues 14 through 25 of *Gay Comix* (1991–98), updating the name of the series to *Gay Comics* to reflect the changing comics publication landscape.[5] When Mangels picked up the *Gay Comix* series, he continued to build on that collective spirit by recruiting equal numbers of gay men and lesbian artists to publish in the comic. Mangels also acknowledged how the series and grassroots press had fostered the success of various artists by dedicating some issues of the comic to spotlight specific cartoonists.[6] The special issues during Mangels's tenure included: a one-off *Gay Comix Special* no. 1 (1992) dedicated to the work of Tim Barela; *Gay Comics* no. 19 (1993), solely featuring the work of Alison Bechdel; and *Gay Comics* no. 21 (1994), split evenly between the work of Roberta Gregory and cartoonist collaborators P. Craig Russell and David Sexton. Aside from Russell and Sexton, all of the featured cartoonists also published work within the *Strip AIDS USA* volume and were active in creating comics that touched on social issues, whether they were publishing in *Gay Comix* or elsewhere in the LGBTQ+ grassroots press. There was an activist impulse embedded within the *Gay Comix* project throughout.

When Don Melia and his partner, Lionel Gracey-Whitman, produced *Strip AIDS* (1987), their anthology comic represented one of the first comings-together of LGBTQ+ artists in print in the United Kingdom. There was no British analog for *Gay Comix*, from which Melia and Gracey-Whitman could recruit their artists. Melia continued this community-building work in subsequent years, creating the *Buddies* (1991) series in the year before his death from HIV/AIDS. *Buddies* was meant to be a continuing series in the vein of *Gay Comix*, with a rotating grouping of artists meditating on LGBTQ+ experiences (Melia 1991a, 1991b). Indeed, from his position as founding editor of *Gay Comix*, Cruse wrote the introduction to *Buddies* no. 1 (1991), solidifying the connection and positioning the new series as a "fledgling cousin to *Gay Comix*" for a British audience (Cruse 1991). The creation of *Buddies* was made all the more difficult by a politically conservative landscape in the United Kingdom, exemplified by the enactment of Section 28 in 1988, which barred authorities from "intentionally promot[ing] homosexuality" and stifled the production of much work until the law was fully repealed in 2003 (Clews 2017, 111, 136).[7] In fact, a number of artists who participated in *Strip AIDS* (1987) came together again a year later to protest Section 28 in comics form in the *AARGH!* (1988)

("Artists Against Rampant Government Homophobia") anthology that cartoonist Alan Moore edited. These anthologies following *Strip AIDS* (1987) highlight its importance in bringing together a community of cartoonists in the United Kingdom, committed to LGBTQ+ social justice.

The *Strip AIDS* volume itself came together rapidly over a handful of weeks in mid-1987 as a fundraiser for London Lighthouse, an organization helmed by Christopher Spence that was fundraising to build residential care facilities and support systems for people living with HIV/AIDS. Melia and Gracey-Whitman raised money by selling the comic and its original art at charity auctions and exhibits across the United Kingdom. Featuring the work of eighty-eight artists, the comic, unlike its later American cousin, welcomed comics in a broad array of styles. The aesthetic variety of the collection issues from Melia's recruitment of a diverse range of cartoonists—from those involved in the gay press and burgeoning alternative scene to those publishing strips and political cartoons in more mainstream papers—as well as a handful of musicians, visual artists, and public figures. The fundraising efforts benefited from this coalition whose perspectives offered a glimpse into the varieties of knowledge and experience around HIV/AIDS that existed at the time. As a point of context, the first antiretroviral drug, AZT, had only been approved in the US by the FDA that same year in March 1987, and it was almost a decade more before the introduction of combination therapy as fairly effective treatment (US Food & Drug Administration [FDA] 2019a, 2019b). Melia himself explained the need for the collection in a short statement printed on the inside cover of the volume where he notes how the project arose in response to a newspaper cartoon that "perpetuate[d] ignorance, fear and prejudice" around HIV/AIDS. He explains his rationale for inviting a wide range of creators to contribute:

> Sooner or later, one way or another, we are all affected. In the five weeks that it took to compile this book, several of the contributors had friends who were either hospitalised with or died of AIDS. It couldn't have hit the message home harder. The spirit of *Strip AIDS* is non-political, non-sexist, non-racist, and, most importantly, non-judgmental. AIDS transcends all these barrier[s]. Everyone involved in this book—from the artists through to you, the readers—has also transcended these barriers. (Melia 1987)

Melia highlights how the disease "transcends . . . barrier[s]" and has "affected" the many contributors in different ways, which provided them with an understanding of the gravity of the situation. In characterizing the comic's ideology as "non-political," he implies that HIV/AIDS has been inappropriately politicized by "judgmental" forces, so this volume seeks to rebalance representation with a "non-sexist" and "non-racist" account. Though there are comics in the volume that represent the crisis from a gay and lesbian perspective, a greater number frame the matter as a public health concern for all and prioritize safe sex through condom use. American cartoonists Trina Robbins, Bill Sienkiewicz, and Robert Triptow adopt Melia's framework when they put together a new collection, *Strip AIDS USA* (1988), the following year.

The transatlantic connections between Melia and these artists were integral to the formation of the American volume and shaped its approach. When both Sienkiewicz and Robbins expressed interest in creating an American edition, Melia connected the two artists together. Melia included advertisements for both volumes in the new comics magazine he created and edited, *Heartbreak Hotel* (1987–88), which ran for six issues across two years. In every issue, Robbins penned a column about the comics industry, writing about the process of creating *Strip AIDS USA* in the fourth issue. In that same issue, Melia ran half-page ads for *Strip AIDS* (1987) and *Strip AIDS USA* (1988) together on the same page, emphasizing the interconnections between the two projects.

Also conceived as a fundraiser comic, *Strip AIDS USA* (1988) raised $11,500 to support HIV/AIDS-related workshops and services at the Shanti Project. It took three cartoonists with different backgrounds to replicate Melia's impressively diverse contributor list. As Robbins reflects in her recent memoir: "We divvied it up: Bill Sienkiewicz got the mainstream guys, Robert [Triptow] edited the gay cartoonists, and I got the underground and the women" (2017, 183). All told, the volume ended up containing the work of 121 artists, meaning that the two collections together encompass the work of over 200 artists, providing a snapshot of attitudes and knowledge around HIV/AIDS in the late 1980s both from artists who were themselves activists and also from those whose work had otherwise rarely veered into the political. Within this sizable volume, the LGBTQ+ artists show an unparalleled depth of knowledge and understanding of the crisis, and their approaches to representation demonstrate varied understandings of how comics might operate as affective activism. Their comics illustrate how LGBTQ+ people support each other in response to the mounting losses due to HIV/AIDS, modeling how this emotional labor undergirds and sustains them in their daily life and in any activist work in which they also engage. *Strip AIDS USA* (1988) extends earlier work in *Gay Comix* and from a decade or more of creative projects across various grassroots and gay periodicals where artists honed their treatment of visual politics of LGBTQ+ issues in rarely studied materials that merit a fuller appraisal.

AFFECTIVE ACTIVISM WITHIN ANTHOLOGIES:
STRIP AIDS USA (1988)

Comics in *Strip AIDS* (1987) and *Strip AIDS USA* (1988) have a weightiness and depth of understanding to them. For LGBTQ+ artists especially, they were not only encountering HIV/AIDS as part of their daily lives within their communities, but they were processing it again and again on the pages of the LGBTQ+ grassroots publications where they worked and published comics. This section will examine the work of four of these artists—Tim Barela, Jerry Mills, Gerard P. Donelan ("Donelan"), and Leslie Ewing—who published widely in the LGBTQ+ press, contributed to *Gay Comix*, and created poignant work for *Strip AIDS USA* (1988) that document this moment and reflect on what opportunities exist for action in ways large and small.[8] These comics allow the artists to reflect on how the epidemic was upending their culture and to share the resiliency of their communities in the face of this tragedy. Their comics argue for the importance of the social bonds between individuals and assert that this togetherness is just as vital for survival as more organized forms of activism.

Though there are comics within *Strip AIDS USA* (1988) that follow and center the experiences of those who are ill, all four of these artists deal instead with the community of support surrounding those individuals, insisting on the survival of those who died through the memories and work of those who remain. In their comics, both Barela and Mills document the parameters of their community under threat as they reflect on the loss of named individuals, while Donelan and Ewing use their pages to advocate for specific activist endeavors to memorialize the dead. These comics operate as individual episodes within longer-running strips featuring familiar, recurring casts of characters that were regularly published elsewhere in grassroots and underground newspapers and comics. They leverage these characters to insist that this support is a continuing community effort that features familiar individuals.

Tim Barela's contribution is an episode of the long-running *Leonard & Larry* strip entitled "Little Victories" that shows both titular characters coming to terms with death in their community. Barela developed *Leonard & Larry* across the 1980s in various gay periodicals and *Gay Comix* and later published the strip opposite Howard Cruse's *Wendel* and Donelan's *It's a Gay Life* in the national gay magazine *The Advocate* at the end of the 1980s. The *Leonard & Larry* strip often features the domestic life and quibbles of the titular monogamous couple, Leonard and Larry. The humor hangs on the odd-couple nature of their pairing as Leonard is an uptight introvert who works in the art world, while the bubbly and extroverted Larry runs a sex shop. This particular strip subverts these expected personality types as Leonard arrives home full of fury over a minor parking infraction and finds Larry uncharacteristically despondent and lying fully clothed on their shared bed. When Leonard finally asks Larry why he is distressed, he replies, "—Sigh—Chuck died today." The disclosure in the final panel of the second page of a two-page comic shifts the topic and tone of the piece into more serious territory.

Over the next page, as Leonard joins him in bed, the two talk about the fact that they have both lost a lot of friends to HIV/AIDS in their overlapping industries. Leonard does his best to comfort his partner while recognizing the dire circumstances, at one point comparing Larry's survivor's guilt to that of his own Jewish ancestors who were the only ones in the family to survive the Holocaust. Working to counter Larry's feelings of helplessness, Leonard reminds him, "Well, like sticking together and claiming all the little victories . . . helping one another, comforting each other, keeping up the fight . . . you've done better than you think." This sentiment in the penultimate panel is the key takeaway that undergirds the whole exchange: it is what everyone needs to do to support one another. Though Larry does important community work in running the sex shop, Leonard affirms that this emotional care work is of the utmost importance, especially in the face of continual loss that makes Larry feel that all his efforts are "useless."

Of the two *Poppers* strips that Jerry Mills contributes to the volume, one of them neatly parallels the plot of Barela's *Leonard & Larry* episode. Mills's *Poppers* strips are filled with a recurring cast of friends who often enjoy the liberated pleasures of gay sexual permissiveness. The strip's very title, which is the slang term for a recreational drug used by gay men, nods to this fact. Different characters and social spaces show different kinds of loss. Looking beyond Barela's monogamous couple, Mills's group of friends widens the scope and deals with the loss of people and locations for sexual pleasure, as the baths are closed due to public health concerns. Mills's career and rise as an artist is indebted to and deeply tied to this scene as he began his *Poppers* strips in 1982 with encouragement from his coworkers while working on staff at *In Touch*, a gay men's erotic magazine that represented and supported gay sexual liberation.

Like Barela's strip, this comic is heavy on dialogue that speaks to the enormity of loss. The strip also begins in a similar way as Yves and Andre arrive to a quiet dwelling where the normally ebullient and outgoing Billy sits alone in the dark. When they ask him what is wrong, Billy, like Larry, names individuals—Mike and Joey—who have recently died. That opening part of the exchange takes place across a single row of panels, and the comic then pivots from these deaths to discuss the larger ramifications. The friends begin grappling with how their community spaces—the baths, bars, and parties—are also under threat. They collectively reach a dark and hopeless place in the middle of the strip, marked by a fully black panel. From this darkness, Andre lights his cigarette and begins to rally their spirits, reminding them that "people will always need

Figure 4.1. "Leonard & Larry: Little Victories," Tim Barela, in *Strip AIDS USA*, edited by Trina Robbins, Bill Sienkiewicz, and Robert Triptow (Last Gasp, 1988), n.p.

to dance and party and laugh!" and getting them back into a frame of mind where they can go out and enjoy partying together.

The formally interesting part of this exchange is that because it happens in a dark interior, the figures of the characters are not very prominent. In fact, a number of the panels only features their dialogue in speech bubbles set against a fully or mostly black background. This tactic allows Mills to sidestep

Figure 4.2. "Poppers," Jerry Mills, in *Strip AIDS USA*, edited by Trina Robbins, Bill Sienkiewicz, and Robert Triptow (Last Gasp, 1988), n.p.

the visibility of his characters' fit and muscled bodies, which often act as a source of pleasure for their fellow characters and readers alike. We see their muscled bodies only in shadowed outline aside from the panel where we gaze upon Andre's physique as he lights his cigarette. This absence of their bodies, which allows them to confront the emotional toll of the disease, is countered by Mills's other *Poppers* strip contained later in the volume. Topless, sexualized, and muscled gay bodies overwhelm the panels as Billy walks the streets of Los Angeles alone and is barraged by these images on covers of books and billboards; adjacent to each encounter, he sees reminders of the HIV/AIDS crisis, which dampen his mood. The only utterance in the comic happens in the final panel as a distressed Billy reflects in a thought bubble, "Boy, it's not easy living in an age where you have to be a good boy just when men have finally been accepted as sex objects!" His friends are not present in this vignette, so we encounter Billy feeling alienated by his own culture and without the support of his community of friends to help him process his experiences and feel more grounded.

Barela's and Mills's work foregrounds the importance of intimate communities of friends and partners to counter the isolation that one can feel, as evidenced by the dour demeanors of Larry and Billy at the beginning of their respective strips and as additionally evinced by the emotional turmoil that Billy experiences when out by himself on the streets of Los Angeles. Donelan and Leslie Ewing's comics further emphasize the importance of community in their comics that depict characters participating in the NAMES Project AIDS Memorial Quilt. This undertaking involved people across the nation making quilt panels to commemorate individuals whom they knew who had died of HIV/AIDS. This project was in the forefront of people's minds as the first full version of the quilt was displayed on the National Mall in Washington, DC, during the 1987 March on Washington for Lesbian and Gay Rights (Ruskin and Herron 1988, 9–10). Donelan's six-panel comic, *The Quilt*, departs from the style he is most known for: quippy one panel cartoons that ran in *The Advocate* and other periodicals and that commented on gay and lesbian lifestyles in punchy and sometimes erotic ways, depending on the publication venue. Ewing's *The NAMES Project* strip echoes the aesthetics and approach of her other strips that she published in *Wimmen's Comix*, *Gay Comix*, and elsewhere and which often featured discussions of sexual wellness and safe sex. Both of these comics also reflect on the emotional toll as characters work through the tears remembering their lost friends and family as they participate in the quilt project.

Donelan's comic illustrates the emotional impact of the disease and death by showing a man grieving at the sewing machine while creating a panel for the quilt. We understand what he is doing from the outset from the comic's title, but it is not until the final panel that we see the creation itself, which

Figure 4.3. "The Quilt," Gerard P. Donelan, in *Strip AIDS USA*, edited by Trina Robbins, Bill Sienkiewicz, and Robert Triptow (Last Gasp, 1988), n.p.

names the individual, Steven, and proclaims, "We miss you." This sentiment affirms what both Barela and Mills showed in their strips—that a community of care surrounds each loss even though we only see one individual portrayed in this particular comic. Ewing's four-panel comic pairs with Donelan's to portray the emotions present while volunteering at a site where the quilt is on display. Her comic is a primer for volunteers and likely draws from her own

Figure 4.4. "The Names Project," Leslie Ewing, in *Strip AIDS USA*, edited by Trina Robbins, Bill Sienkiewicz, and Robert Triptow (Last Gasp, 1988), n.p.

involvement with the NAMES Project. In the first three panels, we watch the lesbian protagonist provide comfort to the teary, distraught people around her until she requires and receives emotional support herself when she starts to cry in the final panel. Her comic also affirms the participation of lesbians as vital community members during the HIV/AIDS crisis—a fact that other comics in the volume, Alison Bechdel's included, also reflect on. These two comics show the affective quality of activism, much as Barela and Mills reveal the emotional reality that underlies the day-to-day lives of gay men. These comics assert a hope in the power of community to support individuals in organizing against the despair of HIV/AIDS.

In the years since their creation, Strip AIDS (1987) and Strip AIDS USA (1988) have rarely been acknowledged, and the existing criticism has been overwhelmingly negative regarding their overall quality (Rodi 1989; McAllister 1992; Ferguson 2016), even though as Kevin Ferguson notes in Eighties People (2016), "the nature of these collections necessitates a fragmented, occasion-ally incoherent voice" (70). Still, these comics act as a valuable snapshot of a historical moment, presenting different understandings of the syndrome and its ramifications that are shaped by the diverse artists creating the comics. A number of the comics, including the ones discussed in depth, also document and preserve representations of gay and lesbian culture and activism in the face of HIV/AIDS. Within that scope, they not only safeguard the memories of dead individuals like those named in the comics themselves, but also those individual creators lost to HIV/AIDS in subsequent years, including Melia who died on August 21, 1992, and Mills who died on January 28, 1993.

The direct participation of the comic itself in activism places these works within a broader framework of art created in order to raise money for HIV/AIDS organizations specifically but also for other causes. For London Light-house, the organization that Strip AIDS (1987) supported, the arts were a major source of funding. An individual fundraising for the organization reflected on the power of the visual arts, writing for the newsletter, "The visual arts, especially, deal with making manifest an emotional feeling, an intuition, without written language" (Orient 1992). Though comics do contain "written language," these works leverage this language to reinforce the emotional impact of the visual work. This sentiment pinpoints the ultimate power of Strip AIDS (1987) and Strip AIDS USA (1988) in capturing the feelings of their moment. We see that in each individual strip, but we also glimpse it across strips where we can trace how emotions are wielded to build and support community in incidental and organized ways. The anthology format situates these sentiments side by side, serving as an outline of the moment, but also as a map towards other histories that still have yet to be fully written about LGBTQ+ cartoonists and concerns.

Notes

1. Earlier issues of Matt Black played with how the superhero comic could be a campy space, especially in how they created the personas and superpowers for each hero and villain.

2. The alternative and mainstream comics industries are defined by a number of comics publishers like Fantagraphics and Drawn & Quarterly, and Marvel and DC. For overviews of the history of these industries, see Charles Hatfield's Alternative Comics (2005) and Shawna

Kidman's *Comic Books Incorporated* (2019). The comics anthologies that I discuss were produced independently and drew upon gay grassroots publications, which have been fruitful spaces for queer cartoonists to develop, as Justin Hall identifies in *No Straight Lines* (2013) and as I further discuss in the following section.

3. This is not the well-known painter and educator, but a gay man also named Bob Ross who is most well known in activist circles for founding and publishing the *Bay Area Reporter* newspaper in San Francisco.

4. Cruse's correspondence with Kitchen is collected as part of the *Gay Comix* Records located at the LGBT Community Center National History Archive, New York. I discuss these archives in an article where I survey the duration of Jennifer Camper's career and Cruse's role mentoring her when she was starting out (Galvan 2018a).

5. The "x" in *Gay Comix* connected the title with the underground publishing scene, which had been in decline for many years, so Mangels wanted to remove that association and bring the work to a new, broader audience, writing in his editorial in *Gay Comics* no. 15 (1992): "The comic world has changed over the last few years and I felt that one of the ways to bring *Gay Comix* 'out of the underground' was to change its name to reflect the attitudes of the day." Though Mangels changed the name of the series to *Gay Comics*, when discussing the series collectively in following paragraphs and throughout this essay, I will refer to it as *Gay Comix*, since that is the founding title and the title through which most people are familiar with the series.

6. Triptow published one special issue during his tenure where he dedicated *Gay Comix* no. 9 (1986) solely to the work of Jerry Mills.

7. Despite the existence of Section 28, the UK government provided some financial assistance to HIV/AIDS organizations. Compare this with the nonresponse of the Reagan administration in the US and and its refusal to acknowledge or deal with the crisis.

8. All four of these artists are white and are based on the West Coast. While non-white artists like the Hernandez Brothers and Jennifer Camper contributed to *Strip AIDS USA* (1987), the majority of the contributions are from white artists and represent mainly white experiences. This ethnically unbalanced perspective was also true of the cartoonists who published in *Gay Comix* and elsewhere in the grassroots press. Moreover, they all published in Los Angeles or San Francisco venues and represented that perspective to the exclusion of other regions of the country.

Works Cited

Barela, Tim. *Gay Comix Special*, no. 1. Edited by Andy Mangels. Bob Ross, 1992.

Bechdel, Alison. *Gay Comics*, no. 19. Edited by Andy Mangels. Bob Ross, 1993.

Burk, Tara. "Radical Distribution: AIDS Cultural Activism in New York City, 1986–1992." *Space and Culture* 18, no. 4 (2015): 436–49. doi:10.1177/1206331215616095.

Campbell, Andy. *Queer X Design: 50 Years of Signs, Symbols, Banners, Logos, and Graphic Art of LGBTQ*. Hachette UK, 2019.

Clews, Colin. *Gay in the 80s: From Fighting Our Rights to Fighting for Our Lives*. Troubador Publishing Ltd., 2017.

Crimp, Douglas. *Melancholia and Moralism: Essays on AIDS and Queer Politics*. MIT Press, 2004.

Cruse, Howard, ed. *Gay Comix*, no. 1. Kitchen Sink Enterprises, 1980.

Cruse, Howard, ed. *Gay Comix*, no. 4. Kitchen Sink Enterprises, 1983.

Cruse, Howard. "Introduction." In *Buddies: A Pretend Family Production* no. 1, edited by Don Melia, Fiona Jerome, Richard Hansom, and Howard Stangroom. Pretend Family Productions, 1991.

Cvetkovich, Ann. "AIDS Activism and Public Feelings: Documenting ACT UP's Lesbians." In *An Archive of Feelings: Trauma, Sexuality, and Lesbian Public Cultures*, 156–204. Duke University Press, 2003.

Ferguson, Kevin L. "The Person with AIDS: Graphic Humor and Graphic Illness." In *Eighties People: New Lives in the American Imagination*, 57–78. Palgrave Macmillan, 2016.

Finkelstein, Avram. *After Silence: A History of AIDS Through Its Images*. University of California Press, 2017.

Galvan, Margaret. "Archiving Grassroots Comics: The Radicality of Networks and Lesbian Community." *Archive Journal*, no. 5 (2015). http://www.archivejournal.net/issue/5/archives-remixed/archiving-grassroots-comics-the-radicality-of-networks-and-lesbian-community/.

Galvan, Margaret. "'The Lesbian Norman Rockwell': Alison Bechdel and Queer Grassroots Networks." *American Literature* 90, no. 2 (2018b): 407–38.

Galvan, Margaret. "Making Space: Jennifer Camper, LGBTQ Anthologies, and Queer Comics Communities," edited by Michelle Ann Abate, Karly Marie Grice, and Christine N. Stamper. *Journal of Lesbian Studies* 22, no. 4 (2018a): 373–89.

Gould, Deborah B. *Moving Politics: Emotion and ACT UP's Fight against AIDS*. University of Chicago Press, 2009.

Gregory, Roberta, P. Craig Russell, and David Sexton. *Gay Comics*, no. 21. Edited by Andy Mangels. Bob Ross, 1994.

Hall, Justin. "No Straight Lines." In *No Straight Lines: Four Decades of Queer Comics*, edited by Justin Hall. Fantagraphics, 2013.

Hatfield, Charles. *Alternative Comics: An Emerging Literature*. University Press of Mississippi, 2005.

Kidman, Shawna. *Comic Books Incorporated: How the Business of Comics Became the Business of Hollywood*. University of California Press, 2019.

Mangels, Andy, ed. *Gay Comics*, no. 15. Bob Ross, 1992.

McAllister, Matthew P. "Comic Books and AIDS." *Journal of Popular Culture* 26, no. 2 (1992): 1–24.

Melia, Don. "Strip AIDS: The Reason." In *Strip AIDS: A Charity Project for London Lighthouse*, edited by Don Melia and Lionel Gracey-Whitman. Willyprods/Small Time Ink, 1987.

Melia, Don, Fiona Jerome, Richard Hansom, and Howard Stangroom, eds. *Buddies: A Pretend Family Production*, no. 1. Pretend Family Productions, 1991a.

Melia, Don, and Howard Stangroom, eds. *Buddies: A Pretend Family Production*, no. 2. Pretend Family Productions, 1991b.

Melia, Don, and Lionel Gracey-Whitman, eds. *Strip AIDS: A Charity Project for London Lighthouse*. Willyprods/Small Time Ink, 1987a.

Melia, Don, and Lionel Gracey-Whitman, eds. *Matt Black, Charcoal*, no. 6. Willyprods/Small Time Ink, 1987b.

Melia, Don, and Lionel Gracey-Whitman, eds. *Heartbreak Hotel*, no. 1.1. Willyprods/Small Time Ink, 1987c.

Melia, Don, and Lionel Gracey-Whitman, eds. *Heartbreak Hotel*, no. 1.2. Willyprods/Small Time Ink, 1988a.

Melia, Don, and Lionel Gracey-Whitman, eds. *Heartbreak Hotel*, no. 1.3. Willyprods/Small Time Ink, 1988b.

Melia, Don, and Lionel Gracey-Whitman, eds. *Heartbreak Hotel*, no. 1.4. Willyprods/Small Time Ink, 1988c.

Melia, Don, and Lionel Gracey-Whitman, eds. *Heartbreak Hotel*, no. 1.5. Willyprods/Small Time Ink, 1988d.

Melia, Don, and Lionel Gracey-Whitman, eds. *Heartbreak Hotel*, no. 1.6. Willyprods/Small Time Ink, 1988e.

Mills, Jerry. *Gay Comix*, no. 9. Edited by Robert Triptow. Bob Ross, 1986.

Moore, Alan, ed. *AARGH!* Mad Love Publishing, 1988.

Orient, Anatol. "The Arts Work." *Lighthouse News*, September, 1992.

Reed, Thomas Vernon. "ACTing UP against AIDS: The (Very) Graphic Arts in a Moment of Crisis." In *The Art of Protest: Culture and Activism From The Civil Rights Movement to the Streets Of Seattle*, 179–217. University of Minnesota Press, 2005.

Risky Business. San Francisco AIDS Foundation, 1988.

Robbins, Trina. *Last Girl Standing*. Fantagraphics Books, 2017.

Robbins, Trina, Bill Sienkiewicz, and Robert Triptow, eds. *Strip AIDS USA*. Last Gasp, 1988.

Rodi, Rob. "Bigot-Bashing: Rob Rodi on Strip AIDS USA and AARGH." *Comics Journal*, no. 126 (1989): 43–46.

Ruskin, Cindy, and Matt Herron. *The Quilt: Stories from the NAMES Project*. Pocket Books, 1988.

Safer Sex Comix, nos. 1–8. 1986–87. Gay Men's Health Crisis.

Sammond, Nicholas. "Meeting in the Archive: Comix and Collecting as Community." *Feminist Media Histories* 4, no. 3 (2018): 96–118.

Shamsavari, Sina. "Gay Ghetto Comics and the Alternative Gay Comics of Robert Kirby." *Queer Studies in Media & Popular Culture* 2, no. 1 (2017a): 95–117.

Shamsavari, Sina. "The History of Gay Male Comics in the United States from Before Stonewall to the 21st Century." *International Journal of Comic Art* 19, no. 2 (2017b): 163–201.

Triptow, Robert. *Gay Comics*. Plume, 1989.

US Food & Drug Administration (F.D.A.). "HIV/AIDS Historical Time Line 1981–1990." *FDA*, April 2019a. http://www.fda.gov/patients/hiv-timeline-and-history-approvals/hivaids -historical-time-line-1981-1990.

US Food & Drug Administration (F.D.A.). "HIV/AIDS Historical Time Line 1995–1999." *FDA*, April 2019b. http://www.fda.gov/patients/hiv-timeline-and-history-approvals/hivaids -historical-time-line-1995-1999.

Chapter 5

DESIRE WITHOUT END
ON THE QUEER IMAGINATION OF SEQUENTIAL ART

ALISON HALSALL AND JONATHAN WARREN
IN CONVERSATION WITH RAMZI FAWAZ

In January 2020, we enjoyed a lovely afternoon with the literary scholar and comics critic, Ramzi Fawaz, at Stanford University's Center for the Humanities where he was a 2019–20 Visiting Fellow. That setting was as splendid as our conversation about comics was dynamic, thought-provoking, and wide-ranging. Beginning over lunch among the center's other researchers, we chatted about queer families, superheroes as mutant outcasts, queer maneuvers in comics, comics pedagogy and way-finding, *Watchmen*, camp, "Designing Women," and, within a few idea-packed hours, we found ourselves happily knee-deep in shared queer and comics sensibilities. Indisputably a powerhouse teacher whose students are very lucky, Fawaz was our magnetic tour guide to comics' queer history and historicity, reception and fandom, affect and force, and importance. Fawaz's current research is focused on the women's and gay liberation movements and their influence on American popular culture in the 1970s and after. He is a gracious host and generous thinker. What follows here recounts many of the topics we covered during a memorable afternoon together.

Alison Halsall and Jonathan Warren: You've written that the history of sexuality and the history of comics can be thought of as mutually constitutive. What kinds of sexual history do comics propose? Readers of superhero comics will be familiar with the ages, Silver, Golden, Bronze, and so on. Do LGBTQ+ comics specify their own periods of sexual history? Which examples stand out most for you? What kinds of history do they propose?

Ramzi Fawaz: When I first made this claim, it was meant as a provocation to scholars of visual culture and sexuality to think about the ways that comics form has participated in expanding how readers imagine or conceive of desire, intimacy, and erotic attachment across time. Historically, comics have either been studied for the ways they directly represent sex, especially in pornographic ways (think of the Tijuana Bibles or Tom of Finland's gay male erotic utopias), or else been understood as an unsophisticated form of lowbrow culture that reproduces dominant ideas about normative gender and sexuality (think of the stereotype of the superhero genre, which is commonly thought to celebrate white, muscular, virile male bodies, and hypersexualized female ones). I aim to shift the focus of these approaches by asking how distinct uses of the comics medium at different historical moments allowed artists to depict emergent or developing social transformations in sexuality—the increasing visibility of gays and lesbians, for instance, or expanding interests in alternative sexual practices like BDSM—and to experiment with new ways of representing what it means to be a desiring subject. In other words: how has comics form allowed readers to refigure sexuality—what it is and can be—in the mind's eye? I think that a predominant focus on sexual representation and ideology (what kinds of bodies and desires are represented in comics and what is their presumed political message) often obscures the *imaginative* potential of comics to shift how people think, see, and feel sexuality as a lived experience.

Central to my claim lies the idea that comics, because of their formal investment in seriality, frequently present sexuality itself as an unfolding experience. Sex and sexuality are only occasionally punctual: we may experience an intense or powerful sexual act, or be able to identify critical moments when our sexual identity was influenced or shaped by immediate events (coming out to a loved one, being bullied, meeting someone with the same desires, etc.), but ultimately, sexuality takes shape over time. In this sense, sexuality—understood broadly as the entire realm of intimate and erotic relations and identifications—is a fundamentally serial experience. Sequential or serial movement is a central formal conceit of comics that articulates beautifully to a view of sexuality not as a fixed essence but as a ceaselessly unfolding arena of intimate or erotic possibility. Now, every particular expression of this is different, so when I claim that the history of sexuality and the history of comics are co-constitutive, my point is not to say that the history of comics tells *one* story about the history of sexuality, but that the affordances of the comics medium allow for telling and showing what sexuality and eroticism can be in numerous ways at different historical moments.

Perhaps the most celebrated example is William Moulton Marston's *Wonder Woman* comics of the late 1930s and 1940s, which famously depicted countless scenes of bondage and submission between its Amazon warrior with a Golden "Lasso of Truth" and her many opponents. In part because of historian Jill Lepore (2014), it is now widely known that Wonder Woman's creator was a Harvard-educated psychologist who believed that social harmony could be achieved through the complete sexual and emotional submission of men to women; scandalously, Marston was also part of a long-term polyamorous BDSM relationship with two women, Elizabeth Marston and Olive Byrne, with whom he raised his children. Comics artist Phil Jimenez (2018) and cultural critic Noah Berlatsky (2017) have brought critical attention to the fact that Marston's ideas and lived experiences with nontraditional heterosexual intimacy appeared everywhere in the *Wonder Woman* comics, particularly in his frequent representations of the hero using her lasso of truth to bind or tie up both men and women in scenes highly reminiscent of bondage play—the serial quality of comics allowed Marston to represent bondage as a recurrent or unfolding experience of pleasurable submission that was never permanent or fixed but enacted by all parties over time. Wonder Woman often finds herself chained, caged, and bound, always seemingly energized by these brief but exciting moments of danger before reversing roles and tying up those who would attempt to contain her. Marston's comics circulated to Americans during the last years of the Great Depression, a period that saw women increasingly taking on service work and odd jobs to make up for men's lost income, and in which perceived "feminine" values like sharing, caregiving, and mutual aid became widespread in the face of collective economic deprivation. Seen in this context, Wonder Woman both captured the increasingly powerful role that women were playing in American social and cultural life, but also allowed Americans to imagine this transformation as tied to a pleasurable change in heterosexual relationships. In other words, Marston's own idiosyncratic erotic desires collided with comics' serial form to present sexual bondage and submission not only as an individual kink, but as a desirable and playful metaphor for shifting social relations: in Marston's serial narratives heterosexuality starts to evolve into something approximating queerness.

The key here is to see that a comic book series like *Wonder Woman* did not merely reflect dominant sexual mores. BDSM was not a dominant or publicly celebrated sexual practice in the American 1930s, if it ever has been. Rather, *Wonder Woman* actively participated in shifting how people imagined what heterosexuality could be in a moment when every entrenched idea about proper familial roles was in flux.

Other historical moments are also instructive. In the 1970s, the serial anthology *Gay Comix* collected the comic strip work of numerous gay and lesbian comics artists who had vastly different aesthetic styles, political commitments and stories to tell. In *Gay Comix*, gay identity and experience were presented as kaleidoscopic not only by the variety of stories each issue included but in the different ways that creators would draw or give shape to queer affect, same-sex emotional and sexual intimacy, and gay social life. Consequently, the real-life sexual diversity of queer people was formally captured in myriad approaches to drawing gay and lesbian lives on the page: from highly stylized cartoonish representations of flamboyant gay male sexuality, to hyper-realist depictions of gay and lesbian sex, to quotidian or ordinary renderings of conversations between same-sex couples about their sex life, social calendar, and careers. These comics were obviously responding to contemporary social transformations in American society catalyzed by the movements for women's and gay liberation; but they were also trying to visualize many other possible configurations of what gay sexuality could be beyond either activist circles or dominant straight stereotypes.

We need to study comics as a key site where contemporary conceptions about sex, sexuality, and gender expression (among many other identities and lived experiences) are literally *redrawn* or rendered in new and surprising ways. I'll give one more example: in a fascinating essay on gay erotic superhero comics, Darieck Scott briefly analyzes the pornographic comics of Japanese artist Gengoroh Tagame. Tagame's stories represent extremely explicit scenes of domination and sexual submission between muscular, hairy Japanese men—the comics are surprising because they depict pornographic encounters that are at once highly violent and disturbing, but also erotically thrilling because of their sexual intensity and aesthetic beauty (2014). Tagame is an extraordinary craftsman, and he manages to illustrate the messiest exchange of bodily fluids, hard fucking, and bondage in ways that make every sexual act look like a work of art. Scott focuses on a single aesthetic innovation in Tagame's oeuvre: through the comics form, Tagame frequently represents a dominant male "top" ejaculating inside his sexual partner. This image is often drawn in the form of a visual cross-section of the receptive bottom's anal canal flooded with semen. As queer theorist Tim Dean has discussed, internal ejaculation remains the impossible fantasy ideal that real life gay male pornography can never capture with cameras (2014). As a medium that requires every image to be fabricated from whole cloth, comics allows for this intensely intimate (or up close) drawn depiction of the exchange of semen. These scenes open up a world of erotic fantasy, allowing readers of any sexuality and gender expression to picture fluid exchange in the mind's eye, potentially expanding their affective relationships to sex as a kind of primal act, as a vulnerable opening up to another person, as an intense exchange of bodily matter. Tagame's work doesn't simply tell us something about gay male sex, but visually transforms how readers can think about erotic encounter altogether.

All of these examples stress the importance of moving away from a "reflective" study of comics that sees comics art as a mirror for already formed historical realities, cultural trends, or subcultural practices. No doubt, comics reflect the historical conditions of their production, but they also invent or create that world *anew* in the ways they shape, inform, or influence how people see themselves, their bodies, desires, and attachments. We need a much more robust understanding of how comics *constitute* social relations—in the ways they expand people's imaginations, draw together unexpected publics, produce new kinds of aesthetic projects and artistic communities—rather than simply reflecting existing ones.

Because individual comic strips or series are circulated in print or digital formats, they frequently get reproduced across historical time, so that audiences re-encounter the same stories and images in completely different contexts. Like the serial quality of comic strips themselves, the frequent reprinting of various comics texts allows them to unfold in new ways, accruing unexpected meanings and responding to new sexual histories. So Marston's Wonder Woman of the 1930s *returns* to the cultural scene in the 1970s when feminists like Gloria Steinem take up the Amazon superhero as an icon of women's liberation; but in this new context, feminist activists and cultural critics conveniently overlook the series' representation of bondage and submission, focusing instead on Wonder Woman's ability to exercise agency and her sisterhood with fellow Amazon warriors.

Consequently, I think it's crucial for us to talk about how particular expressions of sex, sexuality, and gender expression in comics have many lives across time and space. Comics capture the recursive quality of embodied experiences of sexuality and gender. What happens when a nonbinary trans* man living in rural Texas reads reprints of Stan Lee and Jack Kirby's *The Fantastic Four* series from the early 1960s? What kind of meanings are produced when an Asian American feminist reading group in San Francisco decides to include the work of Tagame and his gay erotic manga contemporaries among their selections? What kinds of aesthetic possibilities are opened up when a gay male artist in 1970s New York City reinterprets the classic 1930s comic strip character Nancy as a butch lesbian? These kinds of questions make it impossible for us to ever claim that any comic strip, series, or character ever means one thing, or reproduces a single ideological understanding of sex, sexuality or gender; instead, we can study how different comics proliferate a range of ideas about erotic and intimate bonds and sexual and gender identity in various contexts. As a result, the way we study the relationship between comics and sexuality can itself be modeled on the serial, open-ended, multiplicitous quality of our objects of study.

I think this is why there is still so much more to be illuminated about comics generally, but especially about LGBTQ+ comics. Not only do we need to explore various comics in their original contexts of emergence and circulation, but we must endlessly follow their travels across time and space, through their cultural adaptations, reproductions, appropriations, and reinventions in venues big and small, in the hands of a single reader or circulated among millions.

AH and JW: With that call for more studies of LGBTQ+ comics reader reception in mind, we're curious to hear about your own experience as a reader, as a critic of these comics. Do you find that comics have mapped the history of your sexuality? You've written about the significance of *X-Men* in your childhood and early adolescence. What do you think about your life *after that* in relation to particular comics as modes of imagining sexuality?

RF: This is a very significant question for me, as I suspect it is for most people who end up studying comics. This is because for many of us, at some point we chose to research and write about a cultural object that we originally formed some of our most powerful childhood and adolescent fantasies around. I've now spent more years studying superhero comics than I was a childhood fan of them; but that first period when I read superhero comics purely for pleasure, from the ages of thirteen to twenty-one, was also a hugely formative time when I came out as being gay but also struggled to translate that into significant gay relationships. I was a late bloomer in a lot of ways: I wasn't deeply connected to gay community and didn't have any serious gay male romantic relationships until my mid-to-late twenties. In that sense, I often say I felt I had a gay *identity* for years before I had a gay *sexuality*. Rather, I lived my gayness as an affective orientation toward queer family or kinship.

As you mentioned, the most foundational relationship that my sexual orientation had to comics was in my teenage years when I was reading *The X-Men*. And I think that has everything to do with my sense of being a member of a queer family. My mom is a lesbian, my brother is gay, my uncle who passed away when I was six was gay—we were queer Middle Eastern migrants to the US, bonded not only by blood but also by a shared experience of multiple forms of minoritization. As a teenager, I was very invested in the value of queer kinship, of chosen bonds, which I understood as a rebellious alternative to the socially sanctioned heterosexual nuclear family. And the superhero team was the most potent metaphor for that kind of social relationship that I'd ever encountered in American popular culture. The idea of a collective of people bound together by mutual outsiderness was incredibly compelling to me. And that's one example of the recursive circulation of comics that I mentioned earlier: a comic book about mutant outcasts that only metaphorically referenced gayness in the 1960s and 1970s, could land in the hands of a gay Lebanese boy in suburban Orange County, California, in the 1990s, who would immediately read the *X-Men* as a story about queer family and go on to write a book based on that experience (2016). The series allowed me to make sense of the family I was growing up with, but it also introduced me to an imaginative world where my own queer commitments could come to attach to an incredibly diverse range of fictional characters whose bodies appeared in wildly divergent shapes, sizes, and colors. These were characters whose queerness hinged less on their sexual orientation or gender expression per se, but inhered in mutant bodies that shape-shifted, teleported, regenerated, merged, and sometimes wholly dissolved on the comics page.

Figure 5.1. "The Fantastic Four Pin-Up Page," Stan Lee (writer) and Jack Kirby (penciler), *The Fantastic Four*, no. 15 (June 1963): n.p.

When I was growing up, I didn't understand my attachment to these bodies in erotic terms; instead, I felt deeply affectively or emotionally attached to mutant bodies in flux. The distinctly gay or queer dimension of that attachment actually became more visible to me years later, when as a scholar, I discovered a glaring gap in my knowledge of superhero comics: like a charlatan, I had never read *The Fantastic Four*! When I read the first hundred issues of this brilliant series, I couldn't believe that it was even more of a story about queer family than *The X-Men*. Every member of the Fantastic Four—the stretchy Mr. Fantastic, the translucent Invisible Woman, the fiery Human Torch, and the rock-like Thing—exhibited bodies that were completely out of joint with their "proper" or presumed gender and sexual identities. You have a patriarch, Mr.

Fantastic, who is supposed to be symbolically "hard" on Communism and the staunch leader of the group, but he's literally a flexible rubber band, endlessly soft and pliable. You have this hardened rock person, the Thing, who is supposed to be the paragon of virile masculinity but is a blubbering (yet lovable) emotional mess. You have a putatively straight male teenager who's supposed to be a lady's man but is quite literally a "flamer." And you have a woman who can turn invisible, but who, over time, becomes the most visibly powerful and indispensable lynchpin of the group.

These incredible contradictions around sexual and gender roles and identities were exhibited directly on the page in the visual clash between how each member was drawn and how they behaved—this mapped onto my own sense of being someone who combines a variety of masculine, feminine, and androgynous qualities in my manner of dress, my voice, my affect, my performative style. And so there was a way in which I felt incredibly *seen* by *The Fantastic Four* because it was a narrative about living in a body that projected competing internal desires and identifications, which is really what the experience of gender and sexuality is about: negotiating an endless series of contradictions about your relationship to those categories and how society enforces them. When I read *The Fantastic Four* for the first time, it felt like a deep exhaling: I suddenly understood that the Marvel universe and the countless superhuman bodies that inhabited it had been central in helping me define a queer sense of self because it was a fictional world that allowed for, even visually celebrated, endless bodily contradiction and multiplicity. *Unstable molecules* are what the Fantastic Four's bodies are made of, right? Reading that comic book, I began to see that my own desires and fantasies about superhuman bodies had to do with fictional characters that were deliciously unstable and always in flux.

AH and JW: Are there comics that you read now that don't fit into your academic or critical, intellectual practice, that you read for pleasure or that you wouldn't write about? Where do comics fit into your life, more broadly?

RF: After years of reading only mainstream superhero comics, and then spending nearly a decade writing a book about them, I now have a much more curated relationship to comics: I no longer follow any regular series or read contemporary superhero comics. I read reprints of classic superhero stories, and I am fascinated by abstract, avant-garde, or experimental comics. I selectively seek out comics that are aesthetically unrecognizable to me like Edie Fake's *Gaylord Phoenix* (2010), Jesse Jacobs's *Crawl Space* (2017), or Rodrigo Muñoz Ballester's *Manuel no está solo* (1985). Each of these creators render fictional worlds that combine seemingly contradictory aesthetic styles like hyper-realism, minimalism, abstract expressionism, surrealism, and psychedelia to tell stories about gender transitivity, unrequited gay love, travels to higher dimensions, and all kinds of queer intimacy. I find these aesthetic adventures to be really dazzling. For me, comics used to be an imaginative escape; then they became cultural texts to theorize and think with. They are now more objects of aesthetic curiosity and enchantment. I sometimes get lost for hours online researching weird comics that "break my brain," as I like to put it: they might scramble my perception of what comics are supposed to be by eliminating the use of traditional sequential panels (I love comics like David Wojnarowicz and James Romberger's *7 Miles a Second* [1996], which are almost entirely composed of massive full-page spreads so that each page is a "panel" unto itself); they might mix collage with drawing and photographs; they might have no representational figures or dispose of narrative storytelling altogether. I really like seeing how people push the medium to its absolute limits, which allows me to expand my own ability to read and make sense of texts that don't fit any ideas I already have about what comics are and can be. And in that sense comics usually serve the purpose of bringing *beauty* into my life, which feels incredibly necessary in dark political times.

Of course, I also have collections of all the comics I loved when I was a child and that I studied to write my book, *The New Mutants*. But ultimately, I'm not invested in comprehensiveness—I think comic book reading becomes rather dull when the aim is to absorb every page, every issue, every series in its entirety. I believe in a committed eclecticism, an energetic jumping around between texts; you might say I take an associational approach to reading comics, following the trail from one set of comics to another that allows me to make surprising connections between series, characters, creators that would never be apparent through a linear approach to reading.

JW: Would you say that there's something queer about the style or aesthetic that you're drawn to?

RF: I've written extensively about the queer affordances, or aesthetic possibilities, of comics form. By this, I mean the ways that the formal qualities of comics—like sequential visual panels, the combination of image and text, and the ability to draw anything one can imagine—*lend themselves* to representing sexual and gender nonconformity. None of the formal qualities of comics are *inherently* queer; rather, they share a variety of features that allow them to be articulated to queer investments, experiences, or sensibilities. As I mentioned earlier, for instance, the serial quality of comics lends itself to a queer view of sexuality or desire as a series of unfolding erotic possibilities with no obvious end or terminal point. Similarly, the necessity of drawing a character multiple times across many panels in a sequential comic strip means that every depiction of that figure will be slightly different, multiplying or proliferating representations of a single body across visual space. Queer and trans* comics artists often exploit this feature of comics form to underscore the socially constructed nature of gendered bodies. For example, Fake's experimental trans*

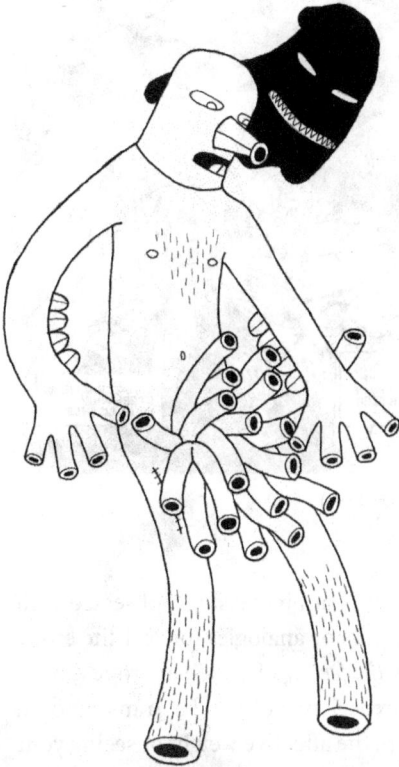

Figure 5.2. *Gaylord Phoenix*, Edie Fake (Secret Acres, 2010), 117.   Figure 5.3. *Gaylord Phoenix*, Edie Fake (Secret Acres, 2010), 149.

comic *Gaylord Phoenix* features a title character who is a mythical genderless wizard and sexual trickster. Across the arc of the narrative, Gaylord embarks on a painful but transformative adventure of sexual and gender self-discovery, that involves countless bodily transformations, surreal erotic encounters with magical creatures, and psychedelic travels through different lands. On nearly every page of the two-hundred and fifty-page epic, Fake depicts Gaylord taking on a different bodily shape. In each image, they appear with new appendages and orifices that completely confound traditional male or female genitalia and multiply or reorganize traditional human limbs. In one instance, Gaylord appears as a floating cloud with eyes; in another, they sprout a bouquet of tubes from where we would expect to see a penis or vagina; in another, their arms grow small wings that allow them to float across magical landscapes. This visual disorientation allows us to imagine gender transitivity as a thrilling kind of shape-shifting that can take numerous forms and expressions, even in the same body.

Figure 5.4. *Stuck Rubber Baby*, Howard Cruse (Paradox Press, 1995), 190.

In terms of my own personal fascinations, I am increasingly obsessed with how comics artists innovate visual metaphors or analogies for real-life erotic or intimate experiences. How do you draw *the feeling* of same-sex erotic desire? How do you give shape to the visceral experience of gender transitivity in drawn form? How do you formally capture the affective weight of seeing your friends die of AIDS? What shapes or forms adequately convey or translate what it means to be queer, to be trans*, to be nonbinary in various contexts?

Two instances always stand out in my mind. I've written before about a scene in Howard Cruse's monumental graphic novel *Stuck Rubber Baby* (1995), which narrates a gay white man's coming of age in the civil rights South: the white protagonist Toland Polk stares into the eyes of an African American friend who has barely survived the racially motivated bombing of a local motel. In a series of adjacent panels, Cruse first draws Toland's face as he locks eyes with his friend, who wears a bandage around his head, followed by a surreal image of Toland's head shattering apart like a broken jigsaw puzzle with long rebars radiating outward from its center. Here, Toland encounters white supremacy not as an abstract ideology, but as the murderous obliteration of Black bodies, an encounter so horrific that it prompts an immediate identification with the body of someone who has experienced and barely survived such brutality.

That identification is materialized in the form of a literally fractured head, indexing Shiloh's actual head wound and the psychic shattering inflicted by racist violence (2019, 592). The scene captures the affective intensity of a cross-racial and cross-sexual identification between a white gay man and a straight Black man; it is distinctly queer not only because Toland is gay but because it

Figure 5.5. *7 Miles a Second*, David Wojnarowicz, James Romberger, Marguerite Van Cook. 1996 (Fantagraphics, 2013), 60–61.

visualizes a moment of such heightened psychic intimacy that it destabilizes Toland's sense of self to the point of annihilation.

Similarly, in Wojnarowicz's graphic memoir *7 Miles a Second*, drawn by James Romberger and painted by Marguerite Van Cook, the creators represent the devastating moment when Wojnarowicz witnesses his lover Peter Hujar die of AIDS in a hospital bed. At the center of a double-page spread, Romberger draws a surreal image of Wojnarowicz and Hujar's bodies exploding into one another. It is a visual rendering of Wojnarowicz's fantasy of a final union between himself and his former lover. Around the central panorama are a series of smaller panels depicting moments of quiet intimacy, including Wojnarowicz grazing Hujar's limp hand, and presumably later sitting alone to eat. Here the artists use representational *density*, the frantic accumulation of smaller panels around an explosive fantasy scenario, to capture the affective experience of rapidly losing lovers, social communities, and one's own physical health in the face of the epidemic.

When I first read *7 Miles a Second*, I was completely disoriented and emotionally unraveled by the experience. With the exception of Bill Sienkiewicz's art in *The New Mutants* series, I had never encountered a comic book story told with such visual ferocity, intensity, and rebelliousness. It formally captured the disorganizing experience of being psychologically shattered, and physically degenerated, by the twin traumas of homophobia and AIDS. The story is largely told in bold, double-paged panoramas that depict hallucinatory episodes or dream sequences where Wojnarowicz imagines drowning in a tsunami; fantasizes riding a massive train toward the end of history; dreams he is a dog being eviscerated by the police; and experiences his body decomposing under the eyes of a woolly mammoth skeleton. In many of these displays, people's bodies are depicted violently colliding, exploding, smashed, broken or dismembered. Van Cook paints the narrative with watercolors that frequently bleed across the borders of Romberger's drawings, blending into one another to produce odd and surprising hues that are often not "appropriate" or natural to the scene (in one instance Wojnarowicz's skin appears purple, while in another the sky is painted bright red). Alongside the charged images of bodily disintegration, Van Cook's watercolors affectively invoke the feeling of drowning or hallucinating. When I first read it, I remember thinking: "What I'm seeing on the page is making me viscerally feel what it must have been like to live during the height of the AIDS epidemic." This particular reading experience catalyzed my fascination with the ability of comics artists to transmit the affective force of a distinctly queer experience, but to do so *non-representationally*. *7 Miles a Second* doesn't always directly or explicitly *represent* people with AIDS; rather, it provides a vast range of visual metaphors or analogies that seem to formally describe what living with, and fighting against, the disease might feel like. For instance, many of the panoramas in *7 Miles a Second* present elongated diagonal panels that cut through an entire page at odd angles like an X-acto knife finely slicing a scene into jarring segments. This formal strategy visually invokes the feeling of being fragmented, cut up, or disarticulated by the violence of government neglect or mistreatment by medical professionals.

In sum then, I am less invested in any single distinct queer comics style and more invested in any aesthetic *sensibility* that attempts to translate queer affect, embodiment, or lived experience into visual form.

JW: So, comics are a portal to a historical sensibility. Not a representation of one.

RF: Yes.

JW: And you're drawn to those that have the most affective power.

RF: Absolutely—after all, the combination of text and image in comics is intended to pump up the volume on the affective or emotional force of whatever is being displayed on the page. If you could convey the same intensity of an idea, story or image with only words, or only images, then you'd do that. In comics, the intentional concatenation of multiple modes of visual representation—not only text and image, but colors, the texture of the paper, the different scales of comic book panels, the shape and size of the material text in your hand—creates a heightened affective intensity that is a unique and powerful feature of the medium. Reading comics is mentally straining because of the number of variables you are juggling as you process visual and verbal information simultaneously. But it is also thrilling because so much is happening all at once—the rush of visual information through your mind can be made to articulate with an endless variety of lived experiences of bodily intensity or heightened states of consciousness. Sex, sexuality, and gender are deeply embodied and viscerally felt, whether they are linked to immediate material experiences (like having sex or taking hormones) or social identities and performances. To my mind, the most exciting comics art harnesses the visual intensity of the medium to transmit or translate particular felt, lived, or embodied experiences of gender and sexual nonconformity to wide audiences.

At a conference presentation by queer comics scholar, Michael Harrison, I remember being blown away by Ballester's *Manuel no está solo*, an astonishingly beautiful Spanish comic about a gay man's unrequited love for his handsome, straight male friend Manuel (2013). Though the two men become socially intimate, they never have sex. At one point, the protagonist (an avatar for the author) sees Manuel out on a date with a woman. It emotionally obliterates him. Ballester depicts a hallucinatory scene in which Rodrigo runs to an ice cream store, buys a massive banana split sundae, and quite literally "eats" his emotions—with each bite, the panels wobble, melting like ice cream, while Rodrigo's own body contorts, liquifies and *becomes* melted ice cream. At some point, we can no longer tell if Rodrigo's body looks like the soupy remnants of a banana split or an ocean of tears. Perhaps he becomes both. Ballester's visual style repeatedly combines a precise, *hyper-realistic* depiction of bodies and urban landscapes with a hallucinatory, *surrealist* depiction of feeling states like this one. In so doing, he attempts to capture the passionate queer emotions that roil beneath the surface of one gay man's body—in other words, comics form becomes a space for visualizing the interior psychic life of queer desire on the page. After all, the page literally looks like the wet, messy, porous liquidity of the tears we shed over unrequited love; Ballester then provides a potent visual metaphor for the way our minds and hearts can become figuratively porous or lose their boundaries in the face of our love and attachment for another. Through this visual metaphor, the scene makes the particularity of one gay man's emotional struggle translatable to many other affective contexts and experiences regardless of one's sexual identity or gender expression.

AH and JW: So many of the comics that you discuss are about diversity. Are they for, or do they imply, a readership that is *not* as diverse and that needs to be instructed on the value of diversity, or do they take a queer readership as a given?

RF: Let me just say unequivocally: I don't believe in the idea of instructing audiences about anything. I just don't think it works. People do not read comics to be taught how they are *supposed* to view the world; they read comics to

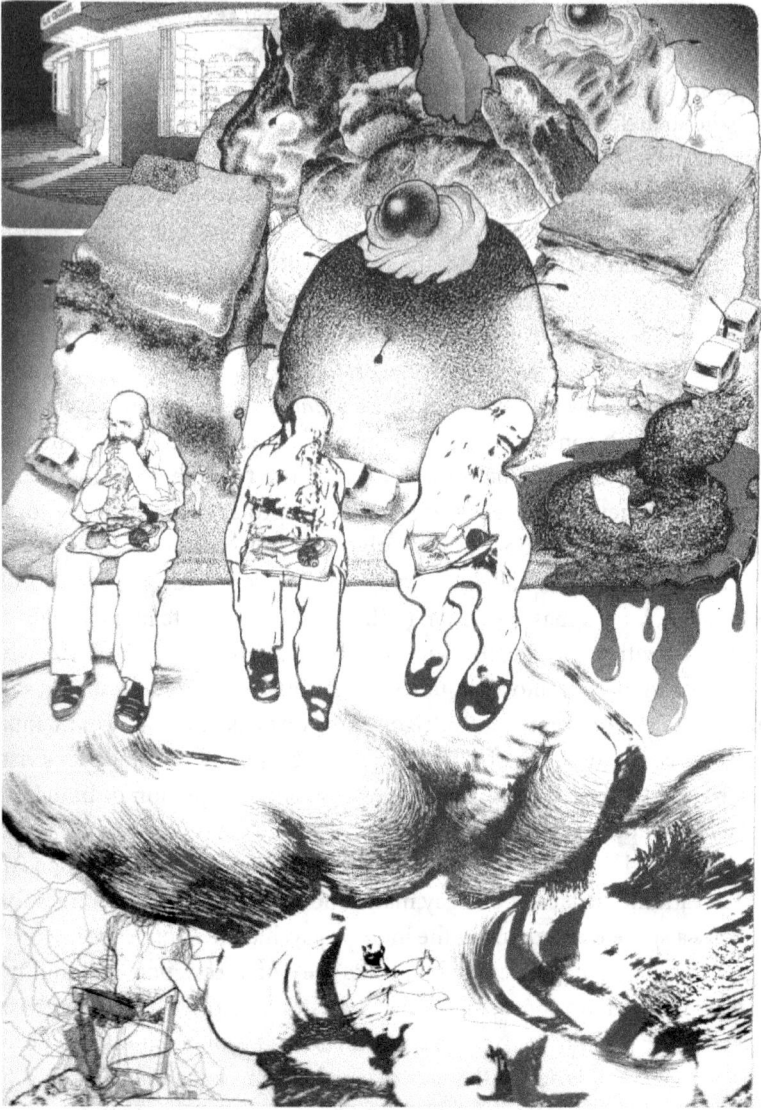

Figure 5.6. *Manuel no está solo*, Rodrigo Muñoz Ballester (Ediciones Sinsentido, 1985), n.p.

discover new ways of interpreting, making sense of, or *imagining* the world otherwise. The distinction is a fine but important one. One mode of storytelling is didactic or aims to inform, the other aims to expand the imagination. I believe cultural production has the most impact on audiences when it works on readers' imaginations, allowing them to see and think differently. Consequently, comics are at their best not when they provide a clear definition of what diversity is, but offer readers unexpected, enchanting, or unusual creative frameworks for understanding the *idea* of diversity anew. For instance, I've published on the masterful superhero comic book series, *Legion Lost* (1999), which I often consider to be a case study in comics diversity: this twelve-issue miniseries tells the story of a team of teenage superheroes who find themselves lost on the other side of the universe. There, they discover a genocidal god-like being, the Progenitor, who is intent on wiping out all life in this uncharted galaxy. The genius of the series was that it addressed the problem of diversity from numerous angles—not only are the characters diverse in terms of their gender, race, and even species identities, but each issue of the series is narrated from the perspective of a different character. The series then not only depicts a "legion" of superheroes but trains readers how to *think like a legion*, that is, to approach questions of collective concern from multiple, competing perspectives. At the same time, by centering the value of complex character development alongside rip-roaring space adventure, the series showed readers how a variety of differences between the teammates—including those of temperament, spiritual belief, emotional responses to stress, and past life experiences—are as important to their struggle for survival as their distinct gender, racial, and species identities. Finally, by pitting this heterogenous team against a singular genocidal monster, the series presented the Legion's collective fight as a struggle against a god-like force intent on *reducing or eliminating diversity* from his part of the universe. In *Legion Lost*, then, diversity comes to have multiple meanings, and is addressed at every level of text: in its cast of characters, its plot, its narrative address, and its formal elaboration on the page. To read the text is to imaginatively conceive of the problem of diversity from a kaleidoscopic perspective.

Similarly, when I was growing up, my attachment to the Marvel Comics universe had everything to do with its innate heterogeneity. Diversity, understood as the simple fact of human variety, was a totally organic part of the Marvel universe—every character looked distinct from all the others and there was an endless font of different species, superhuman types, geographical locations, intergalactic conflicts, teams and alternative families that comprised this creative world. But more than that, the *ethos* of the Marvel universe was one of cosmopolitan encounter between unlike people who were always productively transformed by meeting strangers from across the globe, the galaxy, and the universe. The ongoing discourse on representational diversity is often concerned with the *underrepresentation* of minoritized people in fictional comic book worlds. And lest I sound equivocal on this, I will say without reservation: it is absolutely imperative that comics directly depict the widest range of queer, trans*, Black, Asian American, Latinx, Indigenous, and disabled characters and lifeworlds, and that the comic book industry highlight the creative talent of equally diverse writers and artists. Beyond simply being nice or ethical, this is a necessary step in making comics accountable to the world we actually live in. With that said, if you introduce "diverse" characters to a creative world largely lacking in an ethos of cosmopolitan encounter and exchange, their presence will mean nothing more than the mere numerical fact of depicting lots of different kinds of people on the comics page. Merely nominal diversity would have no meaningful impact on the ways characters respond to and negotiate their differences.

I've remained attached to classic Marvel comics for so many years because the fundamental conceit of the Marvel imaginative universe was simply that it is filled with different kinds of people and it's awesome to get to know them. When you hitch that to an *ethos of care for the world*—which is a central value of superhero comic books—then you are linking a diverse cast of characters to the value of negotiating, making meaning out of and responding to human difference. In other words, you create a fictional world that is organically diverse, filled with many kinds of people (just like the world we actually inhabit), and you set them to dynamic interaction. By its very structure, this kind of cosmos hails or draws in a diverse readership, that includes self-identified queer people, as well as others who simply see or interpret the world in queer ways regardless of their sexuality or gender.

AH and JW: Your introduction to your special comics issue of *American Literature* (2018) proposes that there's something queer about comics in three ways. As an outsider medium, comics elicit attachments from outsider audiences, outcasts and minorities. Comics' representational capacities enable them more than other modes of art to make queerness visible and believable. And comics' serial narrativity—repetition with a difference—fosters opportunities for queer stories to emerge. So, if *all* comics are always queer in these ways, are there useful ways to distinguish the queerness of LGBTQ+ comics in particular?

RF: There are numerous ways to distinguish the queerness of LGBTQ+ comics: you can reconstruct the history of self-identified LGBTQ+ comics creators, identify distinct styles, track representations of characters, study reception by self-identified LGBTQ+ readers, compare visualizations of LGBTQ+ sex, sexuality, and gender-expression across time and place. The list could go on. Each approach is necessary and valuable. And yet, in order to capture the capaciousness of queer gender and sexuality we cannot presume a stable ground of "gay" or "lesbian" or "bisexual" or "transgender" identity; all of those terms have multiple meanings in different contexts. I agree with Eve Sedgwick that whatever we call "queer" must in some way be grounded in the lived experience of self-identified LGBTQ+ people; but *also* her follow-up claim that queerness will always exceed the particularity of LGBTQ+ lives to describe a range of experiences of gender and sexuality that do not follow the line of heterosexual normativity. Queer is elastic, evolving, and ultimately not hitched to any specific identity.

You can look at comics texts written and drawn by anybody, regardless of their sexual orientation or gender expression, in which questions of alternative gender and sexuality are either central to the text or circulate peripherally at the edges of the narrative. I often think of Mariko and Jillian Tamaki's beautiful and strange graphic novel *Skim* (2005) as a queer text in the most potent sense of the term. It is a story about a precocious Asian Canadian teenage girl who identifies as a witch and is struggling to be seen and heard by her friends and family. The queerness of the text is extremely subdued: in a shocking and unexpected moment, the character Skim shares a kiss with her English teacher, a beautiful, intelligent middle-aged woman who is one of the only people who admires and recognizes Skim's brightness. This moment is brief but powerful, and it is never described or talked about in the terms of "lesbian" identity. Skim feels more attached to her identity as a witch than to any other social category including lesbian, Asian or Canadian. If we expect a coming out story, or a clear articulation by Skim that she is an "Asian Canadian queer girl," we won't find it. Queerness appears instead in the breaking of inter-generational taboos, in the surprising intimacy and recognition between a student and her loving mentor, in Skim's disinterest in almost all identity categories. The brief kiss never blossoms into a romance. It is ephemeral and fleeting, yet transformative; this is also an accurate description of the way the text is drawn. There is a fine-art quality to Jillian Tamaki's rendering of each scene, using long flowing lines, a black-and-white color palate, and depicting bodies and faces in a distinctly Japanese style that invokes the theatrical make-up of Kabuki theatre and Geisha culture. The delicate, extremely detail-oriented, and, dare I say, self-consciously "feminine" quality of the art feels intensely *gay* to me, but it can't be described as "camp" because it is so restrained and lacking in excess (for example, see figure 14.4 on page 223).

You couldn't easily categorize *Skim* as an LGBTQ+ comic if you were committed to the idea that its author has to be a self-identified gay or lesbian person. So, we need to leave room for different versions of queerness in comics production, circulation and reception, from the most self-consciously gay, lesbian, bisexual, transgender, and nonbinary comics to the most ephemeral, fleeting, and even completely unnamed expressions of *queer being or affect* in sequential visual art. This might simply involve producing many different kinds of genealogies, reading lists, and definitions of queer comics that deploy different criteria for what counts as a distinctly *queer* aesthetic intervention in sequential art. I think this work is already happening in comics studies and it is making for an incredibly exciting moment when the entire field of international comics production is being reappraised as a vast archive of queer aesthetic practices. I am basically of the mind that, if you can provide a compelling description of what you mean by "queer" and make an argument for the value of one comic or another as uniquely so, then I'm here for it.

To paraphrase Sedgwick: if what we want is to create a world in which a vast range of queer desires and embodiments are valued and celebrated, then why shouldn't we have endless definitions of what counts as queer? I think the point is not to ultimately decide what is and is not an LGBTQ+ comic (frankly, I think *The Fantastic Four* is one of the queerest comics ever produced and there isn't a single self-identified LGBTQ+ character in the original run). Rather, our task is to continually *extrapolate what could be a queer aesthetic act or practice* in a given comic text, and then to see what theoretically unfolds from naming it as such. In this sense, I am less interested in identifying what is distinctly queer about LGBTQ+ comics and more invested in thinking about queerness as an experimental, theoretical, or conceptual possibility that unfolds from comics' seriality. A queer sequence if there ever was one.

Works Cited

Ballester, Rodrigo Muñoz. *Manuel no está solo.* 1985. Ediciones Sinsentido, 2005.

Berlatsky, Noah. *Wonder Woman: Bondage and Feminism in the Marston/Peter Comics, 1941–1948.* Rutgers University Press, 2017.

Cruse, Howard. *Stuck Rubber Baby.* Paradox Press, 1995.

Dean, Tim. "Introduction. Pornography, Technology, Archive." *Porn Archives*, edited by Tim Dean, Steven Ruszczycky, David Squires, 1–26. Duke University Press, 2014.

Fake, Edie. *Gaylord Phoenix.* Secret Acres, 2010.

Fawaz, Ramzi. "Legions of Superheroes: Diversity, Multiplicity, and Collective Action against Genocide in the Superhero Comic Book." *Social Text* 36, no. 4 (2018): 21–55.

Fawaz, Ramzi. *The New Mutants: Superheroes and the Radical Imagination of American Comics.* NYU Press, 2016.

Fawaz, Ramzi. "A Queer Sequence: Comics as a Disruptive Medium." *PMLA* 134, no. 3 (May 2019): 588–94.

Harrison, Michael. "Queering Comic Spaces in *Manuel.*" Society for Cinema and Media Studies National Conference. Chicago, IL, March 6–10, 2013.

Jacobs, Jesse. *Crawl Space.* Koyama Press, 2017.

Jimenez, Phil. "Wonder Woman, Feminist Icon? Queer Icon? No, Love Icon." *Journal of Graphic Novels and Comics* 9, no. 6 (2018): 526–39.

Lepore, Jill. *The Secret History of Wonder Woman.* Knopf, 2014.

"Queer About Comics." *American Literature* 90, no. 2 (June 2018).

Scott, Darieck. "Big Black Beauty: Drawing and Naming the Black Male Figure in Superhero and Gay Porn Comics." *Porn Archives*, edited by Tim Dean, Steven Ruszczycky, David Squires, 183–212. Duke University Press, 2014.

Tamaki, Mariko, and Jillian Tamaki. *Skim.* Groundwood Books, 2005.

Wojnarowicz, David, James Romberger, and Marguerite Van Cook. *7 Miles a Second.* 1996. Fantagraphics, 2013.

II.

GLOBAL CROSSINGS AND INTERSECTIONS

Chapter 6

GLOBAL CROSSINGS AND INTERSECTIONS

SECTION INTRODUCTION

ALISON HALSALL AND JONATHAN WARREN

Comics historians and aficionados know well that comics have always been a global medium without a singular national root, a many-branched rhizome with prominent outcroppings in Europe, Asia, North America, Latin America, and, well, everywhere.[1] From French and Belgian *bande dessineé* to the German comics that develop out of *Bilderbogen* and *Bildergeschichten,* from the thrilling superabundance of Japanese manga to the American juggernaut of newspaper strips and comic books, superheroic and otherwise, comics belong to the world and have long been heralded for welcoming migrants as they travel around it and make homes in new places. Comics' accessibility to the il- and semi-literate and to new language learners has long been cited to account for their popularity, reach, and value as a literature that supports global migration and which thrives, in part, as a measure of such ceaseless human movement. Nonetheless, we are also familiar with the fact that comics' global reach is, in English-language commentary, often acknowledged by way of a passing reminder.

In April 2018, a special "Cartoon Times" issue of the *Times Literary Supplement* announced that "the comics age is upon us" (Bulson 2018, 7), what with the plethora of graphic novels, anthologies, collections, reprints, and critical works about comics that are emerging: "Some of the most popular adult comics and graphic novels may still be coming out of the United States, but the medium is and always has been global" (7). The *Times'* Eric Bulson boldly labels the era while feeling the need to remind those living in it not to forget its key attribute. His welcome impulse is nonetheless indicative of a continuing worry that readers and critics still assume that the most significant comics output comes from the United States even as comics' global aspect is increasingly apparent on the shelves of comics connoisseurs and casual readers alike. The growing availability of comics from around the world for the "us" in Bulson's pronouncement is undeniable. *Barefoot Gen, Baddawi, Safe Area Goražde, Zenobia, A Game for Swallows, Persepolis, Aya, The Arab of the Future, Deogratias,* among many others: the genres of auto/biography, testimony, documentary, and slow journalism are some of the most recognizable in the global comics industry, visualizing local communities by means of a medium that crosses national and cultural boundaries. However, the availability of such works might not on its own make them as legible as one might hope given their susceptibility to interpolation within a market-driven globalism that risks flattening or obscuring cultural distinctness.[2] In a late-capitalist environment of superabundance, the nationally diverse voices on the comics bookshelf must contend with the irony that the fact of their more ready availability, in the absence of well-attuned critical curation, may subsume their other values, leave them opaque, or annex them to hegemony. Publication strategies to avoid licensing material with potentially offensive content or to adapt that material by eliminating or changing images and words (such as shrink-wrapping comics or mailing them under a plain cover) signal how comics as transnational commodities can take different forms as they are adapted to suit the particular local cultures in which they find themselves (Pagliassotti 2009, 31).

That the *TLS* chooses still to advise its readers to remember that the rest of the world exists flags to us that comics readers need also not to take for granted that they know what the rest of the world is, even as they buy stories from the vast diversity of far-flung localities abbreviated under the rubric "global." Offering an important corrective to such a homogenizing tendency, Gillian Whitlock instead pictures "a global network of sequential art" ("Autographics" 2006, 969) by means of which different forms, formats, genres, and storytelling traditions across cultures and from around the world come into contact. In such a network, varieties of storytelling engage with one another transculturally and transnationally, thanks to the accessibility and adaptability of comics art.

So, for example, in this section of the *Reader*, William Armour's chapter considers Gengoroh Tagame's erotic manga as a Bildungsroman, a sexual formation story by Japan's preeminent gay manga creator that is strongly influenced by American gay author John Preston's *Mr. Benson: A Novel* (1983) in its depiction of university student Ōhashi as a studly *tabula rasa*. Tagame amalgamates transnational literary elements in a tale about the erotic pedagogy and taming of a particular BDSM slave, in part, to generalize about the distance between mainstream Japanese social norms and gay sexual liberation and to reveal how ironically close acceptable Japanese regulatory opprobrium is to BDSM's codes of role play and uninhibited shamelessness. Moreover, Tagame maps the story's interest in such distance and proximity geographically. Extreme sexual rites of passage initiate Ōhashi into a world of newfound fulfillment, allowing Tagame to ponder a literal world where such BDSM satisfaction is possible and sustainable. After master Shibazaki climactically humiliates Ōhashi in front of his students, Shibazaki flees the constraints of mainstream Japanese society. The pair relocate to ostensibly more sexually liberated and permissive Berlin.

The specificity of the German capital stands also for the idea of a more general world of erotic freedom but one revealed as such inextricably within the circuit of Japanese sexual becoming. Ultimately, Ōhashi and Shibazaki together emerge into BDSM's future, a "kinkily ever after" that Tagame renders as a transnational voyage, one already anticipated by Tagame's own storytelling technique itself with its intertextual borrowing and incorporation of Western elements.

Comics' accessibility—their shared formal familiarity—is as important to their worldwide appeal as it is to their provision of opportunities for cross-cultural interaction and understanding. Nonetheless, readers' comfort with the meaning-making image-and-text dynamics of comics form and their capacity to represent, translate, adapt, and map complex ideas and experiences does not, of course, guarantee easy dexterity with a comic's cultural specificity. It is worth remembering to be cautious in the face of comics' often friendly positing of readers' familiarity or of the premise that no cultural complication will be so thorny, no nuance so fine that it cannot be made easily legible. Similarly, as LGBTQ+ status ramifies differently in different places, to read the world's queer comics obliges us not to presume that any local gayness, for example, will be the common ground of LGBTQ+ people everywhere. Remembering to note the interplay between apparent ready accessibility and cultural specificity is especially relevant as the internet's circulation of electronic comics produces the illusion of the whole world's instantaneous, immediate nearness.

ArtQueerHabibi, for example, devises some of the most compelling comics taking up this dynamic. The pseudonymous Instagram-based artist's single panels feature easily recognizable queer scenarios, inflected by the style, locales, and sensibility specific to the artist's Arab milieus. Moody and fierce, they mingle amorousness and celebration to feature and flout homophobic stigma, the comics' transnational language of love always appearing in images that are local, specific, and particular, their evocation of queer tenderness presuming or serving as a primer for readers' facility with the important sweet nothings of LGBTQ+ Arab life. "Habibi," Arabic for "my love," "my sweetheart," or "my darling," is the most common term of endearment and affection in the Arab world. *ArtQueerHabibi*'s eye-catching images of LGBTQ+ life and love in the Middle East—queer romance, sensuality, flirtation, cruising, gender fluidity, nightlife, family, fashion, and intersectional solidarity—visualize and fantasize about the vibrancy of queer Arab life for his 50,000 followers around the world while affirming the specificity of lived experiences and the semiotic vocabulary of queerness in the Middle East and its diaspora. Hundreds of young people reach out to the artist, seeking advice about coming out and reconciling LGBTQ+ identity with religious beliefs and cultural expectations.

The chapters in this section of *The LGBTQ+ Comics Studies Reader* show how comics depict and narrate LGBTQ+ identity, sexuality, gender, politics,

Figure 6.1. "Tinder 2018," *ArtQueerHabibi*. @artqueerhabibi.

and desire across different geographical and cultural contexts while attending to how ideas about comics' legibility and LGBTQ+ visibility oblige a reckoning with local specificity. The chapters collected here denote key comics histories and conceptual achievements within their local contexts (Germany and Japan, here) and contend with, and exemplify, the complicated valences of reception and appreciation by audiences well outside of them (specifically with regard to Japanese erotic manga). Susanne Hochreiter, Marina Rauchenbacher, and Katharina Serles's overview of German-language LGBTQ+ comics deepens and complements current studies of the European comics and *bande dessinée* scene. Comics emerged in Germany after World War II, thanks to the popular culture imported by soldiers from the American and British occupying armies. The emergence of lesbian and gay subcultures in Germany continued in spite of the Nazis' blanket persecution and eradication of lesbians and gays, and later with the continued spying on homosexual and trans* people. In important respects, German-language comics commented on the zeitgeist, tracking the gradual

Figure 6.2. "Rainbow Street Amman," *ArtQueerHabibi*. @artqueerhabibi.

process towards social and political acceptance of LGBTQ+ people in Germany, Austria, and Switzerland. Gender and genre produce exciting translocal synergies, as Keiko Miyajima's chapter demonstrates. Focusing on Hagio Moto's science-fiction manga, Miyajima explains how they provide an innovative, gender-fluid space to encourage readers to liberate their imaginations from the constraints of gender and sexual norms within a future-oriented arena of possibility, unconstrained by national or cultural boundaries. Hagio posits a state of betweenness for her characters, surpassing the gendered conventionality of other Japanese male and female comics characters. As with Tagame's evocation of Berlin as the hoped-for alternative to Japan's restrictiveness, Hagio imagines even more remote locations on the edge of different galaxies and dimensions for the realization of her comics' dismantlement of gender and sex binaries and sexuality categories. For Hagio, binaries can only be rejected by means of the crossings that characters make between and among spatialities, temporalities, and identities; Miyajima helps us to see that Hagio's comics imply

Figure 6.3. "Disco Saudi," *ArtQueerHabibi*. @artqueerhabibi.

a story about the queer benefits of global movement and comics circulation while imagining such advantages through what is nonetheless a specifically Japanese evocation of alterity.

While many contemporary discussions of globalization have focused on the one-way flow of Western cultural products into other nations, "the flow has never been unidirectional" (Pagliassotti 2009, 1). Ernest dit Alban explores the provocative and productive erotic queer exchange between the creators of a French gay fanzine (*Dokkun*) and Japanese amateur comics. *Dokkun's* participation in fanzine conventions in Europe and Japan, he argues, shows the potential of amateur pornographic comics to create "contact zones" among gay communities around the world. Local, regional, and global cultures meet in the transnational circulation of images, books, artists, and alumni of gay comics. In this instance, gay manga becomes a tool for inventing queer social spaces through transcultural and translocal dynamics.

Given the rising prominence of queer voices, it is easy enough to fantasize about a fully active transnational LGBTQ+ network of comics readers, each locality having easy access to, and enjoying comics from, every other, with France, Mexico, Latin America, the Philippines, Scandinavia, India, Spain, etc., winding all of the world's comics queer localities into a vast skein of cross-connections, but our contributors suggest that such an LGBTQ+ comics commons is still largely the stuff of tomorrow and that cross-cultural, cross-regional, and translocal reading will inspire the future of LGBTQ+ comics scholarship. From what we already see of transnational LGBTQ+ comics, international crosscurrents, patterns of influence, international adaptations, and other transmissions between and across geographical, regional, and cultural boundaries, it is clear that we are on the cusp of it.

Notes

1. See John Lent's 10,200-entry scholarly guide, *Comic Art in Africa, Asia, Australia, and Latin America through 2000: An International Bibliography* (Praeger, 2004) for one important indicator of comics' worldwide reach.

2. In a usefully similar way, Antonia Levi invokes Iwabuchi Koichi's concept of "cultural odorlessness" to allude to efforts made to promote Japanese products abroad by reducing or erasing marks of a Japanese cultural identity.

Works Cited

Bulson, Eric. "Wiping the Windshield of Your Mind." *Times Literary Supplement*, April 27, 2018.

Levi, Antonia. "The Sweet Smell of Japan: Anime, Manga, and Japan in North America." *Journal of Asian Pacific Communication* 23, no. 1 (2013): 3–18.

Pagliassotti, Dru. "GloBLisation and Hybridisation: Publishers' Strategies for Bringing Boys' Love to the United States." *Intersections: Gender and Sexuality in Asia and the Pacific* 20 (April 2009): n.p.

Whitlock, Gillian. "Autographics: The Seeing 'I' of the Comics." *MFS Modern Fiction Studies* 52, no. 4 (Winter 2006): 965–79.

Chapter 7

QUEER VISUALITIES— QUEER SPACES

GERMAN-LANGUAGE LGBTQ+ COMICS

SUSANNE HOCHREITER, MARINA RAUCHENBACHER, AND KATHARINA SERLES

INTRODUCTION

This article strives to provide an overview of German-language LGBTQ+ comics as well as an insight into a scattered and precarious scene. Unlike their Anglo-American counterparts, for example, German-language LGBTQ+ comics have not been collected and studied extensively, as comics and queer theory are not intrinsically linked and do not share the same kind of tradition (see section II). Thus, research within this cross-section of fields cannot be conducted easily: there is no database like queercomicsdatabase.com; there is no institutional recognition like *Comicosity*'s rubric *Queer Visibility* or the *Queers & Comics* Conference; the archives and bibliographies we consulted (*Stichwort*, "Keyword,"[1] in Vienna and the *Bonn Online Bibliography of Comics Research*) focus on either the genre/theme or the medium. The fact that efforts to describe German-language LGBTQ+ comics systematically have been sporadic (Reitsamer and Zobl 2011; Pfalzgraf 2012)—single articles, chapters, or issues within anthologies, rather than whole specialized collections and studies—points toward German-language LGBTQ+ comics still being on the margins of the discourse.

Relevant projects with a broader public have taken up work only after the mid-2010s (cf. the professional network's *Comic Solidarity* lobbying for independent artists in the field). In 2019, the German "inclusive" comics award *GINCO* started to honor "artists from marginalized groups"; the same year, Markus Pfalzgraf and Martina Schradi formed the network *Queersplaining* to promote a European queer comics scene.

The following rundown of key developments, influences, artists, comics as well as topics and formal elements can thus only scratch the surface of a field yet to take off. First, some milestones of historical development will be introduced, on the basis of which, secondly, brief analyses of crucial contemporary examples will be presented and theoretical approaches from visual culture studies, gender/queer studies, and cultural studies will be proposed.[2]

HISTORICAL DEVELOPMENTS

Politics after World War II

Due to the pop culture that was imported by soldiers of the occupying American and British armies, comics experienced an upswing in the German-speaking world after World War II. Pop music, fashion, films, and comics became part of a new youth culture, but it was not until the 1980s that comics culture gained broader attention. One reason might be that the Weimar Republic's 1926 *Gesetz zur Bewahrung der Jugend vor Schund- und Schmutzschriften* ("law to protect the youth from trashy and dirty writings"), which essentially prohibited comics, lived on in the Federal Republic of Germany's 1953 *Gesetz über die Verbreitung jugendgefährdender Schriften* ("law on the distribution of writings harmful to young persons") and in equally restrictive and normative practices of the GDR up until the 1970s. To a certain extent, this classification of comics runs parallel to political, social, and cultural struggles in Austria, Germany, and Switzerland after World War II (Dolle-Weinkauff 1990): as a consequence of the Nazis' blanket persecution and expulsion of gays and lesbians, connections to the vibrant culture of the Weimar Republic were almost completely lost. The destruction of lesbian and gay subcultures by the Nazis, as well as the long ideological indoctrination by fascists and National Socialists, had the effect that the vast majority of homosexual people lived closeted throughout the 1950s and 1960s (Aldrich 2007). Again, both the FRG and the GDR initially copied the restrictive Nazi paragraph 175 (criminalizing homosexuality). Whereas the GDR abandoned the policy earlier than its western neighbor, it continued long after to spy on homosexual and transsexual persons (Setz 2006; Dennert 2007; Reiter-Zatloukal 2014).

Visibility and Visualization

In the 1960s, emancipatory forces finally regained momentum in the German-speaking world, with the arts and media being important instruments for analyzing and criticizing discourses on gender roles and power especially within the lesbian and gay liberation movement. In this context, the arts have been valuable not only in the sense of self-expression but also as crucial elements of discourse and critical reflection of political aims and strategies. Demands and strategies revolved around three central topics: visibility, recognition, and (equal) rights. In particular, "visibility" was a central concern for gays, lesbians (and women*)[3] as it offered opportunities to claim and define one's own image. Especially for lesbians who experienced their situation as a double discrimination, the need to become visible within the women's movement and the gay liberation campaign was at the center of their discussions and actions. In 1968, in the context of feminist protests against the board of the Socialist German Students Union, plenty of feminist women* groups and so-called *Weiberräte* (Councils of Broads) and gay initiatives like the famous *Homosexuelle Aktion Westberlin* (HAW; Homosexual Initiative West Berlin) were founded. In 1972, the Austrian *Aktion unabhängiger Frauen* (AUF; Initiative of Independent Women) was formed in Vienna. New feminist groups such as the *Frauenbefreiungsbewegung* (Female Liberation Movement) and the *Organisation für die Sache der Frau* (Organization for the Woman's Cause) also emerged in Zurich. One means of gaining "visibility" in a broader sense were (periodic) print publications.

Comics in Feminist and Lesbian Media

The most prominent example of such a feminist publication is Alice Schwarzer's magazine *Emma*. Comics, cartoons, and illustrations played a crucial role since the first edition was published in 1977. An overwhelming number of these works originates from Franziska Becker, who is known for her use of irony and humor to establish a somewhat playful perspective on pressing political issues. However, Becker's works—as well as Schwarzer's political statements and *Emma*'s political focus—are increasingly becoming objects of criticism for being heteronormative, racist, and performing a colonialist perspective (Vahabzadeh 2019). In 1978, *Emma*'s first edition on lesbianism was published (no. 3)—but the included comic does not take on the general topic of the issue which points towards the precariousness of representing lesbian identity.

In contrast to *Emma*, which developed into a commercially successful magazine that—despite all critique—remains so to the present day, the magazine *AUF* was not commercially oriented and started in 1974 with an expressive graphic illustration by Inge Opitz. In the early editions, comics by Marie Marcks were frequently integrated. Lesbian love was first thematized in *AUF*'s fourth issue in 1975—without any comics or illustrations. An extensive exploration of sexuality, including lesbian life and love, is part of issue 13 (1977), illustrated with ornamental floral motifs. Certain motifs are part of a historic lesbian code: specific flowers and colors were understood as references to lesbian love and have been elements of a lesbian communication network (Hacker 2015, 290). It took another year until the first depiction of lesbians was included: in *AUF*'s fifteenth issue (1978) a drawing is displayed, depicting two women*

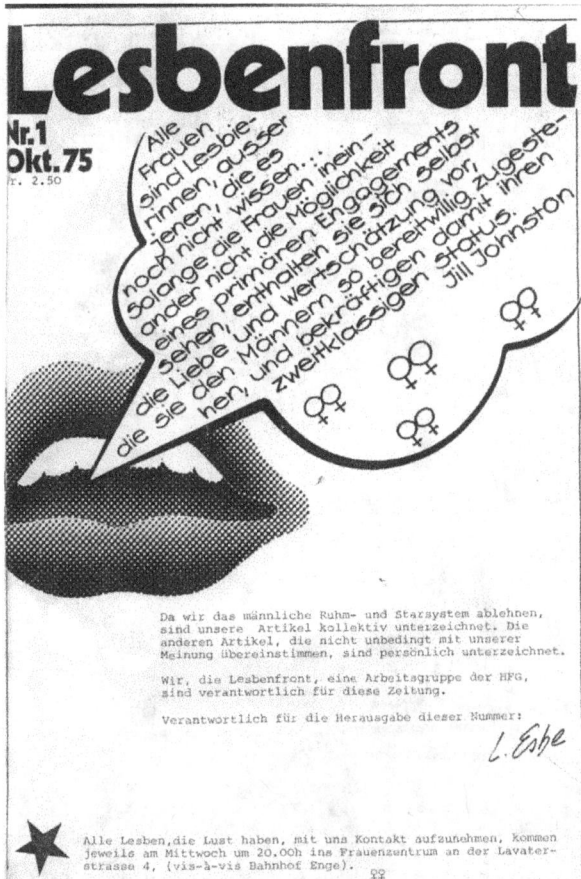

Figure 7.1. *Lesbenfront*, no. 1 (1975), cover.

whose lips are almost touching (25). Strikingly, a lot of feminist media in the 1970s depicted lesbian sexuality in a trivialized or somewhat romanticized and illustrative way, whereas most lesbian publications thematized desire and eroticism more openly. It seems that this different attitude also creates a ground for comics in lesbian media. Comics[4] supports the narrative of lesbian desire as well as the depiction of nonheteronormative bodies and looks. The verbal and visual celebration of the female* body in feminist media did not include sexual desire or lust. Thus, the debate on sexuality was charged with a certain distrust stemming from the need to undermine the male* gaze and to reject the objectification of women*. This might be a reason for the lack of lesbian comics in feminist media.

After World War II, the first lesbian magazine in the German-speaking world was *UKZ* (*Unsere kleine Zeitung*; "Our Small Newspaper") in February 1975, edited by the group L 74, and was followed by the Swiss magazine

Figure 7.2. Gabi Szekatsch (1984), n. p. © Lesben-Rundbrief/Gabi Szekatsch.

Lesbenfront[5] (1975–2005; "Lesbian Front") and the Berlin-based *Lesbenpresse* (Lesbian Press) the same year. As for most feminist magazines, collectivity was awarded high value; the noncommercial orientation and the meager production budget opened up potential for a form of "do-it-yourself" creativity. This is linked to the development of underground comics in the United States in the 1960s insofar as artists veered out into new thematic and aesthetic directions and positioned themselves independently from publishers (Knigge 2016, 23).

In terms of graphic work, illustration, and comics, there are pieces by both amateurs and experienced artists in these magazines. Most featured handwritten, hand-designed elements and typewritten texts and were reproduced by copy machines. The collective production process was based on a political understanding of solidarity and involvement to create a nonhierarchical, non-repressive space for cooperation. *Lesbenfront* presented a declaration on the cover of its first issue stating that most contributions were signed collectively as a protest against the patriarchal celebrity system (Herzog 1997). Lesbian love was now no longer a controversial issue but was strongly supported and significantly more a matter of pride than a cause of shame. Similarly, the later Viennese *Lesben-Rundbrief* (1984–93; "Lesbian Circular") was a local resource for lesbians to discuss ideas and express themselves. Whereas the Swiss publication offered illustrations, collages, and cartoons, the Viennese equivalent offered comics, too. In 1984, artist Gabi Szekatsch contributed the first comic of *Lesben-Rundbrief* (Hacker 2000), making fun of patterns of jealousy and desire in lesbian subculture. The comic is situated in "a well-known place,"[6] supposedly a bar. The present women's* mood just reaches a "high point"[7] (of boredom) as the door opens and another woman* enters the room. She immediately gains everybody's attention; the fourth caption reads "'fresh blood!' (yummy!)."[8] Subsequently, the comic makes fun of the (expected) jealous reaction of the couples and demonstrates irony as well humor, illustrating an established and self-confident lesbian dating scene.

Comics in Gay Media

The layout and content of gay magazines in the early 1970s demonstrate a different style than lesbian and feminist publications. They were often commercial and lifestyle-oriented, and the mainstream professional design was based on erotic and pornographic photography. After the first reform of §175 of the German Criminal Code in September 1969, several magazines were founded: *Du & Ich* (1969; "You and I"), *him* (1970), *DON* (1970), and *unter uns* (1972; "among us"; later: *unter uns ADAM*).

The most obvious difference in terms of visual representation is the depiction of bodies and sexuality. Whereas lesbian publications focus on texts about relationships and politics, many gay magazines offered overtly sexual content and personal ads. They also had different ideas and concepts of cooperation for their editorial work. It was not until the 1980s, when the AIDS crisis drastically changed attitudes and triggered political urgency in gay media work, that publications increasingly started to refocus on legal matters and critical identity politics (Theis 1997, 327). In Jón Jónsson, Andreas C. Knigge, and Annie Goetzinger's *Die verlorene Zukunft* (1992; "The Lost Future"), for example, a partner's positive AIDS test causes fundamental fear: "And in case I am . . . too?!"[9] (1992, 19). This self-confrontation is visualized in a mirror scene. Ralf König drew comic strips for HIV prevention campaigns (Pfalzgraf 2012, 116) and reflected on homosexuality and HIV more extensively in the renowned comic

Super-Paradise (1999). The notably different and deconstructive approach of Wolf Müll (Wolfgang Müller) elaborates on identity politics in light of being gay and coming from a Catholic environment (Müll 1980; Pfalzgraf 2012, 110–15).

Illustrations, comics, and cartoons were contributed by local artists; often international work by renowned artists like Tom of Finland, who had published since the 1950s, were included too. The most important German-speaking comics artist is the aforementioned Ralf König who began his work in the context of the political wing of the German gay movement and contributed critical comics to the underground comix magazine *Zomix* (1979–83) and the gay magazine *Rosa Flieder* (1979–89; "Pink Lilac"). He has been publishing since 1981, when his first comics *Sarius, Das sensationelle Comic-Book* (*The Sensational Comic Book*) and the first edition of *SchwulComix* (*Gay Comix*) were released.

Introducing: Queer

It was not until the early 1990s that the term "queer" arrived in German-language lesbian and gay media. Patu and Antje Schrupp refer to this development meta-reflexively in their comic *Kleine Geschichte des Feminismus im euro-amerikanischen Kontext* (2015, 76–79; *A Brief History of Feminism*, 2017, 73–75). Alison Bechdel's *Dykes to Watch Out For* (1983–2008) had a significant impact on the German-language lesbian and feminist comics scene. The fact that Bechdel's comics have been translated into German since the early 1990s proves the intense and lasting interest in her work that is inspired by the queer theoretical discourse in the United States.

The first major exhibition of queer comics in Europe accordingly focuses on this very relationship: *Superqueeroes—Our LGBTI* Comic Book Heroes and Heroines* was first shown at the Schwules Museum (Gay Museum) in Berlin in 2016, and at the University of Cologne in 2018. Displaying a wide array of comics, it carved out how "independent queer comics challenge dominant histories by bearing witness to an astonishing plurality of queer experience" (Kong 2016, 132). The "gallery" of contemporary examples of German-language LGBTQ+ comics we present below aims to carry forward this approach.

CONTEMPORARY DEVELOPMENTS

Welcome to the Mainstream?

Over the years, both comics as a medium and LGBTQ+ topics have gained ground in the German-speaking mainstream.[10] In his preface to the "gay" issue of the comics anthology *Die Batterie* (2015; "The Battery") published in Kassel,

Figure 7.3. *Der Grüne Jaguar*, Thilo Krapp (EPSILON, 2008), 12. © Thilo Krapp/Epsilon Verlag.

Ralf König states, "Today, both 'gay' and 'comics' have become easier to digest. [. . .] There's not much underground left there anymore" (2015, n.p.).[11] Consequently, bestselling artists like Ulli Lust or Reinhard Kleist have portrayed queer characters (Kleist's *Knock Out!*, 2019) or have depicted a variety of sexual desires (Lust's *Airpussy*, 2005); König is being published by the renowned publishing house Rowohlt (*Herbst in der Hose*, 2017; "Autumn in the Pants").

However, the majority of works in the field are still either mostly published online (cf., e.g., Illi Anna Heger's crucial works, among others, *Minicomics*, 2010–16);[12] self-published (cf., e.g., Elke Renate Steiner's *Love Migration*, 2019);[13] with small/independent publishers—often after having been published online, as is the case with Joris Bas Backer and Nettmann's *Familienjuwelen*, 2019; "Family Jewels"; or in magazines, respectively. This vivid independent scene is difficult to survey in its entirety and scatteredness, especially online. Lists provided by interested individuals (such as on Heger's website) help but are not exhaustive; academic attention, institutional/professional representation, and public campaigns are fairly new.[14]

Even if the specific German-language context has doubly prevented LGBTQ+ comics from catching on in the mainstream, a "normalization" of homosexuality and comics might be identifiable: Thilo Krapp's two volumes about Damian and Alexander (*Der Grüne Jaguar*, 2008; "The Green Jaguar"; and *Dschungelliebe*, 2013; "Jungle Love"), a couple of gay adventurers, exemplify this. By integrating queerness into influential genres such as adventure and jungle comics (cf. *Tintin* and *Tarzan*), their love functions more as a backdrop to the action. The extent of the unchallengeable normalcy of their sexuality becomes apparent in volume 1, where the characters simply assume their relationship to be visible: when a third person does not "read" them as gay, they are utterly bewildered. Both are depicted within an eye-shaped panel, with Damian's eyes just as wide open in surprise as the panel, asking, "Are you blind? We have been together for two years!" (2008, 12).[15] The panel is framed by ornamental floral motifs at the bottom, attempting to support the notion of a readable "queer iconography" and connecting it back to early attempts at visual representation (Kleist 2019, 51–52; cf. *Historical Developments* section above).

Now, what about the subversive power of the underground? As if trying to disprove König's statement about gay comics and the mainstream, the afore-mentioned collection in *Die Batterie* assembles all kinds of politically incorrect or provoking pieces: from, for example, playing with racist clichés in Lukas Kummer's *Sex Safari in Swasiland* (9–12) to slurs against gays and lesbians in Sebastian Gneiting's *Am Strand* (*On the Beach*, 16–20) to the "taboo" of an aging homosexual in Florian Biermeier's *Born to Be Wild* (21–31) (cf. further examples of gay comix in Pfalzgraf 2012, 88–111).

König's own work is an example of how formerly "underground"/"disruptive" comics may be identified as blatantly racist and sexist once they have entered the mainstream: three years after its unveiling in 2015, his "LGBT fresco," which is part of Brussels' "comic strip walk" and the exhibition project *Out in the Street* commissioned by *RainbowHouse*, Brussels, was tagged with the words "transphobia" and "racism." After some debate and calls for replacements of the fresco, *RainbowHouse* decided to keep it as is, with the tags and a pedagogical slab (2019).

Didactical Approaches and a "Queer Archive"

With the increasing popularity of comics in the German-speaking world, didactical approaches are gaining in importance too. Concerning LGBTQ+, above all, two projects are of interest: Imke Schmidt and Ka Schmitz's *Ich sehe was, was du nicht siehst oder: Wer sieht hier wen? Lightfaden für Bildermacher-innen* (2010; "I Spy with My Little Eye or: Who Sees Whom Here? Guideline for Picture-Makers") and Martina Schradi's *Ach, so ist das?!* (2 vols., 2014/2016 and 2018; *Oh, I see?!*, 2017). Schmidt and Schmitz focus on didactical aspects regard-ing processes of discrimination in an intersectional way.[16] *Ich sehe was, was du nicht siehst* was created in the course of the Berlin-based research project *GenderCompetenceCenter* (2003–2010)[17] and examines the visual strategies of intersectional identity attributions/concepts in a broader sense. Schmidt and Schmitz run through various ideas of how societal diversity could be visually realized without reproducing stereotypical or discriminatory patterns. This is a change in perspective from the vital, positive, and political notion of "visibility" in historical contexts of queerness (the opportunity to create one's own images and the commitment to produce self-defined visibility, as discussed in section II) to a precarious and potentially dangerous notion of "visibility" in contemporary contexts. Schmidt and Schmitz find a rather sophisticated way to present the—nevertheless fruitful—insolubility of this problem. With one exception, each page has two parts: a series of five small panels in one row at the top of each page presents two characters adorned with different attributes. The rest of each page displays the two avatars of the artists discussing and experimenting. At a certain point, these two layers are interwoven on a graphic and a meta level: one of the (frustrated) artists throws their pencil up and right into the last panel of the series of five panels on top of the page. That is when the two figures start to transform themselves playfully into fantastic creatures and therefore concretize the creativity and power of visual concepts. The last page displays one panel at its center and the speech bubble reads, as an appeal to self-empowerment: " . . . but we keep this one!"[18] (i.e., the pencil) (2010, 19).

Whereas Schmidt and Schmitz concentrate self- and meta-reflexively on concepts of visualization, Schradi follows a quasi-documentary approach. The subtitle of the first volume, *Biografische Comicreportragen von LGBTI* (*Biographical Comic Reportages of LGBTI*), strives to classify the project as graphic life writing with the goal of recording queer lifestyles and identities in comics and, above all, creating visibility and awareness.[19] Each of the two volumes consists of several short comics, each being introduced by a splash page presenting the main character(s) and a motto like "this binary-gender world just isn't for me!" (2018, 47).[20] Schradi has also created didactic material for schools to be downloaded from her German website,[21] and an English translation of a "best of" of her comics was published (Schradi 2017). Schradi's work is a notable educational project but has to be examined critically: she states that she writes about "true stories"[22] (2016, 3) and therefore purports an imitative function for her works. In the very sense of counteracting "non-visibility"[23] (2016, 3), Schradi strives to conceive a "queer archive."[24] However, this falls short of any obvious self-reflection; to the contrary, the subtitle of the second volume even evokes the idea of "an LGBTI world," creating an exclusive and excluded space. Nevertheless, the medium of comics itself, as well as the chosen structure, constantly refers to its conditions of representation, pointing to artificiality and thus subverting the idea of authenticity.

In-Between and At the Margins: Third Spaces

Considering the potentially heteronormative and therefore limiting discursive contexts of "mainstream" and "archive," we strive to establish an alternative cultural-analytically oriented concept for the analysis of LGBTQ+ comics. Homi K. Bhabha's notion of the "third space" describes a "space of negotiating differences with a view to overcoming hierarchies and hence a space of possibilities of hybridization" (Babka and Posselt 2012, 12).[25] "Hybridity" does not merely describe "the state of the subject"[26] but instead concentrates on the "constitution of subjectivity between the poles of power and authority"[27] (Bhabha 2012, 62).[28] Bhabha highlights the quality of the "third space" as a space for interaction. In this context, the appearance of the "hermaphrodite" opens a "third space" and therefore "a kind of aporetic condition,"[29] which, as a next step, must entail "the ability to act," to have at hand a certain scope (2012, 66).

Due to its specific form (e.g., panels, gutter) and its inter-/transmediality, comics fundamentally operates in an in-between (McCloud 1994, 60–93; Postema 2013, 27–53); it points to its persistence on a threshold, ultimately realized through the gutter (Rauchenbacher and Serles 2020, forthcoming). Bodies are (re)produced via the constant reiteration of "body signs," serially and "not identical but recognizable" (Klar 2014, 171).[30] The trans-/multi-/inter-/meta-mediality (Mitchell 2014, 260) of the comics medium elaborates on this multifaceted process and gives scope for encounters as necessary conditions for the negotiation of identity in a "third space."

One obvious example for this subversive dimension of comics and its creation of a "third space" is Suskas Lötzerich's *Hexenblut* (2014; "Witch Blood") which is the first (autobiographical) German-language comic on intersexuality. The opening splash page shows the birth of Suska; after the delivery, the nurse is not sure about the baby's sex, and the doctor cuts off a so-called "malformation" (2014, 7).[31] The subsequent bleeding is explained to the mother as "witch blood," a kind of "first menstruation" (2014, 8).[32] *Hexenblut* tells of Suska(s)'s[33] search for identity and therefore focuses episodically on crucial moments of their overall traumatization and their transformation to a male* body. This production of different narratives is representative of narrations of intersexuality on a meta-reflexive level (Baier and Hochreiter 2014, 18). The cover already designates this process and compiles the different stages within a pentacle, an encircled pentagram, with the screaming newborn at its center. As a (superstitious) symbol of magic shelter, the pentacle ironically quotes the title and emphasizes the significance of the unauthorized medical intervention into Suska(s)'s life. Concurrently, this montage displays the convertibility or rather modifiability of bodies and points to the inevitable gaps in displaying this body/these bodies at the very same moment. The pentagram is outlined with thick black lines—referencing panel lines—that divide and separate the individual stages of Suska(s)'s development while each "panel" shows parts of their body. What cannot—and is not even attempted to—be shown, is the "malformation," the ultimate symbol of Suska(s)'s intersexuality, which is *ex negativo* represented

Figure 7.4. *Hexenblut*, Suskas Lötzerich (Luftschacht, 2014), cover. © Suskas Lötzerich/Luftschacht.

via the title naming the violation only. This narration of intersexuality realizes an ultimate "third space" insofar as what is—on principle—untold as well as the undepictable is realized by the structure of the comics medium.

Nacha Vollenweider's *Fußnoten* (2017; "Footnotes") may serve as another example of the creation of "third spaces," in this case with a concentration on the formal/structural aspect as a vehicle for reclaiming narration, history and memory. *Fußnoten* is conceived as a story of footnotes, at the citational and literal margin of things. The frame narrative follows Nacha, the protagonist, and her girlfriend on a train ride through the suburbs of Hamburg; inserted as footnotes into that frame are flashbacks to Nacha's Argentinian family as well as to the couple's past together. This begins logically: panels are equipped with superscript numbers and repeated some pages later to initiate a flashback. Notably, this is inverted at the approximate center of the book, from which point the footnotes come before the superscript numbers. The margins have been inverted, have become the core, and vice versa. One of the initial captions conclusively reads, "Somehow, I'm living simultaneously in two worlds"[34]

(2017, 14), which is performatively true on many levels: Nacha lives as an Argentinian lesbian in Germany; her intersectional state of an in-between could not be more aptly mirrored by the structure of the narrative.

Trans* Identities

Sarah Barczyk's *Nenn mich Kai* (2016; "Call Me Kai") tells the story of Andrea, a trans* person who starts to transition into Kai and hence takes up speech and hormone therapy. Whereas the narrative recounts a transition, the comic formally purports distinct and finite states of identity as it is, for example, steeped in stark black and white contrasts. Framed by an illustration of the same bathroom but equipped with iconic female* insignia on the inside of the front dust jacket and stereotypically male* icons on the back, the dust jacket presupposes a clear and fixed beginning as well as end point. It is the gutter that adds subversion: in the first outing scene to his friend, Kai's utterances about "simply having always known"[35] (2016, 12) are positioned within an extended blank space between two panels. This composition is mirrored by another key scene, in which Kai has to decide between a female* and a male* dressing room. Just like the gutter before, the wall space between the doors takes on the form of a capital "T." In it, much like Bhabha's notion of the "third space," there is room for the "negotiation of differences," "hybridity" (see above and cf. Barczyk 2016, 71), and consequently for Kai, which is why he is depicted at that exact spot. Instead of exploring this space or expressing the transgressive violence that the other two spaces exert on him, however, Kai simply concludes, "Oh no, I hadn't even thought about that" (2016, 71).[36]

The infamous trope of the dressing room or toilet scene as one possible visualization of nonbinarity and—in the context of gender transition—as an actual "third space" is also used in the comparatively widely discussed comic-zines *Trouble X* (2005–2016), published anonymously.[37] In **träume* (2007; **dreams*), the eponymous nonbinary/trans* protagonist dreams about a third door between binary restroom doors; the multilinear textual arrangement in the accompanying thought bubble offers various readings: "I can't think," "I can't think me," "I can't really decide right now," and so on.[38] This ambiguity and elusiveness pervade the *Trouble X* comics (except for its strict black-and-white opaqueness)—and even the title itself oscillates between identification and deconstruction of meaning: "The X in Trouble X stands for the questionable X chromosome" (quoted in Reitsamer and Zobl 2011, 370).[39]

Another artist working with dismal black-and-white drawings and subverting binary gender concepts is Franz Suess. Whereas his panels are neatly structured and in symmetrical order, his characters and their "body signs" (Klar 2014) clearly are not. They defy (hetero-) normative classifications. His newest

Figure 7.5. *Nenn mich Kai*, Andrea Barczyk (Egmont Graphic Novel, 2016), 71. © Sarah Barczyk/Egmont Graphic Novel.

Figure 7.6. Anonymous [Yori Gagarim], "*träume." 2007. © Yori Gagarim.

publication, *Paul Zwei* (2019; "Paul Two"), features a dislikeable protagonist, who suddenly discovers that his penis has grown inward and he now "looks like a woman" (2019, 92).[40] While he then experiences dysphoria and dissociation, his roommate Christoph shows interest in the peculiar state of Paul's gender/genitals, which ultimately leads to Paul's only "successful" intimate experience as the two sleep with each other. The discourses and concepts of homo-, bi-, and transsexuality are never made explicit, just as genitals are never depicted even though the protagonist's attention focuses on sex.

Dietmar Dath's and Oliver Scheibler's *Mensch wie Gras wie* (2014; "Human Like Grass Like") can be read as a radical queer project, questioning binarity

Figure 7.7. Dietmar Dath and Oliver Scheibler, *Mensch wie Gras wie* (Verbrecher Verlag, 2014), n.p. © Dietmar Dath and Oliver Scheibler/Verbrecher Verlag.

in general and not only with regard to gender concepts. The title refers to the main idea of a dystopian world, characterized by illness, laboratory experiments, and sheer madness; human beings, as well as flora, are manipulated. The transgressive approach becomes apparent through Scheibler's graphic work where shifting queer identities are visualized and human beings and animals/beasts merge. These border crossings mark both a reference to (possible) results of the experiments and the visualization of emotions, fear, or even madness and result in a "visual uncertainty," which serves as a constitutive structural element of this comic (2014, 196). In light of the overall content, the interwoven plot of the queer relationship between Elin and Martin/Martina almost seems conventional. The shifting identification of Martin/Martina as male* or female* is a paradigmatic placeholder for the challenge of (binary) identities in this dystopian world. Concerning the visual identification of women* or men*, Scheibler experiments with rows of head-on presentations focusing on one character and presenting several medium close-ups or full close-ups in line with different hairstyles, hats, jewelry, or tops. He thus underlines the interconnection of visual attributes and gender identification.

Maurizio Onano's *Oma Herbert* (2019; "Grandma Herbert") reads as a utopian counterpart of *Mensch wie Gras wie* and a continuation of Schmidt and Schmitz's *Ich sehe was, was du nicht siehst* as it juggles the tensions between heteronormative restrictions of society and the performativity/variability of identity. Among others, the portrayed family around elderly trans* woman Berta (formerly Herbert) consists of nonhuman characters whose gender is conventionally codified by their names (such as talking potted plant Gabi) or certain stereotypical attributes (such as a bowtie on Sebastian the cat). This constant pressure of a binary gender system is also visualized by the red and blue color scheme. When questions about Berta's gender come up during a joyful role-playing game, the children make sense of her to be "something like a shape-shifter,"[41] admiring her power to subvert the notion of a steady visual identity.

CONCLUSION

The described "double precariousness" of comics and LGBTQ+ issues within German-language contexts, rooted in censorship and historical defamation, is of utmost importance to understand queer comics. The same holds true for the clash between specific developments in feminism, lesbianism, as well as gay culture in Austria, Germany, and Switzerland in the twentieth century—and the trailblazing impact of international theoretical discourses such as queer theory since the 1990s. This compilation of German-language LGBTQ+ comics, artists, and topics on the basis of a historic contextualization thus offers the groundwork for further elaborations, and suggests a theoretical framework for in-depth analyses of LGBTQ+ comics in general.

Notes

1. Translations of titles and quotes in double quotations are ours; the original wording is quoted in the corresponding endnote.

2. Section II was written by Susanne Hochreiter; Section III by Marina Rauchenbacher and Katharina Serles.

3. An asterisk is used to subvert the collective nouns "woman"/"women" and "man"/"men" as well as the attributions "male"/"female" representing and performing the heteronormative/binary system.

4. We follow Hillary Chute's proposal to use the plural form "comics" as singular if we refer to it as a medium (Chute 2008, 462).

5. The title changed three times: *Lesbenfront* (1975–86), *Frau Ohne Herz* (1986–95; "Woman Without Heart"), *die* (1996–2003; "the"—feminine definite article), and *Skipper* (2004–2005).

6. "[. . .] an einem bekannten Ort."

7. "Höhepunkt."

8. "'Frischblut!' (Lechz!)"

9. "Und wenn ich auch . . . ?!"

10. Anna Beckmann analyzes strategies of ambiguity in German-language comics and elaborates on the queer potential of comics; she presents detailed analyses of comics discussed in this chapter (Beckmann, forthcoming).

11. "Heute ist sowohl aus 'schwul' und 'Comics' etwas leichter verdauliches geworden. [. . .] Underground ist da nicht mehr viel."

12. Cf. https://www.annaheger.de. Accessed March 30, 2020.

13. This comic is originally published in English which fits the overall theme of lesbian love across borders between Germany and Russia.

14. Since 2019, a multitude of comics and scholarly publications have expanded and somewhat institutionalized the topic in the German-speaking world. The publishing house *Jaja Verlag*'s small focus on editing LGBTQ+ comics continues with works such as Peer Jongeling's *Hattest du eigentlich die Operation?* (2020; "Have You Actually Had the Operation?") and Joris Bas Backer's *Küsse für Jet* (2020; "Kisses for Jet"). Conference panels like "Queering Family" (see http://www.nextcomic.org/online-comic-symposium-2021; accessed March 30, 2020), part of the symposium "Eine Familie, wie sie im Buche steht?" (2021; "A Textbook Family?") in Linz, Austria, enrich recent academic discussion.

15. "Sind Sie blind? Wir sind seit zwei Jahren zusammen!"

16. Cf. further information: http://ka-schmitz.de. Accessed May 14, 2019; http://www.123 comics.net. Accessed May 14, 2019.

17. Cf. http://www.genderkompetenz.info/eng/gender-competence-2003-2010.html. Accessed May 14, 2019.

18. " . . . Aber den behalten wir!"

19. Cf. http://ohisee.org. Accessed May 15, 2019.

20. "Diese zweigeschlechtliche Welt is' einfach nix für mich!"

21. Cf. https://www.achsoistdas.com. Accessed May 15, 2019.

22. "[. . .] wahre[] Geschichten."

23. "Nicht-Sichtbarkeit."

24. Cf. the critical take on a "queer archive" by Rohy 2010.

25. "Ort des Aushandelns von Differenzen mit dem Ziel der Überwindung von Hierarchisierungen und damit Ort und Möglichkeit der Hybridisierung."

26. "[. . .] die Verfasstheit des Subjekts."

27. "Konstitution von Subjektivität im Spannungsfeld von Macht und Autorität."

28. "Macht besitzt eher eine statische Qualität, während Autorität etwas ist, das ausverhandelt werden muss" ("power has a static quality, whereas authority has to be negotiated" [Bhabha 2012, 72]).

29. "[. . .] eine Art aporetischen Zustand."

30. "[. . .] nicht identisch, sondern wiedererkennbar."

31. "Fehlbildung."

32. "[. . .] sowas wie die 1. Monatsblutung."

33. As part of the transformation the female* form "Suska" is changed to the male* form "Suskas."

34. "Irgendwie lebe ich in zwei Welten gleichzeitig."

35. "[. . .] also ich weiß das einfach. Schon immer irgendwie . . ."

36. "Oje, da hab ich noch gar nicht dran gedacht."

37. The author, Yori Gagarim, has since, however, allowed for the name to be printed.

38. Some of the polysemy is lost in the English translation provided. Original wording: "ich kann nicht denken," "ich kann (mich) nicht denken," and "ich kann (mich) doch jetzt nicht entscheiden."

39. "Das X bei Trouble X steht für das fragliche X-Chromosom."

40. "Ich sehe aus wie . . . wie eine Frau."

41. "Also so etwas wie ein Shape-Shifter?"

Works Cited

Comics

Anonymous [Yori Gagarim]. "*träume" (2007). http://troublex.blogsport.de/download.

Barczyk, Sarah. *Nenn mich Kai*. Egmont Graphic Novel, 2016.

Bas Backer, Joris. *Küsse für Jet*. Jaja, 2020.

Bas Backer, Joris, and Nettmann. *Familienjuwelen*. Jaja, 2018; originally published: http://familienjuwelen.blogspot.com.

Dath, Dietmar, and Oliver Scheibler. *Mensch wie Gras wie*. Verbrecher Verlag, 2014. *Die Batterie*. 2015, 5.

Heger, Anna. 2010–16. *Minicomics*. http://www.annaheger.de.

Jongeling, Peer. *Hattest du eighentlich schon die Operation?* Jaja, 2020.

Jónsson, Jón, Andreas C. Knigge, and Annie Goetzinger. *Die verlorene Zukunft*. Carlsen, 1992.

Kleist, Reinhard. *Knock Out!* Carlsen, 2019.

König, Ralf. *Das sensationelle Comic-Book*. Vogel Verlag, 1981.

König, Ralf. *Herbst in der Hose*. Rowohlt, 2017.

König, Ralf. *Sarius*. Vogel Verlag, 1981.

König, Ralf. *SchwulComix*. Verlag Rosa Winkel, 1981.

König, Ralf. *Super-Paradise. Dicke Dödel 2*. Salzgeber Buchverlage and Männerschwarm Verlag, 1999.

Krapp, Thilo. *Damian & Alexander 1. Der grüne Jaguar*. EPSILON, 2008.

Krapp, Thilo. *Damian & Alexander 2. Dschungelliebe*. EPSILON, 2013.

Lötzerich, Suskas. *Hexenblut*. Luftschacht, 2014.

Lust, Ulli. *Airpussy*. 2005. http://www.electrocomics.com/airpussy.htm.

Müll, Wolf [Wolfgang Müller]. *Comic-Trips*. Rosa Winkel, 1980.

Onano, Maurizio. *Oma Herbert*. Jaja, 2019.

Patu, and Antje Schrupp. *Kleine Geschichte des Feminismus im euro-amerikanischen Kontext*. UNRAST-Verlag, 2015.

Patu, and Antje Schrupp. *A Brief History of Feminism*, translated by Sophie Lewis. MIT Press, 2017.

Pfalzgraf, Markus. *Stripped*. Bruno Gmünder, 2012.

Schmidt, Imke, and Ka Schmitz. *Ich sehe was, was du nicht siehst oder: Wer sieht hier wen? Lightfaden für Bildermacher-innen*. Genderkompetenzzentrum am ZTG, Humboldt-Universität zu Berlin, 2010.

Schradi, Martina. *Ach, so ist das?! Biografische Comicreportagen von LGBTI*, vol. 1, 2nd ed. Zwerchfell, 2016.

Schradi, Martina. *Ach, so ist das?! Weitere Lach- und Sachgeschichten aus der Welt der LGBTI**, vol. 2. Zwerchfell, 2018.

Steiner, Elke Renate. *Love Migration*. self-published, 2019.

Suess, Franz. *Paul Zwei*. Luftschacht, 2019.

Szekatsch, Gabi. "Eines Abends an einem bekannten Ort . . ." *Lesben-Rundbrief* 3 (1984): n.p.

Vollenweider, Nacha. *Fußnoten*. avant-verlag, 2017.

SECONDARY SOURCES

Aldrich, Robert, ed. *Gleich und anders: Eine globale Geschichte der Homosexualität*. Murmann, 2007.

Babka, Anna, and Gerald Posselt. "Vorwort." In Homi K. Bhabha. *Über kulturelle Hybridität. Tradition und Übersetzung*, edited by Anna Babka and Gerald Posselt, translated by Kathrina Menke, 7–16. Turia + Kant, 2012.

Baier, Angelika, and Susanne Hochreiter. "Einleitung." In *Inter*geschlechtliche Körperlichkeiten. Diskurs/Begegnungen im Erzähltext*, edited by Angelika Baier and Susanne Hochreiter, 9–33. Zaglossus, 2014.

Beckmann, Anna. "Strategies of Ambiguity—Non-Binary Figurations in German-Language Comics." In *Comic Art and Feminism in the Baltic Sea Region: Transnational Perspectives*, edited by Kristy Beers Fägersten, Anna Nordenstam, Margareta Wallin Wictorin, and Lena Romu. Routledge. Forthcoming.

Bhabha, Homi K. *The Location of Culture*. Routledge Classics, 1994, 2004.

Bhabha, Homi K. "Round-Table-Gespräch." In Homi K. Bhabha. *Über kulturelle Hybridität. Tradition und Übersetzung*, edited by Anna Babka and Gerald Posselt, translated by Kathrina Menke, 59–77. Turia + Kant, 2012.

Chute, Hillary. "Comics as Literature? Reading Graphic Narrative." *PMLA* 123, no. 2 (2008): 452–65.

Dennert, Gabriela. *In Bewegung bleiben. 100 Jahre Politik, Kultur und Geschichte von Lesben*. Querverlag, 2007.

Dolle-Weinkauff, Bernd. *Comics. Geschichte einer populären Literaturform in Deutschland seit 1945*. Beltz, 1990.

Hacker, Hanna. "Austria." In *Lesbian Histories and Cultures: An Encyclopedia*, edited by Bonnie Zimmerman, 85–87. Routledge, 2000.

Herzog, Sabine. "'Es wird Zeit, dass wir unsere eigenen Bücher und Texte schreiben . . .' Stationen einer Lesbenzeitschrift: *Lesbenfront—frau ohne herz—die*." *Rosa. Die Zeitschrift für Geschlechterforschung* 14 (1997): 23–24.

Klar, Elisabeth. "Transformation und Überschreibung: Sprache und Text in ihrer Beziehung zum Körper-Zeichen in den Comics von Alfred." In *Bild ist Text ist Bild ist Text*, edited by Susanne Hochreiter and Ursula Klingenböck, 169–89. Transcript, 2014.

Knigge, Andreas C. "Geschichte und kulturspezifische Entwicklungen des Comics." In *Comics und Graphic Novels. Eine Einführung*, edited by Julia Abel and Christian Klein, 3–37. J. B. Metzler, 2016.

Kong, Carlos. "Exhibition Review: SuperQueeroes—Our LGBTI* Comic Book Heroes and Heroines at the Schwules Museum*, Berlin, January 22–June 26, 2016." *Contemporaneity: Historical Presence in Visual Culture* 5, no. 1 (2016): 130–35.

McCloud, Scott. *Understanding Comics: The Invisible Art*. HarperCollins, 1994.

Mitchell, W. J. T. "Comics as Media: Afterword." *Critical Inquiry* 40, no. 3 (2014): 255–65.

Postema, Barbara. *Narrative Structure in Comics*. RIT Press, 2013.

RainbowHouse. "Press Release—Ralf König's Fresco," June 20, 2019. http://rainbowhouse.be/en/article/press-release-ralph-konigs-fresco.

Rauchenbacher, Marina, and Katharina Serles. "Fragmented and Framed. Precarious 'Body Signs' in Comics by Regina Hofer, Ulli Lust, and Barbara Yelin." In *Spaces Between: Gender, Diversity and Identity in Comics*, edited by Nina Heindl and Véronique Sina, 79–94. Springer, 2020.

Reiter-Zatloukal, Ilse. "Geschlechtswechsel unter der NS-Herrschaft. 'Transvestitismus', Namensänderung und Personenstandskorrektur in der 'Ostmark' am Beispiel der Fälle Mathilda/Mathias Robert S. und Emma/Emil Rudolf K." *Beiträge zur Rechtsgeschichte Österreichs* 1 (2014): 172–209.

Reitsamer, Rosa, and Elke Zobl. "Queer-feministische Comics. Produktive Interventionen im Kontext der Do-It-Yourself-Kultur." In *Theorien des Comics. Ein Reader*, edited by Barbara Eder, Elisabeth Klar, and Ramón Reichert, 365–81. transcript, 2011.

Rohy, Valerie. "In the Queer Archive. *Fun Home*." *GLQ* 16, no. 3 (2010): 341–61.

Setz, Wolfram, ed. *Homosexualität in der DDR. Materialien und Meinungen*. Männerschwarm-Verlag, 2006.

Theis, Wolfgang. "AIDS – oder die teuer erkaufte Professionalisierung." In *Goodbye to Berlin? 100 Jahre Schwulenbewegung: Eine Ausstellung des Schwulen Museums und der Akademie der Künste, 17. Mai bis 17. August 1997*, edited by Andreas Sternweiler, 327–39. Rosa Winkel, 1997.

Vahabzadeh, Susan. "Von der schwierigen Sorte." 2019. https://www.sueddeutsche.de/medien/franziska-becker-cartoons-1.4501806.

Chapter 8

XX, XY, AND XXY
GENDERQUEER BODIES IN HAGIO MOTO'S SCIENCE FICTION MANGA

KEIKO MIYAJIMA

The 1970s were a revolutionary period in the history of shōjo (or girls') manga in Japan. The pioneering female manga artists born in 1949, often referred to as the "Year 24 Group," ventured into new genres that shōjo manga hadn't yet explored. In particular, Hagio Moto, one of the leading figures in the Group, expanded shōjo manga's narrative field far beyond its conventional romantic formulas by including elements of science fiction and *shōnen-ai* (literally, "boy love"). Hagio is probably best known as one of the founders of the *shōnen-ai* genre that emerged in the 1970s. As precursors of BL (Boys' Love) manga, her works such as *The Heart of Thomas* (1974) and *The Poe Clan* (1972–76) opened up a gender-fluid space for shōjo readers to liberate their imaginations from the constraints of gender and sexual norms (Fujimoto 2004; Welker 2006).

Similarly, science fiction, previously a male-dominated genre, functioned in Hagio's works since the 1970s as a device to separate characters from the social obligations and gender roles expected as part of the ideological ideal of *ryōsai kenbo* (good wife, wise mother) persistent in Japan since the Meiji period. Hagio's sci-fi works have frequently been analyzed by critics in terms of their ability to imaginatively depict female experience and to transcend the stereotypes found in traditional shōjo manga. For example, C. J. Suzuki points out that Hagio's sci-fi narratives often cast a critical light on society from the alien, "marginal position . . . as a 'woman'" (2011, 68). Rob Vollmar writes in a 2005 essay on "X + X" that "Hagio effectively scrambles gender awareness until little is left to prejudge the dynamic growth of the characters" (135). Depicting gender-ambiguous characters is a way to avoid the gendered expectations that readers bring to both male and female characters. But Hagio does not merely use gender ambiguity as a metaphor for women's marginality or as a way to avoid falling back on gender stereotypes. Rather, her works valorize trans* identities, including those that are fluid and resistant to being defined or conclusively described. The ineffable nature of her characters' gender and sexuality makes them a site of resistance to any coercive gender norms, whether those of the characters' home worlds or of our own.

Figure 8.1. *They Were Eleven* in *Four Shōjo Stories*, edited and translated by Matt Thorn (Viz Media, 1996), 63.

A key example is *They Were Eleven* (1975). Hagio foregrounds the clash between gender stereotyping and fluidity by introducing into an all-male spaceship a character whose sex is not easily definable. As the narrative opens, a team of ten male applicants from various planets are to take the final test to enter the prestigious Galactic Academy. But once on board the ship where the test is to take place, they realize that their team has eleven members. Adding to their confusion is the appearance of one of the applicants, Frol, whom they at first assume is a woman.

Figure 8.2. *They Were Eleven* in *Four Shōjo Stories*, edited and translated by Matt Thorn (Viz Media, 1996), 121.

On this isolated spaceship, the members constantly try to decode Frol's identity by placing it in a known gender category. Frol denies being female, and acts, speaks, and identifies as a man. It is eventually revealed that Frol is neither male nor female but an androgyne who will develop sexual organs as they enter adulthood. Frol came to this spaceship to pass the examination to be allowed to become a man because, on their home planet, men enjoy more freedom and privilege than women. The text's engagement with gender roles is thus complex. It prompts readers to imagine a world with very different gender norms than those of Earth (androgyny is an accepted stage of life), suggesting the arbitrariness of those norms we may take for granted. At the same time, social roles for women on Frol's world are even more rigidly constrained than those on Earth.

Another protagonist, Tada, proposes to Frol that they get married and move to Earth, where women and men are equal in status. Frol eventually consents: "I don't mind becoming a woman if you want me to" (Hagio 1996, 170). This ending, becoming a woman to marry a man, seemingly conflates gender identity with sexual orientation. It is a playful riff on the heteronormative narrative convention that if one is a woman, one must desire a man; here, instead, it is Frol's desire for a man that makes them willing to be a woman, revealing the convention's constructedness.

Gender for Frol is presented as a choice, rather than destiny. By ultimately passing the exam, Frol obtains the right to choose a gender but is willing to be a woman in a particular relationship or environment. True, Frol's declaration of gender choice is determinative within a heterosexual dyad. However, in the work's sequel *Horizon of the East, Eternity of the West* (1977) and related short side stories, Frol is never described as having become a woman. Rather, they continue to defy expectations, acting and speaking as a man. In other words, Frol's performative speech act (declaring they will become a woman) does not produce a "proper" outcome. The choice of gender is thus suspended as a purely future-oriented possibility or, to use Judith Butler's words, a "free-floating artifice" (1999, 10).

Hagio blurs the lines not only between genders but also between sexualities. Though Tada expects Frol to become female eventually, he is attracted by Frol's unfeminine, reckless behaviors and androgynous body. Frol thus remains eternally "undeveloped," at once shōnen and shōjo, maintaining a queer relationship with Tada in a state of in-betweenness.

In 1987's *Marginal*, Hagio further complicates representations of gender and sex by describing non-normative pregnancy. *Marginal* is set on an infertile, all-male Earth where, due to environmental pollution, no females survive or are born. Men form sexual partnerships with adolescent boys, with these partnerships serving as the basic family unit. Older men, called *nenja*, play a parental role, offering protection, and the younger boys, *iroko*, not only sleep with them but also do domestic chores. The propagation of the species depends on the planet's only remaining woman, the Holy Mother, who occasionally gives birth to children. The symbolism of heterosexual procreation is soon revealed to be elaborate theatre, staged by the corporate giant Company. The religious icon of the Holy Mother is in fact a trans* woman with XXY chromosomes without any procreative ability, and behind the curtain, all the eggs are fertilized and raised artificially.

At a glance, the homosocial and homoerotic partnership of *nenja* and *iroko* appears to be a metonymic reiteration of binary gender and heterosexuality, since *iroko* are described as outwardly feminine and taking the receptive role in bed. However, the couples' relationships are not based on stable gender assignments but rather on age difference. In this age-based sexual and familial system, once *iroko* grow up, they in turn form new partnerships with younger boys, revising and reversing their sexual, gender, and familial roles. By depicting an all-male society, Hagio radically revises gendered and sexual assignments in family systems as changeable over time.

In *Marginal*, we see a love triangle quickly form among three men, the younger Kira and the two older men Grinja and Asijin. It is later revealed that Kira is an androgyne with XXY chromosomes, one of a set of quadruplets

Figure 8.3. Moto Hagio, *Marginal* (*Mājinaru*), 5 vols (Shogakukan, 1999), 188.

genetically engineered by their scientist father, at once female and male, endowed with extrasensory power. In appearance, Kira is a boy with male genitals, but when empathetically and sexually awakened, they undergo a bodily transformation: the penis disappears, and the womb opens up to accept Grinja. As a result, Kira becomes pregnant. However, their physical transformation is temporal and voluntary: their genitals remain male during sex with Asijin. Thus, as Kazue Harada points out, while Kira and Asijin form a male-male relationship, Kira and Grinja form a female-male relationship (2015, 100).

Critics have located the significance of this work in its depiction of "unisex reproduction," a trope that, in Akiko Ebihara's words, serves to question ideas of maternity and critique the sexist idea of "a woman's personality . . . growing straight out of her womb or vagina" (2002, 22). But it is not the text's depiction of pregnancy without gender difference that sets it apart; rather, it is its depiction of both maleness and femaleness as unstable and fluid.[1] Kira's shifting body challenges established heteronormative categories in favor of an emphasis on the polymorphous and performative dimensions of sexuality.

At the end of the story, Earth's infertile soil is submerged in water, and the pregnant Kira is washed away in a flood, suggesting that the Earth, merging with Kira's pregnant body and empathetic power, will become fertile again. After Kira's death, one of their siblings, previously frozen, comes back to life. The story ends with the creation of a three-way partnership between this second Kira, Asijin, and Grinja, pointing to the "potential to deconstruct the dyad between either a man-woman or a man-man" (Harada 2015, 102). *Marginal* thus rejects monogamy as a symbol of the Earth's rebirth. It revises twice-told tales about the creation of a new world through heterosexual dyads (like Adam and Eve, or Izanami and Izanagi in Japanese mythology), ending instead

Figure 8.4. Moto Hagio, *Marginal* (*Mājinaru*), 5 vols (Shogakukan, 1999), 146. [Translation: Grinja is stunned at the sight of Kira's male-to-female transformation. "Your body . . . has changed . . .? I saw it when you had a fever, but it looks different now.""Has it? It's because of Kira."]

with a neatly balanced triangle at once queer and straight. Through Kira's transformative, volatile sex and sexuality, Hagio offers a postmodern, queer model of romance, family and procreation that rejects reductive gender, sex, and sexuality binaries.

The trope of queer pregnancy as a symbol of hope can also be seen in *Star Red* (1980). This story takes place on what was once a penal colony on Mars. Years after Mars was first colonized by Earth, the descendants have become Martians, endowed with supernatural powers. The Earth's government views Martians as monstrous and tries to wipe them out. Sei, a fifth-generation Martian, is also born with psychic powers. In her desperate attempts to save Mars, her body disappears from the universe while her consciousness remains, wandering through space and time.

Star Red offers a critical commentary on the domination of colonizer over colonized and on the imperialist abjection of foreign bodies. Hagio's critical imagination further envisions reproduction outside heteronormative logic as a means of resistance. At the end, a male Martian, Yodaka, becomes pregnant with Sei via their telepathic communication so that Yodaka can give birth to Sei and bring her back to Earth. In order for Sei to be reborn into this world, the plot requires a male body to undergo a sex change: Sei's consciousness, entering Yodaka's body, creates a womb and impregnates it. The pair's psychic, empathic power destabilizes and overcomes the boundaries of self and other, male and female. The story foregrounds this queer, transsexual pregnancy as a symbol of regeneration, embodying hope for the Martians' survival.

In *Marginal* and *Star Red*, extrasensory perceptions that break down the boundary between self and other, subject and object, pose a threat to the consolidated power trying to control human bodies and minds.[2] This depiction of empathic power resonates with the concept of the abject, as defined by Julia Kristeva: the power of primitive horror that invites cognitive dissonance and breaks down the distinction between subject and object. The abject, according to Kristeva, originates in the leaky maternal body, or what she called a "dual and alien space," in which the borders of the self and other dissolve (1980, 237). In this sense, the alien spatiality of empathy, encompassing others, is as disturbing as a maternal body.

In Kristeva's theory of the abject, the original abject mother is always already gendered as female. However, in Hagio's work, the abject and its boundaryless nature is more complex, as it is located in genderqueer bodies. The womb, according to Kira's scientist father, is an "alien space in one's body" (Hagio 1987, vol. 3, 23): "The womb—this mysterious black box captures a foreign body and becomes a room for it" (10). Pregnancy itself destabilizes the boundary between inside and outside, the self and the other. Transsexual pregnancy, then, with its deeply disturbing power of the queer abject, goes a step further toward breaking down binaries, not only of self/other but also male/female, native/foreign, homo/heterosexual. In *Star Red* and *Marginal*, empathy and queer pregnancy are equally envisioned as sites of subversive counternarrative—sources of hope and resistance through which the world can renew itself.

The depiction of non-normative bodies and reproduction is not new in science fiction; since Mary Shelley's *Frankenstein*, sci-fi has questioned the ideological boundaries that divide bodies and identities into neatly defined categories. In the words of Wendy Pearson, "Queer, with its denaturalization of master narratives and its movement towards subcultural and subaltern understandings of texts, operates, by analogy, on some of the same levels as sf" (1999, 4). Indeed, science fiction is a perfect narrative device for queer themes, as seen in Hagio's works. A pioneering female voice in the traditionally male realm of sci-fi, Hagio has challenged narrative conventions, describing characters who construct selves and bodies that refuse reductionism. Invariably, Hagio's protagonists are not afraid of sex changes or gender fluidity in their bodies. Instead of dramatizing identity crises, she focuses on the transformative potential of gender fluidity, further suggesting the transformation of the world itself. Hagio envisions gendered bodies as volatile, voluntary, and always in the process of being formed. By describing nonbinary trans* subjects and subjectivities, she opens up a queer space in which bodies and identities are constantly redefined, rendering sex, gender, sexuality and even reproduction something far from given, axiomatic concepts.

Notes

1. Similarly, Ōtsuka Eiji argues that *Star Red* transfers the burden of reproduction onto the bodies of men, so that women can return to a state of presexualized infancy (1990, 181). However, Hagio's depiction of queer pregnancy offers, rather than an escapist fantasy, an affirmation of transformative, volatile identities and subjectivities, including those of women.

2. As Margherita Long posits, extrasensory power in *Star Red* is presented as a (re)productive force that enables the rebirth of Sei and a dead planet.

Works Cited

Butler, Judith. *Gender Trouble*. Routledge, 1999.

Ebihara, Akiko. "Japan's Feminist Fabulation: Reading *Marginal* with Unisex Reproduction as a Key Concept." *Genders*, no. 36 (2002). Accessed March 13, 2019. http://www.genders.org/g36/g36_ebihara.html.

Fujimoto, Yukari. "Transgender: Female Hermaphrodites and Male Androgynes." *U.S.-Japan Women's Journal*, no. 27 (2004): 76–117.

Hagio, Moto. *The Heart of Thomas*. Translated by Matt Thorn. Fantagraphics, 2013.

Hagio, Moto. *Marginal* (*Mājinaru*), 5 vols. Shogakukan, 1999.

Hagio, Moto. *The Poe Clan*. Translated by Matt Thorn. Fantagraphics, 2019.

Hagio, Moto. *Star Red* (*Sutā Reddo*). Shogakukan, 1980.

Hagio, Moto. *They Were Eleven*. In *Four Shōjo Stories*, edited and translated by Matt Thorn. Vis, 1996.

Hagio, Moto. *They Were Eleven Sequel: Horizon of the East, Eternity of the West* (*Zoku Jūichinin Iru!: Higashi No Chihei, Nishi No Towa*). In *They Were Eleven!* [*Jūichinin Iru!*]. Shogakukan, 1994.

Harada, Kazue. "Japanese Women's Science Fiction: Posthuman Bodies and the Representation of Gender." PhD diss., Washington University, 2015.

Kristeva, Julia. *Desire in Language*. Columbia University Press, 1980.

Long, Margherita. "Hagio Moto's Nuclear Manga and the Promise of Eco-Feminist Desire." *Mechademia* 9 (2014): 3–23.

Ōtsuka, Eiji. *Kodomo Ryūritan* [*Tales of Wandering Children*]. Shinyousha, 1990.

Pearson, Wendy. "Alien Cryptographies: The View from Queer." *Science Fiction Studies* 26, no. 1 (1999): 1–22.

Suzuki, C. J. (Shige). "Envisioning Alternative Communities Through a Popular Medium: Speculative Imagination in Hagio Moto's Girls' Comics." *International Journal of Comic Art* 13, no. 3 (2011): 57–74.

Vollmar, Rob. "X + X." *Comics Journal*, no. 269 (2005): 134–36.

Welker, James. "Beautiful, Borrowed, and Bent: 'Boys' Love' as Girls' Love in Shōjo Manga." *Signs* 31, no. 3 (2006): 841–70.

Chapter 9

AN EXPLORATION OF THE BIRTH OF THE SLAVE THROUGH ERO-PEDAGOGY IN TAGAME GENGOROH'S *PRIDE*

WILLIAM S. ARMOUR

INTRODUCTION

Tagame Gengoroh[1] (b. 1964), "the great master of gay pornographic Japanese comics" (Hall 2017, 156), is a prolific author and his attention to detail and the depth of his narratives provide the reader with not just an erotic experience but also aesthetic and epistemic ones, thus making Tagame's MANGA[2] worthy of academic study which adds to the paucity of academic research and writing on erotic comics that Hall (2017, 154) laments.

PRIDE was serialized in *G-men* no. 12 (January 1997) through no. 47 (December 1999), and republished in three collected volumes in 2004 (used here). This work provides us with insights into Tagame's *hontō no jibun* or true self through how he draws on his own fantasies,[3] such as bondage, discipline, muscles, and most importantly for my argument, taming. Tagame (2004, vol. III, 248) notes that *PRIDE* "is a fantasy I wrote as fundamentally a practitioner of SM play." He seems to be writing for readers, gay and other sexual minorities "who are caught by what is called the limits of self in real society beyond SM" (Tagame 2004, vol. III, 248), a point that is explored below. Furthermore, despite its title, *PRIDE* is not a story indexing the notion of gay pride per se. Tagame overtly explores gay pride (*gei puraido*) in *Otōto no otto*, a four volume non ero-MANGA, in which he broadly defines it as not being ashamed of oneself and not losing one's self respect (*jisonshin*[4]) (Tagame 2016, vol. III, 101–2). These issues are not explicitly featured in *PRIDE*.

How simply does *PRIDE* work as porn? Tagame notes that he wanted to "produce an ero-MANGA that could function as a Bildungsroman" (Tagame 2004, vol. III, 248). How Tagame does this is of interest here. Furthermore, *PRIDE* could also be read as a how-to book (Manga), a pedagogical manual (or at least guidelines) for would-be sexual adventurers wishing to culti-vate either the master or slave within.[5] My overall purpose is to explore the ero-pedagogical relationship between Ōhashi Tetsuya who, at the beginning of the narrative, is represented as a conceited topman,[6] and the older Shibazaki, a psychology professor who just happens to be an authority in BDSM, and how this relationship contributes to Ōhashi's transformation, one that may resonate with Tagame's intended audience.

This is my second engagement with Tagame's work (see Armour [2010] for a discussion of three other MANGA set around the time of the Pacific War). My *hontō no jibun*, a motif emerging from a conversation between Shibazaki and Ōhashi, centers around my scopophilic tendencies to observe whatever I encounter as a gay white man in his early sixties. As Hall (2017) notes, "[C]omics readers may be more able to experience eroticism outside of their own sexual desires" and the comics themselves are interesting due to "narrative, concept, character and setting as well as the act of sex" (157). I am not "into" BDSM play, however, I am "into" what Hall calls the "manifestation of fantastical representation . . . [as] . . . the utopian element in all erotic art" (160). Ōhashi's trajectory from proud topman to humble slave is an endearing story, one that makes him such a lovable character. However, I am acutely aware that *PRIDE* is a product of Tagame's imagination and the graphic depictions of what Ōhashi endures on his quest for self-cultivation[7] are naturally fantasies, ones that may, in the end, reveal my own erotic truth. It is with this scopophilic gaze, one not necessarily unique to me (think superhero comics and how they can cultivate a homoerotic gaze[8]), that I approach Tagame's work.

The chapter is structured into three parts. The first part, *Kaikō*, provides an overview of the story. Here I also explore how *PRIDE* functions as a Bildungsroman ero-MANGA. The second part, *Shiiku*, explores the ero-pedagogical relationship between Shibazaki and Ōhashi. I am interested in how Shibazaki "tames" Ōhashi to teach (*chōkyō*—literally to train [an animal]) him humility and how Tagame imagines an implied reader through the erotic roles of the tamer and the tamed. Here I argue that *PRIDE* could also be read as a how-to manual. I foreground the concept of authority to account for how Shibazaki tames Ōhashi, a concept that seems to be a key component in any BDSM relationship. The third part, *Shuppatsu*, is a short conclusion in which I revisit "pride" in the context of Tagame's work.

KAIKŌ—A CHANCE ENCOUNTER

PRIDE consists of seventeen chapters, 582 pages, and almost 3500 panels or *koma* (based on an average of six *koma* per page). Tagame tells us that his story was strongly influenced by American gay author John Preston's novel *Mr. Benson: A Novel*, published in 1983, which concerns a young man's quest for the perfect master (Tagame 2004, vol. III, 248). The motif of pride is also explored in that novel. The narrative arc in *PRIDE* spans about eighteen months and begins by depicting the arrogant and judgemental Ōhashi having sex at a local beat. He is a handsome, muscled, hairy third-year university student whose aloofness, erotic anxieties, and apparent feelings of superiority to the other men there have caught the eye of an unknown figure lurking in the background. The following day Ōhashi is called to Professor Shibazaki's office. After declaring their sexual interest in men, they have sex in the professor's office and again at his home after which Ōhashi, who believes that it was the best sex he had ever had (vol. I, 24), is told by Shibazaki, "You're such a naïve/simple guy." This angers Ōhashi, who storms out and goes to have rushed sex with his *kōhai* (junior) Sakai. At a local beat a few days later, however, Shibazaki's comment makes Ōhashi self-conscious and inhibits his sexual performance. Indignant, Ōhashi confronts Shibazaki who tells him he has become impotent. Ōhashi reacts angrily. The professor responds, "You don't get it, do you? That is the entire cause. Both your impotence and the boring sex is because of that *foolish pride!*" (vol. I, 35).

Ōhashi is told he needs to know his *hontō no jibun*. From this point, Ōhashi and Shibazaki enter into an experiment to show Ōhashi that he is actually a masochist (*mazo*). Through the professor, Tagame constructs how he wants the reader to perceive authority which is so central to the overall narrative. It manifests in all of the encounters between the two protagonists. Surviving a number of minor encounters, Ōhashi finally submits and, prostrate in public, says "Please rape/fuck m . . . my arse-cunt." Shibazaki responds by urinating on him and orders him to walk home drenched (vol. I, 101). This is when he first calls Ōhashi his slave (vol. I, 103). He says to Ōhashi, "And think about it really hard again overnight and if your resoluteness hasn't changed, come to my office first thing tomorrow morning. Your real training begins then" (vol. I, 104).

Tagame crafts a story around this notion of resoluteness (*kakugo*, experiential understanding or, better, experiential enlightenment) and how Ōhashi must act on it to make his transformation authentic. Shibazaki exercises authority (over Ōhashi in particular), while Ōhashi demonstrates resoluteness (to/for the professor), thus creating an interesting erotic binary carried through until the final *koma*. Ōhashi comes to Shibazaki's office as ordered. Here we have probably one of the most significant turning points in Ōhashi's transformation represented in the following sequence (vol. I, 106)—*Koma* 1: Shibazaki is in the background in his office with his back to us and Ōhashi in the foreground at the doorway/threshold, also with his back to us; *Koma* 2: the professor turns his head, "You've come"; *Koma* 3: "Yes"; *Koma* 4, 5, and 6 show Ōhashi closing the office door and also closing the door on his previous life as the brash top. The sequence redefines Ōhashi as *tabula rasa*, a point raised in Preston's novel.

Shibazaki knew he would come since Ōhashi *is* resolute. The moment-to-moment transition between these *koma* requires very little closure (McCloud 1993, 70), creating a poignant moment.

Tagame then proceeds to place Ōhashi into numerous positions of bondage, fear of being caught at the university while being bound, sex with Shibazaki, and being anally cleaned with an enema. Chapters 5 and 6 in volume I detail Ōhashi's *chōkyō*. He is called *mesu inu-me* (fuckin' bitch) and "slave" (*dorei*). Such name-calling is part of the sex play and is also indicative of Ōhashi's path to anonymity. He is subjected to anal penetration (by the professor and with toys that are used to stretch his anus and rectum), and is whipped on a St. Andrew's Cross; he endures public and private humiliation; he wears a chastity belt and drinks the professor's urine. When he transgresses, the professor thrashes him with his belt.

Volume II reminds us that Ōhashi is still a university student (that is, he also participates in a world outside BDSM) and introduces us to Gamō (another student) who learns about Ōhashi's relationship with Shibazaki and wants in. The professor agrees, to Ōhashi's dismay—"My master isn't Gamō! Professor! It's only you!" (vol. II, 77). Volume II introduces us to further sexual encounters between Ōhashi and many others and more name-calling—*mazo butayarō* (fuckin' masochist pig) and *mesu buta* (sow). Ōhashi is treated like a dog, and learns to eat the professor's excrement and to be fisted. His nipples are pierced. Shibazaki tells Gamō, "This guy has already completely become a real masochist slave" (vol. II, 147).

At the beginning of volume III, Tagame provides us with a respite from the visceral depictions of Ōhashi's taming. Pages 15 through 48 are set about one year after Ōhashi met the professor in the park and made a commitment to follow his orders. The significance of these pages lies with Tagame allowing Ōhashi to speak to us directly and to reflect on his own self-cultivation and resoluteness. Tagame has presented Ōhashi's indenture to the professor episodically to show his readers both the steps involved in becoming a masochist slave as well as Ōhashi's resoluteness. Through the same narrative arc, Tagame also fashions Shibazaki's steely authoritative energy necessary to be a BDSM master, providing readers more than one position with which to identify.

Despite Ōhashi's admission that the professor's training/discipline has been strict (vol. III, 16), he also delights in the consistent patterns which have comprised his training but laments a possible future after graduation when he may not be Shibazaki's slave. Tagame draws Ōhashi divided into two possible selves (vol. III, 48). On the right, he is dressed in a leather vest, shirt, jeans, and sneakers—as an average young Japanese man—and on the left, he is stripped naked to reveal a gay erotic possibility: he is wearing a dog collar, chained at the wrist and bound with ropes; his cock sports his Prince Albert. Interestingly,

Tagame does not overtly illustrate Shibazaki's identity quite in the same way. His demeanor must manifest authority through actions and words; the reader can see Shibazaki's methods of training and also overhears how he speaks specifically to Ōhashi. Through the relationship between the two men, Tagame has offered his readers a story about the solace associated with control and the erotic capacity afforded by discipline.

Ōhashi's final humiliation occurs in front of Shibazaki's students. Later that night, he is taken to a private party where he services several young men. Sakai has also been invited. Ōhashi says to Sakai, the *kōhai* whom he would regularly top, "Please . . . please drive your cock into my (lit. this sow's) cunt, Mr. Sakai!" (vol. III, 88). However, Sakai is unaware of Ōhashi's tranformation and to see his *senpai* being fisted and violated is too much; he calls everyone perverts (*hentai*) then leaves. Sakai represents the *sekentei* (decency, appearance in the eyes of society); therefore, the *hentai* comment is not out of place here. Ōhashi insists that everyone else continue what they are doing, motivating the professor to say, "You've really grown up! That's my slave!" (vol. III, 99).

The episode in the psychology class has not gone unnoticed by university management, which results in the professor quitting to take up a position in Berlin, a suggestively erotic destination. Shibazaki decides to flee, ironically, the constraints of mainstream Japanese society, seeking only to be reborn in a more homosocio-culturally liberal foreign setting. This alarms Ōhashi since he believes he is being abandoned only to be invited to go with him with this warning: "But if you want to go together you will resign yourself to a certain amount of resoluteness. It will be different from now than it has been so far!" (vol. III, 107). This reestablishes Shibazaki's authority and reminds his slave that his identity is always under incremental construction and cannot be willed into existence simply and punctually.

The final act that the professor performs before their departure is to brand Ōhashi's left buttock with an S—Shibazaki's slave, a graduation gift perhaps? In another poignant scene, the professor addresses Ōhashi using his first name: "You've become a good slave, haven't you! Tetsuya!" (vol. III, 116). Shibazaki rarely uses Ōhashi's name throughout the narrative. For example, "You're Ōhashi Tetsuya the 3rd year from the Arts Faculty . . . aren't you?" (vol. I, 16) functions only as a way to identify him. Ōhashi is actually shocked, saying that he thought the professor did not know it. Ōhashi has been treated as a thing. That is, the story is not about *who* Ōhashi is but *what* he is. Shibazaki responds, "Where is the master who doesn't know the name of his adorable slave?" (vol. III, 116) and then he kisses Ōhashi. The story ends with the professor saying, "We truly don't know what will happen in the future. Anyhow . . . because the journey is just about to begin!" (vol. III, 121–22). Here Tagame offers the reader an until now hidden side of the professor's seemingly tough and demanding character; his uncertainty implies vulnerability. They flee Japan carrying different things: Shibazaki is carrying his authority as a professor and a BDSM master, while Ōhashi is carrying his resoluteness.

This summary provides a basis for claiming that *PRIDE* is more than simple print porn. It is a tale of hypermasculinity, male voluptuousness, and virile youth and I am certainly not dismissing these aspects of the comic—reading *PRIDE* is an erotic experience. However, Tagame offers his readers much more than that. Considering Ōhashi's transformation, it is apparent that *PRIDE* is a Bildungsroman ero-MANGA. Emerging from the German experience, there are rare instances of *Bildungsroman* in the Japanese literary context: e.g., Miyoshi (1974) suggests Sōseki's *Sanshirō* and Ōgai's *Seinen* (Youth) as examples. Miyoshi (1974) notes that authentic Japanese Bildungsroman are "not so much about the self's discovery of the self as the self's discipline of itself into a production model hierarchically classified and blueprinted in detail by society at large" (xi). Conversely, Mortimer (2000) points out that "[I]f Japanese tradition does not favor the *Bildungsroman*, this is not because, as Miyoshi claims, there is too little involvement with the self but because there is too much of it" (223, italics in the original). She cites Kurt Singer who "is perhaps nearer to the truth than Miyoshi when he asserts that in Japan, 'life means surrender, not fulfillment'" (Mortimer 2000, 223). I read *PRIDE* as "much more than a bland synonym for any story of personal formation . . . what is vital about the genre [following Mikhail Bakhtin's formulation] is that at its heart is a person in the process of becoming someone who 'emerges' *along with the world* and [who] reflects the historical emergence of the world itself" (Graham 2019, 3; italics in the original). For Ōhashi and Shibazaki, this "world" is the world of BDSM, one that transgresses the status quo—the bifurcation of (Japanese) "society" into *seken* and *shakai* that Ōhashi mentions in his reflection in volume III.[9] Tagame portrays a Japanese story of surrender, self-discovery, and discipline, tropes which pervade a larger system of authority, a system in which many of his readers[10] dwell and one that has successfully created a national mythology surrounding its own reinvention and rebirth.

I note the relevance to *PRIDE* when Washburn (1995) observes that Ogai's *Seinen* "successfully fuses a German narrative model with elements of a native narrative type, the quest for manly virtue" (1). He argues that Ōgai crafted "a quest in which the development of the individual moves toward, and in the process is defined by, an ethical code of behavior embodied in the Japanese words *masurao* and *masuraogokoro*" which "denote a socially determined concept of masculinity, the proper, ideal role for which each man should strive" (Washburn 1995, 13). The quest for Ōhashi is to find his *hontō no jibun* (an interior quest), while the quest for the professor, an exterior one, is to tame Ōhashi. The quest for Tagame's readers is to choose with whom they could align, Shibazaki or

Ōhashi, based on their own internal sexual positioning or simply to revel in discovering their options and seeing them depicted. The professor (as a classic archetype) diagnoses that Ōhashi's problem lies within himself and therefore reins in Ōhashi's freedom to fuck as a conceited topman and obliges him to accept his (gay/masochist) *masuraogokoro* nature. *PRIDE* deals with the education of Ōhashi, not in terms of an intellectual experience but in terms of physical and psychological ones. Tagame does not reduce Ōhashi or Shibazaki to an ideological type, and he relies heavily on a gay fantasy of a knowing, older man who steers a younger man to actualize his desires. Ōhashi's quest for manly virtue draws him and Shibazaki together not just as master-slave but in a much more general form of manly love.

Tagame directs a story that is psychologically inward and socio-sexually outward and in which "pride" (*puraido*) is demonized, while "pleasure" is not. Pleasure, however, is not something that the slave should crave but something the master controls and gives. Therefore, Ōhashi realizes a selfhood for the satisfaction of the professor and that sense of contentment functions within a sexual and power matrix obliging the participation of others for its actualization. In *PRIDE*, Tagame crafts neither autobiography nor thriller/horror but something erotic that allows him to explore Ōhashi's physical, mental, and sexual development, from a man who does not want to grow up but does.

SHIIKU—TAMING

The professor is teaching[11] Ōhashi and the reader how to see a particular version of the world and, perhaps, beyond it. Therefore, *PRIDE* can also be read as a how-to manual transforming it from MANGA (entertainment) into Manga (education). When *PRIDE* is read this way, the links to *Bildung* in the sense of "a process of formation or [. . .] the form imparted in such a process" becomes clear (Geuss 1996, 154).[12]

Shibazaki "tames" Ōhashi, and Tagame thereby imagines an implied reader through the erotic roles of the tamer and the tamed to explore possibilities and potentials for would-be readers, slaves or masters and on-lookers, to explore their erotic selves. Harmon (1983) sets out at least fourteen functions of popular culture including to provide (new) role models; to project possible futures; to perform a therapeutic function; to aid emotional and social growth; to explore the boundary between the permitted and the forbidden and to experience in a carefully controlled way the possibility of stepping across that boundary; and to put us in touch with our repressed selves (10–13). Tagame explores all of these in *PRIDE*. It is clear that this MANGA/Manga is a fantasy depicting some impossible scenarios. Yet much of the literature discussing BDSM documents most if not all the subcultural practices Tagame draws upon. Tagame wants his readers to transcend "the limits of self," so he imagines a *Bildungsroman* ero-MANGA that instructs readers to invest in one or several of the functions listed above. A more in-depth discussion of how Professor Shibazaki tames Ōhashi will account for such a reading of this text.

The motif of taming (*shiiku*[13]) is the central pivot on which Ōhashi's identity transformation[14] (his *Bildung* or indeed *shugyō*) spins. Taming depends on intersubjective relatedness and responsibility that points to its ethical dimension. Near the end of the story, the Professor exhibits Ōhashi's debasement in front of his university class, a powerful erotic humiliation that contributes to Ōhashi's physical pleasure but that also prompts the scandalized school administration to recommend that the professor retire. The master and his slave leave Japan. The professor establishes relationships with Ōhashi and with others (Gamō and the other masters to whom Shibazaki lends out Ōhashi) who contribute to Ōhashi's taming. Taming also establishes relationships to *Bildung* through how the professor exercises authority and how he constructs an ero-pedagogy designed to draw out the masochist slave.

A grateful slave, the otherwise unnamed coauthor of the treatise on consensual erotic servitude (2002), outlines four principles of being a slave: identity, obedience, transparency and humility. He asserts that "[T]his isn't about who has 'Power.' It's my belief that both Master and slave must have 'Power.' The Master/slave experience is all about Authority" (a grateful slave 2002, 29). Shibazaki tames Ōhashi by exercising his authority which can be broken down into epistemic and deontic authority: control over what and how things are known and control over another's future actions.[15] Shibazaki exercises epistemic authority as a professor—his students and Ōhashi accept what he says as true (or at least probably true). Ōhashi also eventually accepts Shibazaki's diagnosis regarding his pride. Furthermore, Shibazaki is also an expert in BDSM techniques and training which Ōhashi also has to accept. That is, he needs to trust his master. While these techniques lean more to subcultural practices than any epistemological-based discipline such as psychology, they construct a body of knowledge for the master to invoke and the slave to accept.

Epistemic authority relies on learned declarations to encourage such acceptance. Tagame represents such epistemic authority by connecting Shibazaki's professorial credentials to his authority as a BDSM master, constructing his expertise from both bodies of knowledge. At the university, he draws upon a collection of declaratives that converge into a discipline (psychology), and his role as a professor simmers below the surface even as his role as the BDSM master is foregrounded. However, unlike the declarative performance of professorial authority, BDSM authority derives more from the bodily enactment of erotic practices. So, Tagame offers his readers multiple *koma* containing images of such enactment—whipping and bondage, etc.—offering a different mode of authority for the reader to appreciate, one that functions more powerfully in its way than succinct, declarative authority. Groensteen (2007) notes of comics visuality that "the panel is easily contained by and takes part in the sequential *continuum*. This signifies that at the perceptive and cognitive levels the panel exists longer for the comics reader than the shot exists for the film spectator" (26; italics in the original). The reader can linger over each *koma* and sequence of *koma* that build the enactment of whatever BDSM practice Shibazaki has chosen to use to tame Ōhashi because the *koma* provides what Groensteen (2007) calls "the affective investment" that transforms it "into some sort of fetish" (26). Verbal declaratives are replaced with visual *koma* (images) to tell the story and to construct the epistemic authority required by Shibazaki to fulfill his roles.

Furthermore, and just as importantly, the professor also exercises his deontic authority through the use of imperatives (to Ōhashi) as part of the taming process. As comics readers, we read them in the speech balloons, that is we overhear what is being said. In *PRIDE* and perhaps in the BDSM world in general, the imperative is itself just as binding as the ropes and chains we see on Ōhashi's muscular body. When Ōhashi begins his initial training, Shibazaki barks, "From now on I will not forgive any disobedience at all! Obey all my absolute orders! Can you do that?" (vol. I, 99). Ōhashi unequivocally executes his orders. The professor decides that Ōhashi fulfill some order, task, activity, etc., and Ōhashi does so because it will please the professor and will help him to overcome his foolish pride.

SHUPPATSU—DEPARTURE

In this chapter I have discussed Tagame Gengoroh's *PRIDE* as a MANGA for adults who have an interest in BDSM. Moreover, following Tagame, I have explored how *PRIDE* could be considered an example of a *Bildungsroman* ero-MANGA. Furthermore, I have also suggested that *PRIDE* is a how-to manual that carefully documents many of the subcultural practices of BDSM through the *koma* which take the reader on an erotic journey that presents what is required of a slave to achieve personal cultivation and a master to exercise authority.

I would like to make some final comments about pride itself in the context of Tagame's story and how Tagame mixes languages to construct his view of what the work's title might mean. To do this I consider one key scene that occurs towards the end of the narrative one month before Shibazaki and Ōhashi leave for Germany (vol. III, 111–13). Shibazaki asks Ōhashi whether his "foolish pride" (*kudaranai puraido*) has completely vanished. He answers that he has been "reborn as a true slave" (*shōshin shōmei dorei toshite umarekawarimashita*). Shibazaki then says, "If that is the case . . . from now on have pride in that fact!"—exchanging *puraido* (a word written in *katakana* indicating its non-Japanese roots) with the Japanese word *hokori* (written in *kanji* or Chinese characters). Ōhashi is surprised. The professor says, "To own a slave who has been completely trained is the master's pride and joy (*jiman*) and an honor (*hokori*). That you have become a *genuine slave* (*honmono no dorei*), that is the slave's pride (*puraido*)!" Tagame devises a story of gay pride not in the sense of "I am somebody" but something quite the opposite.

At the beginning of the story, *puraido* is appraised negatively, akin perhaps to hubris, a vice or a pathology, whereas *hokori* is a positive virtue, even for a slave to cultivate. By juxtaposing all three words—*puraido, hokori, jiman*—all of which can be translated as "pride," in this dialogue Tagame refashions *puraido* into something positive, mirroring Ōhashi's commitment to his consensual debasement and erotic becoming. In this sense, this slave's pride is more along the lines of "I am nobody," and *this* is something to be proud of. Tagame's Shibazaki strips off Ōhashi's foolish pride, taming him. Ōhashi struggles with his identity at the beginning of the story and at the end, but the struggles are different. He too distinguishes between the worlds he belongs to. Through his inurement in the world of BDSM, in the end Ōhashi seems comfortable and mature. Therefore, Tagame provides his readers with a metaphorical departure, one that if taken may open up opportunities to, as Tagame hopes, free the self from the limits of society and therefore reconfirms his reputation of grand master of Japanese ero-MANGA.

ACKNOWLEDGMENTS

I would like to thank editors Alison Halsall and Jonathan Warren and the anonymous reader of this chapter for all their comments, insights, and support.

Notes

1. Japanese word order is used for names here.

2. Following Armour (2011) and Armour and Takeyama (2015), "manga" is used to refer to Japanese comics in general, while MANGA is used when "manga" are read for entertainment (including for erotic pleasure). Manga is used when "manga" are read as a medium for the distribution of information and educational uses. The reasoning behind this kind of taxonomy is based on social purpose rather than a "manga" genre, e.g., *shōjo manga*. An argument could also be made that Tagame has actually produced a type of *gekiga* or "dramatic pictures," that is, "adult manga that explores serious topics" (Johnson-Woods 2010, 9).

3. These fantasies are listed on his website http://tagame.org/aboutme/profile-e.html, accessed May 5, 2019.

4. Translation between languages is about making choices. Self-respect, self-esteem, even pride could be possible choices here. In the context of *Otōto no otto*, a MANGA that explores issues such as interracial same-sex marriage, "pride" might be the best choice.

5. In discussing personal encounters with comics of their youth, Scott and Fawaz (2018, 205) note that Scott's engagement with Nubia Wonder Woman "was also, significantly, and in the paradigmatic manner in which comics provide sources of fantasy for their readers of whatever age, an *education* instantiating such desire . . . we see here a comic operating precisely as a queer orientation device," one that directed Scott and other readers "toward new desires for fantasy counterworlds that rebel against the constraints of everyday life" (italics in the original). *PRIDE* functions in a similar manner.

6. On the dust jacket surrounding vol. I, we can see how Tagame captures this through his depiction of Ōhashi—dressed only in jeans, shirtless to reveal his muscularity. His face shows an arrogant demeanor and his right hand, thumb in his pocket, adds to his brashness.

7. I am following Yuasa's discussion of *shugyō* or personal cultivation here: "cultivation is to impose on one's own body-mind stricter constraints than are the norms of secular, ordinary experience, so as to reach a life beyond that which is led by the average person" and "[C]ultivation's ultimate goal is wisdom (*prajñā*), seeing the true profile of Being in no-ego" (Yuasa 1987, 98).

8. Scott and Fawaz (2018) also make this point when discussing Fawaz's encounter with *X-Men* no. 80: "the fantasy of standing atop the arm of a muscle-bound Adonis surrounded by powerful mutant women, in pink holographic form, was at least one gay boy's dream come true" (208).

9. Scott and Fawaz (2018) note that "[C]omics is a medium that . . . hails counterpublics" (200). Following on from this and also Kampourakis's discussion of "subaltern counterpublics," I argue that the world of BDSM portrayed in *PRIDE* critiques normative Japanese social relations.

10. Tagame's readers are not limited to Japanese nationals. Rosenbaum (2012) notes that "[I]t used to be easy to read a comic, but with the global advance of manga as a cultural hybrid, readers now need to be familiar with a range of academic discourses, for manga are intertextual, address gender groups, are delineated into genres" (3) and what is relevant here, Tagame's "manga" convey a specific sense of (usually) male homosexuality.

11. Rucker (2019) understands teaching to be "a specific basic form of education" which is "an aid to enculturation" and thus learning culture (n.p.). He argues that enculturation "depends *firstly* on the assumption that people must acquire patterns of orientation (knowledge, abilities, norms, value judgments, principles, etc.), to participate in cultural practices" (italics in the original). His second point regarding education is that "there are situations in patterns of orientation that cannot be learned through everyday interaction." This makes sense in how Tagame presents Ōhashi's training to his readers: episodic, visual, and detailed.

12. It is beyond the scope of this chapter to explore the framework of *Bildung* in any great depth (see Geuss 1996; Nordenbo 2002; and Rucker 2019 for further discussion). I mentioned above that I am also interested in the Buddhist practice of *shugyō*. While *Bildung* has its origins in Greek culture (Nordenbo 2002, 343), my reading of both shares the view that they index "practical training aimed at the development and enhancement of one's spirit or personality" (Yuasa 1987, 85). In *PRIDE* Tagame, whether deliberately or not, draws together aspects of Western and Eastern thought. It is perhaps no coincidence that Shibazaki and Ōhashi travel to Germany where *Bildung* has been theorized the most.

13. *shiiku* is a combination of two Chinese characters *shi* (to keep, raise, breed, rear) and *iku* (growth, upbringing, breeding). The first character can also be read as *kau* and links to *kainarasu*, to tame. The online Japanese-Japanese dictionary, *Kotobanku* (drawing upon the *Daijirin*) provides two useful definitions of *kainarasu*: "1. keep (a wild animal and wild bird, etc.) and train/discipline (teach it how to behave) it so that it will follow a person's instructions; and 2. (metaphorically) treat a person well and so that they do what they are told. Tame (or win over)." How submission, training, and discipline cluster together in the narrative is of interest here.

14. The concept of ritual liminality (Turner 1987) is also useful here. Turner draws on Van Gennep's notion of *rites de passage* in which he shows that all rites of passage consist of three phases: separation, margin (limen) and aggregation (Van Gennep 1960). Early in *PRIDE*, to overcome his sexual dysfunction, Ōhashi must transcend his "foolish pride" by detaching himself from the state of being a brash topman. During the liminal period, which comprises most of the story, Ōhashi becomes a metaphorical passenger travelling through "a realm that has few or none of the attributes of the past or coming state" (Turner 1987, 4). Shibazaki's branding of Ōhashi's buttock indicates that the passage is consummated and has become stable. What we read in *PRIDE* is a BDSM ritual that is transformative.

15. This section is based on ideas posited by Józef Maria Bocheński and expanded on in Brożek (2013).

Works Cited

a grateful slave, and Guy A. Baldwin. *SlaveCraft: Roadmaps for Consensual Erotic Servitude: Principles, Skills, and Tools*. Daedalus Publishing Company, 2002.

Armour, William S. "Learning Japanese by Reading 'manga': The Rise of Soft Power Pedagogy." *RELC Journal* 42, no. 2 (2011): 125–40.

Armour, William S. "Representations of the Masculine in Tagame Gengoroh's Ero SM Manga." *Asian Studies Review* 34, no. 4 (2010): 443–65.

Armour, William S., and Yuki Takeyama. "Translating Japanese Typefaces in MANGA: Bleach." *New Readings*, no. 15 (2015): 21–45.

Brożek, Anna. "Bocheński on Authority." *Studies in European Thought* 65, nos. 1–2 (2013): 115–33.

Geuss, Raymond. "Kultur, Bildung, Geist." *History and Theory* 35, no. 2 (1996): 151–64.

Graham, Sarah. "Introduction." In *A History of the Bildungsroman*, edited by Sarah Graham, 1–9. Cambridge University Press, 2019.

Groensteen, Thierry. *The System of Comics*. Translated by Bart Beaty and Nick Nguyen. University Press of Mississippi, 2007.

Hall, Justin. "Erotic Comics." In *The Routledge Companion to Comics*, edited by Frank Bramlett, Roy T. Cook, and Aaron Meskin, 154–63. Routledge, 2017.

Harmon, Gary L. "On the Nature and Functions of Popular Culture." *Studies in Popular Culture*, no. 6 (1983): 3–15.

Johnson-Woods, Toni. "Introduction." In *MANGA: An Anthology of Global and Cultural Perspectives*, edited by Toni Johnson-Woods, 1–14. Continuum, 2010.

Kampourakis, Ioannis. "Nancy Fraser: Subaltern Counterpublics." Accessed September 12, 2019. http://criticallegalthinking.com/2016/11/06/nancy-fraser-subaltern-counterpublics/.

McCloud, Scott. *Understanding Comics: The Invisible Art*. HarperPerennial, 1993.

Miyoshi, Masao. *Accomplices of Silence*. University of California Press, 1974.

Mortimer, Maya. *Meeting the Sensei—The Role of the Master in Shirakaba Writers*. Brill, 2000.

Natsume, Sōseki. *Sanshirō*. Translated by Jay Rubin. Penguin, 1908–1909, 2009.

Nordenbo, Sven Erik. "*Bildung* and the Thinking of *Bildung*." *Journal of Philosophy of Education* 36, no. 3 (2002): 341–52.

Rosenbaum, Roman. "Introduction: The representation of Japanese history in manga." In *Manga and the Representation of Japanese History*, edited by Roman Rosenbaum, 1–17. Routledge, 2013.

Rucker, Thomas. "Teaching and the Claim of Bildung: The View from General Didactics." *Studies in Philosophy and Education*. Published ahead of print, June 24, 2019. https://doi.org/10.1007/s11217-019-09673-0.

Tagame, Gengoroh. *PRIDE*, vol. I. III vols. Furukawa Shobō, 2004.

Tagame, Gengoroh. *PRIDE*, vol. II. III vols. Furukawa Shobō, 2004.

Tagame, Gengoroh. *PRIDE*, vol. III. III vols. Furukawa Shobō, 2004.

Tagame, Gengoroh. *Otōto no Otto* (*My Younger Brother's Husband*), vol. III. IV vols. Futabasha, 2016.

Turner, Victor. "Betwixt and Between: The Liminal Period of Rites of Passage." In *Betwixt & Between: Patterns of Masculine and Feminine Initiation*, edited by Louise Carus Mahdi, Steven Foster, and Meredith Little, 3–19. Open Court, 1987.

Washburn, Dennis. "Manly Virtue and the Quest for Self: The Bildungsroman of Mori Ōgai." *Journal of Japanese Studies* 21, no. 1 (1995): 1–32.

Van Gennep, Arnold. *The Rites of Passage*. University of Chicago Press, 1960.

Yuasa, Yasuo. *The Body: Toward an Eastern Mind-Body Theory*, edited by Thomas P. Kasulis, translated by Shigenori Nagatomo and Thomas P. Kasulis. State University of New York Press, 1987.

Chapter 10

GAY FANZINES AS CONTACT ZONES
DOKKUN'S ADVENTURES WITH "BARA" MANGA IN BETWEEN JAPAN AND FRANCE

EDMOND (EDO) ERNEST DIT ALBAN

"In Japanese comics dokkun is the 'sound' (onomatopoeia) of a man ejaculating."
—**Fabrissou,** Facebook message to the author, February 25, 2012

I first met *Dokkun*'s team in 2010 during a modest Japanese *dôjinshi* (amateur comic or manga) convention held in Paris.[1] At the time, their participation in the event was an enigma to me: they were the only LGBTQ+ pornographic fanzine creators and the only French circle at this small venue. Why would a French gay fanzine circle identify so much with Japanese amateur comics? My question was later answered, beginning in May 2012, when I worked as a translator for *Dokkun*'s creator, Fabrissou, and organized his participation at an amateur gay manga convention (the *Yarô Fes*, the Dudes' festival) held in Ikebukuro (Tokyo). The prolific underground circulation of Japanese amateur comics inspires the style, narratives, production models and media forms created by *Dokkun*'s team. Over the ensuing three years, following *Dokkun*'s adventures in France and Japan, I came to see the erotic queerness of *Dokkun*'s European and amateur Japanese gay manga in mutually generative creative complementarity.

In France, a precarious media environment for LGBTQ+ content obliges *Dokkun* mostly to present and distribute its explicitly pornographic books and fanzines at well-known anime conventions, such as the Japan Expo in Paris and the Yaoi Yuri Con in Lyon. Beyond such Japan-related conventions, gay comics in France circulate via a confined network of LGBTQ+ bookstores including *Les mots à la bouche* in Paris's gay village. As a result, although mail-order selling and online platforms (such as Patreon) support the emergence of new artists and contents, access to gay comic books in France remains relatively limited. Websites and publishing companies dedicated to the genre tend to survive for a few years, as the European platform animagay.com did in the mid-2000s. The French gay comics and fanzine market nevertheless remains limited but stable by maintaining a presence in the francophone LGBTQ+ amateur publishing scene and with European anime and manga fandoms via conventions.

Figure 10.1. *Dokkun 11*, Fabrissou. Dokkun (self-published, 2018), cover.

In this way, the peculiarity in the distribution particulars of LGBTQ+ work in France obliges the commingling of creators and distributors from different comics contexts, cultures, and vantage points, generating a noteworthy transnational dimension among fan communities that access these comics via such a diverse marketplace. *Dokkun*'s fanzine influences and format testify to a mixed appropriation of northern American gay comics, French-Belgian *bande dessinée*, and girls' manga typical of the local French fan communities.[2] Each annual issue published every July assembles pornographic short pieces from fluctuating groups of international francophone authors that exemplify this variousness, including Fabrissou, DY, Art by Fab, Silencio, Gigan, Hakujin, Doctor Anfelo, and Logan who worked in the Canadian gay comics scene with Patrick Fillion during his publications for Class Comics in the 1990s.[3] *Dokkun* furthermore officiates as an amateur publisher for many authors by producing artwork books for them.

In tandem with the mixing of comics cultures, fandoms, and influences at work in its distribution scene, since its creation in 2010, *Dokkun* has served as a platform for gay creators to meet and exchange graphic tips and techniques;

it has supported multiple projects looking at how gay art is produced daily in America and Japan. While minor, a *Dokkun* community-at-large has emerged from the transcultural exchanges brought about by the circulation of pornographic gay comics online and at fan conventions. Being part of an audience that is itself increasingly accustomed to a mixture of global comics voices and modalities—via the importation of foreign books, the search for (sometimes pirated or otherwise illegal) digital copies of gay comics online, and the production and consumption of new content for francophone audiences from France and its overseas territories, Belgium, and Switzerland—*Dokkun*'s participation since 2012 in fanzine conventions both in Europe and Japan shows the potential of amateur pornographic comics to help create contact zones (Morimoto 2013) among gay communities across the globe. The transnational circulation of images, books, artists, and alumni of gay comics produces intricate territories where local, regional, and global cultures meet. This highlights intricate phenomena, especially: 1) the emergence of urban and online sites for foreign gay cultures to meet; and 2) the confection of common sets of techniques of visual expressions, narratives, and characters.

Dokkun's roles as a concatenator of diverse comics content—as a possible generator of hybrid comics modalities, as a forum for diverse creativity, as a liminal site with regard to *bande dessinée*, comics, and manga influences—prompted discussions within its circle of participants about how to distinguish between and among emerging comics modalities. What cultural markers were salient in the emerging blend? Which specificities or particular styles and techniques could still be said to exemplify specific cultural areas? And what preconceived notions about LGBTQ+ power and liberation in Europe vis-à-vis the rest of the world might need to be reformulated? A first way into these questions was to think about the divergent fanzine associations and publishing systems across the global scene of gay comics. For example, although the Japanese gay artists whom *Dokkun* most loved live in Japan, where the equality of rights for LGBTQ+ people was not openly discussed back in 2012, those creators seemed nonetheless to benefit from a more extensive media distribution network than *Dokkun* enjoyed in Europe where LGBTQ+ acceptance and advocacy are supposed to be more integrated into the social and political norm. The comparatively wider circulation of gay manga in Japan looked like an impressive advanced cultural system that they could not even dream of reproducing in France. Noting such a structural irony, in which Japan's ostensibly less liberated queer voices benefit from a distribution network that provides them a platform for self-expression that outdoes France's, *Dokkun* started to look into the artistic prerogatives and economic realities of French and Japanese amateur gay comics more broadly: how are they produced? By whom and why? Do they have an influence on mainstream culture?

FAN-MADE "ETHNOGRAPHY": GAY COMICS' CIRCULATION AND TRANSCULTURAL QUEER SPACES

When discussing LGBTQ+ media production, we often question the adequate representation of queer lives (Risner 2010; Morris 2001; Shugart 2003). Comics are no exception. Controversies about gay characters in DC and Marvel comics are often the starting point when discussing LGBTQ+ representation (Palmer-Mehta 2005). Although the issue of queer visibility in comics has also been taken up by focusing on their response to the AIDS crisis (Greenblatt 2019), considerations of gayness in mainstream/corporate comics tend to dominate how we think about LGBTQ+ issues in comics (e.g., how to broach homo-sexuality in a superhero narrative). Because of its grassroots context, *Dokkun*, on the other hand, focused on the specifically LGBTQ+ social and cultural preconditions within which comics production happens and in which comics are circulated, read, and understood. Thinking about queerness in comics tends to emphasize the depiction of LGBTQ+ visually, and scholarly and popular investigations have tended to neglect the preconditions of such eventual visual depictions: the production of a cultural space within which LGBTQ+ comics or manga is made possible.

Dokkun's limited network of circulation in comparison to the Japanese gay fanzine scene invites us to think about comics creation and distribution as the very source of what Halberstam calls a *queer space and time* (2005). Following *Dokkun*'s adventures in Japan between 2012 and 2013, we can discover the trans-national territories of gay manga (often called "Bara" manga online) between Paris and Tokyo. In *The Production of Space* (1974), Lefebvre reminds us that social space is often too obvious to be noticeable. The transcultural exchanges associated with amateur gay comics may help us to notice and explore such underexamined queer spaces. *Dokkun* assumed that Japan was superficially more closeted but far more expressive in its distribution network for queer art than is Europe: amateur Japanese gay art occupies "more space" across cities and fanzine events. Although this might be the result of French queer com-munities choosing other media to express themselves, the hypothesis that gay comics' Japanese circulation produces greater queer spaces relative to those in Europe remains significant.

Transcultural exchanges, necessitated by the online distribution networks of pornographic gay comics, are furthermore not limited to local communities and produce interconnected queer times and places. While these exchanges may not always bring equal contributions on both sides, what emerges from such transcultural sharing is vast in terms of techniques, genres, representa-tions, as well as models of comics bookstores and fanzine events. This phenom-enon hence exceeds the realm of the mere inspiration or reappropriation of foreign cultural forms to bridge and provoke dialogues between communities, and to spur discussion on the local, national, regional, and global territories mobilized by gay comics. Through their potential to disclose opportunities for common practices, representations and media production models, transcultural exchanges may support networks like *Dokkun*'s to recreate their own local gay communities by emulating Japan's so called "Bara" art.

But what is "Bara"? *Dokkun* team members see "Bara" as a genre of manga inspired by gay pornographic art in which buff male characters have graphic gay sex. But on closer inspection of examples, that superficial description feels inadequate. A more thorough answer takes form in the short pieces, entitled "Bara Logics" by the Latin American artist Doctor Anfelo, which appear in *Le Bara ça n'existe pas* (*Dokkun* 2013) and which parody recurrent narrative features and graphic stereotypes identified by foreign fans of Japanese gay comics in the work of Takeshi Matsu, Mizuki Gai, Ittô (Mentaiko), and other famous artists. Anfelo specifies Bara tropes (beards, large muscles, hair, and scars), improbable plot twists (bi-curious stepdads, intimidating but cute wrestlers, overaged high school students), and Japanese character terminology (*megane* for a character with glasses). The pornographic aspect—buff male characters and graphic sex—is only the beginning, and *Dokkun* strove to acknowledge and celebrate the deeper potential of the genre and style.

For example, to celebrate the French release of the publications about their "Bara" adventures in Japan, in 2014, *Dokkun*'s new number featured Fabrissou's "You work well," a piece previously published only as *dôjinshi* (fanzine) at Japanese conventions, as well as Doctor Anfello's "King in Tartan," two short comics by non-Japanese artists that pay homage to Japanese gay comics: they present a love story between buff, hairy, and macho men, discovering a sweet side of their partners through sexual intercourse, and the appropriation of *komawari* (comic strips design or manga montage), onomatopoeia, and other semiotic tropes of manga to express emotions. Fabrissou's "You work well" unfolds through the hybrid format of *komawari*, using rapid cut techniques from the cinematographic style of boys' manga as well as some instances of girls' manga inner-thought stillness. Other artists, including DY, Anfello, and Art by Fab, also experiment with cartoon and manga-like character design, a phenomenon close to what Suan has called the anime performativity.

The "Bara" terminology and its features provide an instructive way to track transcultural interactions. The label "Bara" usually describes manga "made by gay men for gay men in Japan" (in opposition to slash manga made by women) and is frequently used online—on Twitter and image boards like 4chan—by gay artists across the globe to label or classify their art. With the popular impact of "Bara" art, comics, and illustrations on online networks of distribution, *Dokkun*'s community also tends to use the term as a shorthand to describe their

Figure 10.2. *Le Bara ça n'existe pas*, Edo and Fabrissou. Dokkun (self-published, 2014), cover.

production and to build their local network in Europe. "Bara" was a keyword in the early 2010s for the francophone artists to describe their hybrid art style and to attract new readers of and contributors to zines. Conversations and correspondence with artists from Japan, however, discouraged use of the term. Artist Gengoroh Tagame in particular reminded the team that gays in Japan do not use the term because of its history as a slur that is equivalent to "pansies" or "fag." For this reason, *Dokkun* launched a series of interviews and developed gay village maps and fanzines entitled *Bara ha Bara Bara Da* (a phrase that can be translated both by "Bara manga is all over the place" and "There is no such thing as Bara manga") to remind its members and audience of their participation in a controversial cultural appropriation.

If there is indeed *originally* no such thing as "Bara manga" in Japan, the label for the genre was created by the international circulation of Japanese pornographic gay comics (Ishii et al. 2015) which, in turn, was accommodated by some Japanese creators as a kind of uncomfortable convenience.[4] In this context, *Dokkun* sought to examine and explore the meanings of the genre via loosely "ethnographic" work that identifies its media, interviews people associated with it, and maps the geography of gay manga in Tokyo. *Dokkun* published interviews of Japanese artists describing gay manga in their own words and urban zine-collecting maps of queer spaces mobilized by gay manga in Tokyo. Mixing art, pornography, interviews, accounts of urban experiences, and media history, *Dokkun's* project tried to question how "Bara" communities use gay manga to produce their own art and space locally, internationally, and online.[5] Their main concern was to discuss the potential impact of that kind of production on mainstream media. But it is also useful to note the impact that transcultural or trans-local exchanges have on the production of local, interconnected queer spaces; comics creates queer spaces in their stories, in between the sites of their distribution and around their audiences.

Recently, Alvaro Hernandez-Hernandez and Hirai have shed light on how Japanese (fan)zine and amateur comics communities cultivate what they call "translocality" (2015). Hernandez-Hernandez (2016, 2018) invites us to envision international cultural networks of amateur media production as *trans-local geographies*: amateur or fanzine communities reusing similar content, techniques, and technologies that travel from one location to another while adapting to local audiences' needs. Gay comics circulate, in print and online, and local communities produce their own gay pornographic media in relation to them. Interconnected localities emerge, each with its own sense of place and of history, contemporaneity, and futurity, as well as with their geographic influences and linkages legible in the gay comics they emulate, produce, and exchange.

Dokkun's identification with Japanese amateur comics exemplifies such a trans-local dynamic. Via in-person and mediated transnational contacts, the *Dokkun* team met and embraced a Japanese aesthetic mode of sexual representation as well as an advantageous publishing and distribution system. As Hernandez-Hernandez and Hirai highlight, in the Japanese fanzine scene the goal of the amateur media production milieu is to produce a "place of leisure" (*asobi no ba*), where multiple persons can participate in the creation of a specific project (Hernandez-Hernandez and Hirai 2015). "Bara" manga is such a trans-local queer "place of leisure (and pleasure)" and inscribes its territories in cities, bookstores, and conventions across the world. Such trans-locality produces interconnected spaces of circulation rather than the mere importation of or inspiration by a foreign culture. Gay manga can be a tool for inventing queer social space through transcultural and trans-local dynamics.

The transcultural circulation of "Bara" manga can help to conceptualize how gay fanzine communities can interact and envision art's inscription in and production of a new, queer society. In particular, *Dokkun's* project proposes a trans-local community in Paris and Tokyo between 2012 and 2013. Following the provocations of McNeil, Wermers, and Lunn (2018) we may map gay comics' transcultural expressions and spaces of queerness artistically (genres, techniques) and socially (communities, territories, and projects), noting the coexistence of similar expressions and techniques along with divergent local strategies of pornographic comics production and circulation. Referring to *Dokkun's* amateur work contributes to our understanding of the frequently understudied social space produced by a specifically amateur sector of LGBTQ+ comics, one far less tethered to corporate bulwarks, mainstream mass-market sales considerations, or national readership affiliations and expectations than commercial comics. Furthermore, close attention to amateur practitioners themselves helps to preserve precarious and vital queer creativity and spaces for further scholarly attention.

"BARA" MANGA IS ALL OVER THE PLACE: THE CONTRASTED EXPERIENCES OF TWO LOCAL MARKETS

While carrying out research for the Japanese edition of their "ethnographic" fanzine, "Bara manga is all over the place" (2013), *Dokkun's* team and I tried to understand the ambiguous origin of the term "Bara" by mapping the media, people, and places of gay manga through interviews with creators. Our goal was to understand the impact of transcultural exchanges on the lives of different gay communities. How is the circulation of gay manga changing society?

Although there may be no such thing as "Bara" in Japan, the term is associated with the origin of modern gay publishing there. The term is linked to *Barazoku* (薔薇族, the rose tribe), ostensibly Japan's first gay magazine (beginning publication in the 1970s). The phrase "薔薇" (*bara, rose*) refers to the magazine and comes from a post-World War II phrase for describing gay men. Publishing erotic and pornographic art, novels, and photography made by mostly anonymous gay men, *Barazoku* also featured the work of famous illustrators and manga artists like Mishima Gô and Yamakawa Jun'ichi. The former editor of the magazine, Ito Bungaku, also mentioned the emergence of a "bara komi" (Barazoku Comics) genre in his 2010 autobiography.

However, today's amateur gay manga scene has left this terminology behind completely, following current gay sexual slang instead; that is to say, terminologies refering to body types (slim, muscular, chubby).[6] Pioneer gay artist Gengoroh Tagame also explained that connotations of "bara" transformed in the early 2000s as a new nomenclature, made by heterosexuals to refer to homosexual erotic representations online, emerged (Ishii et al. 2015). The visibility of Japanese gay media after the gay boom of the 1990s on national television moreover prompted the gay community to reorient its own production, often to caricature queer representations on television and elsewhere. For example, as the online video platforms 2Chanel and Niconico appropriated gay pornographic imagery for humorous purposes, many gay artists sought new terminologies that would describe their work in counter-distinction to the use of queerness as a mainstream joke. In 2012 and 2013, at the annual gay fanzine convention Yarô Fes, Japanese artists tended to define their art depending on the type of men they drew. The words "*gachimuchi*" (super buff), "*ossan*" (or *oyaji*, old-man), or "*yarô-kei*" (dudes or "bro") came up repeatedly in conversations, but "Bara" was nowhere to be found. *Dokkun*'s attendees at these conventions concluded that the "Bara" label endured mostly as a relatively insensitive appropriation by foreign online communities of an outdated term for the Japanese gay comic scene primarily established in Tokyo and multiple fanzine conventions, including the annual Yarô Fes and Yarô Kingdom or the biannual Comic City Spark and Comic Market.

Despite any insensitivity in their outdated labeling, the passion of foreign audiences for gay manga speaks to their need of a similar flourishing system of queer media production, articulated around multiple, yearly events. Many regional attempts to recreate a similar media ecology in Europe come up against the fact that most publishers and associations there lack local infrastructure and cannot sustain publication frequency to implant themselves in the "rhythms of everyday life" (Lefebvre 1974). It is therefore difficult to replicate the kinds of gay manga consumption one sees in the Japanese scene where all kinds of manga, from fanzine to industrial magazines, flourish. The persistent lack of queer representation and media in Europe is a challenge for LGBTQ+ communities. Facing the difficulty of maintaining niche economies supported by self-published art and lacking access to the relatively elite publication venues of *bande dessinée*, European manga fans understandably see the flourishing Japanese manga subcultures and their industrial production and circulation model as an attractive example to emulate for queer people to gain visibility. In Japan, the "Bara" label connotes an outdated mode of gay self-representation while in Europe it stands for an attractive possibility for expanding gay visibility. The definitions of "Bara" are quite different, but they illustrate complicatedly connected strategies for using comics as a tool for gay representation.

This comparison invites us to reflect upon the situation in France where gay comics production similarly originated in gay villages and grew via fan networks. In the late 1990s and early 2000s, even as French politicians alleged the unpleasant effects of foreign popular cultures on young people, a lack of French youth content for LGBTQ+ audiences drew Japanese Yaoi and Boys' Love slash manga to the center of queer French fan community attention (Nouhet-Roseman 2011). Despite the vibrant legacy of such gay *bande dessinée* artists as Alex Barbier, Frédéric Lère, and Dominique Leroy, since the early 1980s their work has generally been available only in small publications and magazines like *Gai Pied*. While originally intended for female audiences, Japanese slash manga, on the other hand, enjoyed distribution in regular bookstores and was therefore an easily accessible and relatively inexpensive option for LGBTQ+ audiences. Japanese manga—popular narratives and characters but also political messages—have exerted an influence in France, just as many French gay artists used slash manga as a first entry point into Japanese comics.

Moreover, the monthly release of Japanese content contrasts with the more slow-paced publishing schedule of *bandes dessinées*, so the proliferation of Japanese materials abounds at French fan conventions. Legendary artists of the German and French comic gay scenes like Ralf König or Tom de Pékin who engage directly with French (and European) politics and social issues give way to emergent, Francophone pornographic comics translations of American and Japanese gay comics in the early 2000s.[7] Small amateur communities further extended the production of pornographic gay comics at fan conventions and within fanzines like Gigan's Belgian *Themalicious*. The incremental spread of Japanese gay manga—via small publishers, exhibitions by art collectors, and collaborations by French and Japanese circles during fan conventions—transformed the Francophone scene, making it very much an intermediary within a trans-local geography extending to other comics ecologies under similar development, as with Class Comics in Canada and Tom of Finland in Finland, and infused with Japanese gay manga.

These developments were not geographically isolated. Rather, they show transcultural and trans-local influences on new strategies, new expressions, and new modes of social visibility. The clearest transcultural influences tend to be formal. The main format for gay comics in Japan varies between forty-page, A4-sized fanzines (*dôjinshi*) and B5-sized manga comic books (*tankobon*). *Dokkun*, like many artists and artistic circles influenced by "Bara," tend to reproduce these formats that originally mark the difference between amateur and professional gay manga. Moreover, the blurring of that distinction is also relevant in both Japan and Europe, and it is formally visible. In Japan, most authors working for gay magazine publishers like Furukawa, G-Men, or Badi also contribute to amateur fanzines. In interviews, Japanese authors lament the heavy hands of professional editorial teams on graphic styles and content, including forced explicit nudity (*Dokkun* 2013), to account for wanting to work

Figure 10.3. *La Piscine*, Fabrissou. Dokkun (self-published, 2014), 4.

in both spheres. Amateur work affords relative editorial freedom and puts artists in closer proximity to the reading public, helping to generate grassroots experiments and new topics and styles. Japanese artists mix professional and amateur production, complicating the ways in which their work formally appears and circulates in gay villages, at fan conventions, and sometimes in general bookstores. Even though such professional affiliations do not always exist for gay comics creators in Europe, circles like *Dokkun* preserve the use of A4 and B5 formats, depending on the demand of local bookstores. Although this detail of the book formats could seem merely cosmetic, it cites and pays homage to an important attribute of the Japanese gay comics scene: the diverse opportunities and comics modalities available to gay artists in the vibrant Japanese manga market. Understanding formatting, graphic styles, and *komawari* (panel layout) typical to Japanese gay manga helps to realize a trans-local exchange that replicates the look of Japanese materials and that alludes to the meanings of such formatting, so as sometimes to underscore the smallness of the European gay comics scene relative to Japan. Similar cross-cultural meanings can be traced via the use of similar digital tools for image editing (such as Manga Studio) signs attesting to pornographic content (the "R18" mark), the use of introductions and "postfaces" written by authors, and *komawari* techniques. Amateur gay manga and its imbrications in a Japanese industrial system propose an expression, a product, and a model for other grassroot communities to emulate when making their "own" manga that also cites the Japanese example and contexts.

This iteration of common techniques of expression represents the basics of the phenomenon described by Hernandez-Hernandez and Hirai as translocality (2015) or Suan as anime performativity (2017). Exchanges driven by the creation of trans-local spaces of play (and pleasure) (Hernandez-Hernandez, 2016) focusing on fanzines, moreover, have an impact on the respective interconnected locations. In Japan, Gengoroh Tagame (2017) and Saito Takuya (2019) explain the recent augmentation of stories to include references to marriage equality, parenthood, and less frequently transgender lives, as an influence of western media on gay manga. Tagame also points out that one source of gay manga in Japan is the limited importation of the American magazines like *DRUMMER* and its BDSM comics. This complicates the history and techniques of the genre by extending its roots to the trans-local circulation of gay magazines and transcultural, indeed transcontinental, exchange. More recent iterations of these dynamics may be apparent in the tendency of amateur Japanese gay manga to refer to foreign television when alluding to political action and activism. Such sources may have helped to prepare the ground for the so-called LGBTQ+ boom in Japan in the late 2010s, introducing a new vocabulary of marriage equality, adoption, and trans* lives into amateur gay manga.

Such transformations in the discourse and content of gay manga leads us to the crucial element that grabbed *Dokkun*'s attention in the first place: the vast retail networks distributing gay comics. In Tokyo, Japanese gay manga mainly circulates via local networks of gay bars, sex shops, and bookstores in Shinjuku, Ikebukuro, Ueno, and Shinbashi. Nonetheless, its proximity in content and techniques with the female slash scene of Boys' Love manga (McLelland et al. 2015) and its availability at fanzine conventions underscore its incremental assimilation of some more mainstream artists whose work is sold in more general bookstores. In this way, the gay manga scene of the Yarô Fes is in fact in itself always a rather mixed community of gay artists and straight women often publishing under male pen names. Since the early 2000s, Yarô Fes's artists have served a passion shared by both their gay and female audiences for old men (*oyaji*) or muscled men (*nikutaiha*), something we see in recurrent exchanges between gay and slash publishers; the industrial production and distribution model of gay comics magazines and the amateur compilation approach of slash anthologies like *Aquaboy* often relies on and exemplifies such collaboration.

Exchanges among straight female and queer communities are pervasive in gay manga. Baudinette notes the salience of this appropriation of slash manga by gay communities in Japan (2017). Although none of the artists we interviewed thought (at the time) that their work was directly affecting an evolution for LGBTQ+ people's rights in Japan (*Dokkun* 2013),[8] their continuous implication in niche manga markets eventually infiltrated more mainstream genres and production models. In sum, while maintaining essential queer spaces inside of gay villages, the circulation of gay comics also extends beyond them, transforming the urban space occupied by the art of manga pornography into local contact zones with local female fandoms, women's manga publishers, and fanzine communities. Gay manga, its techniques, genres, representations, and topics can slowly spread across the media environment.

As Paris's gay village (Le Marais) gradually disappears, yielding to gentrification and *haute couture* shops, it is urgent to raise the question of how trans-local gay comics might sustain everyday gay life. As "Bara" manga's global distribution has mapped out new connections through the circulation of gay comics, multiple communities have learned to create their expressions, their media environment, and to emulate their vibrancy in their own space. Comparing Japanese and French gay comics' media ecologies highlights two different contexts of creative production and sociopolitical stakes. In France, gay communities have struggled to establish durable structures to publish their work. To find an alternative to the established editorial system of *bande dessinée*, comics learned to address local marginalized audiences from the emergence of grassroots, self-published comics. In Japan, while confronting occasionally demeaning mainstream exploitation of "Bara" terminology, LGBTQ+ comics were able to take advantage of Japan's expansive network of comics publishing, especially within the Japanese media ecology of pornographic comics. That Japanese experience, legible in gay pornographic comics, and by extension, available transculturally and trans-locally, might not first seem like "activism" or "political action." However, Japanese gay manga supports a wide range of artistic developments including transcultural exchanges among foreign gay niche communities, the local visibility of which depends, in turn, on queer people in Japan, circulating their own media production.

CONCLUSION: TOWARDS THE STUDY OF QUEER COMICS AND ITS SOCIAL SPACE

Since the physical and imaginary contact zones produced by the circulation of pornographic comics contribute to transcultural emulation of sexual representations and of comics production models, it is finally worth reflecting on future possible approaches to study the emergence of transcultural and translocal gay comic production. First, one might explore their specific techniques of expression. Fabrissou's style in *Dokkun* brings to mind recent debates in manga historiography about the emergence of *komawari* (strips) techniques in the 1970s to describe inner space, and sexual drives and subjectivity (Ishida 2008; Ôtsuka 2007). Despite the emphatic *bande dessinée* format of his pages, Fabrissou's manga-inspired lines and character design question the inner voice of protagonists even in sex scenes. His approach to pornography recalls the legacy of Hagio Moto and Takemiya Keiko in amateur girl manga, specifically the propensity of filmic sequences to yield toward immobility and the arrangement of strips onto one page, something frequently discussed by scholars and practitioners as a strategy to insert introspective pauses in narratives.[9]

Fabrissou balances rapid shorts describing the movement of bodies and wide angles reflecting upon intimate moments of reflection, gaze, and sexual desire.[10] This dichotomy of body and mind movement nonetheless echoes two strategies that induce a sense of continuous movement in between strips, but also reminds us of the complex origins of the *komawari* techniques associated with amateur Japanese gay comics. The (in)famous art of Yamakawa Jun'ichi for *Barazoku* magazine in the 1980s testifies to an interesting controversy surrounding the "girlish" status of his style. Ito Bungaku often mentions how poorly Yamakawa's work was received by gay audiences who were more interested in realistic and virile figures than ostensibly childish, effeminate main characters (2010). Inspired by Mori Naoko's work, I argue that the systematic use of inner monologue techniques in Yamakawa's pieces contributed to and helped to shape pornographic comic representational conventions in Japan and overseas (2010, 2012). The evolution of slash and gay manga's strategies of sexual representation appear to have happened simultaneously via exchanges between the two communities. As the erotic art of shōnen-ai transformed into the fanzine scene of Yaoi and the industrial Boys' Love market over the years (Azuma 2015), the inner monologue techniques evolved towards mixed representations of the conjoined sexual pleasure of both partners (Mori 2010).

The recent evolution of gay comics' *komawari* also testifies to similar transformations leaving the focus on bottom characters' response to the sexual intercourse (as in Gengoroh and Yamakawa's early works) to focus on the couple's mutual pleasure (Saito 2019). Responding to the contemporaneous

Figure 10.4. *La Piscine*, Fabrissou. Dokkun (self-published, 2014), 5.

metamorphosis of gay and slash manga, the online "Bara" genre extends such emphasis on subjective aspects of sexuality, by pursuing pleasurable erotic images, lovable hairy macho characters, and the subjective development of characters through sexual intercourse. The trans-local circulation of gay manga has therefore entered the door opened by the global exportation of manga cultures to build common narratives, techniques, and characters that focus on sharing common representations of gay intimacy, psychology, and subjectivity. The history of the circulation of girls' manga, slash manga, and then gay manga in France might have gradually shaped the expressions of local grassroots artists communities.

Second, one might explore the political aspect of the reworking of queer representations in comics as well as its diffusion through its physical and online distribution. Azuma Sonoko's thoughts about the female communities of slash manga (2015) may also be applicable to the context of transcultural and trans-local LGBTQ+ communities: if love and sex are the mere alibi for individuals to discuss intimacy and construct grassroots communities based on shared modes of representation, "Bara" manga appears to afford a similar opportunity and related graphic techniques. A potential hypothesis is that the quest to find sexual images that "feel good" (Mori 2010) empowers trans-local communities to reimagine sexuality and to represent bodies with the strength to change heteronormative society. Beyond recognizing gay comics as a *body genre* (Williams 1991) interested in reimagining sexualized bodies, *Dokkun*'s fascination with Japanese "Bara"—its contents and systems of production and circulation—orients and equips their quest to create a queer space that "resembles them" socially and interpersonally as bodies with one another.

Notes

1. Japanese onomatopoeia for the sound of a man ejaculating, *Dokkun* is a French gay comics fanzine with a particular interest in Japanese gay manga, founded in 2010 by the Parisian gay artist and "comicker," Fabrissou. This chapter uses the word to refer to the title of that publication series itself and to the team or circle responsible for its creative direction, production, and distribution in which I have played a part.

2. *Dokkun* (Fabrissou and Edo). *Bara ha Bara Bara Da* (self-published, 2013).

3. Fabrissou and DY are a couple of Parisian artists who have participated with *Dokkun* since its creation. Art by Fab is a gay artist from Nouméa mostly active online on Facebook and Instagram. Silencio is a French gay artist living in America. Gigan is a Belgian artist who created the fanzine *Themalicious* in the 2000s. Hakujin is a French gay illustrator. Doctor Anfelo is a Latino gay artist active online on his Patreon. Lastly, Logan is a famous French gay artist with an international career in Canadian and American gay comics.

4. See the interviews of gay mangaka in Ishii, Anne and Kolbeins, Graham and Kidd, Chipp. *Massive: Gay Erotic Manga and the Men Who Make It* (Fantagraphics, 2015).

5. See glossary in *Dokkun* (Fabrissou and Edo). *Le bara ça n'existe pas* (self-published, 2014).

6. For more information about this aspect, see Marc J. McLelland, "Male Homosexuality in Modern Japan: Cultural Myths and Social Realities." *The Journal of Japanese Studies* 28, no.1 (Winter 2002): 157–61 and Thomas Baudinette, "An Evaluation of Physicality in the Bara manga of Badi magazine," in *Manga Vision*, eds. Sarah Pasfield-Neofitou and Cathy Sell, 107–24 (Monash University Press, 2016).

7. This movement includes publishers like H&O, a French participatory publishing company created in 2000 to support Francophone gay literature, erotic fiction and comics.

8. Artists including Tagame Gengoroh, Draw2, Ebisubashi, Kazuhide Ichikawa, Masanori, Moritake, Killer Bambi, Suv, Noda Gaku, Matsu Takeshi, and Mizuki Gai described their

influences and creative process, and reflected on the impact of the production model of gay comics on Japanese society.

9. The pioneering work of Mori Naoko (2010, 2012) demonstrates how the feminine techniques of erotic and pornographic manga spread across multiple genres and audiences in Japan.

10. In "La Piscine," the hybridity of Fabrissou's trans-local expression ties the following elements together: 1. the dichotomy between cinematographic manga for the body movements and girls' manga inner monologue in subjective moments (the dive scene and gazing scene); 2. floating characters typical of anime and manga; 3. manga graphic conventions including filters and onomatopeia mixed with *bande dessinée* conventions of the same type; 4. mixed character design reusing the graphic style of French cartoons transformed through the treatment of character mobility in manga (erasing the eyes to hide the facial expression of characters, the transformation of characters from one art style to another from one shot to another); 5. a narrative following the usual tropes of "Bara" or gay manga with a sexual experience leading to self-discovery.

Works Cited

Azuma, Sonoko. *Takarazuka, Yaoi: Ai no yomikae josei to popyûrakaruchâ no shakaigaku.* Shinyôsha, 2015.

Baudinette, Thomas. "An Evaluation of Physicality in the Bara manga of Badi magazine." In *Manga Vision*, eds. Sarah Pasfield-Neofitou and Cathy Sell, 107–24. Monash University Press, 2016.

Baudinette, Thomas. "Japanese Gay Men's Attitudes toward 'Gay Manga' and the Problem of Genre." *East Asian Journal of Popular Culture* 3, no.1 (2017).

Califia, Patrick. *Speaking Sex to Power: The Politics of Queer Sex.* Cleis Press, 2002.

Dokkun (Fabrissou and Edo). *Bara ha Bara Bara Da.* Self-published, 2013.

Dokkun (Fabrissou and Edo). *Le bara ça n'existe pas.* Self-published, 2014.

Franklin, Morris E. "Coming Out in Comic Books: Letter Columns, Readers, and Gay and Lesbian Characters." In *Comics and Ideology*, edited by Matt McAllister, Edward H. Sewel, and Ian Gordon, 221–50. Peter Lang, 2001.

Greenblatt, Jordana. "The Banality of Anal: Safer Sexual Erotics in the Gay Men's Health Crisis' Safer Sex Comix and Ex Aequo's Alex et la vie d'après." *Journal of Medical Humanities* 40, no. 1 (March 2019): 33–51.

Halberstam, Jack. *In a Queer Time and Place: Transgender Bodies, Subcultural Lives.* New York University Press, 2005.

Hernandez-Hernandez, Alvaro. "The Anime Industry, Networks of Participation, and Environments for the Management of Content in Japan." Special Issue about "Japanese Media Cultures in Japan and Abroad: Transnational Consumption of Manga, Anime, and Video Games," *Arts* 7, no. 3 (2018): 42.

Hernandez-Hernandez, Alvaro. "The Japanese Amateur Textual Production Scene: Activities and Participation in Dōjin Cultures." *Revista Gremium* 3, special issue SI1 (December 2016).

Hernandez-Hernandez, Alvaro, and Hirai Taiki. "The Reception of Japanese Animation and its Determinants in Taiwan, South Korea and China." *Animation* 10, no. 2 (July 2015): 154–69.

Ishida, Minori. *Hisoyakanakyôiku, BL yaoizenshi.* Rakuhoku, 2008.

Ishii, Anne, Graham Kolbeins, and Chip Kidd. *Massive: Gay Erotic Manga and the Men Who Make It.* Fantagraphics, 2015.

Ito, Bungaku. *Yaranaika: Barazoku henshûchô ni yoru gokushiteki gei bunkashi ron.* Sairyusha, 2010.

Ito, Gô. *Tezuka izu deddo: Hirakareta manga hyôgenron he.* NTT, 2005.

McNeil, Elizabeth, James E. Wermers, and Joshua O. Lunn. *Mapping Queer Space(s) of Praxis and Pedagogy.* Palgrave Macmillan, 2018.

McLelland, Marc J. "Male Homosexuality in Modern Japan: Cultural Myths and Social Realities." *Journal of Japanese Studies* 28, no. 1 (Winter 2002): 157–61.

McLelland, Marc J., Kazumi Nagaike, Katsuhiko Suganuma, and James Welker. *Boys Love Manga and Beyond: History, Culture, and Community in Japan.* University Press of Mississippi, 2015.

Mori, Naoko. "Manga hyôgen no shiten kara mita yaoi." *Eureka* 44, no. 15 (2012): 88–94.

Mori, Naoko. *Onna ha poruno wo yomu josei to seiyoku to feminizumu.* Seikyusha, 2010.

Morimoto Hitchcock, Lori. "Trans-cultural Fandom: Desire, Technology and the Transformation of Fan Subjectivities in the Japanese Female Fandom of Hong Kong Stars." *Transformative Works and Culture,* no. 14 (2013). https://doi.org/10.3983/twc.2013.0494

Nouhet-Roseman, Joëlle. *Les mangas pour jeunes filles, figures du sexuel* à *l'adolescence.* Éditions Eres, 2012.

Ôtsuka, Eiji. "Manga ga inanishite bungaku dearoushi bungaku ha ikanishite manga tarienakattaka." *Saburaruchâ bungakuron.* Asahishinbun, 2005.

Palmer-Mehta, Valerie. "A Superhero for Gays?: Gay Masculinity and Green Lantern." *Journal of American Culture* 28, no. 4 (December 2005): 390–404.

Risner, Jonathan. "'Authentic' Latinas/os and queer characters in mainstream and alternative comics." In *Multicultural Comics,* edited by Frederick Luis Aldama and Derek Parker Royal, 39–54. University of Texas Press, 2010.

Saito, Takuya. "Ren'ai kara miru gei dansei no aidentiti: gei manga ni egakareru nayami to shakai." *Kokusai kôhô media kankô gaku journal,* no. 29 (2019): 37–53.

Shugart, Helene. "Reinventing Privilege: The New (Gay) Man in Contemporary Popular Media." *Critical Studies in Media Communication,* no. 20 (2003): 67–91.

Stevie, Suan. "Anime's Performativity: Diversity through Conventionality in a Global Media-Form." *Animation: an interdisciplinary journal* 12, no.1 (2017): 62–79.

Tagame, Gengoroh. *Gei karuchaa no mirai he.* Ele-king books, 2017.

Williams, Linda. "Film Bodies: Gender, Genre, and Excess." *Film Quarterly* 44, no. 4 (Summer 1991): 2–13.

III.

RESILIENCE:
BECOMING QUEER

Chapter 11

RESILIENCE
SECTION INTRODUCTION

ALISON HALSALL AND JONATHAN WARREN

Even in recollecting a pre-Stonewall 1950s New York that was "purely hell"—its stifling, straight homogeneity, its obligatory gay circumspection and discretion, its social stratification, its racism, its apparent scarcity of other Black women that loved women—Audre Lorde writes, "A lot of it was fine, feeling I had the truth and the light and the key":

> There were no mothers, no sisters, no heroes. We had to do it alone, like our sister Amazons, the riders on the loneliest outposts of the kingdom of Dahomey. We, young and Black and fine and gay, sweated out our first heartbreaks with no school or office chums to share that confidence over lunch hour. Just as there were no rings to make tangible the reason for our happy secret smiles, there were no names nor reason given or shared for the tears that messed up the lab reports or the library bills. (1982, 176)

Loneliness weighs on Lorde, but it also impels her to explore and to discover, "sometimes in secret, sometimes in defiance." Though the closet imposes a heavy solitude—what Lorde calls "a greater aloneness"—those "pretty imaginative tough women" who survive it do so wielding the truth and the light and the key (177). They navigate hostile territory, detect and decode the city's ubiquitous and thick queer subtexts—"('Why are those little Black girls always either whispering together or fighting?')" (177)—and find friends, "buddies," "a loose group," "sisterhood," "little pockets that almost touched," "really sisters," "a place to sleep," a "crew," "a community of sorts," inventing a queer world, learning that they are more adept at world-building than those whose relative complacency about the ready-made one prompts them less to think to, to need to, or to try. Around and in addition to same-sex desire, queerness manifests as a panoply of aptitudes and ingenuities, coping tactics and fluencies in coded talk and conduct, affiliations and intersections.

Lorde's "biomythography" is remarkable in part for its notation of the range and value of the benefits of "being young and Black and gay and lonely." Among the inextricable extensions of her queer selfhood:

the capacity to transmute experiences of isolation and ostracism into
   speculations that queerness's seeming rarity implies its great value
   ("Perhaps our strength might lay in our fewness, our rarity") (177);
a liberating detachment from and suspicion of conventionalism and
   tradition;
an aptness and aptitude to question or defy restrictive gender norms;
a propensity to discern queer possibility hidden in plain sight ("we
   were always on the lookout . . . for that telltale flick of the eye, that
   certain otherwise prohibited openness of expression, that definite-
   ness of voice" (180);
an openness to varied, impromptu, and ad hoc kinds of family;
a heightened acuity to intersectional resonances and their limits;
a geographical imagination whereby the city is mapped into various
   gay scenes;
an access to shared queer folk wisdom, gossip, and strategy; and
a less competitive relationship with straight women.

Reflecting on such experiences and benefits of queerness, Lorde obliges us
to remember that just as gay identity is never merely punctual, never just a
moment's self-regard or declarative utterance, gay pride is irreducible to any
"love is love" truism meant merely to acknowledge the adequacy of gayness
relative to straightness. Resilient and exceptional on its own terms, queer selfhood is an ongoing and evolving way of being in the world whereby tactics of
survival verge on and blend into distinct modes of knowing, and orientations
of desire and gender experience correlate to and enrich every other register
of sociality. To be queer is to come out again and again in ways fleeting—the
daring, say, implied in wearing that scarf or those boots, the cunning in discerning the *double entendre* that others miss—and lasting. To feel the electric
circuit that links the former to the latter and that recharges a sense of queer
buoyancy, strength, and specialness is the core of pride. Together and individually, the essays gathered in this section of the *Reader* imagine and attest to the
plenitude of queer becoming, taking up important touchstone ideas about the
expansive registers of LGBTQ+ selfhood within and across LGBTQ+ comics
and their history, to show how representations of particular LGBTQ+ individuals, incidents, and experiences propose features of a recognizably resilient
and protean queerness.

Justin Hall's landmark volume, *No Straight Lines: Four Decades of Queer
Comics*, anthologizes many key comics from North America and around the
world to chart their complex and variegated presentation of queer selfhood.
Hall's title evokes the visuality of queer comics art and its freedom from regi-
mentation or obligation to norms. It also makes us think about the precious

filaments that connect queer comics, their creators, and their readers to one another: a tangle of influences and associations and a rhizomatic sprawl. Cataloguing and showcasing exemplary aesthetic, historical, and representational comics, Hall acknowledges a mutual queer recognizability without needing to assert fixed lineage or straight lines between and among a treasure house of comics that evoke the lively multiplicity of queer lives like his own fantastically various one: champion of queer comics, multiple award-winning comics creator, university professor, porn star, art curator, Fulbright scholar . . . Hall's conversation with Hillary Chute, included here along with a selection of images that Hall generously allowed us to reproduce, describes the evolution of his 2012 anthology out of the world's first museum show of LGBTQ+ comics held at the Cartoon Art Museum in San Francisco in 2006, including its inspiration for a feature-length documentary, directed and produced by Peabody Award-winning and Emmy-nominated filmmaker Vivian Kleiman. Cultivating and catalyzing the field of queer comics, Hall stands out as much for his own creations as for celebrating and drawing attention to other queer artists' achievements, demonstrating the value of extended family building and the satisfaction and ongoing discovery of LGBTQ+ recognition as core features of queer life.

Sheena Howard takes us to the pages of *BLK* magazine, an American monthly that was published from 1988 to 1994 and their many single-panel comics visualizing African American lesbians. Mingling investigative journalism, news coverage, and profiles of major contemporary Black LGBTQ+ figures—including Audre Lorde, Marlon Riggs, Ivy Young, Dr. Marjorie Hill, RuPaul—*BLK* magazine spoke to a Black LGBTQ+ readership and, in its comics, addressed what Howard describes as a void in comics representation of Black lesbians with comics that depict characters' queerness in dating and flirtation, in experiences of lesbian pregnancy, in activism, in light of safe-sex practices, and with reference to the other queer people. *BLK* magazine's comics affirm their characters' lesbian selfhood through specific engagements with their 1980s and 1990s contexts to help show that queerness inheres in everyday registers of social interaction: from familiarity, alienation, or interest to perturbation or bemusement.

Similarly, Matthew Cheney considers how Howard Cruse's *Wendel* allows the queer humanity of that strip's characters to emerge via their different responses to shared experiences of gay alienation. Visualizing characters' variations in outlook, privilege, race, age, physicality, and self-esteem draws them together as queer friends who can relate to one another's experiences of precarity and know the solace and exhilaration of trying to. Understanding and channeling the restorative, edifying, and unifying power that comes from seeing aspects of oneself in others' experiences of difference, oppression, and self-affirmation are central to Cruse's magisterial, long-form comic *Stuck Rubber Baby* (1995), the first queer graphic novel to be published by a mainstream press. A meticulously crafted story of Toland Polk's gay coming of age and coming out in the Jim Crow-era American south, Cruse's comic correlates his white protagonist's conflicted awakening to his homosexuality with his contemporaneous experiences and evolving but plausibly partial comprehension of Alabama's racist turmoil and its resistance. Narrated retrospectively and interrupted occasionally by a husband whose presence helps to signal his own queer future, Toland connects the idea of overcoming homophobia with the civil rights history of overcoming racial violence and injustice. Initially desperate to "cure" himself of his homosexuality, Toland's "will" to be straight and his "not very political" disposition (Howard 2020, 29) are transformed by his witnessing of and adjacency to racist injustice and violence that such white aloofness helps to sustain. "It could've been me" (Cruse 2020, 193), Toland tells the grieving crowd at the funeral for his friend, Sammy Noone who was hanged by the Ku Klux Klan for integrationist and queer ideals that Toland had come to share. Seeing himself in Sammy allows Toland to see himself anew and as though for the first time. His political consciousness emerges in tandem with his ability to understand himself in relation to experiences of racialized victimization and survival. Toland sheds his early self-loathing by virtue of an invigorated political engagement that, for Cruse, is one of the most salient features of his protagonist's queerness. At the novel's climax, it buoys him up, providing serenity and a sense of deep empowerment, accepting himself as a gay man by knowing to discover support, love, and acceptance in a life of social activism.

The Canadian LGBTQ+ comics scene features perspectives from many different communities—Cherokee and Two-Spirited; Japanese Canadian and queer-questioning; Hindu, transgender, and nonbinary—as Alison Halsall's chapter explores, showcasing the personal experiences of intersectional insight and agency that queer characters encounter. The particular visual formats of Daniel Heath Justice's comics parable, Vivek Shraya's comic *Death Threat* (illustrated by Ness Lee), and Mariko and Jillian Tamaki's young adult graphic novel, *Skim*, consider queerness as an aspect of gender identity, race or ethnicity, and spirituality. Tongva illustrator, Weshoyot Alvitre's rainbow palette colors Justice's parable about two Two-Spirited men finding one another and using their "defiant song" (Justice 2017, n.p.) to spread "loving beauty too long denied" (n.p.) to transform their world through vibrant colors that convey a joyous message. Likewise, Ness Lee's illustrations transform Vivek Shraya's tale of transphobic cyber-hate into images of vivid strength to diminish hatred through humor and aestheticism. In the Tamakis' *Skim*, the teenaged, Japanese Canadian protagonist's resilience in the face of racial prejudice dovetails with her feelings of queerness that begin to stir yet remain unspecified except as a corollary to her general fortitude. As Ramzi Fawaz reminds us, *Skim's* queerness inheres as a definitive, self-sustaining resource in just such registers. It is in the breaking of inter-generational taboos, in the surprising intimacy and recognition between a student and her loving mentor, in Kim's disinterest in almost all identity categories (see page 103). In these Canadian LGBTQ+ comics, queerness is at work at the interstices of other modes of accounting for selfhood, as their brightening and invigorating feature.

Comics for younger readers are taking up such ideas about queer selfhood more and more, as we see in graphic novels as diverse as Hubert and Marie Caillou's *Adrian and the Tree of Secrets* (2013), Melanie Gillman's *As the Crow Flies* (2017), and L. Nichols's *Flocks* (2018). Recently, Ari North's *Always Human* (2020), Tee Franklin's *Bingo Love* (2018), and Hope Larson and Brittney Williams's *Goldie Vance* (2016–) series imagine "coming out" less as a singular event or punctual challenge and more as a continuous exploration of the exhilaration and empowerment that a young person can feel in discovering and accepting that they are queer. Tee Franklin's charming story about two young Black women who fall in love at a bingo game in the 1960s chronicles the transformations in same-sex life and politics that have come to safeguard queer lives. While religion, social expectation, and homophobia kept Mari McCray and Hazel Johnson apart as young people, as grandmothers they reconnect and choose love over convention after fifty years spent apart, enjoying a new social mobility that the comic underscores with the dynamism of its visual celebration of their joy, fulfillment, pride, and resilience. Likewise, as Lara Hedberg and Rebecca Hutton explore in their chapter about *Goldie Vance*, that young adult comic series about the adventures of a sixteen-year-old queer, Black feminist who dreams of being a detective redeploys genre tropes and historical contexts from its civil rights- and Cold War-era setting to propose a historically plausible, self-possessed and self-determined, intersectional queer girl detective. Recent LGBTQ+ comics like these move beyond merely normalizing queerness and coming out, simply to celebrate those aspects of queerness that Audre Lorde long ago found so fine. So, detection is an overdetermined trope in *Goldie Vance*; Larson and Williams's hero uses it to solve mysteries and her stories play up the fun that queerness affords us to detect our world's sexual coding and to crack it. Vance's queer resilience gives her special aptitudes to solve crimes and produces a compelling distinctness about her, Black and fine and gay, for the next generation of young queer readers to admire and emulate. Talk about the truth, the light, and the key!

Reproductions of artwork by Alison Bechdel appear at the end of this section with her generous permission.

Works Cited

Cruse, Howard. *Stuck Rubber Baby: 25th Anniversary Edition*. First Second, 2020.

Franklin, Tee. *Bingo Love*. Art by Jenn St-Onge. Image Comics, 2018.

Gillman, Melanie. *As the Crow Flies*. Iron Circus Comics, 2017.

Hall, Justin, ed. *No Straight Lines: Four Decades of Queer Comics*. Fantagraphics, 2012, 2015.

Hubert and Marie Caillou. *Adrian and the Tree of Secrets*. Arsenal Pulp Press, 2013.

Justice, Daniel Heath, and Weshoyot Alvitre. "The Boys Who Became the Hummingbirds." In *Moonshot: The Indigenous Comics Collection*, vol. 2, edited by Hope Nicholson, n.p. Alternate History Comics, 2017.

Larson, Hope, Brittany Williams, and Sarah Stern. *Goldie Vance*, vol. 1. Boom! Box, 2016.

Lorde, Audre. *Zami: A New Spelling of My Name*. Persephone Press, 1982.

Nichols, L. *Flocks*. Secret Acres, 2018.

North, Ari. *Always Human*. Yellow Jacket, 2020.

Chapter 12

CRITICS AND CREATORS
THE LGBTQ+ COMICS ECOSYSTEM

HILLARY CHUTE IN CONVERSATION WITH JUSTIN HALL

The cartoonist, professor, and editor Justin Hall (born in 1971) has spent a large part of his career shining a spotlight on other creators—namely, on queer cartoonists working from the 1960s to the present tense, a period during which the very notion of a "queer cartoonist" or the field of "queer comics" has developed meaningfully. His 2012 anthology *No Straight Lines: Four Decades of Queer Comics* (Fantagraphics), a deeply significant and popular volume, offered readers a vibrant history of queer comics. *No Straight Lines*, which won a Lambda Literary Award, sold out its first print run; its success demonstrates the hunger and excitement around contemplating queer comics as a rich and multifaceted body of work over time. The book, which opens with a survey essay by Hall, presents the work of eighty-six different artists. It gives readers a cultural and aesthetic trajectory for queer comics where none had previously existed, between covers, with the same breadth (although earlier titles such as *Gay Comics*, the 1989 collection edited by Robert Triptow, and *Dyke Strippers: Lesbian Cartoonists A to Z*, the 1995 collection edited by Roz Warren, charted vital queer work).

A fascinating creator and cultural figure in his own right, Hall has shaped a sense of the possible in comics, queer communities, and elsewhere. Hall attended the State University of New York at Purchase, where he—like many cartoonists for whom cartooning was not an option—majored in printmaking. When he was younger, he told me, he "didn't know a single other cartoonist," but he eventually won funding—a famed Xeric Grant to support self-publishing—to produce a work about the Dead Sea Scrolls, *A Sacred Text*, inspired by his travels in Israel (he worked on the story while in West Jerusalem). A travel fanatic who counts *True Travel Tales* among his other early comics, Hall has been to over seventy countries.

Hall has racked up numerous "firsts" through persistent, on-the-ground dedication to the field, and enjoys the sense of game-changing those accomplishments bring: he was, for example, the first Fulbright Scholar of comics, in 2016, for the project "Comics in the Czech Republic," during which time he taught as a member of the Faculty of Arts at Masaryk University in Brno. In his ongoing day job, he helped to start the MFA program in Comics at the California College of the Arts, where he is currently Associate Professor of Comics. Crucially, Hall was responsible for the first queer comics programming at the widely admired and important Alternative Press Expo (APE), a vital cultural venue for up-and-coming independent cartoonists, and organized twelve years of panels there, building a sense of community around the creation and analysis of queer comics (his panels, among many other participants, included Alison Bechdel and a young Erica Moen).

Perhaps most importantly for the focus of this interview, Hall curated the world's first museum show of LGBTQ+ comics at the Cartoon Art Museum in San Francisco, where he lives, in 2006 (with the museum's Andrew Farago). "No Straight Lines: Queer Culture and the Comics" became the seed for what would eventually be the award-winning *No Straight Lines* anthology. Hall recognized his own energy for presenting—and the ongoing need to showcase—histories of queer comics across different media. (He also went on to co-curate the exhibit "Superqueeroes" at the Schwules Museum in Berlin in 2016, the largest such show of queer comics on record.)

Hall has created erotic comics, as in the collaborative series *Hard to Swallow*, with Dave Davenport, and he has also himself worked in porn (along the "firsts" line, at least for me, he is the only professor and working cartoonist I know who can claim a previous career in porn). In his comics, he explained in our interview, he was trying to create porn that was "sexy *and* good." Hall routinely brings in stacks of DIY porn to show his comics students, trying to inspire them to make the kind of content they want to see. His many other comics include *Glamazonia: The Uncanny Super-Tranny*, and he sits on the board of the nonprofits PRISM Comics, which supports LGBTQ+ comics, and Siewphewyeung (Our Books), which supports Cambodian literature including comics.

Currently Hall is a producer of *No Straight Lines: the Rise of Queer Comics*, the feature-length documentary based on his book. Directed by Vivian Kleiman, the film, now nearing completion, focuses on the stories behind some of the book's most celebrated artists, including Alison Bechdel, Jennifer Camper, Rupert Kinnard, Mary Wings, and Howard Cruse, who died in November 2019. Hall was the last person to publish Cruse, whom he calls the "godfather" of queer comics in our interview. I first met Justin in the context of the film, for which I am an advisor, in San Francisco in 2018 (although earlier, in 2016, I had seen him speak on a panel at the San Diego Comic-Con, where his insight, warmth, and charisma left a lasting impression). In one of my favorite stories from our interview that illustrates both his conviviality and his charmingly nerdy comics knowledge, Justin recalled, in his early days in San Francisco, recognizing an esoteric Spidey tracer tattoo on the barista serving him tea at Peet's in the Castro. (He himself has a tattoo of Winsor's McCay's Little Nemo character.) The two are now longtime friends. The evening after we met, he attended a public conversation I conducted with underground comics legend Aline Kominsky-Crumb at Green Apple Books, where he presented us both with homemade cookies. He's that kind of guy.

I first reached Hall over the phone before he was, characteristically, about to jet off for a month to Denmark for a residency at the Animation Workshop (TAW). I followed up with him via email while he was in Madrid to touch base about his thoughts about Cruse's legacy. Hall is currently working on a long graphic novel, tentatively titled *Castle and Creek*, which takes place in his own San Francisco neighborhood, the Mission. It is an ambitious work, one for which he told me, "it will either be great, or I'll faceplant." He wrote me from Madrid: "The graphic novel was chugging along until I left (I'm drawing a scene now where the Sisters of Perpetual Indulgence, an order of drag nuns that began in San Francisco during the AIDS crisis, are sainting one of my characters on his deathbed—I did research on their actual ceremonies and if I pull it off right the scene will be tear-jerking but also with the sense of campy surreality that San Francisco brings to everything)."

Hillary Chute: What was your angle with *No Straight Lines*?

Justin Hall: I was worried that as the queer bookstores were falling apart and the queer distributors and publishers were folding and all of that infrastructure was falling apart—that so much of the queer comics material was going to get lost forever. And that's what I was interested in for *No Straight Lines*, and what I was focusing on. My *raison d'être* for the book: I don't want to let this material go away.

HC: So then how does that translate? There are three iterations, it seems like: there's the museum show, there's the book, and there's the film. Does that project manifest differently in the different forms that this has taken or will take?

JH: It's not like I intended from the very beginning to have a branded project going across all these different media, but it wound up that way . . . and it's interesting to think of how it *does* change from form to form.

So, the museum show [2006's "No Straight Lines: Queer Culture and the Comics"] I did with the S.F. Cartoon Art Museum: it was important to get that work up on the walls. Honestly, at that point I should have known more than I did, and looking back at that show, I had some gaps here and there that I could have filled. There's always more to know, right? I went and then helped curate the Schwules Museum in Berlin that did the largest show on queer comics, three years ago. I went out and curated that show with a couple of other German curators. That was nice, because it was a little bit of a vindication—I was able to go back, and I thought, some of the things that were missing from the original show, I can shore that stuff up now.

Figure 12.1. Cover of *No Straight Lines: Four Decades of Queer Comics*, edited by Justin Hall. Art by Maurice Vellekoop. Fantagraphics, 2015.

But then the book was really wonderful, because it allowed space to be much more comprehensive . . . and to write that introductory essay, which, as you know, is a pretty condensed little piece about the history of this material. That was really important for me to do, because I needed to get a timeline of this stuff out there that other scholars could have. Because as I was putting it together, I realized, "My God, there's more here than I even expected." I knew this was going to be a really rich world, but it's even richer than I expected. This book can't be comprehensive, because no book could be.

HC: But it can be galvanizing . . . I think it's so great: it can give people the seeds to pursue other creators, or to pursue a creator in more detail.

JH: Yes, and that's what was really clear by the end of putting the book together: this is what the book is *for*. It's to galvanize interest in this world, and then create a kind of structural foundation to look at it, so that other scholars and creators can come to this collection and to this timeline that I've created in the essay. They don't have to agree with everything, but at least they have a starting place to get into it.

HC: You were describing the early 2000s as sort of anemic [for queer comics]. And then why do you think in 2012, people were ready? In a way they might not have been before. There were all of these classics that were being reissued around that time, like the David Wojnarowicz book [*7 Miles a Second*], and the Samuel Delany book [*Bread & Wine: An Erotic Tale of New York*] . . .

JH: But honestly, all that stuff happens after, right after *No Straight Lines*.

HC: Right, it was like a "moment" happening. . . . You can see the ripple effect. But why do you think *then* in particular? What had happened?

JH: Well, it had been a few years since *Fun Home*. *Fun Home* comes out middle of 2006 and it grows, it affects . . . I was actually an Ignatz judge that year as well, for the Ignatz Awards in SPX [the Small Press Expo]. The publisher hadn't sent us *Fun Home* and no one knew about it in the comics world, that it even existed, because Alison [Bechdel] was still a complete unknown in the comics world. I knew this book had come out and was the best thing since sliced bread, so I nominated it . . . and it didn't win. No one had read it. No one knew who she was. But then a few years later, oddly enough, she goes from this "queer comics" tiny little world, and she jumps, she leapfrogs the rest of the comics world and she dives into the mainstream. She takes the attention of the mainstream world, of the book world, and then the comics world catches up to that.

By the time 2012 rolled around: all of that was already firmly established. People were ready. I had Alison as a big crossover name in the book, and so I think that was part of it—the idea that, hey, you know, this Alison Bechdel you know and love did not come out of nowhere. She came out of an entire *ecosystem* of other great comics, and you all need to know about this system. It's time for you to remove your blinders and embrace it.

HC: I promise I won't ask you about specific people [covered in the show, book, and film], because that would just take too long. But what about Howard Cruse, who seems like the other "crossover" figure in the book?

JH: So Howard is the godfather of queer comics and unbelievably important in so many ways. He was the creator and the first editor of the *Gay Comix* anthology series, which began in 1980 and was where so many early queer cartoonists cut their teeth. It was the backbone of the queer comics scene. He also created the seminal gay comic strip *Wendel* for the *Advocate* magazine, which was really the first time the intimate life of a gay couple had been serialized in comics. And of course, if I were going to nominate any book for the Great American Graphic Novel, it would be *Stuck Rubber Baby*. It's such an American classic, but it came out ten years too soon . . . in the sense that it came out in 1995, the world wasn't ready for it the way that the world was ready for *Fun Home* in 2006.

HC: I remember when that book first came out: it was a huge big deal to me. That was after *Maus*. The second volume of *Maus* comes out in '91, so there was a little bit of a context for a serious book-length thing, but it was before there was so much momentum around the scene, so it was always alone on a bookshelf with a couple other titles, for awhile.

JH: And it went through several different publishers and was out of print half the time.

HC: Right, which just seems *ridiculous*.

JH: And also, it was never printed in the way that it should have been. Those original pages—I actually own a couple of the original pages because I'm obsessed with the work—and they are *monumental*, they are massive. I don't have dimensions on them right now, but they're like full wingspan.

HC: It makes sense now, because of the almost pointillist detail, but I didn't know that the originals were so big.

JH: He had to work that big, because as you said he was doing all that pointillism and crosshatching by hand, and of course they're printed way smaller than they should be.

HC: Yes, it's not a huge book, given the range of sizes of graphic novels, even.

JH: First Second Books has just picked up the rights to publish it, and I am crossing my fingers that they are going to do an oversized edition, because that's what it needs. The closest one to it is actually the German language publication, which is another 25 percent bigger than the page size of the largest American edition. And it's *beautiful*. But the original, it took him five days a page, and he was working nine-hour days. The work is monumental and it was never treated right. I mean, it got some awards . . .

HC: . . . it got respect . . .

JH: . . . but it didn't have the kind of bomb-shell impact that *Fun Home* did and that it should have had. And he maxed out those credit cards and went bankrupt.

HC: I was on a panel in New York with him and Alison [Bechdel] a few years ago, at MoCA. I wish that more people had a sense of how important that book is.

JH: *Fun Home* probably wouldn't have happened without *Stuck Rubber Baby*—

HC: As Bechdel says, all the time. She gives credit where credit is due.

You said something really interesting: I think it might be on the Wikipedia page for *No Straight Lines*, where you were talking about how you selected work for the book, and you said there were three different criteria, in decreasing order of importance, and representation was the last one, the third one. I was actually really excited, because it's such an interesting comment, and I feel like we're in such a tricky moment right now—like literally, right now—around questions of representation. And I just wanted to ask you if you remember that quote, if you can remember what you meant to talk about.

JH: I remember the three categories I had: the first one is artistic merit, the second is historical merit, and the third one is representational merit. At the time, in 2012, it felt almost edgy to add representational merit to it [*laughter*]. And now it feels like, wow, you really put representation at the bottom of the list . . . ?—but I would still do it the same way for the purposes of that collection, because I wanted the book to stand out, to grab attention, as a collection of *good work*. Otherwise it doesn't matter how important it is historically and representationally: it wouldn't have a lasting power if it wasn't good work.

It's a history book, first and foremost. But representation has to be part of that, because history is colored by that, entirely. But you're right, things have changed quite a bit. The national conversation around it has certainly changed.

HC: I like the comment so much. I actually didn't know what year you had said it. But it's a tricky thing because I feel like capital I-Identity has become a much more valued part of discourse even than it was a few years ago. But I feel like recognizing the aesthetic value of work can be a political act, too. Of at least as much value as publishing something because of the body or desires or identity of the creators.

JH: Yes, it's really wonderful when all those things line up really well. Sometimes they do, which is lovely, but not always. I run into it constantly as a professor, teaching comics history. It's a survey course of comics history, so there is no way that I can cover all the things that should be covered. And so then I have to figure out my own canon, as there isn't an established canon so much with comics. The field is still pretty open. So I'm still figuring out what I want to show my students, and over the years I've actually gotten smarter, I think, about representation. For example, my lectures on American comic strips, which were an incredibly vibrant artform at the beginning of the 1900s and then became increasingly less so, and more and more anemic. But there was so much incredible work being done back then. There was that [2005] show, *Masters of American Comics*, and there wasn't a single woman creator there. And that's not acceptable on a basic level, and it's also not historically accurate. Because then there's Trina Robbins's response to it: which was *Women and the Comics* [cowritten with Catherine Yronwode]. Because people would say,

"Where are they? Where are the great women creators?" Well, they got erased from history. They were in fact there, but they got erased from history. Rose O'Neill, creator of the Kewpie doll [the most widely known cartoon character before Mickey Mouse]?

HC: And Trina has written a lot on her [including in *Pretty in Ink: North American Women Cartoonists, 1896–2013*].

JH: She was the highest paid woman artist *in the world* at the time. She was considered the queen of Bohemia. She created the characters that created the first mass-produced toy line in those days. If that's not historically important. . . . And she was like Rodin, a real artistic figure. [She learned sculpture at the hand of Auguste Rodin and had several exhibitions of sculptures and paintings in Paris and the United States.] She had the artistic merit, she had the historical merit, and she was denied the show basically because she was a woman. She got erased from the history. So, using representation as a galvanizing force to do better historiography, I think leads to better artistic and historical merit.

HC: I mean, it's something that I encounter in my teaching with comics all the time, too. And I feel like I've learned from my students how important it is. Not that I didn't think it was important before, but when you're teaching comics, you know, there are huge swaths of that history where it's largely white men.

JH: I had a student recently; I was going into the beginning of comics and talking about [Rodolphe] Töpffer and all this stuff, and the person was like, "Well, why aren't we starting with people of color?" And I'm like, "I don't know what to tell you. It started in . . ."

HC: . . . it started in Switzerland in the 1830s! Some things you just can't change.

JH: But there are so many ways one can shed light on diversity. One of the things I talk about is how Jack Kirby was actually Jewish, and that was a huge part of his identity and influences his work. So I think even the way we talk about "white men" is colored now in interesting ways by the issue of representation. Vaughn Bode was experimenting with female hormones and even though he was doing this really misogynistic underground comics work, he might very well have been a closeted trans* woman. So that's interesting. And that wouldn't have come up, I think, until . . . I mean, that's a more modern discussion about his work.

HC: And that's a really great point about the way that as an educator you can call attention to the way these creators were addressing or dealing with identity, and it doesn't have to simply be representation on a syllabus; you can open up the issues of identity in other ways.

JH: What they're producing, how their own identities are working . . . our markers have changed historically, so back in the day being Jewish was not necessarily considered "white."

HC: Right, it's a totally historical phenomenon when that shifted.

JH: And what about all those early cartoonists who then had to hide their Jewish identity—Stan Lee was born Stanley Lieber, Jack Kirby was born Jacob Kurtzburg—so I think representation then colors all sorts of conversations. And then the fact that Jack Kirby, as a Jewish American man, creates the Black Panther as the first major Black superhero is really interesting. But it is incumbent upon us to dig. I do like to find gems. I think it is important for me to find and then point out gems of representational merit that often stay hidden. For example, Henry [Yoshitaka] Kiyama created in the Japanese American newspapers in San Francisco what I would say is the first real memoir graphic novel, with *The Four Immigrants Manga* series [1931].

HC: Yes, that book is so interesting.

JH: And that was completely forgotten by history until Frederik Schodt discovered these strips in the San Francisco library. So it's incumbent upon us as historians and scholars to do the digging, to try to find the gems that were really hidden because of sexism and racism and homophobia—all the institutional, societal problems that can hide this stuff from us. I will also say, though, in terms of representational merit, there are these moments . . . I think of Diane DiMassa . . . *Hothead Paisan* [1991–96] is amazing. It's kind of crappy comics, but it's amazing.

HC: It's like Aline Kominsky-Crumb's work . . .

JH: I think Aline's work is more aesthetically interesting to me, it's lusher. But it doesn't matter with Diane's work, it's so of the moment and it expresses this angry queer id that's just like—oh my God, it's galvanizing and powerful. And it just makes you realize that artistic profundity doesn't necessarily correlate nicely to the craft.

HC: And it's so funny, too.

You spoke about uncovering, and teaching, the "gems" in comics that wide audiences may not know about—what, for you, are the "gems" of queer erotic comics?

JH: Jon Macy's *Teleny and Camille* is a graphic novel adaptation of what's considered the first gay novel, created in secret by Oscar Wilde and his circle of friends. Each man would write a chapter and then bring the manuscript to a bookseller who would keep it hidden, since gay material was illegal. The next anonymous author would then tell the bookseller a codeword, be given the manuscript, and then add his own chapter to it. Macy adapted the book and then created his own original chapter at the end. In this way, he both paid homage to the making of the novel and also spun a positive, celebratory ending to what was an erotic tragedy in its original form.

Colleen Coover's *Small Favors* was my favorite lesbian porn comic and luckily it's been recently collected in a beautiful book by Oni Press. It's a fairly goofy premise, that a sex-crazed young woman is assigned a tiny magical woman as her chaperone of sorts to stop her from masturbating so much. This just results in the two having lots of fun, hot sex. Coover is a master illustrator and visual storyteller and she has fun with some meta cartooning as well, like when one of the characters has sex with her own word balloons.

Brad Rader's *Harry and Dickless Tom* is absolutely fascinating. Rader was an illustrator for DC, and each chapter of this book is an homage to various comics greats, from Hergé to Milton Caniff. It tells the story of a homophobic trucker who wakes up one morning with a vagina, which is both a gift and a lesson from the Goddess. What follows next is a hallucinatory road trip full of sweaty, transformative sex that puts gender theory through a blender.

I have so many more examples! Gengoroh Tagame, Jiraiya, Nazario, Belasco. . . . Gay cis men have dominated the world of queer erotic comics, but we're seeing the emergence of more women, trans* and nonbinary folks, bisexuals, and cartoonists of color making this sort of work on the web and in print, all of which is tremendously exciting.

HC: Do you ever teach erotic comics?

JH: Every semester at some point, I bring in a big stack of erotic comics and slam them on the table, telling the students that they should, at some point in their careers, make pornography. That sex and desire represent one of the great mysteries and profundities of the human experience and we should be making exciting and courageous art about it. Especially if we're a woman, a queer person, a person of color, we should be making our own porn; don't let someone else colonize your sexual space! Make good, authentic erotica, and the world will be a better place for it.

I'm lucky I teach comics at the California College of the Arts . . . I can get away with a lot without getting fired! I was even the faculty advisor for the Sex Worker Student Union on campus, which I believe is the only sex worker student group ever in the country, if not the world.

HC: What's it like discussing porn/erotica in the classroom?

JH: Usually their jaws hit the floor when they hear their professor telling them to draw dirty comics! But they hear me, we have good conversations about it, and then there are even a few who take up the challenge. But I've also taught comics to Buddhist monks in Thailand and I never brought up erotic comics there. . . . So, you have to know your audience!

The majority of alternative comics have become increasingly less sexual since the days of the underground comix. My students now usually omit romantic and sexual plots altogether in their stories; they're seen, I think, as hokey and old-fashioned, as well as a minefield of gender and sexual politics that's just easier to avoid. The exception is usually the LGBTQ+ students. Not surprising, I suppose, since the best and most interesting erotica done in comics

Figure 12.2. Cover of *Hard to Swallow*, no. 4, edited by Justin Hall and Dave Davenport. (Northwest Press, 2016).

now is hands-down the queer stuff. It still feels revolutionary and urgent, as opposed to cliché and problematic.

This sort of sucks for straight comics, to be honest, and I hope straight creators get their erotic groove back. Or rather, push it forward into new, less creepy territories than those explored by the early underground cartoonists. I'm totally into comics like *Junqueland*, which is a collaboration between a woman and a man that gives equal weight to female desire and agency and has a celebratory feel to it.

HC: Tell me about your experience when you started drawing erotic comics—when was it, how did it happen, how did it feel to you, what was the goal for you?

JH: I had been making a series called *True Travel Tales* when my friend Dave Davenport came to me with the idea of doing *Hard to Swallow* in around 2006.

Figure 12.3. "Fluid," in *Hard to Swallow* no. 3, edited by Justin Hall and Dave Davenport. (Marginalized Publications/ All Thumbs Press, 2006), 4.

I hadn't intended to do erotica, to be honest, but I really wanted to work with Dave so I decided to take the leap. We each did half the comic, à la [Jaime and Gilbert Hernandez's] *Love and Rockets*. We also brought in guest artists with each issue, which was really fun to curate.

So much of the stuff we were seeing was boring. It was too safe and didn't dig enough into deeper concerns around sex and desire. I wanted to bring some of the memoir and biographical vibe from *True Travel Tales* over into stories about sex, especially since I had started making porn films around the same time and wanted to tell stories about the real sex lives of people who had public sexual personae.

One of the short pieces I'm most proud of, called "Fluid," tells the story of a femme dyke I met at a porn industry party who used to write gay male porn reviews under a male pseudonym. She told me she used to strap her sizable tits down and put on a hoodie and suck guys off in the back of the Powerhouse, a gay cruise bar here in San Francisco. Even though she's a dyke, she was turned on by the raw sexuality of the place. And once one of the guys she was blowing realized she was a woman, but instead of reacting badly he became even more turned on because of the transgressive nature of having a woman suck him off in a gay bar. It just makes you realize how remarkably expansive and fluid sexuality actually is! I wanted to make a comic that was sexy and you could jerk off to, but that was also challenging and interesting to read.

I really grew as a cartoonist by doing porn comics. Before I made them, I was too stuck in the hyper-restrained indie comics aesthetic of the time. *Hard to Swallow* forced me to break open my cartooning style with tilted panels, decompressed storytelling, dramatic close-ups, and splash pages. No one wants restraint in their porn comics!

HC: How has your own experience working in porn influenced how you draw erotic comics?

JH: Well, as I said, I started doing both around the same time, so my erotic comics were certainly influenced by my experiences in porn. I did at least one autobio story about being on a porn set, called "Porn Star: Long Time Cumming," about trying to get the cum shot at the end of almost eight hours of filming (yup, that's how long it can take to film a twenty-minute scene for the big companies!) I kept going limp and thinking about the bowl of phở that I was going to eat after I was done but had to keep bringing my mind back to the task on hand. Again, I wanted a story that was hot but also thought provoking and even funny. I also did a bunch of biographical stories about the sex lives of some of the porn stars and escorts I worked with.

And now, I'm working on a big graphic novel that takes place in the National Guard Armory [in San Francisco] where I filmed with Kink.com when they

Figure 12.4. Page from *Castle & Creek*, Justin Hall (unpublished).

owned it. The novel takes place in the porn industry of the mid-to-late aughts, so I guess I'm still mining that part of my life for material.

HC: How is erotic/pornographic drawing different for the reader/viewer than erotic/pornographic film or photography?

JH: There are a few things that comics and illustration do differently than film and photography, specifically in regard to pornographic content. First, they have different relationships to their subjects. Film presupposes a subject in front of the camera, creating a voyeuristic dynamic as opposed to one solely

Figure 12.5. Page from *Castle & Creek*, Justin Hall. (unpublished).

about the art. In other words, a comics reader thinks "that drawing is hot" as opposed to "that model is hot."

This allows for more flexibility in terms of erotic appreciation. For example, as a gay man I'm almost never turned on by women-on-women film porn, but I find *Small Favors* incredibly hot. I love seeing how Coover loves viewing women and am turned on by her desire for them. It's Coover's loving linework, compositions, and character designs that are the real turn-on for me and allow me to empathize with her sexual desire.

There are also differences between film and comics in how we engage with them as consumers. At least in this day and age, there's this assumption that to watch porn is to want to get off. There is less of that with reading comics. They also read them for titillation, for expanding their erotic imaginations, and perhaps to use later as inspiration for masturbation or partnered sex. This allows cartoonists to include other elements in their work. We see humor, politics, social commentary, etc., showing up in erotic comics that filmmakers would be worried would take the viewer out of the masturbatory experience. You only have to take a look at comics like *Lost Girls* and *I Want to Be Your Dog* to see that extra level of complexity at play.

An illustrator and cartoonist can also do things beyond the capacity of porn photographers and filmmakers. We can draw unrealistic and fantastical things! Centaurs, giants, mermaids, tentacles.... We can draw penises the size of arms and impossibly bouncy tits. Even more interesting, to my mind, we can draw unrealistic viewpoints. Gengoroh Tagame and the other erotic mangaka are the masters of this. He will often draw a penis ejaculating in a butt or throat as seen from within, for example, or illustrate the full figure of a bottom getting fucked by removing the top from the picture, or drawing the scene from below the floor looking up. In other words, he is drawing a realistic scene and realistic bodies but from angles and perspectives impossible for a camera.

Finally, I would say that the nature of comics itself, which uses panel transitions to move the reader through space and time, is a more interactive and fertile sort of space for erotica than what occurs in film. When there's a cut in a porn film from one position to another or one angle to another, the viewer isn't really encouraged to engage with that. In comics, however, the gutter is precisely where the reader injects their own erotic imagination. A good porn comic becomes a dance between the erotic imaginations of the reader and the creator in a more dynamic way than occurs in film.

I have more thoughts, but I could ramble forever!

HC: What do you think is one of the most exciting things that we're seeing right now with queer comics?

JH: Well, I'm kind of blown away by how queer comics are getting in general. I think of this last Ignatz Awards, for example. *No Straight Lines* didn't even get a nomination for an Ignatz [in 2012]. And the whole time I knew that my work was never going to be allowed up on the stage in that same way. Like, it was just too queer. But now, this last Ignatz round was swept by queer books. Absolutely swept.

HC: Do you feel disappointed or psyched?

JH: So, I mean, absolutely psyched and so excited, and I think it's wonderful. But there's a little piece of me that's like, goddamnit [*laughter*] . . . You know, I remember when *No Straight Lines* was up for an Eisner Award, and I went to

Figure 12.6. "Full Moon," in *Theater of Terror: Revenge of the Queers!*, edited by Justin Hall and William O. Tyler (Northwest Press, 2019), 1.

San Diego Comic-Con. Neil Gaiman and some other people were up on stage, and it felt like the whole night, for some reason, was gay jokes. And Neil Gaiman and some other guy kissed on stage . . . but my book was the only fucking book that was actually queer that was up for anything, and it got passed over for an anthology—a crappy anthology—that had Star Wars in it.

HC: That sounds legitimately depressing.

JH: And of course it's not Neil Gaiman's fault, but the sense of like, oh my God, you just did "gay face" for two hours, and making gay jokes, and then the one queer book is not given anything. When I'm feeling petty . . .

HC: I don't think that's petty. I feel like that makes legible a dynamic that happens a lot. The artificial references get a lot of play.

JH: I am thrilled that that dynamic has lessened, or is not happening in really the same way anymore.

HC: Hey, you took one for the team!

JH: I like being someone who is doing the first of things. A lot of us kind of *like* that position of being out there first and getting more flack than we probably should and, you know, five years down the road they won't be getting the same weird shit thrown at them. I don't know, someone's got to do it.

HC: It's sort of like you have said to me about porn: if you want something to exist and you don't see it, you can't complain about it unless you try to make it exist!

JH: Absolutely. But I do hope—in the same way when I was at the very beginning of my [career] making comics, I was not as cognizant as I should have been . . . I mean, it took me a couple of years to realize that, "Oh my God, there's all this amazing queer content that was created by these pioneers that has changed the world," in a way that enabled me to tell my stories in an easier way. I do hope that that continues: that new queer cartoonists continue expressing themselves, and continue to look back and pay homage to the pioneers . . . to the Howard Cruses and the Mary Wings, and Trina Robbins, who made all this stuff possible.

HC: Well, I think the *No Straight Lines* film will also be a platform to help people do that. It is a way of archiving their voices and lives.

JH: I want these people on film. While we have these people.

• • •

Addendum: Howard Cruse died shortly after Hall and I recorded this interview. Hall wrote to me:

Howard Cruse died on November 26, 2019, from cancer, which has been completely devastating for so many of us. I was actually the last person to publish him—he did a pinup for an anthology of queer horror comics I put together called *Theater of Terror: Revenge of the Queers*.

I feel so lucky we got to film him for the *No Straight Lines* documentary. He's really the backbone of the film in many ways. But it's so tragic that he won't get to see himself up on the big screen!

It's also tragic that he didn't live to see the new edition of *Stuck Rubber Baby*. I hope that this edition, along with our film, will cement his place in the canon of the Great American Cartoonists. Because Lord knows he deserves it for his extraordinary artistry and storytelling, but also for his courage depicting queer lives with empathy and authenticity and for busting open doors for all of us queer comics creators. He was a master artist, a community activist, and a role model all rolled into one and he used all of that to do as much good as he could in the world. He will be missed.

Chapter 13

ACTIVISM AND SOLIDARITY IN THE COMICS OF HOWARD CRUSE

MATTHEW CHENEY

Howard Cruse had been working in underground comix for a few years before he allowed himself to add any gay content to his work, and even after he did so, it took some time for him to embrace his identity as a queer artist. "Even when you know that remaining closeted is a dead end," he reflected in 2009, "it's not easy to discard the strokes that go with being assumed to be heterosexual" (25). Cruse was not assumed to be heterosexual by the underground comics community much beyond August 1979, however, when Denis Kitchen (who would later found the Comic Book Legal Defense Fund) invited Cruse to edit *Gay Comix* for Kitchen Sink Press. Cruse accepted the invitation, and edited the first four issues (September 1980–November 1983) of a series that Hillary Chute (2017) has called "field-defining" for queer comics, noting that it "may have taken longer than other underground titles to coalesce, but its significance has been enormous" (357).

By 1983, when Cruse began drawing his *Wendel* comic strips for *The Advocate*, he was an experienced cartoonist and editor with a clear political vision shaped by the civil rights struggles of the 1960s and the gay liberation movement of the 1970s. In addition to being the year that *Wendel* began, 1983 was also the year the *New York Times* published its first front-page story about AIDS (Pear), and though Cruse had intended *Wendel* to be a "comedic portrayal of everyday life" (2011, 9), it proved impossible to keep tragic subjects out.

Wendel ended in 1989, as Cruse began work on what would become his 1995 graphic novel *Stuck Rubber Baby*, which tells the story of a young white man in Alabama during the early 1960s who slowly comes to grips both with the civil rights movement and his own homosexuality. Though set in an era before AIDS, *Stuck Rubber Baby*'s tale of political awakening, protest, coalition-building, and friendship resonates deeply with anyone familiar with AIDS activism, of which Cruse said in a 2001 interview, "It was like the '60s all over again—it was thrilling" (Duralde). That sense that activism against oppression and tragedy can be thrilling is a primary force within Cruse's comics, whether it manifests in the generally light, everyday present of the *Wendel* strips or the often violent history portrayed in *Stuck Rubber Baby*. Throughout his life and work, Cruse has shown that what allows people to survive tragedy and oppression is a communitarian ethos coupled with a commitment to activism, a radical generosity that actively creates space for refuge and coalition-building.

In this chapter, I will look at a few of the ways that *Wendel* and *Stuck Rubber Baby* represent activism as a necessary tool for building and strengthening communities of outsiders. Both works wrestle with questions of responsibility, complicity, and solidarity, suggesting that though circumstances and goals may differ between eras, activism itself possesses a vital power.

WENDEL

Wendel's serial format made it a chronicle of ever-changing gay male life in a small city somewhere in the Central Time Zone, and as such life changed, so, too, did the comic change. In the introduction to *The Complete Wendel* (2011), Cruse says, "When I was drawing *Wendel* for *The Advocate* during the 1980s, a central premise of the comic strip was that my fictional characters were reading the same real-world news accounts that I, and their fans, were reading each morning" (9).

Despite their differences, both *Wendel* and *Stuck Rubber Baby* propose that in times of crisis, activism is a technique to create not only systemic changes, but, more reliably, to open spaces of refuge within struggle. While such refuge may offer occasional sites of safety, for groups facing existential threat, safety is always precarious, and the refuge of activism works more importantly as a source of energy, companionship, love, and even joy while the necessary struggle continues. Activism creates and strengthens community, and one of the most radical proposals of Cruse's work is that activism can, and perhaps ought to be integrated into everyday life like any other activity. In a comprehensive interview with Jon B. Cooke for *Comic Book Creator* in 2016, Cruse said of *Wendel*, "I think the strip humanized the notion of activism, showing that it's only one side of a rounded life, the way sex is a part of life without being the be-all and end-all" (66). Such a view is not trivializing; rather, it suggests that a healthy, well-rounded life is one that includes activism in it.

Reading *Wendel* in chronological order is a particularly powerful experience because what begins as a light, slice-of-life comedy can't help but reckon with life in an ever more terrifying world, a world of yuppies and Reagan and plague. There's a remarkable *Wendel* comic from the fall of 1987 in which Wendel and friends go to a big AIDS demonstration in Washington (Cruse 2011, 162–63). The majority of the story is given over to a song by a character named Glenn, who has taken on the responsibility of entertaining everybody on the bus from New York City to DC, and who is, he says, wearing the same gown he wore during the night of the Stonewall riots. The comic ends with a large panel made up of a collage of actual photographs of Reagan administration officials above Washington, DC, landmarks mixed with a hand-drawn crowd of protesters (163). Cruse doesn't typically use photographic images in his comics, but here reality invades in the form of Reagan and some of his men. The place and date are specific, and the sense of historical continuity is strong—by having Glenn wear the clothes he wore during the Stonewall riots, Cruse insists on the importance of the current moment for gay history and gay liberation.

This was not the first time politics entered the strip, however—politics was there from the beginning. In the third strip, Wendel and his friend Deb have been elected co-chairs of the Lesbian & Gay Ideological Solidarity Committee, they wonder why nobody ran against them, and then when their first meeting immediately descends into name-calling and denunciations by various factions within the group, they learn how difficult the job is (Cruse 2011, 20–21). They then go out for an ice cream and are mistaken for a heterosexual couple and denounced by people who say such things as, "You two straights have a lot of nerve exhibiting blatant displays of heterosexual affection in the middle of our gay ghetto!" and "Once again we're victimized by the insensitivity of callous heteros indifferent to our historic oppression" (21). This very funny portrait of activism as infighting and knee-jerk response is more negative about the value of organizing and of community identity than any of Cruse's later strips will be, though he never ignores the complexities of various stances and the feeling of futility that can sometimes result from organizing efforts.

Wendel always portrays the personal and political as both interlinked and mutually invigorating. Here, I will look at two particular episodes. The first appears early in the strip's history, depicting people sitting out in a park and listening to speeches for Gay Pride 1984 (Cruse 2011, 54–55). At this point, Wendel and Ollie have just decided that their relationship is pretty serious. At the top, on either side of the title and byline, we see a speaker on a stage saying, "We must stand together against oppression . . ." and then we see Wendel say to Ollie, "I try to stay with these heavy-duty political speeches, but . . . (sigh)" and Ollie replying, "Yeah . . . the mind does wander . . ." Then we move into the central part of the strip, which depicts what seems to be a single moment where everyone's minds are wandering—but wandering in a way that supports the distant speaker's statement that "The Stonewall rebellion is far from over" (54). We see Ollie and Wendel remembering their first meeting (which occurred in the fifth strip), we see people of various ages, genders, and races remembering good times and bad—and the bad include exclusivity within the gay community itself: one character lies with his head on another's leg, the other's hand on his belly, thinking about a time when he was barred from a gay club because "we don't get the cuties here if we let the fatties in" (55).

Toward the end of the strip, Ollie's son, Farley, asks Wendel's mother if they'll get home in time to watch *Knight Rider*, and Wendel's mother, who is wearing a PFLAG (Parents & Friends of Lesbians & Gays) T-shirt, says, "Hush, now, Branman [Farley's superhero name; he named himself after looking at a box of healthy cereal]—Granny's communing with her past." Her thought bubble shows her thinking back to a peace rally and getting screamed at by right-wing anti-communists (55).

And then the strip ends by returning to Ollie and Wendel, both imagining themselves on top of a wedding cake, with Ollie saying, "Well, whaddaya think, Wendel? Do ya think we belong up here on top of this damned cake?" and Wendel replying, with the strip's final words, "I just don't know, Ollie. What do you think . . . ?" (55). The meaning is both personal and political. Are they, liberated gay men that they are, willing to enter into a monogamous relationship with vows of faithfulness (a particularly challenging question for Ollie, who was once married to Farley's mother, and had an awful time of it); but also, do gay people belong in what, in 1984, was the heterosexual (and often heterosexist) institution of marriage?

The question of marriage is answered, more or less, a year later, when the first series of *Wendel* strips ends with Ollie and Wendel sharing a dream of a wedding that is queer in every possible way: they are married out in the woods by Smokey the Bear, who has thrown away his ranger cap in favor of liberation and not being defined by labels, and Ollie, Wendel, and all their friends and family are completely naked. Their vows include such things as, "Do you promise never to forget what it is about each other that you've learned to love, and never to be stingy with the hugs and kind words even if you're not feeling all that horny at the moment?" They are not pronounced man and man or husband and husband, but rather "best friends, lovers, and lifemates." Then Smokey tells them they'll have to work out the details themselves (Cruse 2011, 112–13).

Let's return to Pride 1984, though. I won't belabor the obvious; the strip's meaning doesn't require a lot of explication. The diversity of the community in the park is clear from their thoughts and memories, but also clear is exactly what the speaker says, the words that begin the strip: "We must stand together against oppression. The Stonewall rebellion is far from over" (54). The strip itself provides an aesthetic unification through its depiction of multiple thoughts and memories at one moment. There is a warmth to its vision, a sense of common humanity and possibility. This is a very positive view of the possibilities of activism, if just the rather tame activism of watching a speaker in a park, even when your mind wanders. The key is that the activism of the organizers has created a space of celebration and refuge. Many of the memories depicted are painful—people remember being rejected by their parents, fired from their jobs, and physically attacked—but they are the memories of people now sitting relaxed in the sun, many of them holding hands or resting on each other comfortably. There are many forces in the world arrayed against them, but together they can create a community of their own.

This communitarian idea continues to be reinforced throughout the *Wendel* strips, particularly as AIDS plays more and more of a role in the story. A sequence from 1989 tells the story of Wendel and Ollie's friend Sterno, who falls in love with a bodybuilder named Duncan, who then proceeds to try to make Sterno into what he thinks of as a better person: not only someone who exercises constantly, but also someone who isn't political (238–65). When the sequence was collected in a one-time edition of *Wendel Comix*, the cover depicted Wendel, Ollie, and Farley listening to a radio shock-jock while from the margins hands reach toward them, guns are pointed at them, and it seems like the entire world is threatening their existence. The sequence tells the story of Sterno's infatuation with Duncan alongside the organization of a protest against the shock-jock, Crank Animus, a big hit on the radio station WKKK. At the protest, Wendel stumbles into a group of Crank Animus fans, and they attack him. The protesters run to his aid—"Hurry everybody!" they cry. "Bashers on Tenth Street!" (256)—but it is ultimately Sterno, who can't resist stopping by the demonstration, who grabs the guy who attacked Wendel and delivers him a rather strong beating. This excitement—not just the excitement of violence and macho physical activity, but of being part of a community, of helping friends, of standing up for a cause—invigorates Sterno, even as he fears it will cause Duncan to criticize him. He needn't worry, though; Duncan has found another protégé, and while Sterno is at the protest, Duncan is having sex with the new guy. Sterno walks in on them, Duncan declares he's moving on, and Sterno kicks them out of his apartment (261). Meanwhile, Crank Animus's ratings are skyrocketing even as he doesn't know his own daughter is a lesbian, and the sequence ends with her hearing the siren call of the Lesbian and Gay Chorus in a gay pride parade singing "This land is your land, this land is my land . . ."—an anthem of many political struggles past, a song of freedom and hope (265). If she can find her way toward that parade, perhaps she can end the loneliness and sadness that seem to fill her.

STUCK RUBBER BABY

Wendel ended in 1989, and Cruse began a major new project, his first graphic novel, *Stuck Rubber Baby,* released in 1995 by the DC Comics imprint Paradox Press.[1] It gained notice and won awards, but never had the breakout success of something like *Maus, Persepolis,* or *Fun Home.* Alison Bechdel, *Fun Home*'s author, has often acknowledged the influence of Cruse on her own work (and wrote the introduction to *The Complete Wendel* and the reissued edition of *Stuck Rubber Baby*). She noted in an interview with the *Guardian* that Cruse had "devoted years of his life to it, but it didn't cross over. People weren't ready to identify with a gay hero. That changed in the next decade" (Cooke 2017). Unfortunately, the change came too late, and *Stuck Rubber Baby* has gone in and out of print ever since it was first published, while works it influenced deeply became bestsellers.

Stuck Rubber Baby is a true graphic novel—unlike many other books that get that label, it was not conceived in pieces or published serially; it was always intended to be a long, unified narrative. (Though based on some of Cruse's own experiences, *Stuck Rubber Baby* is not a memoir; it is fiction.) It tells the story of a man named Toland Polk, mostly through his memories of growing up in Alabama during the early 1960s as a white guy who doesn't really know what he wants from the world or his life, coming to grips both with the civil rights movement and his own homosexuality. Partly in an attempt to try to cure his gay desires, he ends up in a relationship with a fiery college student, activist, and singer named Ginger, and she becomes pregnant. Meanwhile, protests against segregation and racism are growing more and more ferocious, and the white establishment fights back, with tragic, horrifying results. Throughout it all, Toland meets queer characters of various races and ages, and finally decides both that political action is necessary and that he can't pretend to be heterosexual any longer. This primary story is framed as the memories of Toland thirty years later, apparently in a stable relationship with a man, living a solidly bourgeois urban gay life, but still haunted by the past. Other characters' stories and fates are woven through Toland's memories, creating a complex view of this past and his remembering of it.

"Once I thought about placing my novel in the early '60s, I started getting excited," Cruse said in 2016:

> That would give me a chance to show parts of the Southern culture, including the pre-Stonewall gay subculture, that hadn't been shown much in fiction—certainly not in comic-book fiction. I could break new ground. So thinking about all of that made it seem that there was the basis for a real novel there, not just an extra-long comic book story. And my feeling was that, if I was going to do a comic that called itself a novel, I would want it to have the richness of a "real" novel. It would have to be like the novels I had really liked during my youth. There would have to be enough facets of the story that when you finished the book you couldn't remember everything that had happened in it. It would be worth reading more than once. (Cooke 2016, 71)

As various critics have shown, *Stuck Rubber Baby* represents and explores the intersections of sexuality and race in ways that challenge conventional ideas of the South, of the civil rights era, and of the history of queer liberation. Cruse's project, Julie Buckner Armstrong (2018) writes, is one of perpetually "queering civil rights movement history and integrating gay history" (124). Gary Richards points out that *Stuck Rubber Baby* draws from and plays with the conventions of "the white southern racial conversion narrative and the coming-out novel" (164), fulfilling the basic expectations of both narrative types while adding elements to complicate our interpretation of *Stuck Rubber Baby* via those genres alone. While Richards sees and appreciates some of the complexities, his interpretation misses other ones that complicate some of his criticisms, as Armstrong points out (2018, 119–22). The limitations of Richards's interpretation point less to any failure on his part than to the richness of Cruse's book, particularly in how it melds history, fiction, and questions of social justice, but does so without any of the simplicities of agitprop.

Stuck Rubber Baby works against forces resulting from what Roderick Ferguson (2019) identifies as "the contemporary mainstreaming of queerness"—forces that "obscure the real and historically productive convergences between queer politics and other forms of struggle" (19). In both its story and its form, Cruse's graphic novel promotes ideas of solidarity across boundaries, of friendship and openness as key traits for progress and pleasure. This is true of much of Cruse's work, certainly including *Wendel*, but in *Stuck Rubber Baby* the ideas gain new power through the interactions of past and present.

The narrative structure overall is basically linear for the major events, but within sequences (and sometimes even individual pages) the movement is more fluid and associational, developing a complex interweaving of time periods, memories, and memories of memories. We're set up for this structure right from the first page, which introduces many of the visual motifs that will reappear throughout the book: the Kennedys, protests, dead bodies . . . In the first three pages, we move from Toland as an adult in the mid-1990s to Toland as a child and young teenager to Toland and his sister shortly after their parents died. The fourth and fifth pages then circle back to develop some of what was glimpsed earlier before using this new information to bring in Ginger, who will become the mother of his child (the baby of the title), standing with Toland at the March on Washington, where she asks him, "Who're you lookin' at?" to which Toland replies, "Just someone I used to know" (5). Ginger understands none of the context, but we do, and we understand it through numerous levels of narrative and time: not only the immediate context that led Toland to stare at one of his first male crushes, but the greater context of who Toland becomes later, which we've seen in enough glimpses up to that point to be able to extrapolate a sense of what sort of life the older Toland lives. The scene offers even more complexities when we look at it from the perspective of race and class, which Cruse emphasizes from the first pages, making it impossible for us to separate Toland's growing understanding of his sexuality from his growing understanding of other aspects of his identity, including the aspects for which he is in a position of majority power (he is white, male, and of some economic privilege in comparison to many people in his milieu). It's an exquisite moment, encapsulating so much of what the book wrestles with, giving poignance to a scene early in the story, and also beginning to develop the characters who will be central to the primary story.

The graphic novel form allows Cruse particular effects that would not be available in any other type of narrative, even cinema, with which comics are often compared. Hannah Miodrag (2015) makes the important point that "unlike film, whose shots are viewed one at a time, comics panels are co-present on the two-dimensional page," and thus, "within the page, simultaneous panels can participate in webs of interrelationships that violate narrative sequence, and it is these non-linear relations that truly distinguish comics from other forms of narrative sequence" (111–12). Cruse takes extraordinary advantage of just such nonlinear relations, far more so than he ever did in *Wendel*, to weave various moments past and present together at once. From the first page, *Stuck Rubber Baby* sets itself not merely as Toland's memories, but as Toland *remembering*. The narrative itself becomes an active process, with memories fragmented, revisited, and revised. Most of the images of Toland in the present sit as a background layer on the page, with memories of past events placed over that background like puzzle pieces on a table. Important events such as Toland's parents' death in a car crash are glimpsed at one place (page 4) and then explained, expanded on, or reinterpreted later (page 12). In the beginning of the book, multiple moments past and present get united by the page itself, for instance page 6, where the top of the page depicts the March on Washington (an event the book returns to repeatedly), the middle of the page is the present, and the bottom of the page depicts a time before the March on Washington, with Toland reading *Playboy* to try to make himself straight.[2] The comics form is perfectly suited to the narrative's need for memories to move freely around and across each other.

It's an extremely talky book. The few panels without text stand out, and their presence inevitably feels either like a relief or a shock. The characters are constantly trying to talk their way through things, to find the right words, and more often than not they fail. At the same time, other characters wield words as weapons, with deadly consequences. Again and again, *Stuck Rubber Baby* returns to ideas of representation and performance, and of how identity, performance, and memory can merge or split. Sometimes words help, but often they do not; they accumulate and obfuscate, they crowd out action and sight. Here, too, the form is particularly well suited to convey this tension between words and action, because within the tight confines of the panels, the words cover, obscure, push up against, spread across, and otherwise get in the way of what we're looking at. It's significant that the book becomes more quiet at the end, as Toland finds ways to reconcile himself to the past, to move forward while preserving memory, to admit his own failures and not simply reduce those failures to stories he tells over and over again later in life. Music weaves through his memories, and it is music that accompanies him in the end: "There's something I wanna show ya," he says, and the panels open up, the music weaves through the images, and we are left with the silent peace of a city snow storm (207–10).[3]

Despite all their talking, what matters most often is what and how these characters look at the world—both metaphorically and literally: where their glances linger, what they notice and what they don't. The question Ginger asks Toland early on ("Who're you lookin' at?") is one that could be asked throughout *Stuck Rubber Baby*. Looking is partly about knowledge, about paying attention to what is around you, but it is also, as we are led to notice early on, about desire, yearning, memory, regret. At the end of the book, Toland speaks at Sammy's funeral and says, "It could've been me" (effectively coming out to the audience) while looking right at Shiloh, who sits bandaged and damaged, having barely survived the bombing of the Melody Motel, the place where Toland had his first experience both of gay sex and interracial sex (193). Toland guesses what Shiloh must be thinking and feeling, but he has no way to know, nor do we, because Shiloh doesn't speak. In a book so filled with conversation, that absence is immense, suggesting a gulf of communication that Toland does not possess the knowledge, skills, or power to cross. And yet, while we know that whatever Shiloh thinks at that moment is mediated through Toland's perception and memory, there is some bond, some sense of solidarity, some connection. It is the bond produced by shared experience and openness.

Shiloh is first introduced to Toland the same night that Toland first meets Ginger; indeed, their names are linked for Toland from the first moment he sees them singing folk songs together at a party at the Melody Motel (27). Because of that party, the motel becomes for Toland the first space of open friendship and solidarity. "It'll be an integrated party," he's told, "full of beatniks, anarchists, homosexuals, negroes, vegetarians, drunks, and poets" (23). In a panel just below the one offering this information, present-day Toland gives a brief history of the motel: "At some time in the past the motel may have served as a simple way station for tired black travelers, but by the time I came of age it had become a famous symbol of tenacious activism" (27). When Toland enters the party, we get one of the largest single panels in the book up to that point, a panel that stretches across the entire middle of the page. It is crammed with people, but does not feel as cramped and claustrophobic as many of the panels leading up to it.[4] This is Toland's first taste of a kind of freedom he has not experienced before. It is not just a freedom for himself, though, and that is important to the effect of the place on him and the rest of the story. In fact, closeted and awkward, Toland is particularly more free in those moments than he usually is. But he is experiencing a social space of vastly more freedom than the space outside the motel's walls, and he is welcomed into that space. Liberation of sexuality and race are quickly linked: soon after he enters the party, he sees a gay interracial couple dancing (25). Friendliness is the only criterion for entry: "In the course of the evening, I met Marge and Effie, a lesbian couple who told me they ran a nightclub located on the city's outskirts. It was mainly for blacks, but anybody friendly was welcome" (26). This is the guiding principle for all of the spaces that will liberate Toland's own identity and political consciousness, but though we see this through Toland's eyes, the value of the principle of friendliness is clearly not of value only, or even primarily, to him. The value is to the movement as a whole, a movement for a better, more just, less oppressive society.

Stuck Rubber Baby also shows how a lack of friendliness leads to exclusion. Orley, Toland's brother-in-law, discovers this when he refers to the Rhombus as "the fag bar" (39) and he gets ostracized (not for that comment alone, but also for his blatant racism and boorishness). Orley ends up losing a lot of what he values in life because of his inability to enter into friendship with a diverse group of people, and even after he becomes a hippie, his previous life will haunt him (197).

But friendliness is not a simple concept. It includes dangers, as Bernard discovers when he invites a crowd of strangers to the Alleysax and doesn't realize some of them are going along for some racist gaybashing (81). Aside from the danger that openness to strangers poses, solidarity may be misunderstood or misplaced, as Sammy discovers that a police officer he knows to be gay (and with whom he seems to suggest he has had sex) sides with straight white power, attacks him with his baton, and says, "An' don't you go spreadin' lies about me either, faggot!" (69). For the police officer, it is easier, safer, and more appealing to choose solidarity with racist, homophobic power than to sacrifice that power and risk becoming an outsider.

Community, too, is no simple concept here. There are white gay racists at Rhombus, men seemingly incapable of understanding the solidarity that the place they are sitting in represents (44). The church that originally provides refuge for Sammy kicks him out when he becomes a political liability (122–23). The small community of the Wheelery, which through much of the book provides refuge for Toland and his friends, fractures as people begin to get on each other's nerves and various personal priorities clash. Cruse shows again and again that refuge is provisional, utopia fleeting—and yet still worthwhile, still worth fighting for.

AIDS is not explicitly mentioned in *Stuck Rubber Baby*, but it is an integral context for the story, and it is important to keep in mind how readers in 1995 would have perceived the present-day sequences. The book was published in the same year that the US Food and Drug Administration approved the first protease inhibitor, making possible what got called highly active anti-retroviral therapy, a therapy that over the next few years helped make HIV, for many people, a chronic, manageable disease rather than a death sentence. But when *Stuck Rubber Baby* hit bookstore shelves in September, that progress was just beginning, and morale among many activists was low. Deborah Gould (2009) reports that by the twenty-fifth anniversary of the Stonewall riots in June 1994, "many [ACT UP] chapters had already dissolved, and as a national movement, ACT UP was no longer what it had been. We were moving from the streets into history" (43). Gay people of all backgrounds and beliefs had to come together for political action because their lives were on the line. Silence equals death. Cynicism equals death. Complaisance equals death. Wendel, Ollie, and their families and friends all learn this lesson as the *Wendel* comics progress, and in *Stuck Rubber Baby*, Toland learns a similar lesson. The connection between Toland's world in the 1960s and his world thirty years later did not need to be spelled out to readers in 1995, and the only reference making the connection is a single, tiny, unobtrusive image in a small panel on page 207, where, behind the picture of Ginger holding the baby before it is given up for adoption, there hangs the iconic "Silence = Death" ACT UP poster.

What readers needed, though, was a reason to continue even as it seemed death was prevailing. The slice-of-life style of *Wendel* couldn't provide such a reason, as any hope it tried to propose would likely feel jejune, disingenous, even grotesque. Gould writes that

> in the years of ACT UP's decline many in the movement reached a point of despair about the AIDS crisis; they did not think the movement had succeeded in saving lives, and they were losing hope in its ability to do so. It is important to note that ACT UP declined before the advent of protease inhibitors in 1995–96, drugs that have helped people to live longer. ACT UP's activism was a crucial factor in the development of this new class of drugs, but that extraordinary success was not yet known during the years of ACT UP's decline. (2009, 269)

Despair easily leads to depression, cynicism, and inaction. By providing a diverse historical perspective on activism, *Stuck Rubber Baby* portrays something other than simple progress, because readers at the time would know that while some progress had been made on both civil rights and gay rights, there was still a long way to go, and many, many people were dying. Instead of a sense of inevitable progress, what *Stuck Rubber Baby* offers is a more deeply affecting, and perhaps more lasting, sense of the value of community and activism that *Wendel* had also portrayed. *Stuck Rubber Baby* is a story of political awakening, but it was written as a call to consciousness, not a comforting nostalgia trip.

Simon Dickel (2011) states that after reading Cruse's graphic novel "we cannot think of the politics of black and gay liberation as isolated or separated realms" (633), an insight that points toward what keeps *Stuck Rubber Baby* relevant now: its narrative and emotional representation of intertwined lives and histories. "The clarity with which we understand an intellectual and political inheritance," Roderick Ferguson says, "greatly determines whether we can identify and compel an alternative future" (150). Given the social changes of the last twenty-five years, and particularly the effect of medications for HIV, there is a chasm of experience between the mid-'90s world and now. The way that Cruse structures the telling of the story of *Stuck Rubber Baby* as a story the adult Toland tells in the '90s shows that Toland seems to feel that way about the '60s: he carries its traces and hauntings inside himself, he carries a sense of lived history, one that, in the final pages, becomes a kind of dream of suburban domesticity, warmth, and peace against the cold, snowy solitude of the city. The past is alive in Toland's memory, his intellectual and political inheritance is clear, and so he has reason to hope that life can get better, that congeniality and community might still spark action, even amidst despair. The regenerative power of active solidarity may yet bring a better world.

Notes

1. Cruse had intended for *Stuck Rubber Baby* to only require two years of work. He severely underestimated the challenge of writing and drawing a 200-page graphic novel by himself. He tells the story of the book's creation on his website in a series of pages titled "The Long and Winding Stuck Rubber Road."

2. *Playboy* is a continuing prop throughout the story; Cruse was a cartoonist for the magazine in the late 1970s, and in *From Headrack to Claude* he reports that when he published his first openly gay comic in a major market (*Village Voice* in 1981), only *Playboy* dropped him (2009, 64).

3. For an analysis of Cruse's use of music throughout *Stuck Rubber Baby*, see Dickel (2011).

4. It is important to note that Cruse's pages were shrunk for publication. On his website, in a chronicle of the writing of *Stuck Rubber Baby*, he reproduces a letter he wrote to his agent on June 6, 1993, explaining, "The larger size is obviously better, but it virtually guarantees that the book will never find a place in the fiction section of most bookstores, whose shelves often cannot accommodate books of a greater height than 9-1/4"; but if it's placed in the humor section next to *Garfield*, browsers for fiction will never discover it. The effect of shrinking the pages was not as terrible as Cruse originally expected, but, he said, there was "a clear loss of visual expansiveness" (Cruse n.d.). It is unfortunate that a full-size edition of the book has never

been published, because while the tense, crowded effect of the shrunken art is appropriate to much of the story's content, details get lost and reading is sometimes difficult.

Works Cited

Armstrong, Julie Buckner. "*Stuck Rubber Baby* and the Intersections of Civil Rights Historical Memory." In *Redrawing the Historical Past: History, Memory, and Multiethnic Graphic Novels*, edited by Martha J. Cutter and Cathy J. Schlund-Vials, 106–28. University of Georgia Press, 2018.

Chute, Hillary L. *Why Comics? From Underground to Everywhere*. HarperCollins, 2017.

Cooke, Jon B. "Finding the Muse of the Man Called Cruse." *Comic Book Creator*, no. 12 (Spring 2016): 32–77.

Cooke, Rachel. "Fun Home Creator Alison Bechdel on Turning a Tragic Childhood into a Hit Musical." *The Guardian*, November 5, 2017. https://www.theguardian.com/books/2017/nov/05/alison-bechdel-interview-cartoonist-fun-home.

Cruse, Howard. *The Complete Wendel*. Universe, 2011.

Cruse, Howard. *From Headrack to Claude: Collected Gay Comix*. Nifty Kitsch Press, 2009.

Cruse, Howard. "The Long and Winding Stuck Rubber Road." Howard Cruse Central. Accessed May 15, 2019. http://www.howardcruse.com/howardsite/aboutbooks/stuckrubberbook/longroad/index.html.

Cruse, Howard. *Stuck Rubber Baby*. Paradox, 2006.

Dickel, Simon. "'Can't Leave Me Behind': Racism, Gay Politics, and Coming of Age in Howard Cruse's 'Stuck Rubber Baby.'" *Amerikastudien / American Studies* 56, no. 4 (2011): 617–35.

Duralde, Alonso. 2001. "Cartoonist Howard Cruse." Advocate.com. August 8, 2001. https://web.archive.org/web/20010808070503/http://www.advocate.com/html/stories/840/840_wendel.asp.

Ferguson, Roderick A. *One-Dimensional Queer*. Polity, 2019.

Gould, Deborah B. *Moving Politics: Emotion and Act Up's Fight against AIDS*. University of Chicago Press, 2009.

Miodrag, Hannah. *Comics and Language: Reimagining Critical Discourse on the Form*. University Press of Mississippi, 2015.

Pear, Robert. "Health Chief Calls Aids Battle 'No. 1 Priority.'" *New York Times*, May 25, 1983. https://www.nytimes.com/1983/05/25/us/health-chief-calls-aids-battle-no-1-priority.html.

Richards, Gary. "Everybody's Graphic Protest Novel: *Stuck Rubber Baby* and the Anxieties of Racial Difference." In *Comics and the U.S. South*, edited by Brannon Costello and Qiana J. Whitted, 161–83. University Press of Mississippi, 2012.

Russell, Thaddeus. 2008. "The Color of Discipline: Civil Rights and Black Sexuality." *American Quarterly* 60, no. 1 (2008): 101–28.

Chapter 14

CANADIAN LGBTQ+ COMICS
INTERSECTIONS OF QUEERNESS, RACE, AND SPIRITUALITY

ALISON HALSALL

Canadian transgender musician, writer, visual artist, and LGBTQ+ activist Vivek Shraya frequently addresses personal experiences of homophobia, suicide ideation, and sexual violence in her creative work. In an article that she recently published in *NOW Magazine*, she describes her motivation for writing her first book, *God Loves Hair* (2010): "I wanted to give young, brown gender-creative kids the kind of book I didn't have growing up. Much of the art I have produced since has been inspired by a desire to address gaps in the representations that shaped my childhood in hopes of minimizing the kind of loneliness I felt" (Shraya 2019). A surprising development occurred through this act of writing: Shraya began to unburden herself of the traumas she experienced in childhood and as a teenager.

However, the pitfall, or the "trap" as she calls it, that she inadvertently fell into was that a disturbing correlation between her exploration of personal trauma and her level of success began to develop, measured through the institutional support she received, as well as by the art contracts, funding, awards, and invitations that were extended to her with more frequency. Worse, she came to see herself as a "trauma clown." As a trans* creator Shraya notes how difficult it is to create outside of the expectations that public and private institutions, communities, and audiences have about the topics that they expect to read from her. This is a common experience for marginalized artists, she observes: "our value often seems inherently tied to the suffering we portray in our work." She goes on to speculate whether "the demand that marginalized artists repeatedly perform trauma—becoming trauma clowns—in our art is a way to contain and oppress us, politely or indirectly, from the comfort of a seat, hands clean." Shraya suggests that an ideological slippage has occurred between the concept of diversity in Canada and "marginalized communities," which has in turn become conflated with oppression, an oppression that pigeonholes such creators into crafting stories that only ever explore traumatic experiences. Shraya warns that this exclusive focus given to images and narratives of trauma limits representations (and, indeed, consumers' perceptions) of people from marginalized groups. More to the point, the more pain that is consumed about people from these communities by readers, the "less potential these images have to effect necessary social change" (Shraya 2019).

For this trans* artist, the diversity that has become a catchword for Canadian culture should certainly include diverse voices but also, even more importantly, diverse stories. That comics should tell diverse stories is consistent with the LGBTQ+ comics that are emerging with more frequency on the Canadian scene, both in webcomic and in print form. Vivek Shraya recently published her comic *Death Threat* (2019), which she cocreated with artist Ness Lee, a "meta response," as she calls it, to hate mail that she received. Although *Death Threat* visualizes the personal trauma that such transphobic messages provoked in her, Shraya argues that she didn't feel like a trauma clown in writing it because the project allowed her "to turn hate into art, an alchemy that runs throughout my career, and which has been personally and vitally restorative." What makes *Death Threat* different from trauma work in general is the act of choice, "that I chose to tell this story and to tell it in this form" (Shraya 2019).

Canadian LGBTQ+ comics are certainly very diverse, as my selection of comics suggests. Daniel Heath Justice's parable "The Boys Who Became the Hummingbirds" (2017), Mariko and Jillian Tamaki's *Skim* (2005), and Vivek Shraya's *Death Threat* (2019) encapsulate the diversity of Canadian LGBTQ+ comics, featuring perspectives from marginalized communities: Cherokee and Two-Spirited; Japanese Canadian and queer-questioning; and Hindu, trans*, and nonbinary. Their visual formats provide a platform for their intersectional approaches to matters of queerness, race, and spirituality. While each comic undoubtedly addresses homo- and transphobia, abuse, violence, and suicide, these creators transform hate into art, in the process expressing the distinctive queer experiences that their protagonists live through in their respective communities. In *Reinventing Comics* (2000), Scott McCloud writes: "Comics, like other minority forms, are vital to diversifying our perceptions of our world" (19). These three LGBTQ+ Canadian comics do just that in questioning many of the dominant cultural narratives that define the Canadian nation, and in critiquing the presumptive whiteness of much queer work through their choice of topic and visual approach to representing LGBTQ+ experiences in Canadian society and culture. These comics creators avoid performing as "trauma clowns" by moving past personal traumas to represent the intersectional LGBTQ+ experiences across Canada, offered up and in response to the sociopolitical challenges that distinguish a large and disparate country.

"A TEACHING AND A REMEMBRANCE": DANIEL HEATH JUSTICE'S COMICS PARABLE

In the twenty-first century, Canada's dynamic comics tradition thrives, and is increasingly a focus in both popular and academic studies. Canada's landscape and its hockey ethos, its long history of colonialism and instances of cultural appropriation, as well as its ironic self-identification as "not American" are just some of the preoccupations of Canadian comics, Chris Chikuma-Reyns and Gail de Vos claim (2016, 12–13). Candida Rifkind and Linda Warley's collection *Canadian Graphic: Picturing Life Narratives* (2016) explores the long and varied history of life narrative (memoir, confession, autobiography, biography) in the Canadian alternative comics scene. In their introduction to the volume, Rifkind and Warley note that cartoonists of color and Indigenous cartoonists in particular are under-represented in comics scholarship (4). I would include Canadian LGBTQ+ comics in that assessment.

Comics in Canada about Indigenous[1] political and cultural issues began as recently as 2008 with the publication of David Alexander Robertson's *The Life of Helen Betty Osborne*, a graphic narrative about the abduction and brutal murder of a Cree high school student in The Pas, Manitoba, in 1971, by four white men. Since then, the field of Indigenous comics in Canada expands on an annual basis, extending beyond life narratives into genres of myth, fantasy, realism, and speculative fiction with a particular focus given to educating readers about Canada's troubled colonial past and present. Colorado-born Canadian citizen of the Cherokee nation, Daniel Heath Justice published "The Boys Who Became the Hummingbirds" in volume 2 of *Moonshot: The Indigenous Comics Collection* (2017). Illustrated by Weshoyot Alvitre, a Tongva/Scots-Gaelic artist, this parable represents one of the first explorations of Indigenous Two-Spiritedness in comics form. "Two-Spirit" is an English term that references historical foundations of gender and sexual diversity in North American Indigenous societies, and alludes to the "contemporary interlinking of gender, sexuality, spirituality, and social roles, or a critique of heteropatriarchy in Native and non-Native communities" (Driskill et al. 2011b, 17). Sometimes referring to a person who possesses both masculine and feminine spirits, Two-Spirit is also a shifting term that allows queer Indigenous people to distance themselves from colonial gender binaries and analytical identity labels and categories used by a prior generation's interest in anthropological authority, as well as from generic LGBTQ+ identities that are in turn tied to whiteness (Driskill et al. 2011b, 5). In many respects, "Two-Spirit" and "Two-Spirited" are some terms that Indigenous queer people identify themselves with, terms that are also deeply rooted in histories of Indigenous resistance and decolonial struggles.

The visual register of comics is an especially useful tool with which to address entrenched Canadian and European colonialism. Indigenous comics are responding to the call made by Canada's Truth and Reconciliation Commission (T.R.C.) in its 2015 Executive Summary to educate. "Using the power of the graphic medium to both show and tell" (Wolf 2016, 221), they tackle hard-hitting issues that affect Indigenous populations across Canada, such as chronic poverty, social exclusion, suicide, homelessness, violent death, substance addiction, disease, incarceration, and colonialism.

Daniel Heath Justice and Weshoyot Alvitre's comics parable employs visual and literary storytelling to depict the marginalization of Two-Spirited people within Canadian and Indigenous communities, and yet visualizes their determination to use the spiritual force of love to begin the healing process required by their communities after enduring centuries of colonialism and intergenerational trauma. It is a story about an unnamed "strange boy" who lives in a grey prairie town, a land degraded environmentally and inhabited by people whose self-hatred causes them to lash out in acts of emotional and physical violence. The "strangeness" of this boy is personal and sexual: he is apart from his community, living among them but possessing a knowledge about his sexuality that separates him from them. Alvitre's rainbow color palette calls attention visually to the uniqueness of Strange Boy, distinguishing him from the grey, faceless masses with whom he comes in contact. Beginning and ending with the declaration that it is "a teaching and a remembrance" (2017, n.p.), Justice highlights the comic's larger rhetorical thrust to impart knowledge to contemporary readers. The parable evokes a Cherokee story that tells of a sick people whose sacred medicine (tobacco) has been stolen or possessed by dangerous guardians. In the story, the Hummingbird returns the medicine to the people and helps heal their sickness. Justice redeploys this story in his parable about Indigenous Two-Spiritedness: Strange Boy and his lover transform into hummingbirds, and proceed to heal the communities around them of a different kind of "sickness," this time the sickness of self-hatred and homophobia. A story about metamorphosis, healing comes into Justice's story from the Two-Spirited men/hummingbirds' determination to respond to acts of trauma with love.

"The Boys Who Became the Hummingbirds" also visualizes a return to Indigenous spiritual wholeness through the healing power of eros. Part of the settler colonialism that it disrupts occurs through the act of storytelling, the instruction that Justice and Alvitre convey through their comics parable. In this tale, trauma is not unspeakable or invisible; it is represented through "inventive textual practice" (Chute 2010, 26). And yet Strange Boy does not define himself in relation to this trauma, as one might expect. By means of his resilience, he brings inspiration to those who wish to hear and learn. Strange Boy's distinctiveness is conveyed visually: once he commits to helping the

Figure 14.1. "The Boys who Became the Hummingbirds," Daniel Heath Justice and Weshoyot Alvitre, in *Moonshot: The Indigenous Comics Collection*, volume 2 (Alternate History Comics, 2017), n.p.

community heal, his face is distinguished from the mob around him. His vitality and determination make him targets. Surrounded on all sides by the faceless horde, Strange Boy willingly submits to trauma: inset panels suggest fragmentation and aggression, evidence of violence is suggested by the bandages that decorate his arms.

This brutality, however, to which he submits, is but a means to an end. The erotic emerges as the creative and generative force needed to resist the

self-hatred and homophobia of his community. This is the "sovereign erotics" that Qwo-Li Driskill, Daniel Heath Justice, Deborah Miranda, and Lisa
Tatonetti describe, a resource that provides energy for change from hetero-
patriarchal gender regimes (2011b, 3). Strange Boy connects sexually with Shadow
Boy, a young man with whom he had been intimate previously but who had
never had the courage to accept and declare his identity publicly. Once Shadow
Boy praises Strange Boy's brave acceptance of his own Two-Spiritedness, their
metamorphosis into beautiful, vibrant hummingbirds—symbols of wonder and
peace that suggest the miracle of living—begins. These hummingbirds exceed
the parameters of the panel on the page and are the bright and colorful points
that draw a reader's eye.

United by "sovereign erotics," the hummingbirds begin the process of awakening their communities to the hope and beauty that lie within, visualized in
the beautiful hummingbird that each individual holds captive in their chest
cavity. Metamorphosis provokes visual distinctiveness, as the horde gradually
transfigures into individually rendered characters. Thanks to the efforts of these
beautiful creatures, and their "defiant song" (2017, n.p.), healing begins to occur
across the land through the power of education and a renewed connection with
spirituality and culture. As "a teaching and a remembrance" Justice and Alvitre's
comics parable affirms the transcendent beauty of these avian figures, whose
"gift of healing" centers on the restorative potential of Two-Spiritedness, that
they suggest might help move Indigenous and Canadian communities forward
on their respective journeys towards reconciliation.

THE HIGH SCHOOL AS CLOSET: VISIBLE/INVISIBILITY IN *SKIM*

A collaboration between Mariko Tamaki, a Toronto-based writer and play-
wright, and her cousin, illustrator Jillian Tamaki, formerly of Edmonton, *Skim*
(2005) explores intersections of queerness and race in Canadian youth culture.
This graphic novel tells the story of Kim(berly) Keiko Cameron, a sixteen-year-
old, half-Japanese, half-Caucasian goth girl who lives in Toronto and attends
an all-girls school. It captures in word and image the angst-filled experience
of adolescence. Kim's narrating voice is at times glib, self-obsessed, funny, and
earnest as she wrestles with her identity as a racial minority in her homogenous
high school and, even more pertinently, as queer-questioning. Arguably, the
most interesting (and elusive) narratives in this graphic novel concern Kim
herself and the kiss that she shares with her English teacher, Ms. Archer, and
volleyball jock John Reddear's suicide, which is linked to his closeted homosexuality. However, these narratives about homosexuality and race remain spectral
in the text. The nature of her identity is seemingly a taboo topic, socially and

personally, for Kim herself. Indeed, Kim never comes out at any point in the text as LGBTQ+, and yet her daily experiences suggest that queer-questioning might be the most useful term to describe her strong (yet undeclared) feelings for her English teacher. In spite of this aporia, sexuality is the topic that a reader encounters right from the cover illustration. The cover image (and the only image in color) portrays Kim in the vein of sensual nineteenth-century Japanese woodblock prints, which would frequently depict heterosexual and homosexual encounters between courtesans and their patrons. This cover illustration is significant given the emphasis it places on beauty and sensuality, in spite of Kim's recurrent insistence that she finds herself unattractive. The intersectional nature of Kim's sexuality is what the Tamakis explore in word and image through its silent presence in the graphic text.

High school for Kim, as for many adolescents, is a metaphorical closet, whose oppressiveness provokes radical effects, the most obvious being the burial of her most intimate thoughts (certainly from her acquaintances, and at times even from herself). Kim is deeply private, even with best friend Lisa Soor, concealing her sexual feelings and her complex emotions about her Japanese identity beneath an ironically dismissive persona. Kim has long learned that her peer communities are both heteronormative and racially homogenous. She recalls a particularly traumatic evening when she was invited to Julie Peters's thirteenth birthday party, and she and Hien Warshowski, both racial outsiders, were ostracized by the girls, who threw them out of the house. "Maybe she [Hien] thought that's how people left parties in Canada. Asians first" (Tamaki and Tamaki 2010, 86), Kim muses to herself, as she walks home alone, acknowledging the silent (and not so silent) racism that continues to alienate her from her peer group. Kim's Japanese Canadian ethnicity has a discursive and visual life in the text that is very similar to that of homosexuality, "her Japanese features are simultaneously visible and invisible, physically marked on her face but seemingly unremarked by her peers" (Chiu 2015, 30). Silent and overt homophobia also runs rampant in this homogenous and privileged adolescent community: Lisa, Kim's best friend, cruelly describes her as "a freak" (29) and "a spaz" (30) when she begins to suspect that Kim has developed a crush on their English teacher. Go "make out with Ms. Archer" (34), Lisa snarls at her in frustration, you "psycho bitch" (Tamaki and Tamaki 2010, 34).

The Tamakis link these experiences of racial hatred with homophobia, visually and discursively. On one particular splash page, Kim trudges through the newly fallen snow to write in large letters that she "hat[es] everything" (89). Jillian Tamaki parallels Kim's nihilism with an inset image in the lower right-hand corner that depicts John Reddear with the word "fag" scrawled across his forehead (89), an image that draws attention to the fascination that his peers have in labeling him, outing him, and hating him all at once, even after he

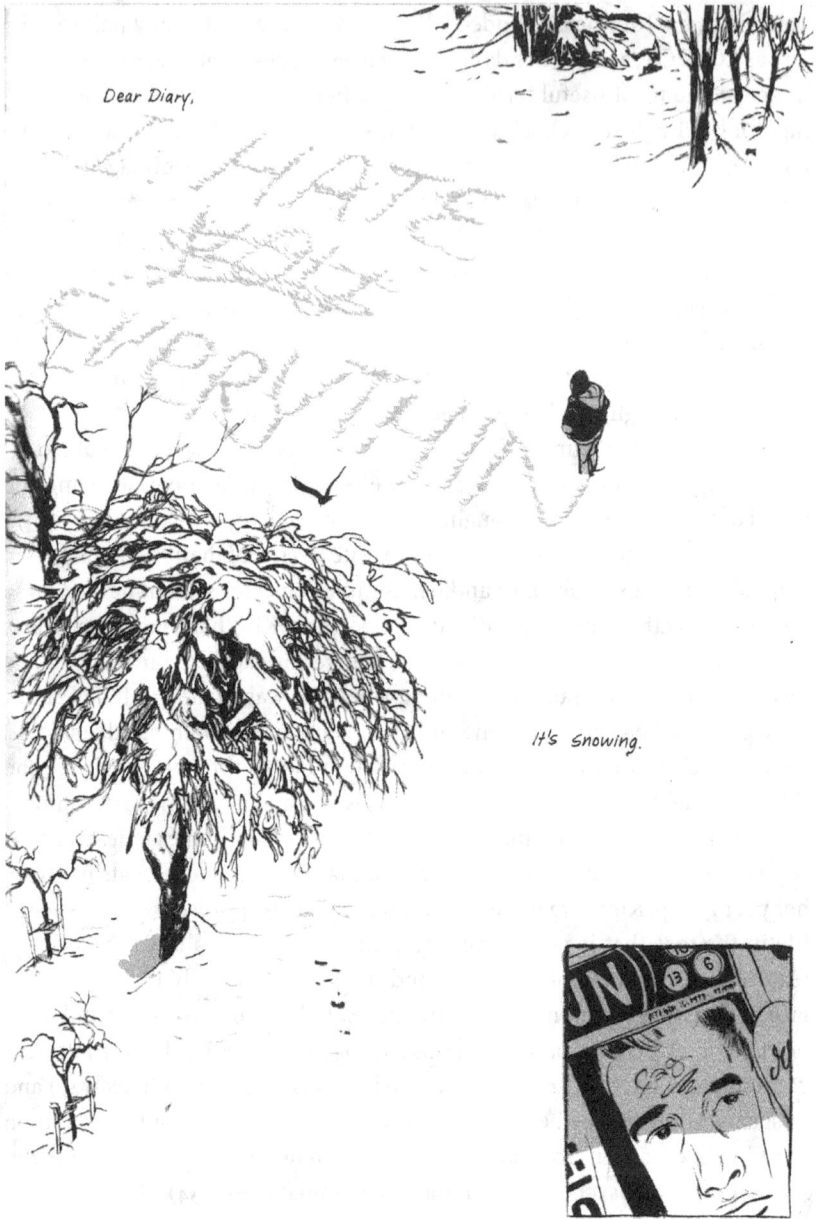

Figure 14.2. *Skim*, Mariko Tamaki and Jillian Tamaki (Groundwood Books, 2010), 89.

commits suicide. As this page reminds readers, both Kim and John share an outsider status, and yet the important questions about race and sexuality are never asked by the communities around them. Ineffective guidance counselors, parents, and students focus on the wrong things, concealing deeply rooted prejudices about sexual difference. Students apply a heterosexual narrative to John after his death so as to "save" him the tarnish of being labeled (publicly, at least) as gay. At his memorial service, the Girls Celebrate Life club focuses on suicide, peer pressure, and depression as challenges that affect their school community, while remaining willfully ignorant to John's homosexuality. Likewise, the guidance counselor Mrs. Hornet targets students like Kim whom she assumes are at risk because of their outward goth appearance, but neglects the people who really need her support (John and his ex-girlfriend, Katie Matthews, both of whom tried to commit suicide).

Skim outlines the complexity of Kim's perceptions and emotions, visually nd literally, as she awakens somewhat reluctantly to her adolescent sexuality. Body and queer-questioning identity are intimately related in the Tamakis' *Skim*, through absence as much as presence. On this page, for example, the top three panels evoke Polaroids that Kim attempts to take of the new cast on her arm. All readers see, however, are disembodied shapes as Kim struggles to manoeuvre a camera with her non-dominant hand. This is followed by another three perspectives of Kim. This time, an establishing shot, an over-the-shoulder shot, and a close-up of her left hand trying to write her name, remind readers about Kim's attempts to capture this moment of her adolescence visually. Together, these six panels provide a metatextual commentary about the elusiveness of Kim's very identity. She writes her name over and over in her diary, teaching herself to write with her non-dominant hand, and insisting in the process that her identity is tied to her "broken" body. *Skim*'s chapters are fractured into diary entries, each providing an assemblage of visual and literary markings that allow an intimate view into her private (and still elusive) thoughts. Likewise, Kim's nickname designates a name and an identity that are not in fact accurate, deepening her elusiveness as a character. Ms. Archer asks Kim what the name "Skim" means: "Because I'm not" (27), Kim answers cryptically. This is an important statement by Kim about her identity. It is, at once, an assertion of herself ("I am"), and a refusal of what the people around her assume her to be ("not"). The Tamakis establish Kim as having shrewdly mastered the narratives imposed upon her by her peers, as she slowly claims her own space within the narrative. This exchange with her teacher is told in dialogue boxes, with only the tips of their heads showing in the panels. In this way, Jillian Tamaki deprives the reader of any visual that might add context to this revealing exchange between teacher and student. "I'll assume you prefer

Figure 14.3. *Skim*, Mariko Tamaki and Jillian Tamaki (Groundwood Books, 2010), 8.

Kim" (27), Ms. Archer declares, quickly dismissing the inaccurate name that Kim's peers have assigned her.

"Skim" is like "fag" in the Tamakis' text, in that it is a label imposed by peers, for the purposes of designation. This is linked to the interest the graphic novel takes in "marking." "I think there are a lot of ways to be marked" (124), Kim muses in an interlude later in the text. For example, one is "marked" (like student Natasha Cake) if she looks strange and is socially awkward. This is like the labeling that Kim and John Reddear experience as outsiders: Kim as Japanese (and queer-questioning) and John as a "fag." "People can also mark you" (124), she continues, remembering the hickey that Scott Bouffant gave her that "slut-shamed" her for a week in grade nine. This line of thinking leads Kim to reflect on how "everything you do and everything people do to you leaves

Figure 14.4. *Skim*, Mariko Tamaki and Jillian Tamaki (Groundwood Books, 2010), 40–41.

a mark, or at least it affects who you are" (125). To "mark" in this context is to "affect who you *are*" (rather than who you are not). In *Skim*, who Kim *is* relates to her queer-questioning perspective, a topic that remains as visibly invisible as Kim's Japanese Canadian identity. Ms. Archer, as an exotic spectacle, "marks" Kim from her first introduction in the text. The rounded, serpentine lines that visualize her suggest vigor and dynamism; the comic's panels barely contain her. Kim describes Ms. Archer as a "freak." "I like her though," she continues. "I'm a bit of a freak" (13). The parallel that Kim quickly establishes between her teacher and herself highlights the strong feelings of kinship she has for this woman, feelings that swiftly become an all-consuming desire. The uninhibited ease with which Kim talks to her English teacher—her effusiveness, even—presents a striking contrast to the silent moodiness that characterizes her interactions with her peers. Kim's fascination with her teacher deepens quickly, captured by the individual close-ups that multiply in the text of particular parts of Ms. Archer's body: the back of her head, her profile, her hairdo, her hand on Kim's cast. These close-ups convey the enormous importance that Kim places on intimate moments that they share. Kim, however, is unsure about how to claim this development in herself, though she admits in her diary: "Ms. Archer and I have this thing now. When we sit for our talks, Ms. Archer holds my cast" (31). Still uncertain and unwilling to define or "mark" what is happening with her teacher, Kim asserts that there is something between them, "this thing" (31), as she calls it, followed up by another (equally ambiguous) insistence: "It's just this thing" (31). This second assertion insists on its existence and yet defines it as something not capable of being designated. In silent contrast to these ambiguous statements is the visual: two splash pages are devoted to the kiss that Kim and Ms. Archer share in the woods. In this vital moment, they share a moment of connection, whose ambiguity in words is equally as ambiguous in visuals, as the kiss ends with an abrupt shift in the narrative.

The nature of this kiss remains unclear for the duration of the graphic novel. Yet, this is the moment that marks Kim, that affects who she is. Immediately afterwards, Kim registers more emotion than readers have previously seen from her, first through poetry: "I had a dream / I put my hands / inside my chest / and held my heart / to try to keep it still" (43). The intensity of emotion is then visualized by Tamaki who represents the beating of Kim's heart as lines captured by an electrocardiogram that overwrite the words and images on the page. For Kim, the kiss represents nothing less than an entire new way of being, of feeling, of breathing even, one that marks her as queer-questioning, as someone who is in the process of stepping outside the norms that discipline behavior and manage human development. From then on, Kim refuses to perform as a "trauma clown" in spite of her personal experiences of racism and homophobia. False feelings of grief and mourning for John Reddear and Katie Matthews (encouraged primarily by the school guidance counselors and her peers) become as sickening to her as overeating; she is disgusted by their excessive affect. Part of Kim's discovery process centers on change, on sloughing off the attributes that have been used to define her. "Mostly I think change is a good thing. Especially when things are crap to start off" (127), she writes in her journal. She bleaches her jet-black hair and abandons her morose, goth identity, smiling more in the final pages of the comic than she did throughout. She offers friendship (and perhaps something more) to Katie Matthews, John's ex-girlfriend. In *Skim*, the Tamakis demonstrate that Kim's identity is in process. Kim's distinctiveness—captured by the visual singularity of the graphic narrative—lies in her claiming a way of being that is unique to her protean Japanese Canadian resiliency.

"YOU'VE GOT HATE MAIL": THREATENING THE TRANS* SUBJECT

As mentioned earlier, Vivek Shraya's comic book *Death Threat* was inspired by the transphobic hate mail that she began to receive in the fall of 2017. Illustrated by Ness Lee, a Toronto-based artist, the comic redeploys this hateful prose to empower the trans* subject, a political choice and act that looks to show how insidiously hate-speak can travel on the internet. The text's visual format provides creative opportunities for the intersectional approaches that

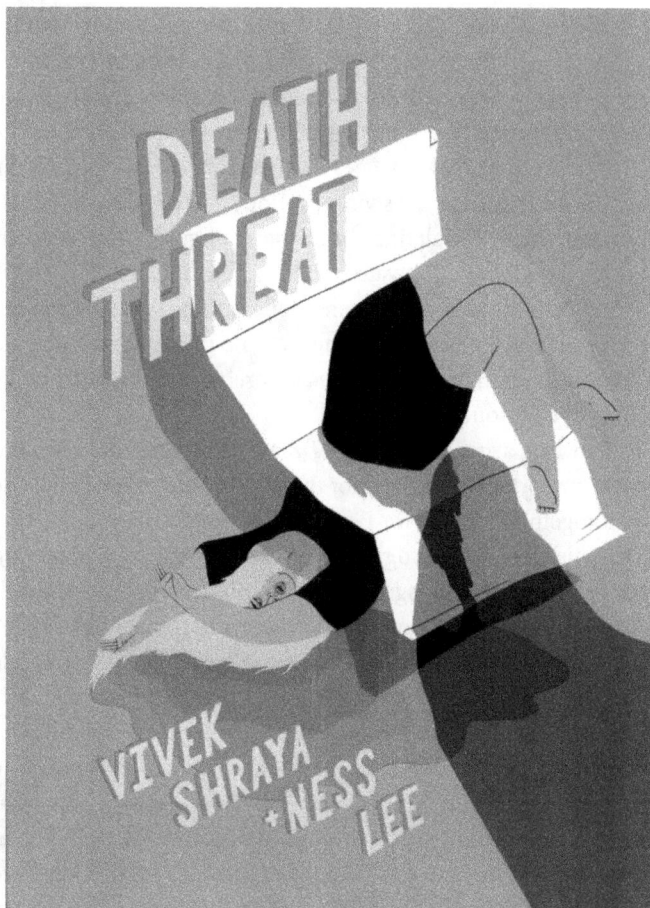

Figure 14.5. *Death Threat*, Vivek Shraya and Ness Lee (Arsenal Pulp Press, 2019), cover.

Shraya and Lee take to matters of transgenderism, race, and religion. In turn, their inventive literary and visual practices help them to rethink dominant tropes of unspeakability, invisibility, and inaudibility, associated with victims of trauma. The cover illustration of *Death Threat* is a particularly apt example of this inventive practice. The comic's interrogation of power is expanded in the visual relationship that Vivek (the character) has with the hateful piece of paper. Fascinatingly, Vivek is visually deployed *as* the weapon, as she penetrates the hate mail, even though she registers trauma in her beautiful body, as the pool of blood beneath her suggests. Her body is also distinctively female, rounded and undulating, clad in a "little black dress," with flowing blonde hair and beautiful brown skin. Who threatens in this text? Certainly, the hate mail writer, at the beginning of the comic. But by the end, what was once perceived as a threat is denied that privilege by means of the restorative power of art. In

Death Threat, Shraya and Lee bear witness to transphobic harassment, their bawdiness/bodiliness becoming a powerful site of exploration in which this visual and literary narrative makes material femininity and sexuality. Just as the Tamakis and Daniel Heath Justice emphasize the importance of eroticism to LGBTQ+ subjectivities, Ness Lee's figures embody an energetic eroticism that is restorative and vital. Lee's visualization of Vivek depicts her in buxom fashion, as a rounded, undulating, and dynamic figure, completely unlike the muscled skinniness Shraya cultivated while still passing as a man. Her feminine sensuality refutes the homophobic insistences that her stalker makes about her "natural" masculine gender. In their comic book, Shraya and Lee make material the trans* body as she defuses and reconstructs transphobic hatred through acts of creation.

As J. Halberstam argues *In a Queer Time & Place* (2004), "transgender" is a shifting term, important not simply for those who want to reside outside gender categories altogether but also for people who want to place themselves in the way of particular forms of recognition, a relation between and among people and communities (49). Transgender thus embraces hybrid possibilities for embodiment and identification. It is still subject to transphobia, violence, and oppression, as events around the globe all too frequently attest. *Death Threat* is an example of the attention that people—in her case, hate mail writer Nain Yoyokama—take in the transgender subject, as Yoyokama attempts to force Vivek to accord with his own (narrow) heteronormative gender categories. Unfortunately, thanks to the reach offered by social media, this transphobic person is granted unlimited psychological access to Shraya. Social media encourages an intimacy between sender and recipient, as messages are posted on a board or sent to an inbox that the recipient then opens; these are messages that can easily bypass some of the more common checks we have in place to protect our privacy. Ness Lee slows down the pace of reading the comic to dramatize the process through which Shraya and Yoyokama come in contact. Counterpointed pages juxtapose Shraya and Yoyokama's perspectives, as their destinies grow closer: the cool colors that distinguish the full-page spreads that feature the vulnerable Shraya contrast with the pages that depict a shadowy figure working over a laptop computer, crafting hateful messages. "Viveka!! Your name was shouted at my place as someone who has to die" (11), Yoyokama ejaculates in his first missive, threatening her with death.

Yoyokama's transphobic letters initially intrigue Shraya, as they are so obviously attempting to subdue the trans* subject. For Halberstam, this is one of the "typical" motivations for representing a trans* life by nontransgender people: "In this narrative project, the destabilizing effects of the transgender narrative are defused by establishing the transgender narrative as strange, uncharacteristic, and even pathological" (2005, 54–55). Yoyokama's letters seek to delimit Shraya's gender through language and faith. He uses the Sanskrit term "Napumsaka," which means "neither man nor woman, emasculate; or neuter gender (Gr.); m. hermaphrodite; eunuch, n. neuter word, neuter gender" (Shraya and Lee 2019, 13), to refer to Vivek, Sanskrit, or Hindi labels that resonated with Shraya, given her Hindu background. The letters also attempt to code Shraya's behavior as strange and pathological. For example, one of the letters advises Vivek to reject same-sex marriage (visualized by Lee as two grooms tumbling off a collapsing wedding cake, their homosexuality incongruous with the comforting matrix of hetero-domesticity), while another proclaims that her physical gender is "likely" male (25). Such letters first inspire confusion on Vivek's part, and then bemused humor. Lee visualizes Vivek's increased preoc-cupation with the hate mail, sleeping on a bed of bloody words that begin to stretch across the page. Increasingly, they amuse her less, so much so that she comes to be defined by and in relation to them. In this image, Lee depicts Vivek *as* the mail: her body contained by the letter, her powerlessness conveyed by her eyes that watch helplessly as a knife cuts her face. Yoyokama's hate mail goes on to pathologize her identity and to offer religious suggestions about how to atone for her trans* identity: "If you go to a forest Āśrama the sages there will help you," he writes. "They may have a Vaidya diagnose you. . . . And then put you in a separate mud hut" (24). From this religious-speak, Yoyokama proceeds to invoke Vivek's mother, advising Vivek to tell her mother that she is not a woman (26). At heart, these hateful letters seek to convince the trans* subject that she is strange and "unnatural," an icon even of Canadian sexual deviance: a Bonhomme Carnaval that wears a red Trump MAGA hat that reads, "Make Vivek a Man Again" (49). Such hate-speak produces the desired results: Vivek's paranoia deepens into an overwhelming sense of powerlessness in relation to the social structures that serve to protect the status quo. She catastrophizes that no one would believe her if she were to take these letters to the police, that she would in fact be arrested for "false accusation" (31) instead.[2]

As in Daniel Heath Justice's comics parable, love overturns hate in Shraya and Lee's comic. Another email—this time from her parents—breaks this pat-tern of transphobic abuse. "We are proud of what you and your brother are doing by his grace. Always know this—You are loved, no matter what," they write (41). Lee visualizes Vivek's intense emotions of gratitude and relief as a cleansing river of tears that pool beneath her laptop, her organ of creativity (43). At this point in the graphic text, *Death Threat* shifts focus, deploying certain formal techniques that give the readers access to the trans* gaze so that readers can look *with* Vivek rather than merely *at* her. The second half becomes metatextual, linking the transformation of hate mail into material for a best-selling comic. As with Justice's parable and the Tamakis' *Skim*, the act/art of storytelling brings power to the member of the marginalized community:

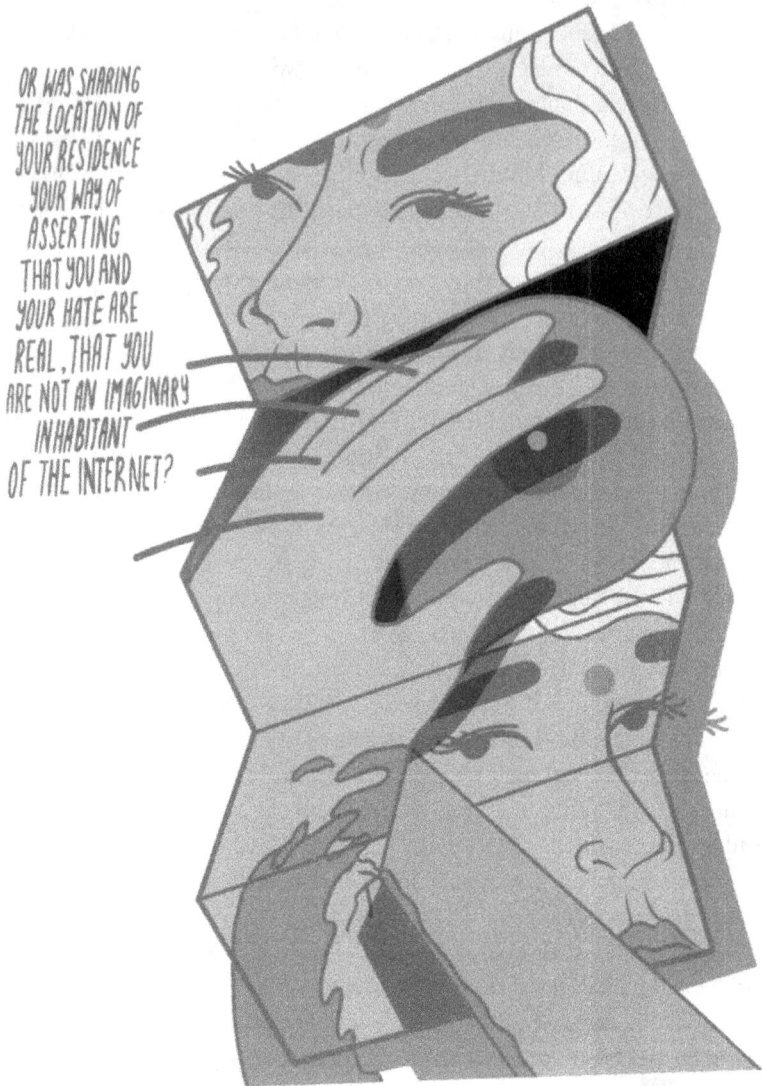

Figure 14.6. *Death Threat*, Vivek Shraya and Ness Lee. Arsenal Pulp Press, 2019, 20.

Shraya and Lee redeploy the hate mail and in so doing claim power over it. Refusing to perform as "trauma clown" for Nain Yoyokama, Vivek Shraya chooses to tell this story in the comics medium, to "turn hate into art," which will in turn lead to further invitations, art contracts, and institutional support.

The dynamic Canadian LGBTQ+ comics scene changes in exciting ways. A country as large as ours with communities with distinct and individual needs is increasingly a focus in the comics mode. These three comics by Daniel Heath Justice, Mariko and Jillian Tamaki, and Vivek Shraya and Ness Lee represent a trend in the Canadian comics scene that fills gaps in visual and LGBTQ+ representation. By disrupting colonially imposed and internalized systems of gender and sexuality, these three comics expand some of the dominant narratives about difference and diversity in the Canadian nation. Although these three comics address personal experiences of homophobia, sexual violence, and suicide, their traumas become instead a vehicle for transformation, visual vessels of empowerment by creators from marginalized communities that are moved to the center so they may begin to create from a place of privilege.

Notes

1. I use the terms "Indigenous" and "Indigenous peoples" to refer to the First Nations, Métis, and Inuit sovereign nations living in what is now called Canada, to honor the hundreds of culturally and linguistically distinct nations, and those of mixed ancestry, that inhabit North America and especially Canada.

2. Shraya never went to the police about the harassment. "The truth is, there is a really contentious history between queer people and the police," she said in an interview. "As a trans person, the last thing I want to do is be on the police radar. I don't completely trust anything would be really done about it. I never felt it was something I was comfortable doing" (Volmers 2019).

Works Cited

Chikuma-Reyns, Chris, and Gail de Vos. "Introduction." *Canadian Review of Comparative Literature/Revue Canadienne de Littérature Comparée* 43, no. 1 (2016): 5–22.

Chiu, Monica. "A Moment Outside of Time: The Visual Life of Homosexuality and Race in Tamaki and Tamaki's *Skim.*" In *Drawing New Color Lines: Transnational Asian American Graphic Narratives*, edited by Monica Chiu, 27–48. Hong Kong University Press, 2015.

Chute, Hillary. *Graphic Women: Life Narrative & Contemporary Comics.* Columbia, 2010.

Driskill, Qwo-Li, Chris Finley, Brian Joseph Gilley, and Scott Lauria Morgensen. "Introduction." In *Queer Indigenous Studies: Critical Interventions in Theory, Politics, and Literature*, edited by Driskill et al., 1–21. University of Arizona Press, 2011a.

Driskill, Qwo-Li, Daniel Heath Justice, Deborah Miranda, and Lisa Tatonetti. "Introduction." In *Sovereign Erotics: A Collection of Two-Spirit Literature*, edited by Driskill et al., 1–8. University of Arizona Press, 2011b.

Halberstam, Judith. *In a Queer Time & Place: Transgender Bodies, Subcultural Lives.* NYU Press, 2005.

Justice, Daniel Heath, and Weshoyot Alvitre. "The Boys Who Became the Hummingbirds." In *Moonshot: The Indigenous Comics Collection*, vol. 2, edited by Hope Nicholson, n.p. Alternate History Comics, 2017.

Luedecke, Patti. "Affect and the Body in Melville's *Bartleby* and Jillian Tamaki and Mariko Tamaki's *Skim.*" *International Journal of Comic Art* 11, no. 2 (2009): 299–321.

McCloud, Scott. *Reinventing Comics.* Perennial, 2000.

Rifkind, Candida, and Linda Warley. "Editors' Introduction." In *Canadian Graphic: Picturing Life Narratives*, edited by Rifkind and Warley, 1–19. Wilfrid Laurier Press, 2016.

Shraya, Vivek, and Ness Lee. *Death Threat*. Arsenal Pulp, 2019.

Shraya, Vivek. "How Did the Suffering of Marginalized Artists become so Marketable?" *NOW Magazine*, May 1, 2019. https://nowtoronto.com/culture/art-and-design/vivek-shraya-trauma-clown/.

Tamaki, Mariko, and Jillian Tamaki. *Skim*. Groundwood Books, 2010.

Volmers, Eric. "Vivek Shraya Confronts Hate and Harassment with New Graphic Novel, 'Death Threat.'" *The Guardian*, April 26, 2019. https://www.theguardian.pe.ca/lifestyles/vivek-shraya-confronts-hate-and-harassment-with-new-graphic-novel-death-threat-305801/.

Wolf, Doris. "Unsettling and Restorying Canadian Indigenous-Settler Histories in David Alexander Robertson's *The Life of Helen Betty Osborne* and *Sugar Falls*." In *Canadian Graphic: Picturing Life Narratives*, edited by Rifkind and Warley, 207–34. Wilfrid Laurier Press, 2016.

Chapter 15

BLK CARTOONS
BLACK LESBIAN IDENTITY IN COMICS

SHEENA C. HOWARD

The front cover of *BLK* magazine, the American monthly that published from 1988 to 1994, usually pictured prominent African American LGBTQ+ people, such as Audre Lorde, Marlon Riggs, Ivy Young, Dr. Marjorie Hill, and RuPaul, to name a few, who were interviewed in its pages. Along with regularly featured sections called Word Up, News, Arts, and Classifieds, investigative journalism articles, and advertisements tailored to the Black LGBTQ+ community, each issue usually included three to four single-panel comics. The magazine's production value increased as it gained popularity. According to founder and editor of *BLK*, Alan Bell:

> BLK was very popular. The Black LGBT community loved us. But, of course, we had the advantage of being the only game in town. But perhaps another way to look at our popularity (or perhaps "significance"), is that during BLK's run, we were the "go to" publication for non-Black LGBT media and organizations. Once Oprah's company called us asking for a referral. (personal communication, 2020)

This popularity led to very impressive print and distribution numbers for a niche magazine that began with little to no budget. "When the magazine was free, the print run was 50,000. When it went paid, the print run dropped to 10,000, of which 75% we sold," according to Alan Bell (personal communication, 2020). Throughout its six-year run, *BLK*'s cartoons represented a concerted and continued effort to engage with and develop a comics ecosystem, in the same way as those in magazines such as the *New Yorker* did, interacting with and alluding to the rest of the magazine's presentation of contemporary Black LGBTQ+ life. *BLK* comics led the way to visual and textual representation of lesbian and gay Black characters within a pioneering publication depicting this community. The last issue of *BLK*, published in 1994, coincides with the first comic book featuring a Black lesbian lead character, published that same year.[1] Even without claiming a direct connection between the two, I'd argue that noticing the features of *BLK*'s comics helps us to see the historical richness

established in LGBTQ+ comics of the late 1980s and early 1990s and the important timeline for the representation of Black LGBTQ+ people in comics.

> Of the decision to include comics in *BLK*'s pages, Alan Bell recalls that,
> while hard news was foremost in my mind, both the cartoons and *Word
> Up* were included as a respite from the magazine's serious side. Plus, they
> were a way of making incisive points through humor. The cartoons in
> the first seven issues were stolen from *Ebony* with new captions written
> by me. Beginning with number eight, the drawings were done by the
> late A. J. Benny (a pseudonym) from captions that I wrote in advance.
> (personal communication, 2020)

Although the magazine was journalistic and political in nature, its comics are
in line with how such publications have used single-panel comics, comic strips,
or "funny pages" for comic relief and to make fun of serious political issues.
Some *BLK* comics were demonstrably political. Others focused on a myriad
of topics—relationships, sex, education, and more—that were not as blatantly
so. Of course, even these comics can be interpreted through a political lens. As
a comics scholar focused on intersectionality who believes that the personal
is political and that ostensibly nonpolitical comics may nonetheless make a
political point, I enjoy and want to feature here *BLK* comics' intersectional
representation and politics.

This chapter considers over twenty single-panel comics that were published
in *BLK* magazine between 1990 and 1994, focusing on an exemplary sample of
nine of them. Through the lens of *Black Queer Identity Matrix*, I contend that
BLK magazine was at the forefront, addressing a void in Black lesbian comics
representation. The *BLK* comics offer radical resistant cultural commentary and
challenge systems of heteronormativity through the representation of a wide
range of Black lesbian experiences, especially within families, educational settings, and relationships. Their representation of Black lesbian lives contributes
to and seeks the empowerment of those lives.[2]

Depictions of Black lesbians in the media have largely been absent, sim-
plistic, or stereotypical. This is particularly true in the comic book industry.
Representations of Black lesbians in media often stereotyped them as masculine
or hyper-masculine or depicted women in submissive-dominant relationships
(Moore 2006). *BLK* challenged and spoke back to these stereotypes, representing intimate experiences of motherhood, family dynamics, and a variety of
interpersonal dynamics between Black lesbians.

In *BLK* no. 20 (July 1990), a single-panel comic depicts two Black lesbian
women at a hospital, looking through the window at a newborn baby. The caption reads, "He's okay. The doctor just left him in the test tube a little too long"

*"He's okay. The doctor just left him in the
test tube a little too long."*

Figure 15.1. "He's okay. The doctor just left him in the test tube a little too long," Alan Bell and A. J. Benny, *BLK* magazine (BLK Publishing Co., 1990).

(17). The couple's baby is pill-shaped. Today, it is more prevalent and acceptable to see lesbian women starting a family. Of course, at the time of this comic's appearance, same-sex marriage and the lesbian and gay communities' ability to serve openly in the military were not legal. In that context, the notion that two lesbian women would start a family would have been taboo, and definitely not represented in the comics industry. This panel represents lesbian women using new technology to start a family as it pokes fun at their own relatable anxieties and thereby disarms homophobic ways of rendering the idea of lesbians and gay men having children as abnormal, predatory, or sinister. This panel acts as a site of radical cultural commentary by depicting and normalizing such an otherwise taboo experience for a Black lesbian couple.

Such powerful *BLK* comics representation appeared during the comic book industry's Copper Age, a period roughly spanning 1984 to 1991, when a new breed of writers and artists took center stage (Howard 2018). Independent comic book publishers like Image Comics flooded the market with typically black-and-white offerings, and artists like Jimmie Robinson and the industry as a whole challenged depictions of white-male superheroes and those who created them. A decade-long self-publishing boom in the 1990s allowed creators much more room to expand the types of stories that were told in comics. *BLK*, publishing in the late 1980s, was a pioneer during this boom in comics for independent comics publishers. The LGBTQ+ experiences depicted in *BLK* were innovative and the comics' representation of gender was expansive, putting *BLK* at the forefront of comics' modern age.

BLK made a concerted effort to depict a variety of gender expressions. In a single-panel comic published in *BLK* no. 36 (1992), a Black lesbian woman with a curvy body and Gumbo-style haircut turns away and makes fun of a young door-to-door salesman with a very assertive tone and comment, "That's very interesting. Now I'm going to tell you the story of the dyke that poked the little Dutch boy" (23). A contrasting gender presentation is evident in a comic from *BLK* no. 38 (1993) in which two Black lesbian women present as very feminine, hugging in bed, one pregnant and waking from a nightmare, while her lover comforts her. The caption reads: "It was just a nightmare. But you are going to have to face the fact that our baby might be straight" (4). Repeating the topic of Black lesbian women starting a family, the comic represented a variety of important types of visibility during a time when Black lesbian women living together and starting a family was otherwise absent in the mass media. *BLK*'s comics represent Black lesbian womanhood as self-possessed and confident, assertive and savvy, tender and loving, maternal and affectionate, and wry and funny.

In a comic set in the world outside the domestic space, in *BLK* no. 37 (1992), readers encounter a Black lesbian woman at an ice cream parlor ordering a sundae from a server who asks, "Whipped cream, nuts and cherry?" The customer replies, "The cream and cherry will do just fine." A placard announces that the shop sells "69 flavors." Representing these women doing taken-for-granted things allows the reader to visualize a society in which Black lesbian women are free to flirt, court, and verbalize interest in other women in the public sphere. Heterosexual men and women might not think twice about flirting. Comics like this one normalize its possibility for Black lesbians, too, and they describe a world in which Black lesbians can be themselves beyond the privacy of domestic space.

BLK's comics help us to remember that representation is important because it reinforces taken-for-granted beliefs about who we are and how we should present ourselves to the world. To underscore the point, some *BLK* comics characters confront the consequences of a lack of such representation. A single-panel comic in *BLK* no. 36 (1992) depicts two Black women after a movie date together, leaving a theatre where they watched *The Addams Family*. One woman asks the other, "Do you think there's any possibility that Thing is lesbian?" (15). As a Black queer woman, I can relate to the humor and commentary in this

Figure 15.2. "Whipped cream, nuts and cherry?" "The cream and cherry will do just fine," Alan Bell and A. J. Benny, *BLK* magazine (BLK Publishing Co., 1992).

panel. During my college years, I'd always hope that certain characters on television or female actors were lesbians so that I could have someone or something to connect to. Though a lack of representation can be harmful, isolating, and demoralizing, this panel treats the subject resiliently and with naughty humor. "Thing" is a hand in *The Addams Family* movie, and the reader is tacitly encouraged to imagine what possibilities the movie-goers might see in its sexuality. Moreover, the subtext highlights the severe lack of lesbian representation across mass media, leading these movie viewers to yearn to see queer sexuality in even the silent and second-tier character. Taking up even non-depictions of lesbian lives in *The Addams Family* and ascribing lesbian possibility allows the *BLK* comic to challenge the erasure of Black lesbian women in the public sphere, in mass media (like Hollywood movies), and in comics (the Addams Family, after all, originated in Charles Addams's single-panel comics in the *New Yorker*).

Attempting to normalize the everyday experiences of Black lesbian women by depicting a breadth of them, *BLK* addressed a sore need for representation during the 1990s, one that is still felt today. Black lesbian women and women of color are yearning to be represented more widely across mass media platforms—this includes in comics (Howard 2014; Muñoz 1991; Bowleg 2008). A

diversity of Black lesbian representation signals acceptance and leads to feelings of coexistence. To flag the importance of "others" and simply to acknowledge that *others* exist are overwhelming aspirations for Black lesbian women
(*BQIM*). Like *Cyberzone* and its Black lesbian superhero, Amanda Gunn, afterwards, *BLK*'s comics begin to fill a representational void, addressing the need
for visibility, acceptance, and acknowledged coexistence.

Beyond its important strategies of representation, *BLK*'s comics propose
examples of Black lesbian empowerment. They reflect aspects of Black lesbian
community empowerment achieved through pride, strength, and protest, by
wearing clothes that are deemed empowering and by staying mentally strong
(*BQIM*) and recognizing that Black lesbian women use multiple communica-
tive strategies to feel empowered within a system that often renders them power-
less. *BLK*'s comics envision empowerment as the ability, as well as struggle,
to exist and overcome internal and external fears through acceptance of self,
solidarity, and affirmation (Howard 2014, 55).

Of course, representation is itself empowering. A *BLK* comic from January
1991 depicts two Black lesbian women at a small restaurant, "'Kickin' Chicken."
As one of them orders, the other who is behind the counter replies, "Would you
like two breasts?" (26). The caption reads, "Karina stifles the urge to give the
obvious answer." Beyond helping Black lesbian women to understand that there
are other Black lesbian women who love women, and that they can be found in
a variety of places, including the neighborhood chicken spot, the comic gives
these women the empowering license to flirt in public. In the world outside
the comic, flirting can feel risky, provoking severe negative reactions or giving
rise to enough fear of such reactions that it is never risked. Depicting a lesbian
woman flirting not only represents the public existence of Black lesbian lives.
It makes it feel as though it is okay to live those lives fully. This is empowering.

A comic in *BLK* no. 21 (August 1990) features just four letters: "HNIC" (22),
relying on its readers' shared cultural understanding to make sense of their
meaning: "Head Nigga In Charge." Its first use in Black media that I recall
(though it might have been referenced earlier in popular culture) is in the cult
classic movie, *Lean On Me* (dir. John G. Avildsen, 1989), in which Joe Clark, a
new school principal in New Jersey, asserts, "This is not a damn democracy.
We are in a state of emergency, and my word is law. There's only one boss in
this place, and that's me—the 'HNIC.'" A well-known phrase with an obscure
origin, widely in use across the Black community, it describes a Black person
in a position of power and authority. Growing up, I understood its meaning.
The *BLK* comic does not explicitly identify the Black woman in the panel as a
lesbian, but it hardly needs to given the magazine's target audience. The comic's
use of the acronym is empowering: it both describes the power of and ascribes
power to its single character. She is on the phone, presumably giving someone an

Figure 15.3. "HNIC," Alan Bell and A. J. Benny, *BLK* magazine (BLK Publishing Co., 1990).

order. In *BLK*, Black lesbian women, a triple jeopardy minority contending with intersectional gender, race, and sexuality discrimination, discover an illustration of what they could be and aspire to, particularly in the workplace.

Beyond picturing empowered Black lesbians living fully in public and taking charge in the workplace, *BLK* further expands the capacity of its comics to imagine lesbian power by including safer sex as a topic. In a *BLK* comic in no. 41 (March 1994), two Black women walk towards a building labeled "Oakwood Vampire Association." The caption tells us, "I hear that nowadays they use dental dams and just pretend to bite." Not imagining safe sex as a limitation, this panel subtly promotes safe-sex practices between lesbian women while it powerfully affirms the existence of lesbian sex and specifies the kinds of safe-sex practices that are available to lesbian women, something that was rare or nonexistent in the mass media at the time. The ease with which the panel's characters refer to dental dams normalizes the use of these safe-sex practices through humor. Black lesbian women are thereby empowered and not at all embarrassed to discuss and practice safe sex.

The kinds of forthrightness and humor that we find in the *BLK* comics model a way of coping with the matrix of homophobia, sexism, and racism that Black lesbian women face, mechanisms that have been defined by Black

"I hear that nowadays they use dental dams and just pretend to bite.."

Figure 15.4. "I hear that nowadays they use dental dams and just pretend to bite," Bell and A. J. Benny, *BLK* magazine (BLK Publishing Co., 1994).

lesbian women in previous research (Howard 2014). By presenting scenes in which characters cope, the comics indirectly depict the intersectionality at the core of Black lesbian identity. *BLK* depicts this intersectionality in various panels. In a comic in *BLK* no. 37 (1992), a woman at a clothing store holds up two outfits with dissimilar styles and fabrics. She turns to the sales associate and says, "Apparently it's row vs. suede" (2), a clever allusion to the United States Supreme Court's 1973 landmark *Roe v. Wade* decision which ruled that the Constitution protects a pregnant woman's freedom to choose to have an abortion without excessive government restriction. This decision is still being challenged today, just as it was at the time when this comic was published. That fact helps to show the continued topicality of the reference and that Black women are and were politically engaged even as the women's rights movement has been criticized for its lack of inclusion and action in support of women of color. In 1989, when *BLK* was being produced and published, Faye Wattleton, the first Black woman president of Planned Parenthood, stood on the steps of the Supreme Court to condemn its *Webster v. Reproductive Health Services* decision to limit abortion access and to divert one's right to choose what happens to one's own body to the state. Vulnerable populations with fewer resources and finances, and less mobility than their white counterparts would be more devastated. That same year, sixteen Black women made history by publishing the first collective statement advocating for equal access to abortion, "We Remember: African-American Women are for Reproductive Freedom." Retired congresswoman Shirley Chisholm, soon-to-be-elected representative Maxine Waters, and civil rights activist Dorothy Height were among the notable signatories (Whaley 2019). The shopping woman in the comic suggests an easy facility with these important political developments that bear on her own bodily autonomy and the power of women more generally. Moreover, it prompts readers to bring to mind the facts of Black women and childbirth: Black women are more likely to die of complications related to childbirth (Oparah and Bonaparte 2015). Restricting access to abortions can exacerbate those vulnerabilities for a group whose health disparities are tied to their lack of economic power (Howard 2014). Considering these interlocking systems of oppression helps to reveal the complicated implications of the *BLK* comic's depiction of a Black lesbian shopper who exercises her financial prerogatives while referencing a judicial decision the restricting or overturning of which could devastate that power.

Such intersectional considerations should be taken into account when reading another comic from *BLK* no. 36 (1992), depicting two Black women looking at a sign that reads: "Session 1: Black Homophobia, Gay Racism [. . .] Groups meet at opposite ends of the same room." Speaking directly to the intersections of race, gender, sexual orientation, and heterosexism, the panel lacks a reference to lesbians, rendering these two women absent in the verbiage, and forcing them to decide where they fit in or have their issues addressed. Aside from the obvious joke about how ostensible homophobia among Black people and racism among gays so polarizes a session convened to contend with those very problems, the panel directly depicts the dilemma Black lesbian women have to contend with in a society that excludes them. Which group is most amenable to Black lesbians and their concerns: homophobic Black people or racist gay ones? This comic identifies the conundrum and speaks back to the cultural norms within a matrix of race, gender, and sexual orientation that excludes Black lesbians.[3]

Such nimble use of intersectional allusion is a regular feature of the magazine's comics. In its January 1991 issue (no. 26, page 30), *BLK* published a single-panel comic that depicts two women talking to one another, while reading the newspaper. Flipping homophobia on its head, the comic pokes fun at heterosexists. This speaks to the matrix of domination around sexual orientation that Black women contend with in a layered and complex way. The humor in this

Figure 15.5. "Session 1: Black Homophobia, Gay Racism," "Groups meet at opposite ends of the same room," Alan Bell and A. J. Benny, *BLK* magazine (BLK Publishing Co., 1992).

cartoon is the bending and challenging of these labels (lesbian, gay, etc.) and the social constructs that precede these labels.

BLK magazine is a fruitful site of exploration for the themes of representation, empowerment, and intersectionality, rarely explored or illustrated elsewhere in the comics ecosystem in the late 1980s and early 1990s, or after. Even during the "Black Age of Comics," also known as the self-publishing comics boom of the 1990s, there was nearly no representation of Black LGBTQ+ people in comics—but there were *BLK* comics panels. These *BLK* comics were at the forefront of Black lesbian representation in the comics ecosystem, even before the publication of the first comic book featuring a Black lesbian lead character.

One might well wonder about their creator. Who was A. J. Benny and what did he contribute to the canon of comics after *BLK* magazine ceased operations? Benny, who signed the cartoon panels in *BLK* as "AJB," used this as a pseudonym to protect his identity; fears of homophobia and backlash prevented him from revealing his real name. As Alan Bell remembers, "Since my initials are AB and his are AJB, we agreed that they would be signed AJB, with the A and B doing double-duty. The initials of the artist's real name are also AJB" (personal communication, 2020). Fascinating and frustrating, it is nearly

"*The politically correct New Yorkers have decided that being lesbian or gay is sexist. They are requiring everyone to be bisexual.*"

Figure 15.6. "The politically correct New Yorkers have decided that being lesbian or gay is sexist. They are requiring everyone to be bisexual," Alan Bell and A. J. Benny, *BLK* magazine (BLK Publishing Co., 1991).

impossible to pin down the comics or artwork of "AJB" before or after the publication of *BLK* magazine. It is certain, however, that AJB passed away and his family is still uncomfortable publicly revealing his identity or more about his work with *BLK* (Alan Bell, personal communication, 2020). However, much is known about editor and founder, Alan Bell, who worked collaboratively with AJB to produce the comics. He recalls that before and after the publication of *BLK*, he dabbled in the realm of comics and was always intrigued by the single-panel format in particular. He says, "A favorite thing to do was to re-write the captions and share them with friends. The re-writes might be black or gay, but they also just might be anything else on my mind that I thought would be funny to friends" (personal communication, 2020). Bell was most inspired by the styles found in publications like the *New Yorker*, and he was attracted both to absurdity and to puns, which is evident in the humor of the single-panel comics he published in *BLK*. Bell, however, did not publish anything comics-related since *BLK*, as he continued as president of BLK Publishing Company, focusing on working with community-based organizations through his graphic design, corporate identity, and custom publishing work.

The collaboration of two Black gay men yielded comics that displayed a variety of gender expressions and opposed single-dimensional and stereotypical representations of Black lesbians. They offered a varied representation of Black lesbian women beyond clichés exclusive to the butch-femme dichotomy (see Moore 2006). The *BLK* comics were forward-thinking and helped make the magazine a site of dominant cultural resistance. They are imbued with a sense of empowerment for Black lesbian women, demonstrating that Black women can be in charge, in the workforce, with regard to their own sexual safety and health, and in everyday private and public experiences.

Across its six-year run, in *BLK*, Black lesbian women were represented alongside Black gay men in comics while Black lesbian women were absent from the larger comics ecosystem. It is not, however, lost on me that Black lesbian women were not a part of the *BLK* creative team. *Black Queer Identity Matrix* places value on Black lesbian scholars analyzing representations of Black lesbian identity, as there is power in tending to the voice, perspective, and analyses of said community. Although Black lesbian women did not create the comics in *BLK*, their inclusion still marks *BLK* as radical and pioneering in the comics ecosystem but also for media in general. As a comics scholar who studies race, gender, and sexual orientation, I was surprised at the inclusion of Black lesbian women in the *BLK* comics as I was used to a more prevalent focus on Black gay male representation and had come to expect that Black lesbian women would be excluded. On this issue, Alan Bell says,

> Black lesbian representation in the cartoons was absolutely intentional. It was always *BLK*'s mission to tell the story of the entire black LGBT community. That meant in all ways: good and bad, Democratic and Republican, female and male, big city and small town, etc. While we might not be able to achieve parity on all these tensions since the news is what it is, we had total control over our ability to even things up in the cartoons. In fact, a favorite thing to do was tell the same joke from both a black lesbian and black gay male point of view, printing both in the same issue. (personal communication, 2020)

As a Black queer woman, I want my experiences and stories to be represented, and I want my community to be depicted in a breadth of ways that speak to the depth and complexity of my humanity. In addition, it is encouraging that more Black queer women today are telling their own stories, including me. I want to further move towards coexistence, and because of that I am appreciative of the intentionality of *BLK* magazine and the editor's concerted effort to be inclusive and to foster coexistence, "learning to live together, accept difference, and make the world a safe place for difference" (Howard 2014, 57). The comics that *BLK* published and the magazine itself represent Black lesbian women in an innovative and pioneering fashion, years before the first comic that featured a Black lesbian lead character. As Audre Lorde reminds us, "it is not our differences that divide us. It is our inability to recognize, accept, and celebrate those differences" (Lorde, 85). *BLK*'s comics do the work of such recognition, acceptance, and celebration.

Notes

1. *Cyberzone* was a comic book self-published by Jimmie Robinson and later published by Image Comics. It features Amanda Gunn, the first Black lesbian lead comic book character.

2. The *Black Queer Identity Matrix* (BQIM) was designed to "allow researchers to begin to explore questions around the Black, lesbian female community" (Howard 2014, xvi). BQIM posits that, the master narrative of American culture has maintained a compulsory heterosexual notion of reality. This dominating and oppressive system is supported and embedded in institutions such as education, healthcare, marriage, etc. (Howard 2014). Reading *BLK*, with a specific focus on the cartoon panels as a Black queer female allows me to interrogate the cartoon panels based on the fundamental assumptions of BQIM. That is, BQIM operates from the fundamental position that queer theory is deficient in addressing the needs and concerns of Black lesbian identity. The framework posits that Black queer women should be at the forefront of any analysis and critical examination of research on Black queer women in academe.

3. Discerning this matrix of domination allows researchers to critique how systems of power, domination, and oppression are produced, reproduced and constrained, according to Patricia Hill Collins (2009). However, according to Sheena Howard (2014), "Collins' matrix of domination is not sympathetic to the specific construct of sexual orientation or the dialectical tension of race and gender for the Black lesbian female" (73). This comic depicts this tension and dilemma, thus challenging the shortcomings around race, gender, and sexual orientation across the LGBTQ+ community and society at large.

Works Cited

Bowleg, L. "When Black + Woman + Lesbian? = Black Lesbian Woman: The Methodological Challenges of Qualitative and Quantitative Intersectionality Research." *Sex Roles* 59, nos. 5–6 (2008): 312–25.

Braun and Clarke. "Using Thematic Analysis in Psychology." *Qualitative Research in Psychology* 3, no. 2 (2006): 77–101.

Collins, P. *Black Feminist Thought: Knowledge Consciousness, and the Politics of Empowerment.* HarperCollins Academic, 2009.

Howard, S. *Black Queer Identity Matrix: Towards an Integrated Queer of Color Framework.* Peter Lang, 2014.

Howard, S. "Situating Cyberzone: Black Lesbian Identity." *Journal of Lesbian Studies* 22, no. 4 (2018): 1–13.

Lorde, Audre. *Sister Outsider.* Crossing, 1984.

Moore, Mignon R. "Lipstick or Timberlands? Meanings of Gender Presentation in Black Lesbian Communities." *Signs* 32, no. 1 (2006): 113–39.

Muñoz, J. *Disidentifications: Queers of Color and the Performance of Politics.* University of Minnesota Press, 1991.

Oparah, J., and A. Bonaparte. *Birthing Justice: Black Women, Pregnancy, and Childbirth.* Routledge, 2015.

Robinson, Jimmie. *Cyberzone* 1, no. 1–4 (1994).

Whaley, N. "Black Women and the Fight for Abortion Rights: How This Brochure Sparked the Movement for Reproductive Freedom." NBC News, March 25, 2019, p. 4.

Chapter 16

GOLDIE VANCE
QUEER GIRL DETECTIVE

LARA HEDBERG AND REBECCA HUTTON

The twenty-first century boom in comics and graphic novels for young readers has brought with it an expansion in the corpus of graphic narratives representing young queer female subjectivities. Christine A. Jenkins and Michael Cart chronicle the "rapid growth" in the number of queer characters represented on the page, and note increases in "the number of female authors and illustrators," contributing to the field as well as in female audiences for graphic narratives (2018, 187–88). There has also been a broadening of the types of intersectional queer representation seen in graphic narratives for young audiences, with Hope Larson and Brittney Williams's *Goldie Vance* (2016–), a popular comic-turned-graphic-novel series for young readers, as one such example. Set in early 1960s Florida, the series features sixteen-year-old protagonist Marigold "Goldie" Vance, a queer, Black feminist who dreams of being a detective. The *Goldie Vance* series uses the graphic narrative form to present an updated, yet historicized revisioning of the girl detective that positions an active, rebellious, and successful young, Black, queer woman at the forefront of crime-solving.

Sheena C. Howard (2018) suggests that the "inclusion of triple-jeopardy minorities (three oppressed identities) in comic books presents a cultural collision with historically dominant narratives in comic books" (412). What is particularly productive in *Goldie Vance*'s approach to representation is the way the text opens up spaces for the recognition and valuation of queer, Black, feminist subjectivities through a blending of "then," "now," and an imagining of what could be. Goldie's work as a valet at the resort her father manages, her love of cars and drag racing, and her prodigious ability as a mechanic are combined with her desire to become a detective and intense crush on "cool" record store clerk Diane Kimura. Goldie's professional and sexual desires are accommodated by the seeming erasure of racial or sexual prejudice in the bright, glossy, liberal alternative history of the series; however, real world histories and politics are not necessarily forgotten. In fact, *Goldie Vance*'s interweaving of historical details and movements avoids simply superimposing contemporary identity politics onto a historical backdrop. From styling Diane in greaser-like attire to Goldie's best friend Cheryl's preoccupation with NASA and becoming an astronaut to drawing on Cold War tensions to having a cast of female characters who point to an array of civil rights movements, this narrative situates Goldie and her friends within a recognizable history at once familiar and unfamiliar. This chapter argues that representations of queerness in this series sit in the nexus between past and present, and between word and image. *Goldie Vance* reclaims space for queer subjectivities and lives in the past while also drawing readers into contemporary queer identity politics. In doing so, the series does not posit a clear demarcation between a "progressive" now and an oppressive past that might lead readers to assume that the work of civil rights, feminism, and gay liberation has reached an end. Instead, the text uses the conflation of then-and-now to offer young readers visions of agential and valued intersectional queer subjectivities.

Prior to readers witnessing her desires for Diane, Goldie is already coded as transgressive, as queering normative conventions of girlhood. As an esteemed race car driver and mechanic, she defies real-world understandings of gender normativity that would likely inform readers' approaches to interpreting her interests and occupations. Goldie is immediately identifiable as a working-class Black teenager through the visuals of the text, in a manner that concurrently disrupts patriarchal systems of power and hierarchy as she actively inserts herself into detective cases and the machinations of resort management. From taking on the role of "assistant" to the official resort detective, Walter Toole, to solving crimes that threaten the resort, her father's position as manager, and even North America itself, Goldie challenges and questions her way through each adventure. Of note is that while the narrative does include (unsuccessful) attempts by men (such as Goldie's father and Walter) to reign in her risk-taking to solve cases, the text refuses to present similar resistance with regard to Goldie's other non-normative attributes. In fact, Goldie's status as race car driver and mechanic are revered (she is the best around, proven by a showdown with the other top driver, Sugar Maple, in volume 3), and she is surrounded by a cohort of other female characters who also occupy non-normative positions.[1] Furthermore, Goldie's romance with Diane is not commented on negatively or discouraged. There is no surprise or disapproval at Goldie's desire for Diane and no demarcation between heterosexual and homosexual relationships.

In *Goldie Vance*, queer desire is depicted as positive and without prejudice for young readers, an audience frequently denied such representations due to assumptions of both sexual "innocence" and compulsory heterosexuality that are associated with children (Pugh 2011). Within the field of children's and young adult literature, the past two decades have seen a notable increase in the number of texts featuring queer protagonists, but queer female characters of color are still a minority within such minority representation. While the visual markers of Goldie's age, gender, race, and even class are visually obvious in every panel, her sexuality is rendered in a manner that relies predominantly on gesture and physical response. Here, the possibilities of the graphic visual narrative, more so than dialogue, champion the series' openness to the representation of queer sexuality. Young readers are offered visual codes that engage with queer sexuality, as neither Goldie nor Diane's sexuality is ever formally stated. Rather, in the first volume of the series young readers follow the visual language of desire (blushing, shared glances, longing looks) and are positioned alongside Goldie as she must work out, or detect, Diane's sexuality and potential attraction. Goldie's relationship with Diane evolves across all four volumes of the series to date, from her crush-at-first-sight to Diane's reciprocated feelings and subsequent assistance in solving crimes to their relationship that survives a potential break up in volume 4. By affording this relationship both the depth and duration that exceeds the fast-paced, easily resolved "case of the week" storylines that appear in each volume, the series offers a vision of young queer desire as significant and worthy of recognition.

The pacing of the narrative further facilitates an emphasis on this relationship even among Goldie's chaotic, action-packed adventures. After Walter is drugged in volume 1, Goldie steals a car and pursues the culprit, witnesses a crash, rappels down a cliff, rescues a woman from a burning wreck, and is then knocked unconscious. The panel design changes to heighten the action, with the often orderly rectangular panels of the preceding pages replaced with a series of sharp-edged trapezoids dominating each spread. The white space between panels reduces on most of these pages, with the black-framed panels often overlapping full page, large-scale backgrounds, asking readers to split their attention as both Goldie and the reader are forced to take in the competing visuals. But the pacing suddenly shifts as Diane comes into Goldie's view. The largest panel on the page features Diane (in a swimsuit and sporting a parasol), and the readers are offered a visual invitation to linger on this sight as Goldie does, offering a queer gaze as the reader's position aligns with Goldie's. This is followed closely by a full page of the two women conversing in the car on the way home. After the quick succession of action throughout the previous pages, the time devoted to conversation between Goldie and Diane conveys this moment of connection as particularly salient.

The representational strategies underpinning the visual presentation of Goldie's desire for Diane (and Diane's returned affections later in the narrative) also eschew the stereotypical "coming out" narrative trope prevalent within narratives for young people. The absence of the "coming out" narrative operates in a dual capacity. First, it avoids the heteronormative assumption of heterosexuality, where being gay is something that one has to articulate as Other. Such narratives of course acknowledge aspects of the realities queer young people face within the heteronormative structures that govern society, but, as Lydia Kokkola suggests, they still often politicize young protagonists' sexuality as the central problem of the text. Kokkola notes that "making sexual orientation the 'problem' that needs to be solved" may "inadvertently reinforce negative stereotypes of same-sex desire" (2013, 98). Second, the omission of a "coming out" narrative for Goldie in the series connects in interesting ways with the political environment of the 1960s, a time infused with the intersecting vectors of the civil rights movement, sexual revolution, and the beginnings of gay liberation. Such openness regarding queer desire in this fictionalized version of the period offers a questioning of the often-assumed primacy of current time periods as politically "advanced."

As a visual medium, the *Goldie Vance* comics are able to circumvent the need to articulate Goldie and Diane's sexuality linguistically through the visual depiction of their attraction to each other. This approach opens up interpretive possibilities around sexuality, as it resists the construction of sexuality as Other through specific identity categorization, and instead situates queer desire within a more open field of interpretation. The first indication of Goldie's crush on Diane comes as she pauses to say hello to her friend, Tony, who is lounging against the record store window. After Tony says he is "waiting for Diane to punch out," readers turn the page to see a panel featuring Diane selling a Beethoven record to an elderly woman.[2] In the same panel, Goldie appears in silhouette pressed up against the window as she utters a wistful "Diane ..." As a femme version of a "Greaser," with short dark hair, red lips, and a black leather jacket with a popped collar, Diane epitomizes Goldie's statement in the following panel: "She's so cool." This is accompanied by a close-up of Goldie staring wistfully through the window, hand pressed up against the glass, a blush on her cheeks as she longs for Diane. In the next panel of the sequence, Tony tells her that he and Diane are going out, and readers see from Goldie's wide eyes that she is shaken. She asks, "What? On a - - a date?" and when his response inadvertently implies a confirmation she deflates, her body slumping forward with her face and eyes downcast. Tony suggests that Goldie come along with them but she refuses, already walking away. She turns her head sadly to add, "Third wheel's not my style." In this scene, while the inference of heterosexual attraction between Tony and Diane is actually born of Goldie's assumptions in response to the language employed to articulate Tony and Diane's relationship (which is later revealed to be platonic), the visual narrative locates all physical vestiges of desire within Goldie's attraction to Diane. Tony displays none of the same infatuation. The narrative thus privileges Goldie's desire for Diane and refuses to confirm the illusion of heterosexual desire between Tony and Diane for readers.

The significance of this initial representation of Goldie's crush is key here. As mentioned, there are no negative reflections, articulations, or repercussions that result from Goldie's desire for another woman. Rather, young readers are positioned through these visual mechanisms to wish, just as Goldie wishes, for her and Diane to be on a date together. This affective engagement is amplified as Goldie rides her bike home, with a triptych panel featuring large thought bubbles that depict Diane smiling in flirtatious ways, each getting progressively smaller as the reality of Diane going on a date with Tony sets in for Goldie. The potential loss of this possibility for Goldie is reinforced as something to lament rather than to feel ashamed of. Unlike queer-baiting, which often sees the audience set up to desire certain character pairings only to have those relationships never come to fruition—and likely never were intended to (Brennan 2018)—*Goldie Vance* builds readers' desire for the possibility of a relationship between the two women and then delivers this as a reality. Queer desire is not doomed to be unfulfilled here. In fact, in a fictional world where a sixteen-year-old can free-dive to an underwater training base, take down KGB spies, and survive the animosity of numerous villains, a same-sex relationship takes the mantle as one of the more realistic outcomes by real-world standards, the byproduct of which is an affirmation of queer desire.

As with any detective narrative, the misdirection around Diane's sexuality is soon unraveled, re-inviting readers to engage with the possibility of a romance between the two. When Goldie next encounters Diane, she hesitantly asks about the date with Tony. Diane's grimace, coupled with her response, "No, no, no. He's not my type," is followed by a panel in which Goldie looks directly at the reader with a sly smile and simply says, "Oh." When Goldie then informs Diane that she is "running from the law," Diane's disclosure that she "always thought [she'd] make a keen accomplice" is followed immediately by a panel that cuts to Goldie grinning and blushing. If Goldie can imagine this as a possible sign of there still being promise for the two of them, this likewise gives the reader permission to do the same. Thus, not only does the reader work alongside Goldie to navigate the cues Diane provides, but they are also in a position outside of the narrative where the combination of Diane and Goldie's responses facilitate their ability to imagine the possibilities for the two. Furthermore, Diane's willingness to race off with Goldie as they work to outsmart the villain of the story and locate a kidnapped client offers readers a romantic story arc that elides any self-doubt or homophobia. The first volume concludes with two close-up panels where Goldie takes Diane's hand and suggests a movie as they drive off into the night. These initial moments of unselfconscious queer desire are reflected throughout subsequent volumes as neither Goldie's family nor friends have any issue with her queerness, nor her dating Diane. Seen kissing, hand in hand, hugging and calling each other "cutie," the queer visualization of their desire for, and engagement with, one another without the need for linguistic articulation of their sexualities across the series is facilitated through the comic medium.

The visualization of queer desires within the medium of the graphic narrative—which is predicated on readers closing the gaps between panels and negotiating the complex inferences that exist between word and image—opens up spaces for reader engagement that encourage investment in the progression of Goldie's relationship with Diane without directly casting them as Other. In offering a young, queer, Black, feminist girl detective depicted without contestation within a revised 1960s setting, and serializing this narrative so as to present Goldie's adventures and relationship as worthy of ongoing engagement from contemporary young audiences, this text concomitantly acknowledges and values queer identities of the past and present.

Notes

1. These non-normative female characters include Cheryl, who is training to be an astronaut and specializes in science; a cohort of female mechanics Goldie works with when she goes undercover in volume 3; recurring character, FBI Agent Layla Ladner; and even Goldie's mother, who facilitates a deep-sea rescue in volume 2.

2. In keeping with the overarching representation of racial diversity across both primary and secondary characters throughout the text, Goldie, Tony, and the elderly woman are all people of color.

Works Cited

Brennan, Joseph. "Queerbaiting: The 'Playful' Possibilities of Homoeroticism." *International Journal of Cultural Studies* 21, no. 2 (March 2018): 189–206.

Howard, Sheena C. "Situating *Cyberzone*: Black Lesbian Identity in Comics." *Journal of Lesbian Studies* 22, no. 4 (2018): 402–14.

Jenkins, Christine A., and Michael Cart. *Representing the Rainbow in Young Adult Literature: LGBTQ+ Content Since 1969*. Rowman & Littlefield Publishers, 2018.

Kokkola, Lydia. *Fictions of Adolescent Carnality: Sexy Sinners and Delinquent Deviants*. John Benjamins Publishing Company, 2013.

Larson, Hope, Brittney Williams, and Sarah Stern. *Goldie Vance: Volume 1*. BOOM! Box, 2016.

Larson, Hope, Brittney Williams, and Sarah Stern. *Goldie Vance: Volume 2*. BOOM! Box, 2017.

Larson, Hope, Brittney Williams, and Sarah Stern. *Goldie Vance: Volume 3*. BOOM! Box, 2017.

Larson, Hope, Jackie Ball, Elle Power, and Sarah Stern. *Goldie Vance: Volume 4*. BOOM! Box, 2018.

Pugh, Tison. *Innocence, Heterosexuality, and the Queerness of Children's Literature*. Routledge, 2011.

Chapter 17

REPRODUCTION OF ARTWORK BY ALISON BECHDEL

INTRODUCTION

Alison Bechdel is a comics legend. Her landmark strip, *Dykes to Watch Out For*, syndicated widely in LGBTQ+ newspapers, became a shared comics touchstone for a generation of readers. Her iconic characters made familiar and relatable LGBTQ+ lives a regular part of the comics and her astonishing productivity provided enough hilarious, topical, political, and romantic material to fill more than a dozen reprint collections.

The *Dykes to Watch Out For* strips that follow are reprinted with Bechdel's generous permission.

Figure 17.1. "A Serious Party," Alison Bechdel, in *The Essential Dykes to Watch Out For* (Houghton Mifflin Harcourt, 2008), 49.

Figure 17.2. "Virtual Interface," Alison Bechdel, in *The Essential Dykes to Watch Out For* (Houghton Mifflin Harcourt, 2008), 129.

Figure 17.3. "Notes on Camp," Alison Bechdel, in *The Essential Dykes to Watch Out For* (Houghton Mifflin Harcourt, 2008), 263.

IV.

SEEN/SCENE: DISCOVERY, VISIBILITY, COMMUNITY

Chapter 18

SEEN/SCENE
SECTION INTRODUCTION

ALISON HALSALL AND JONATHAN WARREN

To look gay. To present queerly. To be proud. To reject stigma. To sparkle. Throughout modern LGBTQ+ history, visibility has been a fundamental tool of political and activist work, a key feature of community building, a catalyst, theme, and credo for social and cultural creativity. Against the dulling presumptuousness of heteronormativity, queer scintillation and flaunting, coded costume and custom, and a myriad of subtle, ever-evolving inflections of self-fashioning have worked as signal flares, alerting us to one another, teaching us to calibrate our gaydar to find our way together, and modeling ways to repurpose and recode heterosexual cultural artifacts and modes with nonstandard, queer meanings (Halperin 2012, 18). Once a critical mass of affinity builds, what is seen starts to feel like a scene, and what might have been provisional, incidental, and ephemeral becomes recognizable, iterable, and sustainable.

Because LGBTQ+ comics are a visual medium, for them queer visibility is axiomatic. All comics coordinate pictures and words for visual impact, but, in form and theme, LGBTQ+ comics generate their particular attention out of specific and shared histories that inform their queer visual modes and references. For example, Diane DiMassa's comic strips unleash lesbian power, with Hothead Paisan claiming space, taking up room, dominating action, and rebuking heterosexist disparagement and silencing of or obliviousness to women, especially queer ones. Hothead makes a scene, raging at her world while remembering always to demand that we acknowledge her presence, visibility, humanity, and temerity (for example, see figures 2.4–6 on pages 38–39, 41). In her comics, Jennifer Camper visualizes communities—passionate dykes; lusty women who look to experiment sexually; household sadists; people living with HIV/AIDS, etc.—while mobilizing communities around her among LGBTQ+ comics creators and critics. Her work is full of women who are passionate, joyful, irreverent, and fiercely funny. "Laughing at enemies is a quick way to take away their power," asserts Camper, whose humor is one of her most powerful weapons in making visible the contradictions of queer lives (1994, n.p.) (see figures 21.1–10 on pages 294–303). In the shame-defying flagrancy of Tom of Finland's comics, exhibitionist voluptuaries ramp up the scopophilic intensity

Figure 18.1. Tom of Finland. "Kake 4: Nasty Nature Trail." 1969. *Tom of Finland: The Comic Collection, Volume I* (Taschen, 2005), n.p.

while also showing how visually hyperbolic masculinity correlates with queer longing in figures both worshipful and parodic. Brazen visibility, in turn, may come across as a trace counter-effect of queer closeting or concealment, of the survival practices of queer furtiveness that Tom often transforms into scenic phantasmagoria of gay cruising, of the fear of being targeted, and of neglect, adumbration, or oppression. As comics like Tom of Finland's propose a fantasy world in which characters' queer agency is accounted for by its ubiquitous and pneumatic beefcake embodiment, their amplified love of uniform men in uniforms should remind us of other LGBTQ+ scenes that they are contrived to transcend, particularly those of gender and sexuality in which being looked at, typed, and construed may belie or obscure selfhood and complicate agency. LGBTQ+ comics always *visualize* queerness and that they are thinking about what it means to do so.

"One of the things that 'queer' can refer to," Eve Kosofsky Sedgwick claims in 1993, is "the open mesh of possibilities, gaps, overlaps, dissonances and resonances, lapses and excesses of meaning when the constituent elements of anyone's gender, of anyone's sexuality aren't made (or can't be made) to signify monolithically" (8). As the chapters collected in this final section of *The LGBTQ+ Comics Studies Reader* showcase, queer comics feature a panoply of images, texts, and characters that visualize possibilities for discovery, visibility, community at every site of their production, and that intersect with other

Figure 18.2. Tom of Finland. "Kake 16: Sex on the Train." 1974. *Tom of Finland: The Comic Collection, Volume IV* (Taschen, 2005), n.p.

identity-constituting discourses like race, gender, and medicine. Lin Young's essay explores the potentialities of webcomics to allow creators to explore queer lives without being explicitly oriented around or defined by political oppression and its resistance. Young proposes that recent narratives of hope and normalization in LGBTQ+ webcomics represent a new type of visibility and community for queers, a depoliticized mode of storytelling that looks to detach its narrative conflicts from any obligation to represent or acknowledge social and/or political oppression. In contrast, remus jackson investigates the community networks that shape the contemporary comics scene, in particular zines self-published or produced DIY (do-it-yourself) by queer people who use the comics format to articulate a non-hegemonic experience of masculinity. The comics work of Victor Martins and Higu Rose highlights a fragmentary positioning of identity, jackson argues, enabling stories of transness to go beyond archetypal stories of bodily becoming (and ending in a "complete" transition from one gender to another), so that gender identity is evoked instead through tensions between cisgender constructions of masculinity and a trans* sense of self. As the emotional and creative responses of fan cultures evince, comics that lack overt LGBTQ+ representation can still shape queer modes of appreciation among readers, as Jonathan Warren's chapter on early American comics attests. Riverdale's sexually charged teen community, the scopophilic excitement offered by Golden Age superheroes, the gender-fluid homoerotic tension governing Krazy and Ignatz's turbulent relationship (in comics and cartoons) provides queer suggestiveness that readers of early comics can discover, recognize, and enjoy.

Because LGBTQ+ lives are so often vulnerable and precarious and, even in the wake of some countries' legal and juridical measures to extend equal treatment provisions to gay people, so irregularly or minimally protected from harm and so routinely the subject of scorn and vitriol, to be seen is still often to risk livelihood, life, or limb. Chapters in this section also explore queer visual coding that attempts to envision selfhoods that resist or enjoy freedom from the hegemonic gaze, and the mobilization of art (networks of self-syndication among LGBTQ+ cartoonists, as well as underground and zine communities) to create a communitarian ethos, one that balances solidarity, responsibility, and activism. remus jackson's chapter shares with Sathyaraj Venkatesan and Chinmay Murali's essay an exploration of the cis-medical institutional gaze and the violences this gaze directs at trans* people and lesbians who are trying to get pregnant, as depicted in A. K. Summers's *Pregnant Butch: Nine Long Months Spent in Drag* (2014). Summers's narrative exposes the heterosexual bias in motherhood, while illustrating how the biomedical discourse categorizes butch pregnancy as "unnatural" and "deviant." Summers's Teek Thomasson is a butch trailblazer whose adventurous instincts are emphasized by the Tintin costume she wears. That Teek spent "nine long months [. . .] in drag" alludes to the cisgender constructions of femininity and motherhood still institutionalized by the medical establishment that jar so unpleasantly with Teek's lived experiences of pregnancy and motherhood.

Alison Bechdel's *Dykes to Watch Out For* addresses in word and image the seen/scene dichotomy that is the organizing conceit of this section. One of the earliest representations of lesbians in popular culture, running from 1983 to 2008, the title of the strip itself is resonant, calling attention to a taxonomy of lesbians that the strip visualizes for readers, queer and straight. One cannot underestimate the importance of Bechdel's strip for LGBTQ+ comics around the world for visualizing and valuing various queer communities over twenty-five years of publication, all set against the changing zeitgeist of the time in the United States. The double meaning of the strip's title exemplifies LGBTQ+ comics' treatment of the multiple senses of queer visuality: on the one hand, Bechdel presents a host of lesbian types for readers to recognize and value, to be seen at the scene, if you will. On the other, Bechdel introduces a subtle suggestion of threat in her taxonomy of dykes to fear or to be wary of, to watch out for, because of the subversions that they actively make to the status quo.

Two particular images call to mind the central thematics—discovery, visibility, community—of this final section of the collection: the drawn photograph of her father's secret lover, Roy, at the center of Bechdel's memoir *Fun Home*

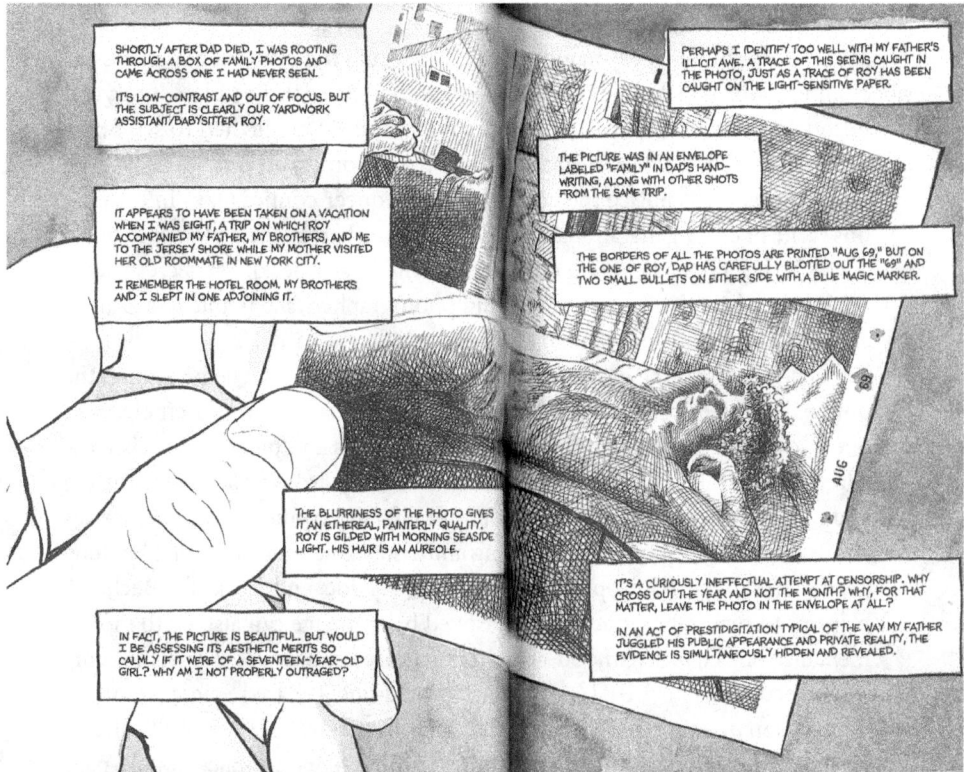

Figure 18.3. *Fun Home: A Family Tragicomic*, Alison Bechdel (Houghton Mifflin, 2006), 100–101.

(2006) and Marvel comics' double-page centerfold of The Thing from *The Fantastic Four* in the program for the 1974 Comic Art Convention. *Fun Home* is a frequent touchstone in LGBTQ+ comics scholarship, and it has quickly become central in the queer comics canon. A graphic memoir about growing up queer, it juxtaposes the development of Alison's lesbian identity with her closeted father Bruce's sexual history with young men. At its center is a photograph of one of those young men, a former student of her father's whom Alison knew as her babysitter and her father's yardwork assistant. Discovering it in a box of family photos after her father's death, Bechdel reproduces it lovingly and meticulously by hand, transforming it into an aesthetic totem, and features it prominently to acknowledge and affirm her father's sexual identity, now uncloseted by his daughter's intervention and tribute. In the photo, Roy, wearing only his briefs, arms curled over his head, "is gilded with morning seaside light. . . . His hair is an aureole" (Bechdel 2006, 100). In its blurry timelessness, its idealized gay masculinity, its evocation of a world before HIV/AIDS and of a time before Bruce's suicide, the image is a potent talisman of queer visibility. Looking at it, Alison senses what must have been her father's "illicit awe" (101) at Roy's beauty, and she assures that the hidden, lost, or forgotten be seen, locating it at the center of her own memoir and thereby making visible a queerness-in-common with her father. As Alison holds the photo in Bechdel's book and Bechdel's readers, in turn, hold the graphic novel, all are invited to see Bruce as a gay man as they see Alison as a lesbian and comics creator. Moreover, we are encouraged to notice the crucial role that queer comics plays in creating this scene of cross-generational queer disclosure whereby the daughter lovingly assists in her father's coming out by including his tender queer secret within the heart of her book: what he saw and photographed, she is able to see anew and adapt and transform in her comics.

Bechdel stresses the importance of pictorial queerness and demonstrates the power that queer comics have to witness, disclose, and transmit emblems of queer love and desire, acknowledging that the risks and pleasures of visuality and visibility link LGBTQ+ lives across time. She is hardly alone in recognizing and rallying the exceptional capacities of LGBTQ+ comics which themselves constitute a nexus of queer storytelling and visual culture. Flaunting it has long been a glorious modus operandi of LGBTQ+ pride, and work like Bechdel's helps us to remember that to be transfixed by an image can also be to monumentalize one's queer selfhood, and sharing those experiences of queer looking can be occasions for LGBTQ+ solidarity, including a shared Spidey-sense for queer resonances across ostensibly dissimilar artifacts. For example, Bechdel's luminous beefcake photograph may bring to mind Marvel comics' double-page spread of The Thing posing nude, which in turn visually references a 1972 issue of *Cosmopolitan* that featured Hollywood icon Burt Reynolds in a similar pose. This particular rendition of The Thing visualizes the multi-dimensionality of LGBTQ+ bodies, their strength, complexity, eroticism, and vulnerability in comics that might not otherwise have had their queerness noted. Ramzi Fawaz (2016) has explored the nonnormative or "queer" effects that *The Fantastic Four* dramatized right from their inaugural issue in 1961, when their bodies were bombarded by "cosmic rays" that altered their molecular structure, and whose deviance from sexual and gender norms of Cold War culture was in turn marked on their very bodies. The centerfold image of The Thing in the program for the 1974 Comic Art Convention is as intimate as Bechdel's photograph of Roy, as The Thing reclines languidly on a spotted leopard print blanket, smoking a cigar, with a rose propped behind his ear. Coy, intimate, masculine, effeminate, genderqueer, and homoerotic, The Thing looks brazenly out at the reader, daring one to see and appreciate the erotic potential of the transgressive superheroic body, a body "in a continual state of political transition or flux" (Fawaz 2016, 69). Burt Reynolds, whose own appearance as a centerfold heartthrob—objectified but not disempowered, acknowledging the feminized trope without conforming to or endorsing its routine misogyny,

Figure 18.4. New York Comic Art Convention program, Jack Kirby (1974), 36–37.

satirizing pinup titillation while also ironically providing it, testing the limits of machismo against homophobic suspicions of merely decorative or feigned manliness, etc.—was itself still a fresh departure from pop cultural norms of visualizing American masculinity, is redeployed in this image as a rocky and monstrous Thing, at once evocative and provocative. The image evokes all the troubled queerness that the evident self-confidence of the Burt Reynolds pinup kept at bay: true to his comic book characterization, The Thing comes off as both hypermasculine and deeply insecure, reminding viewers that, despite his stony appearance, this particular monstrosity fails at the hard masculine social norms (finding a job, getting married, etc.), making him a "sissy" (Fawaz 2016, 77). Marvel readers were especially drawn to The Thing's neuroses, to the implications of unsettled gender correlated with transitions from human to rock form, and to the character's feelings of being "trapped" in his mutated body, all of which seemed to evoke The Thing's visuality in a queerly multiple sense. As the Marvel superhero struggles with how to accept his inescapable identity, one that, like Bruce's in *Fun Home*, torments him as abnormal, The Thing allows Marvel to show "lapses and excesses of meaning" (Sedgwick 1993, 8), that make visible a delight in comics' queer potential.

Beyond acknowledging the themes of LGBTQ+ discovery, visibility, and seeing community in such comics, it is worth noticing how comics' formal processes may extend our understanding of queer visuality. The particular materiality of *Fun Home*, its metatextual referencing of photography and of the process of visual reproduction, directs us to see how the LGBTQ+ artist returns queer humanity to the mechanically produced image. Bechdel retrieves Roy's gayness by creating a drawing of his photograph or by posing herself as the character in the comics panel; both are attempts to *show* readers how she infuses herself into her characters. By letting us see how she sees herself in what her comics present to us, Bechdel correlates her formal interpolation within her images with their stories of disclosure, revelation, and outing (the nature of Roy's relationship with her father, her father's closetedness, etc.). Through such means, Bechdel illustrates that "the end of his lie coincided with the beginning of my truth" (Bechdel 2006, 117), and Alison accepts her own visibility simultaneously as a lesbian and as a comics creator through the same visual gesture.

Bruce Bechdel filed his photograph of Roy in an envelope labeled "family," ironically reminding us that, for LGBTQ+ people, biological family may be an invisibilizing force, bound up with secrecy, anxiety, unhappiness, and oppression. Bechdel sharply contrasts that with other supportive chosen communities, activist groups, her own female lovers and partners; likewise, Bruce's male lovers offer temporary, tantalizing moments of pleasure. Making visible such scenes of queer affirmation is also a priority of Marvel's *The Fantastic Four* which, after all, is named for a biologically unrelated group of non-normative heroes whose identities, affiliations, and experiences of difference and stigma evoke a kinship based on their shared humanity (Fawaz 2016, 72). In what follows, this section's chapters take up the question of how different kinds of LGBTQ+ visibility nurture the formation of intradiegetic and extradiegetic queer communities, affinities, and scenes.

Works Cited

Bechdel, Alison. *Fun Home: A Family Tragicomic*. Houghton Mifflin, 2006.

Camper, Jennifer. *Rude Girls and Dangerous Women*. Laugh Lines Press, 1994.

Fawaz, Ramzi. *The New Mutants: Superheroes and the Radical Imagination of American Comics*. NYU Press, 2016.

Halperin, David M. *How to Be Gay*. The Belknap Press of Harvard University Press, 2012.

Sedgwick, Eve Kosofsky. *Tendencies*. Duke University Press, 1993.

Chapter 19

READING COMICS QUEERLY

JONATHAN WARREN

Ask comics readers, as indeed we did for this volume, about LGBTQ+ comics, and you are more likely than not to hear back about comics that depict LGBTQ+ characters and experiences or that otherwise acknowledge the existence of queer people, if the readers you asked can think of any. A presumptive seeking out of a first-order sort of *representation* informs any such extemporaneous bibliography. Even when such an attempt to generate a list fails to know how to justify a first entry, the reasoning that leads to such an impasse is usually the same: the conflation of LGBTQ+ representation with comics' queerness. Likewise, readers may wonder aloud about the sexual orientations and gender experiences and expressions of particular comics creators. I am very sympathetic to such completely reasonable impulses but note their preponderance as marking an emergent and noteworthy shift from how gay cultural touchstones have often been identified until recently. The emergence of a critical mass of LGBTQ+ representation in comics and beyond them has adjusted how we conceptualize a notional museum or catalogue raisonnée of LGBTQ+ culture. Until recently objects of queer veneration or delight that, even when not always transparently clear products of LGBTQ+ creators or showcases for considerations of queer lives, were inevitably and even reflexively counted in whenever they had piqued an undeniable gay interest, prompted a queer fandom, or travestied heteronormativity in some way that was important to an LGBTQ+ audience. Attending to representation is one important way of seeing culture's queerness, but we risk neglecting an influential attribute of LGBTQ+ readers' relation to comics if we don't also acknowledge the pervasive and continuing power of less witting queer suggestiveness in the comics of our formative reading histories. Comics that lack clear LGBTQ+ representation nonetheless cultivate gay attachments and tastes and shape queer modes of appreciation and discernment.

Without diminishing what can be the tremendous value of discovering details about a creator's LGBTQ+ identity, we hardly need such biographical specificity to discern comics' gayness just as we do not need to rely on comics' plausible depiction of contextually recognizable gay life to suss out their queerness, to find queerness in them, or to attribute queerness to them. Indeed, it has not been until relatively recently that comics readers have sometimes been able to pre-select, as it were, for comics' queerness by way of knowing about their creators' LGBTQ+ status, of their depiction or fictionalization of the lived experiences of queerness and of queer people, and so on. That kind of taxonomy is useful, empowering, and inspiring, but its emerging mode of making LGBTQ+ content visible should not, without better accounting for it, supplant or efface the foregoing, idiosyncratic way-finding that characterized what it was like to read comics queerly.

My childhood connection to comics, though never so committed that any-one would characterize it as fandom, was nonetheless able to sustain a gay fascination via, say, the unstated romantic possibilities and permutations of the Archie-Jughead-Reggie-Moose variety. Though it is safe to say that John L. Goldwater, Archie's creator and a founding force behind, and the energetically conservative president of, the Comics Magazine Association of America, was nowhere committed to depicting his era's LGBTQ+ life or to using *Archie* to realize his own queer vision, my own nascent gay reading practice eas-ily accommodated itself to that comic's world of love-addled teenaged boys whose failure to consummate their ostensible desires with the mostly aloof or otherwise not quite available Betty or Veronica often left them to spend time with one another, sublimating their yearnings through varieties of homosocial intensity that suited my prepubescent, pre-erotic gay imagination. Further-more, the regimented heteronormativity of 1960s and early 1970s comic book Riverdale did not necessarily feel especially exclusive or restrictive to a child who, like so many gay kids of the time, of course, lived in that world (though in nowhere near such a suburban version of it), knew the vocabulary of only its pop culture, and identified his place within it, not (or not yet) as its excep-tion, its antagonist, its outsider, its reprobate, etc. The mode of reading that this entailed included seeing one's selfhood in cultural artifacts that were otherwise apparently thoroughly dependent on speaking to and cultivating a regularized or non-idiosyncratic readership. Without flagged instances of queer representa-tion, it was hardly impossible to use the tools at hand to test any comic's queer possibility just as it was to have G.I. Joe make out with Stretch Armstrong. In a world of comics without today's LGBTQ+ representation, readers were not without gayness. And while in so many big and small ways the post-Stonewall era of visibility has made gay life so indisputably better and more secure, the klieg lights of today's queer metropolis should not risk diminishing our valu-able earlier ability readily to discern and respond to fainter homo starlight.

Indeed, comics' universal silence about queerness did not make me wonder after a franker articulation of gay reality. Rather, it conformed to what was and largely continues to be so much of kiddie pop culture's general blandness with regard to sexuality. That that blandness more than skewed straight isn't news, but it's worth noting that, though it surely did so, this didn't simply foreclose gayness. Sure, comics' penchant for heterosexual story arcs and motivations was most often so routine as to be stultifying, but that universe conveyed important queer messages despite itself. When Archie panted after Betty, that eager sexuality featured most often to power the engine of the comic's consummation-frustration storytelling machinery, and its boys-yearning-for-girls paradigm looked to confirm that it was the dissatisfying story of an eternal impasse. But what of the fact that even without any ultimate culmination the comic was so undeniably saturated in a hetero orientation toward one? Didn't its relentless insistence that boys want to be with girls crowd out, holler over, silence, and deny any queer footing? It didn't seem that way to a child who enjoyed its depiction of a world where boys weren't disparaged for wanting to spend too much time with girls and where masculinity wasn't at issue when it responded to the appeal of femininity. It was entirely possible to read *Archie* as a pop literature of prepubescent queerness in which Riverdale's teenagers were slightly more grown-up avatars of erotically oblivious children. After all, like Jughead, Reggie, Archie, and the rest, I, too, enjoyed the homosociality of witnessing and participating in the emergence of male friends' incipient desires, just as I also appreciated Betty and Veronica both for their providing access to the winsome playfulness and crafty humor of a girls' zone that I was usually scolded for wanting too much of in the actual schoolyard and for making available, maybe for the first time, the ways of seeing boys as desirable. That these characters were straight was no discouragement; compared to their other appeals, their heterosexuality though so obviously pronounced nonetheless always *felt* pretty meagre if it registered at all. It wasn't just that the comics' voluptuous girls were what its frantic boys continually could not ultimately have, whatever that would mean, but that even when their would-be romantic connections did not fail, they also never really succeeded. Dates, car rides together, fleeting smooches, what the comics called "making time": none of these dissipated their ever dissatisfied yearning. As decency norms like those expressed by the Comics Code Authority required the inexorable postponement of such characters' satisfaction and extended the euphemism-strewn narration of their desire, it did not merely tantalize or titillate all readers into accommodating themselves to an obsessively hetero end game while maintaining an otherwise sexless decorum. Such comics' conflation of heterosexuality as axiomatic motivation with their decency obligations to cast panting teenaged horniness as routinized nonevent where no success really satisfies advertised that straight love was only so much fervency covering over the fact that its hetero orientation really looked unceasingly hopeless, certainly its culmination as *beside the point* as the prospect of Wile E. Coyote actually capturing and—what?—eating the Roadrunner, of Elmer J. Fudd murdering Bugs Bunny. The frenzy was the fun, the heteronormativity the flubbed sales pitch.

Heavy-handed normative story formulas, for there were hardly any others, inculcated the habit of looking further to discern eros, queerness, and gay possibility in other silences and indirection. For example, Jughead's relative impassivity marked him as an oddball to the other characters who sometimes marveled at what they took as his inexplicable and blasé indifference to girls. He struck me as mostly a foil for their own monomania, and their sometimes annoying eagerness that Jughead should rouse himself to be more like them disclosed less about Jughead, who remained a cipher, than it exposed the fragility of the boys whose girl-craziness strangely could brook no dissent. Certainly, Jughead offered the possibility of opting out of compulsory heterosexuality or of being a bemused bystander to its displays in the narrative curlicues, gags, and invented delays that built toward the ever unrealized culmination of the other characters' desires. One might posit such a characterization as the comic's gentle mockery of queerness and as a caricature of an often sidelined character's non-productiveness and mystifying opacity, a bafflement moreover that *Archie* would usually position its readers to share. In contrast to his active friends, Jughead's aloof lolling about lacked appeal; his stillness did not seem fun. But if the comics were trying to teach its young readers that being a queer outsider wasn't as desirable as signing on for their energetic heteronormative games, they also prefigured the conclusion of those antics as another death to fun. So, I associated Jughead's quietude not, or not only, with the queer outside to Archie's pursuits but with what would be the dissipation of their energy should they ever get where they ostensibly wanted to go. It all made me suspect that *Archie*'s love plots entailed the eventual, undesirable stoppage of the comic's storytelling and of its mildly daffy seriality of revved up boys without girls, of boys who want girls so badly that their stories therefore need always to keep them apart from one another just enough that that yearning might persist.[1]

What would be the alternative to such serial postponement but the death of the whole enterprise? I think of those truly sinister final moments of *Snow White and the Seven Dwarfs* when dunderheaded Snow White is roused from her poison-apple coma by Prince Charming's kiss, oblivious to all the plot that has intervened, ignorant of what we all know about the evil queen's grandiose trickery and the stunning valor of the dwarves and woodland animals, and, because she has slept right through her story's most exciting bits, believing wrongly that that magic apple really did make her dreams come true. How infuriating that just when the homosocial, working-class, man-children figure out how to collaborate with the anthropomorphic animals, their whole reason for doing so chirpily abandons them all in favor of a man she barely knows, a castle in the clouds, and a storybook closure that looks much like death and definitely shuts down the carnival. Who's dopey, really? The silly dwarf who tries to get a big fat farewell kiss on the lips, or Snow White, who maybe misunderstands the potential scale and nature of the erotic free-for-all that she is exiting as she rotates his head to bestow a chaste goodbye peck on his forehead? Or think of the preposterous conclusion of *The Wizard of Oz* in which Dorothy would have us believe that the scoffing of those incredulous barnyard yokels in the final shots back in black-and-white Kansas is really preferable to the Technicolor movie-musical wonderment of her yellow-brick road phantasmagoria or bearable but for the fact that she can now see through to their gloriously queer subtexts. Obviously, Snow White should have figured out how to stay in the forest. If Prince Charming really loved her, how could he possibly mind? The audio-visual hyperbole of the Disney finale couldn't make its lesson in regimented straightness overcome the fact that it is an annoying foreclosure of the much more exciting fun we see precede it. Likewise, Dorothy appears to have little but homely familiarity pulling her back to Kansas from a dreamworld in which the range of potential experiences is vastly superior.

To be taught that one's fondest desires should naturally entail the end of fun adventures, the pairing of boys with girls, and a return to a dreary Kansan farmstead that hadn't been blown off its foundation after all did not feel especially stifling or censorious to a reader or viewer who had never encountered anything else and who'd become accustomed to noticing when a first-order narrative was undercut by its queer countercurrents and subtexts. Still it was refreshing to discover other queer possibilities. These came not merely via the advent of gay liberation in post-Stonewall pop culture. All that, after all, took so much time to ramify in the newsstand comics to which I had access. And before I was able to come upon much more grown-up LGBTQ+ content, my propensity to associate gayness with implication had found fuel in the pages of reprint collections of *MAD Magazine* comics. When thinking about LGBTQ+ comics, there is a natural tendency to expect much of the future and to watch for a kind of progress as cultural artifacts track forward with queer political empowerment and cultural liberalization. But *MAD*'s delirious satires—I recall being especially provoked by one of Mickey Mouse and Donald Duck as feuding Hollywood celebrities whose customary costumes could be taken off—encouraged me to find queer possibility in the past. What else was there?

One scarcely needs the fretful cautions of the mid-twentieth-century arbiters of comic book decency to notice the queerness of the Golden Age even when its protagonists' psychological complexity was (*pace* Bruce Wayne's PTSD, Clark Kent's intermittent lonesome homesickness) wafer thin, its commitments to the defense of homogeneous and quiescent normality relentlessly square, or its superheroes' general impassivity symptomatic of an affective range that stretched all the way from self-assured to stolid. The visual disclosure of quasi-naked muscularity in Golden Age comics established a conventional pictorial grammar out of relentless masculine exposure and objectification, and subjected male bodies to the sort of scopophilic delectation typically reserved for female ones. Readers became accustomed to an alchemy by which the vulnerability that might otherwise attend public nudity or the hungry, leering gaze was transmuted into hyperbolic brazen strength. The sheer magnetism of heroes accruing, enhancing, or simply indicating their power by galivanting in candy-colored circus tights is queerly at odds with law and order stories so invested in ho-hum normality. Such comics' gayness inheres not in their depiction of LGBTQ+ lives or of same-sex desires, or by virtue of their creators' sexuality but in their ready availability to ascriptions of queerness even before we factor in the genre's conventional dependence on secret identities and fretting about being exposed, sometimes ludicrously campy villainy, or kinky challenges to bodily strength and endurance. That such a wonderful scholarship was waiting to grow up around *Wonder Woman* and the kink-inflected specifics of her creator's unconventional life and career helps to iterate the queerness of Golden Age heroes that was evident in advance of such diagnostic biographical backstories.

In these respects, the Golden Age superheroes' transgressions of normality drew my Cold War-era imagination, inured to a mainstream that afforded an interest in and expectation of implicit queerness, to a past where the fixity of identity seemed even more tenuous and sexuality loopier. The Saturday morning cartoons of the mid-1960s included King Features Syndicate's animated version of *Krazy Kat*—fifty cartoon shorts first aired on television from 1962 to 1964 and then repeated for years after that—providing an entry to the perpetual motion machine that is George Herriman's Coconino County, the southwestern desert world of fluid identity and free-floating signifiers for desire and abuse, pleasure and torment. When, from his endless supply, Herriman's fervent little mouse heaves one of his bricks at the noggin of the hapless Krazy Kat, Ignatz does more than carry on a rich tradition of slapstick comic violence. The brick: so simple, useful, and basic. Although, when hurled by a mouse at a cat, it might seem an obvious metaphor for animosity or cruelty, those cartoons, which in turn led me to the comics, opened up a universe of ambiguity.

The brick—even though it is by its very nature, hard and unyielding, baked to a cruelly, solid fortitude in the ever-burning ovens of Kolin Kelly—is surprisingly and oh so importantly *flexible*. Its hardness is, paradoxically, pliable, and transformable; its meaning varies depending on how you look at it. And while it is well known that its affinity with such Dadaist defamiliarization effects was an aspect of Herriman's creation that excited contemporaneous intellectuals along the lines of Gilbert Seldes's famous homage which, seeing beyond its modernist experimentalism, compares *Krazy Kat*'s qualities to those of the works of Anatole France, Henri Rousseau, Miguel de Cervantes, Charles Dickens, and Charlie Chaplin (1924, 231–33) and concurs with contemporaries who saw in Herriman's whimsies elements from Wolfram von Eschenbach and Shakespeare (236, 238), its instructional value was no less forceful and perhaps even more widespread once it made its way through some inter-generational wormhole to the world of repetitive mid-1960s broadcast television. I remember well how my older brother cheered the relentless viciousness of the abusive mouse, noticing too my different focus on how the infatuated cat, bafflingly, kept wanting it so badly. I knew bullies. That brother was growing into one. So, it seemed preposterous that any character would yearn for their own harm. Of course, the magic of Herriman's invention is that Ignatz's intention with the brick differs from Krazy's interpretation upon its reception; what is thrown in hostility lands with affection. Krazy's love is confirmed. Ignatz's fury is foiled. And Offissa Pupp, who jails Ignatz and defends Krazy whom he also adores, multiplies the miscues, never winning the appreciation of Krazy who, after all, doesn't want Pupp's protection. Here was kiddie culture about a kind of desire to which I could relate, at least in part. Ignatz's axiomatic loathing for Krazy was as inexplicable and familiar as my brother's aggressive menace, but Krazy's appetite for it made sense only as a kind of defensive put-on or mysterious flirtation meant to reinforce parental wisdom about life in the playground which "explained" that sometimes kids are mean because they like you. Intrigued, I worked backwards from cartoon to comic.

Although in the King Features version, Herriman's shifty, mirage-prone, desert southwest has more of a post-World War II, Levittown suburban vibe in the manner of the Flintstones' Bedrock and the Jetsons' Orbit City, the cartoons preserved many of the strip's essentials, with one tremendous exception. In the cartoons, Krazy is female. Her patience with Ignatz's truculence is innocent and wise in the manner of television wives of the era who always saw through to the lovability of grouchy, bigoted, oblivious, or hurtful husbands. In the strips, Krazy's gender varies: sometimes female, sometimes male, and sometimes Krazy does not know. I knew this because, having noticed our interest in the cartoons—which is to say, they were on, and we were watching—my father brought out his copy of the 1946 Henry Holt reprint collection of Herriman's work and enlightened us about the comics' origins in newspaper strips that started before and were still appearing during his Depression-era youth. What ambivalence I had about cartoons that normalized male abuse and female acquiescence, and that egged on my brother's worst impulses, quickly evaporated when met by the strip's greater intricacy, nuance, and commitment to the unsettling, queer force of the arbitrary and the ambiguous. The 1960s cartoons required viewers to accept that Krazy likes Ignatz so much that she will put up with his violence and that dreamy heterosexual romance knows to overlook the occasional brick to the skull. The comics revealed Herriman's more elaborate conceptual blueprint.

In them, Ignatz's incessant determination to hurt Krazy is correlated with his impotence as every missile he hurls betrays him by changing its meaning midair. Rather than what seemed to be the cartoons' justification for the inevitable or excusable violence of straight love, the original *Krazy Kat* print comics instead repeatedly feature vicious little Ignatz's unending bafflement at his lack of authority and force. Meanwhile, wondrous Krazy never acquiesces to, or strives to meet, Ignatz on his terms. Instead Krazy subverts Ignatz's and any reader's expectation that they will submit to a gender designation. By extension, the comics imply that Krazy's desire for the male mouse is sometimes straight and sometimes gay, and, because so protean, always unpredictably queer. In the reprint volume's introduction, E. E. Cummings celebrates Krazy this way:

> Let's make no mistake about Krazy. A lot of people "love" because, and a lot of people "love" although, and a few individuals love. Love is something illimitable; and a lot of people spend their limited lives trying to prevent anything illimitable from happening to them. Krazy, however, is not a lot of people. Krazy is herself. Krazy is illimitable—she loves. She loves in the only way anyone can love: illimitably. She isn't morbid and she isn't long-suffering; she doesn't "love" someone because he hurts her and she doesn't "love" someone although he hurts her. She doesn't, moreover, "love" someone who hurts her. Quite the contrary: she loves someone who gives her unmitigated joy. How? By always trying his limited worst to make her unlove him, and always failing—not that our heroine is insensitive (for a more sensitive heroine never existed) but that our villain's every effort to limit her love with his unlove ends by a transforming of his limitation into her illimitability. If you're going to pity anyone, the last anyone to pity is our loving heroine, Krazy Kat. (1946, 217–18)

Ignatz's would-be assertions forever misfire not because Krazy is stupidly forgiving or smitten, but because the whole universe is on Krazy's side. Krazy exemplifies Coconino County's nature and physics, its ways of knowing and being. Ignatz cannot succeed because his world itself is as ever-shifting as the meaning of his bricks. They will never sustain his meaning or submit to his expectations of fixity; their fluidity is inexorable. On the other side, Krazy always benefits from this setup precisely to the degree that Ignatz himself is so fixed, so unvarying, so reliable, and, as Krazy sees it, so apparently devoted, so evidently in love with the fluidity that Krazy epitomizes. The world is constructed to prevent Krazy from suffering and to confound her/his/their antagonists.

In a characteristically philosophical interlude, when Offissa Pupp and Krazy ponder the essence of the humble brick, Herriman allows them to marvel that the clay upon which they stand, the kiln-fired material out of which their world is built, the conduit by which Ignatz strives to express himself, the basis for palaces and cathedrals (in Herriman's distinctive maybe Yiddish-inflected argot, Krazy is awed by the thought of "pellissis" and "kiddeedrils") is a metonym for their whole world's language and art, in all its range of application and sheer adaptability. As for Ignatz, the brick stands for the walls of the jail house in which he is repeatedly incarcerated for trying to hurt Krazy: solid, delimiting, and punitive. Upon Pupp's mention of jails, Krazy diverts us from ideas of the carceral and the captive, concluding that strip: "Oh yes—prisms is made from them also" (Herriman). While Ignatz is jailed for acting on a narrow desire suggestive of his small-minded, hurtful, and limited understanding, Krazy swoons expansively. Herriman's pun—prisons/prisms—is the comic's verbal approximation of visual refraction.

To see through Krazy's eyes is to delight in the susceptibility of male aggressive energy to queer delectation and to enjoy seeing the determined hostility of its violent prerogative evaporate in the queer gentleness of Krazy's lisping malapropism. In Krazy's adoration, Ignatz's bullyish energy transmutes into a cartoonish pretense. Of what? The irresistibility of the down-low or rough trade? The fronting tough guy who is always on the wrong side of the law because he cannot stop wanting the gender-fluid femme of a different species? The magnetic, naked display of machismo's failure, when the would-be swaggering brute is exposed as the queer character's "l'il ainjil," at once masculinist and feminized, straight and bent? Through Krazy's prismatic appreciation, the brooding, menacing, infantile mouse achieves romantic force despite himself, as though caught up in some vast, invisible queer scene for which there is no safe word.

Krazy demonstrates the capacity of love to transform even antagonists into all manner of desiderata. In Herriman's comic, different kinds of affective intensity, from contempt to adoration, are susceptible to slide into each other and to stand for one another—the love token, still a brick—often more than figuratively. Because *Krazy Kat* came so early in my experience, it was mostly on the basis of the world-defining power of Herriman's comic of queer yearning that I learned to want to read as Krazy sees and to notice when others appeared to see the world like that, too. By the time the high school curriculum got around to, say, Tennessee Williams's Stella and Stanley Kowalski and Edward Albee's George and Martha, *Krazy Kat* had me well set to allow that dramas of heterosexual emotional antagonism might encode queer erotic implications.

By the time I was midway through elementary school, *Annie*, the stage musical adaptation of Harold Gray's long-running, episodic newspaper comic strip, *Little Orphan Annie*, had opened on Broadway. Local New York radio and television advertising was chockablock with the sung refrains of child stars, just about my age, as they belted out "Tomorrow," the first act's showstopper. The musical's tremendous appeal conflicted with that of a comic strip that I found as confusing, inaccessible, and anachronistic as the would-be glamour of *Brenda Starr, Reporter* and which I mostly skipped when looking at the newspaper funnies. The musical took its cue from "little" and "orphan," jettisoning the most maudlin elements of *Oliver!* but still focused on Annie as an emotionally sympathetic, parentless child who pined for a family. The incongruity of such sentimentality with the comic strip with which I was just passingly familiar eventually led me back to the comic.

Any reader of Harold Gray's comic can tell you that his heroine is a very different sort of girl. Indeed, while much of Gray's right-wing agitprop plotting went over my head when I was a child, what did keep me trying to figure out how to engage with his comic was the centrality of a liberated protagonist whose orphanhood was never used to tug at readers' heartstrings and whose family mindedness was either utterly absent or turned up as contempt for its weakening effect on those who suffered from it. Though she looks like a young girl, there is very little childish about Annie unless you count her inexhaustible energy and her zealot's unblemished faith in herself. Like her contemporary Shirley Temple, Annie's status as a child is more mythic than plausible. A comic strip advertisement for American resolve in the face of the Great Depression's economic devastation, *Little Orphan Annie* is understandable as a series of Republican-skewed American tall tales, in the tradition of Paul Bunyan and Calamity Jane, in which Annie heroically overcomes challenges that symbolize those facing the country as a whole through the application of her resilient individual hard work and scorn of handouts. Annie is a combination of muckraking investigative reporter, private eye, and freelance crime fighter. She brooks no self-pity, and there is nothing weepy about her.

Annie's 1933 adventures start with a pretty typical storyline. She is living in Cosmic City with an elderly couple called the Futiles (note Harold Gray's light touch). They are good and meek and easily victimized by unscrupulous con artists. Annie observes a crooked salesman foisting spoiled merchandise on the unsuspecting Mr. Futile, and the first part of the year's strips is devoted to showing how Annie gets to the bottom of it, rooting out corruption, informing the police, and running the crook out of town. A paranoid conservative fantasia, *Little Orphan Annie* imagines an America in which decency is frail and normality is everywhere subtended by rot. Although his heroine knows how to fix things, it is hard enough to ignore the extent of the damage that one comes to expect it as the norm. Gray's strip works against its apparent first-order theme of can-do hardiness to feature that the American façade of greatness is everywhere enfeebled.

Eerily eyeball-less herself, Annie is nonetheless iconically astute, forever noticing problems that others miss, discovering trace evidence, and following up on clues. In a comic strip universe filled with white picket fencing, Annie is the one who regularly peers around to its other shadowy side, confronting the perfidy that is always threatening a world in which the good are mostly oblivious and frail and the wicked, greedy, and corrupt. The hapless good people with whom she temporarily resides fall in love with Annie, taking her actions on their behalf as signs of filial feeling or presuming her susceptibility to treacly sentiments like parental affection. She is regularly, breathtakingly immune. Whereas the Broadway musical presents an Annie who is, from curtain-up to final bows, singularly committed to fitting herself into a family and finding her parents, in the comic strip's episodic format, Gray routinely pivots from one storyline to the next, suddenly uprooting Annie from the family feeling tendrils that creep up around her during her brief sojourns in one place or another. Annie doesn't strive to hold onto family; she shakes off any of its presumptions with an aplomb that is such a marvel of heartlessness, it leaves us to wonder who this kid is who knows so fundamentally that to settle down with normal Americans would simply be unthinkable. Though her adventures often include "Daddy" Warbucks, the industrialist tycoon, his very name signals and ironizes his sporadic paternal function.

The strip's ambivalence about family norms in the conclusion of the Cosmic City storyline is pretty typical. After exposing the town's murderous local corruption, Annie reads all about it in the town newspaper while she and her dog, Sandy, are already headed to their next adventure. Back in Cosmic City, Mrs. Futile worries about Annie, but the girl has vanished without even so much as a goodbye. Annie's abandonment of the old couple who had fantasized about being her parents comes in the July 4th strip, on Independence Day. By July 6th, Annie further reasons out her sense of her own autonomy this way:

> No use lookin' back, Sandy—we're not goin' back to Cosmic City, and that settles it—guess it'd be safe, now—but what's th' use?
> Th' Futiles, and our other friends, are gettin' along o.k.—and I sewed this dough in my dress a while ago, just in case—so we're set for a while—any way, I feel like takin' a trip—don't you? (July 6, 1933)

Then she drops the Futiles a postcard, and she is off.

What of the musical's child with her heartfelt yearning for the simple coziness of a nuclear family? Read against the strips' heroine, the musical seems like a changeling, a counterfeit, and a debilitating corrective. Gray's Annie presents as an orphan in want of a permanent home to those who are in love with the idea of a potential daughter and as a little girl to those who trivialize the magnitude of her threat. Her actual girlhood in Gray's strip is a road-roving oddity, detached from the constraints of normative familial love and villainous, patronizing sexism. Annie's comic strip identity is misconstrued specifically when others understand "orphan" or "little girl" as defects or deficits. Annie is a self-possessed marvel when she is confronting each of the strip's myriad American wastrels, and queerly remote from the normal world's claim to settle her as that world's daughter. A queer superhero in her own right, Annie is attuned to notice and surpass the flaws of a world within which she moves and from which she is nonetheless set apart. Old comics like hers teach readers that queer possibility is not only to be found in the future. It's also wherever Annie's blank saucer eyes conceived of home in an alternative not yet available.

Note

1. Jeffrey P. Dennis reminds us that homosociality in *Archie* likewise extends to the female characters: "When Betty asks Veronica 'What do you find most attractive about Archie?' she responds immediately, 'You!' . . . Veronica's interest in Archie is not predicated upon heterosexual desire, but upon the fun of competing with Betty" (2002–2003, 130). Dennis's reading of *Archie* comics from the 1950s to the 1990s, "reveals that attempts to espouse universal heterosexual desire fail, that discourses presenting heterosexual liaisons as the sole goal of human existence are unstable and contradictory, and that sometimes same-sex desire is acknowledged, permitted, and even celebrated" (126).

Works Cited

Cummings, E. E. "A Foreword to Krazy." *Sewanee Review* 54, no. 2 (April–June 1946): 216–21.

Dennis, Jeffery P. "'Veronica and Betty are Going Steady!': Queer Spaces in the Archie Comics." *torquere: Journal of the Canadian Lesbian and Gay Studies Association*, nos. 4–5 (2002–2003): 125–42.

Gray, Harold. "Little Orphan Annie." July 6, 1933. *Little Orphan Annie, Vol. 3, 1933.* Fantagraphics Books, 1991.

Herriman, George. "Krazy Kat," August 16, 1925. In *Krazy & Ignatz. by George Herriman: "There is a Heppy Land, Fur, Fur Awa-a-ay—" Comprising the Complete Full-Page Comic Strips, 1925–26,* edited by Bill Blackbeard. Fantagraphics Books, 2002.

Seldes, Gilbert. *The Seven Lively Arts.* Harper & Brothers, 1924.

Chapter 20

"BETTER A MAN THAN DEAD?"
RADICAL (TRANS)MASCULINITIES IN COMIC-ZINES

remus jackson

INTRODUCTION

In North American comics studies, the rise of autobiographical queer narratives has generally been linked to the underground comix movement, beginning with Trina Robbins's *Sandy Comes Out,* and Mary Wings's *Come Out Comix.*[1] Though queer underground comix continued well into the 1980s and '90s,[2] generally scholars have traced the evolution of queer autobiographical narratives "beyond the periodical book format" to graphic novels (Kunka 2017, 43) with Alison Bechdel's strip *Dykes to Watch Out For* and later graphic memoir *Fun Home* garnering significant attention as case studies.[3] While a useful starting point for mapping queer comics, a narrow focus on this specific historical narrative can, as Margaret Galvan (2018) notes, overlook grassroots queer comics "because they are often produced outside of comics communities" (409), or, like the comics examined here, are produced in small press communities outside of graphic novel-centered alternative comics publishing. Building on Galvan's call for scholars to be "attentive to original publication histories and to reading across publication contexts" (419), I argue here for scholarly attention on the complicated lineages, influences, local practices, and community networks that have shaped the contemporary comics scene, particularly for creators engaged in self-published or DIY (do-it-yourself)-style comics-making.

This attention is particularly critical when analyzing transgender comics narratives, which intersect histories of comics, zines, and transgender experience. With the exception of David Kottler's 1982 comic *I'm Me,*[4] published in *Gay Comix,* relatively few examples of trans autobiography have been thoroughly examined. Although more work exploring trans autobiographical comics is needed, in this essay I focus on comics by transmasculine authors. Transmasculine autobiographical comics center transness through their depiction of the creators' lived experiences, while simultaneously offering a challenge to the hegemony of cis masculinity. In doing so, comics narratives that feature transmasculine subjectivities become sites of possibility to contest established cis-hetero gender binaries and to explore the inherent fragmentation of identity categories. My understanding of masculinity throughout this chapter draws not only on Butler, Prosser, and other queer/trans theorists, but Raewyn Connell's (2005) definition of masculinity as multiple, intertwined with other social signifiers including race and class, and existing only in relationship to other masculinities and femininities (76–86). Under this model, we can begin to understand how transmasculinities exist in relationship to cismasculinities (and femininities).

In this essay, I examine two transmasculine autobiographical comic-zines, Higu Rose's *Tittychop Boobslash* (2017) and Victor Martins's *You Don't Have to Be Afraid of Me* (2018, shortened to *Afraid of Me*). Both creators take full advantage of the comic form to elude a fixed state of gender identity. Trans prose autobiography has traditionally taken a fixed format that allows the trans body to become "real," mediated through the doctor's office where a transgender subject seeks access to hormone replacement therapy (Prosser 1998, 103–7). As trans scholar Jay Prosser (1998) has argued, through repeated accounts of transition (both published and unpublished), transgender experience "emerges as an archetypal story" (101). Although both creators explore various depictions of masculinity as gendered experience and performance, neither arrives at a unified or cohesive "masculine" experience. Using the comics form allows Rose and Martins to move outside dominant discourses of transgender experience in particularly innovative ways, as autobiographical comics enable artists to play with representation "often by using a range of symbolic elements and rhetorical tropes" (El Refaie 2012, 51). Drawing on the rhetorics of comics and of trans autobiography, Rose and Martins articulate a gendered subjectivity that complicates the relationship between "masculine" and "feminine" bodies and perspectives. Although both creators express a masculine subjectivity, their textual identities are in constant negotiation with the binary categorization of "female" and "male" cisgender identities. Or more simply, how Rose and Martins articulate gender experience *centers* transness, rather than cis ideas of masculinity. In doing so, these narratives become sites of possibility to contest established heteronormative binaries and explore how gender identity is inherently fragmentary.

This essay consists of three parts. The first two parts take up *Tittychop Boob-slash* and *Afraid of Me* as case studies, exploring how each uses the comics format to articulate a non-hegemonic experience of masculinity. *Tittychop Boobslash* is part of a larger lineage of medical transition narratives; however, I argue that the ways that Rose uses comics to probe the complicated valences of seeing and being seen in a trans body allows for an unsettling of the "archetypal" trans autobiography. Similarly, in *Afraid of Me* Martins uses the social aspects of transitioning to examine the complex relationship between misogyny and *male* trans identity, which I argue allows for a reading of how identity is shaped that reveals the inherent tensions in gendered subjectivity. Like transgender autobiographies previously analyzed by trans theorists, both comics end in a kind of gender affirmation for the author, wherein the completion of the narrative affirms the author as now authentically embodying their gender identity. However, I will explore how this affirmation simultaneously works against the idea of a whole, unified gendered subjectivity through each comic. The third part of this essay then puts these texts in conversation with lineages of queer communities in/around comics, examining two things: first, the self-published comic-zine as a specifically situated format that enables an inherently fragmentary positioning of identity; and second, the relationship between contemporary self-published queer comics and various underground publishing networks, particularly the Underground Comix movement, queercore, and riot grrrl zines.

"BODY STOCKHOLM SYNDROME," *TITTYCHOP BOOBSLASH*, AND THE CIS MEDICAL GAZE

Higu Rose's *Tittychop Boobslash* recounts Rose's experience getting top surgery through a loophole in their insurance. The comic is structured episodically, with each vignette depicting a scene from one month leading up to Rose's surgery and their recovery afterward. First-person narratives about pursuing gender-affirming medical procedures are common to trans autobiography, precisely because medical transitioning is part of many transgender people's lives (Prosser 1998, 101–2). Because transgender people seeking access to gender-affirming healthcare need to be able to, as Prosser argues, "recount a transsexual autobiography" (101), transgender medical narratives are mediated through the need to convince institutional figures, such as the doctor or the parent, of the author's authentic transness based on cisgender conceptions of transgenderism.

Although Rose draws on this lineage, *Tittychop Boobslash* differs in several key ways. First, Rose's work challenges cisnormative ideas of masculinity as enforced by medical institutions, by making apparent the "interlocking and intersecting identities" transmasculine people navigate (heinz 2016, 149). Second, Rose works against the "white, middle-class transmasculine discourse" which itself is dominant within transmasculine communities and indeed often reaffirms cisnormative masculinity (heinz 149–50). Thus, *Tittychop Boobslash* both disrupts the cis-medical institutional gaze and shows the transmasculine body beyond the binaries of traditional conceptions of gender. Rose's depiction of their body on the page becomes a productive site for examining their navigation of cis gazes against their own experience of gender. In one important sequence, their full body stretches diagonally across the page, clothed in tight-fitting black fabric that emphasizes the figure they are desperate to be rid of. Their arms, bent, obscure their face, while text cascading around their figure offers reasons to *like* their body: "I have nice legs," "makeup makes me look hot. (fact)." Hiding on-page Higu's face[5] from the viewer detaches Higu from their body while turning their body into an identifiable and knowable object for the viewer. By this point, we understand that this body is not the body Higu wants; the first lines on this page ask "so how do you survive in a body that disgusts you?" But this unwanted body *is* recognizable to "the people [they] love," who "like [their] body more than [they] do." This body, they note, "objectively" fits into a cisgendered body schema as "conventionally attractive." To contend with this tension, Rose evokes the role self-portraiture plays in their actualization, writing "live vicariously through androgynous self-portraits"—but their portrait here rather pointedly eschews androgyny, suggesting Higu "as seen" by (presumably cis) others. The phrase "body stockholm syndrome" captions this page in dense pencil, echoing the heavy marks that give a palpable dimension to their silhouette.

"Body stockholm syndrome" captures Rose's experience of "being seen" against their own self-perception. Here they echo trans activist Riki Anne Wilchins's argument that "in order to grasp our bodies" trans people must "construct" our self-identification through cis others, "since it is in the meanings reflected back at us through culture that we find truth" (1997, 40). "Body stockholm syndrome," then, can be understood as an articulation of how trans self-identification is "held hostage" by cisgender ideas of how bodies should be labeled. At the same time, naming this experience "body stockholm syndrome" suggests a specifically abusive dynamic between cis and trans gender construction which meaningfully builds on Wilchins's claim. In the next sequence, Higu's body disappears, replaced by a four-panel sequence of an ambiguously drawn organic matter—perhaps vines, though Rose's messy marks also evoke raw meat, an important visual motif throughout the comic. From this matter Rose blooms, declaring, "It took me 22 years to accept living in what I was told was a woman's body [. . .] I ain't a woman. I ain't female, either." On the final page of this vignette, Higu's body reappears, the roses now literally bursting from their skin. Roses, traditionally presented as feminine and beautiful, are here grotesque, but their grotesqueness is embraced by Higu: the bottom panel of the page closes in on their expression as they smirk, licking a rose near their mouth with a prominent tongue. These roses signal not an embracing of their body as is or an acceptance of their desire to become conventionally "male"-looking but a turn toward Rose's own conception of their gender, explicitly labeled elsewhere in the comic as "FUCKING FREAK." A literal representation of their body, where they might locate themself as a "site of *truth*

Am I being held hostage by the
Social construction of my own body?

Figure 20.1. *Tittychop Boobslash*, higu rose (self-published, 2017), 9.

to be mastered" (Wilchins 1997, 36, italics in the original), cannot contain the truly freakish body desires Rose expresses. The images of Higu on the page consumed by blooming roses are symbolic in the sense that we, as readers, assume Rose is not actually walking around with roses growing from them, yet narratively Higu interacts with the roses as though they are literally part of their body. Rather than obfuscating their "true" body from the gaze of the reader, Rose's depiction of floral body horror becomes an act of re-situating the "truth" of their lived experiences as a transgender person—their "true" body is not a post-op "male" body, but something that moves beyond the bounds of literal representation.

Throughout the comic they move us to these symbolic representations, incorporating a wide variety of stylistic tools that often both illuminates and obscures their form. Over a collage of panels taken from yaoi manga,[6] they declare "gimme a pair of supple yaoi tits," aligning their ideal body with an explicitly feminized, queer, and erotic male presentation. In a clearer refusal of conventional masculinity, they describe their reaction to the surgeon's warning that their nipples might fall off by pasting in an image of the titular creature from the 1986 film *The Fly*, followed by their exaggerated expression of delight as we see the surgeon note their failure to conform to cisgender masculinity on his clipboard. Because the comics format allows us to see both Higu's personal reaction to the medical institution's idea of gender, and the doctor's reaction to

Figure 20.2. *Tittychop Boobslash*, higu rose (self-published, 2017), 14.

Higu's gender "failure," *Tittychop Boobslash* critiques the trans medical narrative while working within it. Higu's joy comes explicitly at the fantasy of their body being permanently marked as nonconforming. Their cry of "OH!" occupies a significant portion of the panel, surrounded by cartoon hearts that, combined with Higu's wide-blown eyes and drooling mouth, suggest an almost orgasmic response at the thought of losing their nipples. Part of how Rose signals gender identification works through irreverent humor: as with the yaoi images, the identification is unexpected. It is queer and feminine, and evocative of the monstrous body. Rose contrasts this with the doctor, whose reactions to Higu underscore the medical institution's role as enforcers of "acceptable" bodies. That is, although Rose's gender-affirming surgery closely aligns them to an "acceptable" male body (i.e., flat-chested), transmasculine identification in *Tittychop Boobslash* cannot be so easily contained. Moving us between more realistic representations of their body as seen by others, their more stylistically androgynous self-caricatures, and their identifications with a variety of imagery such as the still from *The Fly*, allow Rose to bring forth the inherent limits of binary conventions of masculinity and femininity.

The completion of Higu's surgery in the final vignette does not totally align them with cismasculine expression: Higu does not become a "man." Instead, the final moment of the comic focuses on an exchange of queer intimacy between Higu and a male-coded lover that does not directly address Higu's gender at all. We briefly close in on their chest, squeezed by their lover's hand that recalls the unseen, but described, touch of their doctor earlier. This scene works in two meaningful ways. It reminds of us Rose's earlier explanation of "body stockholm syndrome," where emphasis was placed on how their loved ones gained pleasure through their dysphoria-inducing body. Higu also regains, at least in this moment, control of their body under this gaze through their interaction. Their lover seeks consent to touch their post-surgical chest without disrupting their kissing—after Higu expresses that they "literally can't feel anything," their lover redirects his touch and affirms he "won't do it then." How Higu feels about their body, both literally (the numbness) and figuratively (their lack of dysphoria post-surgery), thus shapes this moment. This scene also entangles gender subjectivity with queer sexuality and desire, as the culminating moment of the narrative maps Rose's embodiment through queer intimacy. This is important because much of the "archetypal" trans narrative rests on an assumption of conforming to *heterosexual* cisgender expression, where alignment of the trans body with cis expectations of how bodies should look and work includes participating in heterosexual desire.[7] By linking their masculine gender subjectivity in *Tittychop Boobslash* with feminine symbolism and eroticism, monstrous others, and queer sexuality, Rose develops a textual transmasculinity that unsettles cis-gender categories and points us toward the fluid, and often disruptive, nature of transgender subjectivity.

YOU DON'T HAVE TO BE AFRAID OF ME AND TRAUMA AS GENDERING

While *Tittychop Boobslash* evokes the well-worn tradition of medical trans autobiography, *Afraid of Me* eludes any reference to medically transitioning at all. Martins instead positions their gender through the repeated acts of gendered violence they faced as a teenage girl. The comic opens on a scene featuring Victor's male teacher on a school bus of high school girls (labeled as such by Martins) as he announces that they are "all so funny and so beautiful." His leering silhouette dominates the middle panel of the page as he leans towards Victor, crowded into the left third of the composition so that their figure presses against the panel border. Through the nearly opaque blue that fills in their forms, we can just make out the lines where the teacher's fingers caress Victor's cheek. Above their heads, Martins narrates, "Oh, but I think you've heard this story before," their followed up "haven't you?" nearly disappearing into the solid blue of their teacher's shape. The male teacher here represents not only a specific individual but the idea of men more broadly, something Martins explicitly calls out by opening the comic with the declaration "let me tell you about MEN." The assumption that their reader is familiar with "this story"—the kinds of microaggressions men perpetuate against women— suggests that Martins wants to claim a collective experience of misogyny. This is further emphasized by the montage of male hands touching Victor, which repeat throughout the beginning of the comic. Close-ups of presumably male hands grabbing Victor's buttocks reoccur across multiple pages, interspersed between other acts of sexual harassment. Here, a hand covers Victor's mouth; here, their guitar teacher pins them to a chair, his hand on Victor's thigh; here, men watch Victor run across the street, their gazes threatening in the context of this gendered violence. I emphasize how this repetition establishes men as a symbol of violence, and specifically sexual violence, because the text ends with Martins *being* a man.

In *Living a Feminist Life* (2017), Sara Ahmed, drawing on Judith Butler's ideas of gender performance, suggests that the act of becoming a girl, or "girling," comes from being "taught what it is to have a body: you are being told; you will receive my advances; you are object; thing, nothing" (25). "Girling" then occurs through a process of repetition, wherein the body marked as "girl" is made to behave in certain ways and accept certain power dynamics, where "violence too is a mode of address." Arguably, Victor's repeated experiences of sexual trauma at the hands of men is a "girling" mechanism, but in my analysis I want to underscore Martins's subtle *transgendering* of these experiences, and how transgendering is crucial to the ways trans creators articulate their own gendered subjectivity. The "archetypal" trans narrative I referenced earlier usually involves a sense of disidentification with the trans person's assigned gender: they are in the "wrong body," and so the way social gender norms shape their development as a child is also "wrong." For instance, think of the young trans man wearing his father's shoes, looking into the mirror and seeing himself as a man for the first time. We see shades of this in *Afraid of Me* as well, as when Martins depicts their dysphoria. Yet importantly, where disidentification

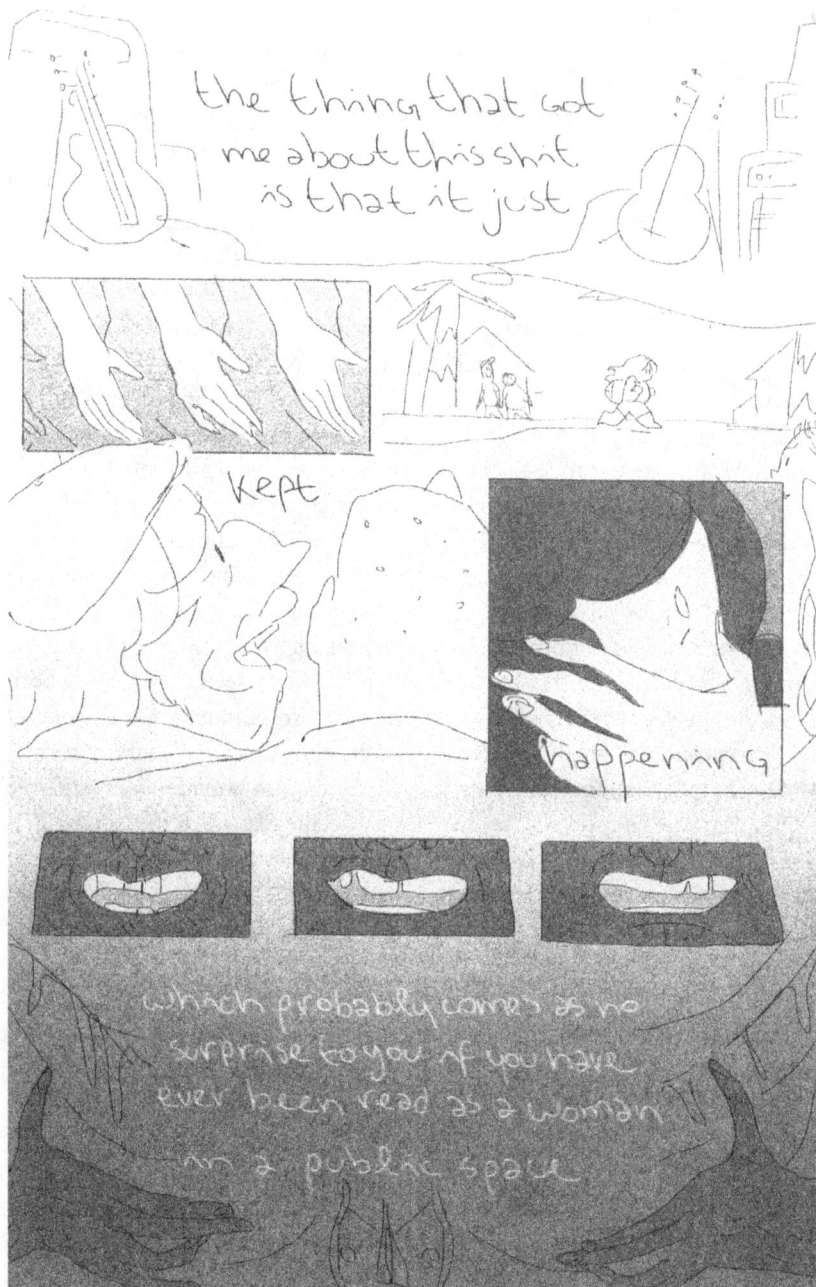

Figure 20.3. *You Don't Have to be Afraid of Me*, Victor Martins (self-published, 2018), n.p.

manifests most prominently is not between Victor and the idea of women, but *men*, precisely because their trauma is so bound up in their treatment *as* a girl at the hands of men.

The narrative's catharsis, Victor's realization of their gender identity, offers a space to unpack this idea further. Following Victor recounting their gendered trauma, a specifically gendered consciousness-raising occurs: literally depicted as descending from the heavens in a biblical-looking tome, complete with halo and wings, comes *feminism*, labeled on the page as "(the answer)." While Martins is not suggesting that men do not engage in feminism; rather, for them, feminism provided a temporary answer to the problem of being *girled*. Victor does not yet conceive of themself as non-girl, as we can see through their encounter with a mirror. Prosser (1998) describes the mirror as capturing "the definitive splitting" between how a trans person perceives themselves internally and how they appear to the world externally (100), which I hinted at above. El Refaie (2012) notes that mirrors manifest frequently in graphic memoir as well, perhaps as a "potent visual metaphor" that suggests the inability to "pin down our fluctuating sense of self" (66). In trans autobiographical *comics*, the mirror allows the trans person to identify themselves *as* an object by temporarily claiming the gaze of others.[8] The mirror enables the trans artist to express this ambiguous relationship between seeing and being seen, as they must both draw themselves outside *and* inside the mirror. Here we must consider whether Martins positions the self in the mirror as the object seen by others or as their own self-understanding; however, the mirror cannot provide an identifiable self to Martins. They do not see themself as we, the reader (or the assumed cis gaze), theoretically would, nor can we see them as they theoretically see *themself* (e.g., "male"). Instead the unbordered bottom of the page fills with scribbled portraits, each subsequent face drawn more distortedly than the last, until they become a mess of tangled lines.

Read against the resplendent arrival of "feminism" we can parse out how Victor starts to shape their gender identity. We go from the failure to manifest an "ideal" self in the mirror—further developed through a literal detachment from the body in the following sequence where Victor, as a ghost, floats away from an intimate encounter—to a series of performative "feminist" gestures. By performative, I mean both literally as a performance of being feminist and as a performance of a particular kind of rebellious gender expression. "I cut my hair short! I don't shave my legs!" floats Victor's voice over accompanying images of Victor cutting their long hair short, of Victor's knees, hairy under the hem of their skirt. The next panel shows a now "feminist"-ized Victor on the bus, proudly occupying multiple seats with their hairy legs deliberately spread, their smile cartoonishly smug as they reflect on "ridiculous men"—"I'll take up room!" Like Rose, how Martins depicts these moments takes on a kind of playful self-irreverence. Their moment of realization comes with a parenthetical header that the "patriarchy sucks" and "internalized misogyny is a thing"— their identity is not a rejection of feminism, described as a "perfectly good ideology" being "misused," or an embrace of the cis masculinity that harmed them. Indeed, it comes as an unwanted shock to Victor, and importantly, is depicted as coming from an external, metaphorical source. Just as feminism descends from the heavens, Victor's gender comes from an angelic cupid, who, interrupting them seemingly mid-drawing, proclaims "ACTUALLY, you're a man" (emphasis in the original). They reply, "Oh shit," and from over their shoulder we see their bemused expression and the paper they were drawing on, which reads: "MEN: the worst." Victor's gender arrives humorously through the exaggerated *unexpectedness* of it: how could Victor, a feminist who *hates* men, be a man?

Ergo, Victor's gender does not come as the embrace of the authentic self as in archetypal trans narratives, nor does it arrive at the expense of womanhood. Though Victor eventually comes to terms with their identity as a man, that resolution does not overwrite their experiences living as a girl. In fact, their maleness becomes a source of pain before it can be reconciled. Martins's drawings give way to a series of text-only pages, the final of which contains only the line "better dead than a man" over and over again until the text overlaps to a point of illegibility, the dark density of words contrasted against the lightening gradient of the page. Though unseen, there is a clear implication of attempted suicide as we return to Victor in a hospital bed, arms bandaged. "Better dead than a man" becomes "better a man than dead?" and thus suggests that maleness here is a final resort, the only strategy left that Victor "hasn't tried." Though "trying" at being a man resolves happily for Victor, I want to call attention to the specific negotiations between womanhood (girling), maleness, and masculinity, happening here. In the previous section I discussed masculinity in terms of presentation, e.g., the flat chest as a masculine chest versus breasts. In *Afraid of Me*, Martins's body is apparent on the page, particularly in the "feminism" sequence, which evokes the visceral drawings by artists in *Wimmins Comix*.[9] However, how the body figures into Martins's negotiation of cisness and transness depends on societal relationships *between* bodies, namely the violence of men against presumed women. Martins shapes the body through repeated violations and through the space it comes to occupy, perhaps reflecting the disassociation between self and body to which dysphoria often leads. Gender then also comes to be formed through these relationships: Victor cannot access cisnormative masculinity precisely because their experiences as a girl permanently transform their ability to relate to masculinity. Thus the masculinity that Martins creates exists in a fundamentally transgendered relationship to cis hegemonic masculinity.

Figure 20.4. *You Don't Have to be Afraid of Me*, Victor Martins (self-published, 2018), n.p.

I began this section by discussing repetition as a gendering strategy: how repeated experiences of violence against women are, indeed, part of what creates the identity "woman." Like in *Tittychop Boobslash*, the kind of transgender subjectivity emergent in *Afraid of Me* may allow us to think through gendering in a way that moves beyond a cisgender framework of analysis. Unlike Higu, Victor *does* "become" a man by the end of the narrative. However, Martins's characterization of transmasculinity through a specific male/female social dynamic reveals the ways that the "male"/"female" dynamic may not be able to explain the particular impact of patriarchy in gender constructions fully.

Or, more simply, transmasculinity in *Afraid of Me* rests on a contradictory relationship between experiences of violence as a woman and experiences of self-actualization, showing how transmasculinity must negotiate masculinity in a way that is markedly different from cisgender masculinity.

TRANS COMIC-ZINES IN THE MULTIPLICITY OF UNDERGROUNDS

Hillary Chute (2017) notes in *Why Comics?* that "zines [. . .] play a crucial role in the history of comics" and echoes the same democratic, anti-establishment ethos of the underground comix movement ("Why Punk?").[10] Expanding on Chute's analysis, I suggest that we can use Martin and Rose's blending of comics and zine techniques to analyze how contemporary trans artists draw on multiple publishing undergrounds as part of their project of developing transgender subjectivities. In the introduction, I noted a particular mapping of queer comics narratives that emphasizes the underground comix movement's role in enabling queer comics to emerge. As much writing on the underground has centered on how marginalized artists were able to break from the constraints of commercial publishing practices, it seemed to me that the natural predecessor should be the contemporary self-publishing scene where many marginalized artists are creating difficult and innovative work, as in the underground. However, the longer I spent working through these comparisons, the more I came to view the underground movement not as a singular, insulated movement, but as one of many underground presses that marginalized artists have flocked to for the freedom to create. Like the underground comix movement, queercore, riot grrrl, pulp novels, and early feminist pamphlets have all enabled queer and trans creators to create work outside of whatever "legitimate" forms of publishing dominate the cultural sphere.

For instance, in addition to being a comic, the aesthetics of *Tittychop Boobslash* strongly evoke riot grrrl and queercore zine aesthetics. The particular collaging of yaoi manga panels echoes riot grrrl zinesters who repurposed "often disparaged" feminine iconography in their zines, as does the collecting of disparate imagery—the manga, the movie *The Fly*, Rose's drawings—in order to construct a "deliberately fragmented" identity (Piepmeier 2012, 228–29). *Afraid of Me*, on the other hand, borrows very little from zines aesthetically, but nonetheless participates, as *Tittychop Boobslash* does, in the social practices of zinemaking. While the formal distinctions between comics and zines are blurry, zines are largely defined through their sociality, as a "radically democratic and participatory medium" (Duncombe [1997] 2001, 7–8) disseminated through trading, gifting, and cheaply selling (Piepmeier 2009, 194–205). Part of this is a method of community building between zinesters, and indeed, much writing on zines has emphasized their role as sites of community between, especially, girls and queer people.[11] For example, Martins ends *Afraid of Me* with their email, Twitter handle, and an invitation for emails, adding "suggested topics: school (sucks), trans stuff, compliments." This sort of community outreach work is common in both self-published comics and zines, where relationships among creators and readers are often forged by sharing contact info in exchanged comics and zines. The deliberate invitation for conversation about "trans stuff" points to a specific community being activated between Martins and other trans people. Though communities have been built with similar strategies in mainstream comics publishing, for instance, through letter columns, this particular community network more closely aligns with zine scenes and feminist pamphlet distribution. At the same time, as both comics fall into the broader category of trans autobiographies, they also share a historical relationship with prose trans autobiographies, which emerged in 1950s pulp novels (Stryker 2001, 81), and with contemporary social narratives of transness across media.

Thus, the consideration of how Martins and Rose fit into overlapping contexts of comics, zines, and other forms of underground publishing allows us to analyze how they shape transmasculine subjectivity in their texts. They illustrate how their bodies and identities are shaped by cultural norms, while leaving, deliberately, fragmentation in their textual gender identities. Part of this fragmentation is in their adaptation of archetypal transition narratives to works that do not end in a "complete" transition from one gender to another, so that gender identity is expressed instead through tensions between cis conventions of gender and a trans sense of self. Another part of this is how Martins and Rose participate in the overlapping comics and zine networks I've gestured towards here. As self-published creators, they occupy a marginal position within the broader comics industry—this position additionally overlaps with contemporary zine scenes, shaped by historical practices of underground press distribution through infoshops, independent bookstores, and comic shops.

Furthermore, their participation in various localized small press comics and zine fests, as well as their use of social media networks for online distribution of their work, highlights how transgender creators forge new communities outside of traditional modes of comics production. Or to put it more simply, their comics are part of a small scene of trans cartoonists, who are often in conversation with each other, or linked by few degrees of separation. In 2017, trans woman cartoonist Carta Monir wrote a review of *Tittychop Boobslash* for the *Comics Journal*, noting that the field of trans cartoonists "is smaller than you might think." Monir would go on to found Diskette Press in 2018 and print another short comic by Martins, *Stay*. These trans-specific printing and distribution networks then shape, at least partially, the process of making trans comics—whom artists are responding to and whom their books are for.

Throughout this essay, I have attempted to demonstrate how transmasculine comics creators articulate transgender subjectivities that enable different modes of masculinity outside of cisnormative gender categories. These subjectivities develop through the on-page techniques employed and through how artists like Martins and Rose participate in trans and queer comics/zine networks. While each text ends in emotional catharsis for the subject, because they do not attempt to recount their entire life, nor present a unified vision of their masculine selves, there is space for the tensions, contradictions, and fluidity that mark the trans experience.

As a transmasculine cartoonist working in the same queer networks as Rose and Martins, my investment in this topic is personal: the techniques I have described here are techniques I myself have employed in my attempts to articulate my own subjectivity on the page. Drawing comics poses a unique set of considerations for trans autobiographers, as drawing opens up different stylistic choices for depicting the self than photography or prose. Because trans autobiography overlaps scholarly discourses about trans history, trans embodiment, queer comics, and comics autobiographies, texts such as *Tittychop Boobslash* and *Afraid of Me* create space for more nuanced analyses of the specific subjectivities transmasculine creators develop through their work. Furthermore, engaging with these transmasculine narratives through their relation to cismasculinity allows us to think about the formation of transgender identity in comics as an act of transgendering that moves beyond a male vs. female discourse. The social patterns their textual identities engage in do not fall along a masculine/feminine axis, or even a masculine/masculine axis, but rather, a transgender/cisgender axis. Or, more simply, rather than seeing these as marginalized masculinities in opposition to hegemonic masculinity, we can think of them as transgender masculinities in negotiation with cisgender constructions of identity.

Notes

1. See Charles Hatfield, *Alternative Comics: An Emerging Literature* (2005); Elisabeth El Refaie, *Autobiographical Comics: Life Writing in Pictures* (2012); Hillary Chute, *Why Comics? From Underground to Everywhere* (2017); Andrew Kunka, *Autobiographical Comics* (2018).

2. *Wimmins Comix* continued until 1992 and *Gay Comix* until 1998.

3. It would be difficult to list all critical scholarship on Bechdel here. Most relevantly, see Chute, *Why Comics?* and *Graphic Women: Life Writing & Contemporary Comics* (2010), and El Refaie, *Autobiographical Comics.*

4. Discussed by Kunka in *Autobiographical Comics,* 111–12.

5. Throughout this essay, I will use Rose and Martins's first names to differentiate between Rose and Martins as authors and Higu and Victor as characters.

6. Yaoi is a genre of Japanese manga that depicts male homoerotic relationships, usually written by women for women to enjoy.

7. For a full discussion of the historical requirements for medical transition, see Julia Serano, *Whipping Girl* (2007), 115–60.

8. This is not necessarily a positive claim: Wilchins describes a friend's experience "imagining how people must see [her]," which makes her feel "just awful" (1997, 40).

9. Both El Refaie and Chute, for instance, describe the intentional excess of the body in Aline Kominsky-Crumb's "primitive" self-portraiture. See *Autobiographical Comics*, 80–83, and *Graphic Women*, 29–60.

10. Chute specifically cites zine work by Gary Panter and Matt Groening, as well as Art Spiegelman and Françoise Mouly's *RAW* (1980–91) in *Why Comics?*

11. See Piepmeier's "Why Zines Matter" in *Girl Zines*, 57–86.

Works Cited

Ahmed, Sara. *Living a Feminist Life*. Duke University Press, 2017.

Chute, Hillary. *Graphic Women: Life Narrative & Contemporary Comics*. Columbia University Press, 2010.

Chute, Hillary. *Why Comics? From Underground to Everywhere*. HarperCollins, 2017.

Connell, Raewyn. *Masculinities*. 2nd ed. University of California Press, 2005.

Duncombe, Stephen. *Notes from the Underground: Zines and the Politics of Alternative Culture*. Microcosm Publishing, 1995, 2005.

El Refaie, Elisabeth. *Autobiographical Comics: Life Writing in Pictures*. University Press of Mississippi, 2012.

Galvan, Margaret. "'The Lesbian Norman Rockwell': Alison Bechdel and Queer Grassroots Networks." *American Literature* 90, no. 2 (2018): 407–38.

Hatfield, Charles. *Alternative Comics: An Emerging Literature*. University Press of Mississippi, 2005.

heinz, matthew. *Entering Transmasculinity: The Inevitability of Discourse*. Intellect, University of Chicago Press, 2016.

Kunka, Andrew. "Social and Cultural Impact." In *Autobiographical Comics*, edited by Andrew Kunka, 99–134. Bloomsbury Academic, 2018.

Martins, Victor. *You Don't Have to Be Afraid of Me*. Self-published, 2018.

Monir, Carta. "Tittychop Boobslash." *The Comics Journal*. Nov. 6, 2017.

Piepmeier, Alison. *Girl Zines: Making Media, Doing Feminism*. New York University Press, 2009.

Prosser, Jay. *Second Skins: The Body Narratives of Transsexuality*. Columbia University Press, 1998.

Robbins, Trina. *From Girls to Grrlz: A History of Women's Comics from Teens to Zines*. Chronicle Books, 1999.

Rose, Higu. *Tittychop Boobslash*. Self-published, 2016.

Stryker, Susan. *Queer Pulp: Perverted Passions from the Golden Age of Paperback*. Chronicle Books, 2001.

Wilchins, Riki Anne. *Read My Lips: Sexual Subversion and the End of Gender*. Firebrand Books, 1997.

Chapter 21

COMICS, COMMUNITY, AND KICKASS WOMEN

**ALISON HALSALL AND JONATHAN WARREN
IN CONVERSATION WITH JENNIFER CAMPER**

In spring 2020, our email conversations with comics creator and graphic artist Jennifer Camper brightened a time that was otherwise increasingly shadowed by the expanding COVID-19 crisis. Though pandemic-related restrictions precluded an in-person interview in New York, Camper's exuberant commitment to support queer comics as a field of creation, innovation, enjoyment, and inquiry was no less evident over email. Camper is a central figure in the world of queer comics. A groundbreaking and influential comics artist and the creator and director of the biennial LGBTQ+ comics conference *Queers & Comics*, Camper spoke with us about the origins and development of her comics sensibility, her sense of the evolving queer comics scene, and the importance of her LGBTQ+ comics community-building work. Her ideas about powerful lesbian representation, "mongrel" identities in comics, how to deploy humor as a weapon, and kickass women delivered exactly the kind of hopeful energy and sense of queer solidarity that will get us all through this challenging time as it has others before. We're grateful that Camper has also allowed us to share some of her definitive work.

Alison Halsall and Jonathan Warren: You've said that one of the reasons you started creating comics was that you didn't find yourself represented in them. What was the comics scene like when you were starting out, and how has it evolved? How do you feel about your place in it, now that there's such a critical mass of LGBTQ+ comics?

Jennifer Camper: Since I was very young, I drew pictures and wrote stories. I never saw people like me in the arts and media, and rarely saw stories that matched my experiences and perspectives. I read underground comics, and then discovered the very few women and queers creating underground comics. That was exciting. But I wasn't seeing comics that reflected my own community of diverse, queer, kickass women who were unashamed, passionate and joyful, and having adventures. I hungered to have stories about those women, so I created those stories in comics.

Figure 21.1. *Rude Girls and Dangerous Women*, Jennifer Camper (Laugh Lines Press, 1994), 9.

I made comics for myself and my friends at home and in school. Later, I contributed comics and illustrations to *Gay Community News* in Boston. I also submitted comics to *Gay Comix*, and met the founding editor, Howard Cruse, who generously mentored so many of us in the craft and business of comics. (We lost Howard to cancer in November 2019, a devastating loss for queer comics and the LGBTQ+ cartoonist community. Howard's comics are spectacular, and his influence is vast.) I also published comics and illustrations in many queer, feminist, and alternative publications like *Wimmen's Comix, Sojourner* [Boston feminist paper], and *On Our Backs* [lesbian erotica magazine].

Eventually I created a self-syndicated, biweekly comic, *Camper*, that ran in a number of queer and feminist newspapers and magazines in the US and Canada. Those comics were eventually collected in my first book, *Rude Girls and Dangerous Women* (Laugh Lines Press, 1994).

I got to know others who were making LGBTQ+ comics. Mary Wings and Roberta Gregory published the first lesbian-made comics, and Rupert Kinnard published some of the first comics with Black LGBTQ+ characters. When Howard Cruse created *Gay Comix,* he published the work of Roberta and Mary along with Lee Marrs, Burton Clarke, Robert Triptow, Trina Robbins, Jerry Mills, T. O. Sylvester, and many others. Later I met other cartoonists who were publishing in the queer press, mini-comics, and zines: Ivan Velez, Alison Bechdel, Andrea Natalie, Diane DiMassa, Robert Kirby, Eric Orner, Joan Hilty, and others.

Figure 21.2. *Rude Girls and Dangerous Women*, Jennifer Camper (Laugh Lines Press, 1994), 82.

Figure 21.3. "Dildo," Jennifer Camper.

Figure 21.4. *Rude Girls and Dangerous Women*, Jennifer Camper (Laugh Lines Press, 1994), 55.

Having these outlets gave me deadlines, assignments, and an audience, but not much money. There were not many queer cartoonists, so we sought each other out and developed a supportive community. We all had unique styles and content. Those of us living in NYC would hang out together. We'd also connect at the OutWrite conferences, the LGBTQ+ Writers' conferences in Boston and San Francisco, sponsored by *Gay Community News*. And I helped organize exhibits of queer comics in New York City. Later, we'd meet at alternative comics conventions like APE (Alternative Press Expo, San Francisco), MoCCA (Museum of Comic and Cartoon Art, New York City), and SPX (Small Press Expo, Maryland).

I organized a lot of group projects for cartoonists as a way to connect and create community.

AH and JW: Irreverence, laughter, and explicit lesbian sex: your comics have always been so frank about lesbian sexuality, and your visualizing women's sexuality has provoked a good deal of comment and critique about the politics of representation (for example, the censorship or self-censorship that queer creators struggled against in the 1980s and 1990s). Are those kinds of pressures still in play? How has the response to your comics' edginess changed over your career? How would you characterize readers' receptiveness today?

JC: I welcome responses to my work—both positive and negative. It means people are reading my comics and thinking about them. There are always gatekeepers in publishing who will have editorial input. (Self-publishing allows

Figure 21.5. *Rude Girls and Dangerous Women*, Jennifer Camper (Laugh Lines Press, 1994), 34.

people more freedom.) And readers will have many opinions. The responses change with the times, but there's usually an emotional reason people get angry with comics.

Some feedback about my comics:

Will make heterosexuals hate us
Sexually objectifies women
Depicts unprovoked violence
Anti-Semitic against Jews
Promotes smoking to children
Depicts sexuality in children

I like to create characters that are not always perfect. In the US in the 1980s and 1990s, there was a concern by LGBTQ+ publishers that my comics would make queers look bad to straight people. Now there are enough queer characters that not all of them have to be saintly role models. But I also make comics about LGBTQ+ Arabs, and my Arab friends living in Arab countries presently have the same concerns about my characters making queers look bad. Creating evil or flawed queer characters is a privilege that comes only with having many opportunities for stories about multitudes of LGBTQ+ experiences.

AH and JW: Your comics are so laugh-out-loud funny. How would you say your comics' sense of humor has developed over the years? Are you especially

Figure 21.6. "The Genius," in *Women's Review of Books*, Jennifer Camper (April 2006), 23.

Figure 21.7. *Rude Girls and Dangerous Women*, Jennifer Camper (Laugh Lines Press, 1994), 75.

drawn to any new topics or targets for laughter? Over time, have you noticed any significant shifts in what it takes to make LGBTQ+ comics readers laugh or in how you and other LGBTQ+ creators use humor to make a point?

JC: In my early comics, humor was often coupled with anger. I like to ridicule people with power who behave badly. There's a catharsis for readers to be able to laugh at their oppressors.

I also poke fun at my own community, because it's important to laugh at ourselves, too. For readers, I think there is a warm and comforting humor in seeing something funny in a familiar experience that mirrors their own lives.

My work is often dark, and in my more recent work my humor highlights the disconnect between the insipidness of mainstream society and the harsher realities of my character's twisted experiences.

AH and JW: We wouldn't want to neglect the importance of rage in your comics. In comics like *AIDS: Bearing Angry Witness*, you bring it to confront injustice, inequities, and the ongoing precariousness of queer lives. How conscious are you of using comics for activism? In what ways do you think comics should take up political and activist work?

JC: I'm very opinionated and naturally my comics reflect my viewpoints. Readers often come to comics with their guard down—because comics seem fun and simple—so cartoonists can sneak in some powerful messages. I'm very aware of using my comics to promote my opinions in the narrative, but also through subtle ways like creating characters with a variety of body shapes, race, age, class, etc., by not using real brand names in my comics, or by exploring stories that are rarely told.

I don't think art has to have an overt political component, but good art causes people to think in new ways—and that is a form of activism.

AH and JW: It's clear from your inspired role in forging the Queers & Comics conventions that you're committed to fostering and supporting a *community* of LGBTQ+ comics creators and readers. What role do you want LGBTQ+ comics to play in teaching readers how to be queer? What part does your communitarian ethos play in that? Can we look for it in your comics' aesthetics?

JC: I created the Queers & Comics conference because I love to throw parties. I wanted LGBTQ+ cartoonists to meet each other and create supportive communities, to document our history, and to inspire people to create new comics.

Why queer comics? First, because I like to read them, and these are fresh stories that haven't often been told before. LGBTQ+ people need the validation of seeing their lives mirrored in the arts and media. Also, readers deserve comics that reflect a wide variety of experiences and voices. They can learn about people who are different from themselves, and this fights prejudice.

AH and JW: From their earliest days, the most groundbreaking and influential American comics have featured characters' hybrid identities and themes of otherness, liminality, or intersectionality, all of which can be especially powerful in disrupting the whiteness of pop culture. Lately, we've been really excited by the sexy humor of *ArtQueerHabibi*'s visualizations of Muslim and Arab queer people living and loving openly. And we love how *theelsalomons* generates thoughtful humor through its depictions of Jewish and Palestinian queer lives lived together. In *Ramadan*, you show the connections between growing up Arab and being a dyke. Can you tell our readers about the importance of what you describe as your own "mongrel," Lebanese American identity for your art? With your heritage in mind, you've described yourself as feeling like an "outsider." How do feelings and ideas of apartness and inclusion contribute to your art and to LGBTQ+ experiences of otherness?

JC: I'm mixed—half-Lebanese—and I grew up in the US without an Arab community except for relatives. Later, I connected with LGBTQ+ Arabs and Iranians in the US and internationally, and we have created a strong community both online and in person. I wanted to include stories of queer Arabs in my comics. For *Ramadan,* I interviewed queer Arab Muslim women, and told a fictionalized story based on their experiences. I'm not Muslim, so I wrote the story in the second person—to emphasize that I was presenting someone else's story back to them.

Queer women navigate between male and female worlds, and mixed-race people also navigate between cultures. It's sometimes difficult because you don't really belong fully to just one tribe, but it is also exciting because you can create

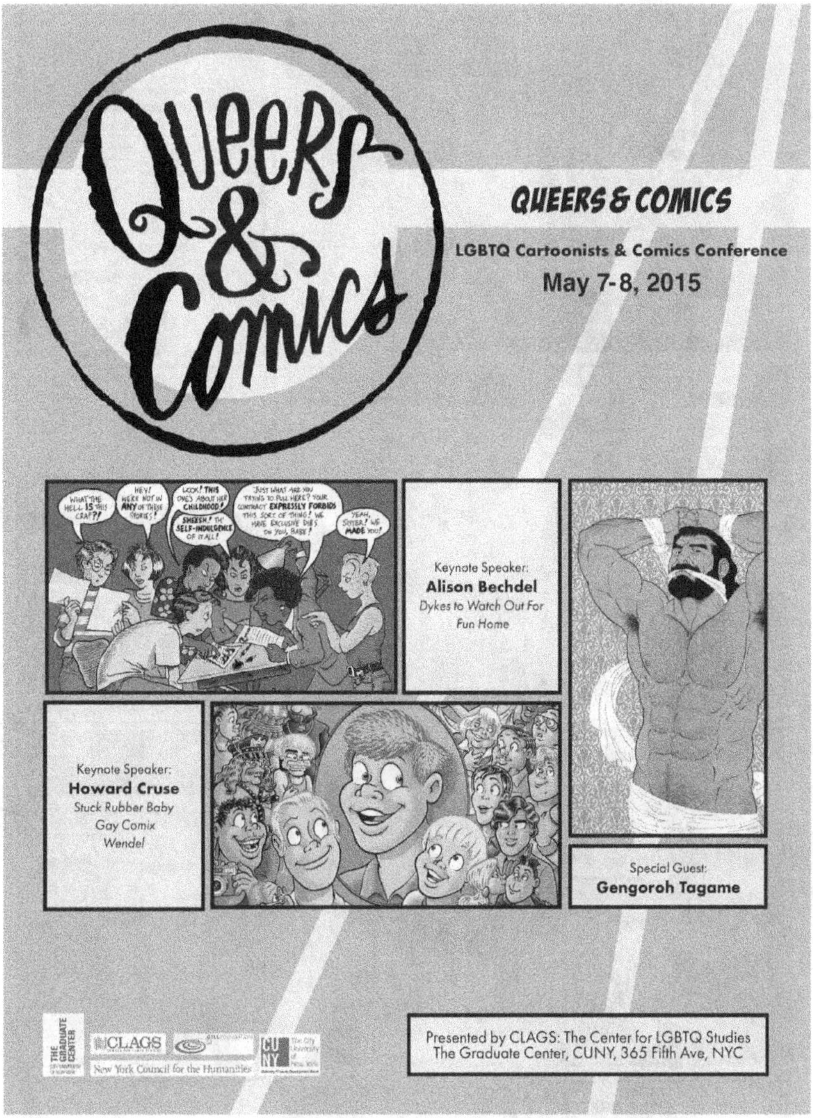

Figure 21.8. Poster for Queers & Comics Conference, May 7–8, 2015.

a new identity that is unique and your own. I often explore and celebrate these mongrel identities in my comics.

AH and JW: The global marketplace would seem to allow more than ever for comics to connect readerships across geographical and cultural distances. Do you think that is happening as well as it could be? What LGBTQ+ comics from outside the North American context turn you on right now? What impediments do you see to the emergence of an LGBTQ+ "world literature" of comics?

Figure 21.9. Revised excerpt from *Ramadan*, Jennifer Camper.

Figure 21.10. Excerpt from "School Girls," in *Qu33r*, edited by Robert Kirby (Northwest Press, 2014), 248.

JC: There are so many great LGBTQ+ comics available now that it is difficult to keep up. There is a wealth of different styles and genres: memoir, literary fiction, journalism, YA, manga, sci-fi, fantasy, erotica, humor, etc. It is a luxury to be able to pick out just what you like and ignore some others. That said, there are still gatekeepers who decide who gets paid for this work, and many cartoonists will not have the financial support to continue making their work over time. The internet is great for self-expression, but we need to find better ways to pay cartoonists.

AH and JW: What are the queer comics that excite you the most right now? What do you think is coming next for LGBTQ+ comics?

JC: Just a few of the comics I'm excited about:

Bishakh Som's recently published comics collection, *Apsara Engine*, and coming this fall, *Spellbound*, her comics memoir about creating comics.

Ajuan Mance's powerful work about violence against Black people, and celebrating queer Black lives.

Stuck Rubber Baby, twenty-fifth anniversary edition, by Howard Cruse. A gorgeous, larger new edition with archival material and extra content.

Ivan Velez is working on a new project, *The Ballad of Wham Kabam*, an epic multicultural American history portrayed in the superhero genre. While we're waiting, check out his groundbreaking *Tales of the Closet*, about LGBTQ+ teens in New York City.

AH and JW: Though they're so labor-intensive to produce, comics have always enjoyed a tremendous payoff in their popularity, powerful accessibility, and loyal readerships. Is that still true in the digital age? What kind of transformations do you see in LGBTQ+ comics' accessibility, creativity, and power as print gives way more and more to exclusively online production and distribution?

JC: Cartoonists will explore new ways to make comics with every change in our culture and technology. And yet there is still a desire for traditional books, and people still love to make and read DIY zine comics. I welcome mixing old and new formats. Publishing will continuously transform itself and always allow some people more access than others. But cartoonists will always find ways to break through the restrictions.

Chapter 22

CONCEIVING THE INCONCEIVABLE
GRAPHIC MEDICINE, QUEER MOTHERHOOD, AND A. K. SUMMERS'S PREGNANT BUTCH: NINE LONG MONTHS SPENT IN DRAG

SATHYARAJ VENKATESAN AND CHINMAY MURALI

QUEER MOTHERHOOD AND GRAPHIC MEMOIRS

When Thomas Beatie, an American public speaker and advocate of transgender fertility and reproductive rights, "came out" as transgender and pregnant in 2008, public responses to his pregnancy "ranged from curiosity to outright hatred to dismissal of his male gender" (Grigorovich 2014, 81). Such a sensationalist and transphobic mainstream response to Beatie's queer pregnancy is not only suggestive of essentially cissexist mainstream conceptualizations of pregnancy but also reveals cultural anxieties surrounding queer motherhood. The social ostracism of alternative versions of experiences, symbolized by Beatie's demonstrates that the institution of motherhood is deeply entrenched within the heterosexual matrix.[1]

The cultural task of *queering* motherhood has been strengthened by an explosion of narratives that destigmatize and render visible motherhood as a queer practice. Such narratives, which have "crossed genre divides between academic, activist, literary, how-to and humour writing" (Gibson 2014, 5), aim to legitimize queer pregnancy and motherhood through layered accounts of conception and parenting from a queer perspective. In addition to Beatie's autobiography *A Labour of Love* (2008), Cherríe Moraga's *Waiting in the Wings: Portrait of a Queer Motherhood* (1997), Amie Miller's *She Looks Just Like You: A Memoir of (Nonbiological Lesbian) Motherhood* (2010), and Karleen Jiménez's *How to Get a Girl Pregnant* (2011) are some of the major autobiographical narratives on queer conception/mothering. Maureen Bradley's comedy-drama film *Two 4 One* (2014) and Cyn Lubow's documentary film *A Womb of Their Own* (2016) are two of the cinematic responses to queer pregnancy/motherhood. As a medium "rife with the social and aesthetic cues commonly attached to queer life" (Scott and Fawaz 2018, 197), comics also has lent itself to queer articulations of the maternal. Alison Bechdel's *Spawn of Dykes to Watch Out*

For (1993), for instance, which depicts a midwife-assisted homebirth in a lesbian community, is perhaps the earliest attempt to use comics to narrate the queer experience of pregnancy/motherhood. Notably, comics about queer pregnancy and motherhood are part of an emerging corpus of graphic medical narratives about female reproductive issues such as abortion, miscarriage, infertility, and postpartum depression. In fact, contemporary queer representations of pregnancy, childbirth, and parenting in narratives such as *The Argonauts* (2015) by Maggie Nelson, *Labor of Love* by Thomas Beatie, *Dykes to Watch Out For* by Alison Bechdel, among others, are exciting in that they challenge pregnancy as an inherently feminine experience. Such resignifications have not only unsettled the prevalent stereotypes about gender nonconformity as unproductive and ineffectual but also have affirmed and made visible gender diversity, and queer maternal identities and imageries.

Notably, there has been a proliferation of graphic memoirs about female reproduction in which women tackle nuanced issues centered on the complexities of female reproduction from their subjective and lived experiences. Phoebe Potts's *Good Eggs* (2010), Endrene Shepherd's *A Significant Loss: The Story of My Miscarriage* (2014), Paula Knight's *The Facts of Life* (2017), and Jenell Johnson's *Present/Perfect* (2018) are among the recently published graphic narratives engaging critically with motherhood and reproductive issues. As such, these visual narratives, as Jenell Johnson in *Graphic Reproduction* (2018) contends, demonstrate graphic medicine's potential to create "a discursive and visual forum where the affective, biological, social, and political complexities of reproduction can exist together in generative uncertainty" (4). While the aforementioned texts explore women's reproductive lives within a heterosexual paradigm, Summers's visual memoir complicates the culture of reproduction by interrogating the heteronormative assumptions that undergird reproductive medicine and by offering the full complexities of butch pregnancy in thought-provoking ways.

Apportioned into three parts that deftly knit together the author's experience as a pregnant butch lesbian in a deeply homophobic and heterosexist sociocultural landscape, *Pregnant Butch* centers on Teek Thomasson (an alter ego of the author, who is frequently drawn in a Tintin costume) who transitions to parenthood and her femme-identified girlfriend Vee. As such, *Pregnant Butch* emphasizes "the negative! The dirt!" of reproduction and thus fills in the "lack of gender-challenged confinement tales" (Summers 2014, iv). Laced with wry humor and witticisms, Summers's culturally resonant narrative also sheds light on a range of issues, including cultural and medical attitudes towards queer motherhood, butch identity, and female masculinity, as well as social expectations about motherhood and heteronormative hegemony. This chapter's reading of Summers's graphic memoir brings into sharp relief the way the pluripotent space of the comics medium allows the author not only to foreground her "queer" experience of pregnancy in a heteronormative context, thereby interrogating (cis)normative constructions of motherhood in multiple ways but also to accentuate "queer mother knowledge," to use Sierra Holland's phrase (2019). It also seeks to investigate the ways in which the narrative arraigns the discourses of obstetrics, midwifery, and childbirth education for their insistent heterosexual and gender-dimorphic bias that alienates queer maternal subjectivities.

"GROAN, SQUEAK, RUMBLE . . .": THE HETEROSEXUAL MATRIX

Alluding to the cultural scripts that entwine pregnancy and femininity, Summers observes in an interview: "a lot of people are just going around with a very standard script in their head that links pregnancy to this ultimate expression of femininity . . . when you disrupt that, those associations and that kind of typical pattern, you freak people out and they feel uncomfortable" (Bendix 2014). Given such a context it is not surprising that Summers's memoir launches a strident critique of the heterosexual matrix. *Pregnant Butch* opens with a splash page in which the protagonist firmly asserts her sexual identity by confidently identifying herself as a pregnant butch lesbian. Teek's poised affirmation of her butch identity is further reinforced by the title "Pregnant BUTCH" (appearing at the top of the page), bolded and capitalized. Interestingly, the protagonist is pictured waiting for a subway train at Lexington Avenue, between a locked-down building structure on one side and an arriving train whose sound is reproduced as "groan, squeak and rumble," on the other (Summers 2014, 1). Further emphasizing her dyke identity, Teek is introduced in masculine attire (short-sleeved shirt, trousers, and a cap) sporting a baby bump as she stares directly at the reader. The low-angle shot of the image amplifies the protagonist's imposing and arresting posture. The positioning of Teek and the setting of the scene (a subway system infrastructure that is caged) together are suggestive of a person in transit or someone underground, and capture Summers's own embodiment of a resolutely butch lesbian. The subterranean fullness of the city is also linked metaphorically to the pregnant body of Teek.

Censuring mainstream popular culture, Teek laments thus: "[a]s a butch dyke I am accustomed to feeling exempt from most things covered in your glossy women's magazine," such as "hair, makeup, Mars-Venus commentary" (Summers 2014, 1). The protagonist's angry stare at the reader also implicates her/him in gendered assumptions and stereotypes that ostracize non-normative heterogenous sexual subjectivities. The author's criticism of women's magazines continues the implications of being in the underground and deepens the

Figure 22.1. *Pregnant Butch: Nine Long Months Spent in Drag*, A. K. Summers (Soft Skull Press, 2014), 1.

visibility/concealment theme introduced in the first few panels of the memoir. Read in this context, Summers suggests how heterosexual hegemony conceals desires, embodiment, as well as the material aspirations and needs of the LGBTQ+ community. As a non-privileged group, queers are unacknowledged and unrecognized and are often placed outside the symbolic and material economies of representation. After all, subjectivity and personhood, in a sense, are textually produced, discursively constituted and mediated through representations, an issue that finds expression in the introduction thus: "If you don't get it down, it didn't exist" (Summers 2014, v).

In its critical scrutiny of heteronormative popular culture, *Pregnant Butch* also deploys parody and subversion as a queer aesthetic trope in multiple instances in the text. For instance, Teek's confident and assertive posture as a pregnant butch dyke at Lexington Avenue subway has a resonance (and hence a subversive parody) to one of the most iconic cinematic moments, in which actress Marilyn Monroe's white halter dress is blown up over her hips. This image from *The Seven Year Itch* (1954), which captures Monroe in her seductively ravishing manifestation of feminine sensuousness is deftly rewritten and parodied by the artist through a heroic display of her butch identity. By deliberately inserting herself and, thus, rewriting the mise-en-scène of the much-touted sequence in *The Seven Year Itch*, the narrative not only exposes heterosexual imperatives in the mainstream discursive order that deny symbolic legitimacy and intelligibility to non-normative sexual and gender subjectivities but also unleashes a strident critique of such cisnormative order.

"WHAT DO YOU MEAN BY 'ARTIFICIAL'?": OBSTETRICS, MIDWIFERY, AND HETEROSEXISM

Summers's narrative not only exposes the heterosexual bias in motherhood but also illustrates how the biomedical discourse intersects with the moral universe of the mainstream by categorizing butch pregnancy as unnatural and deviant. Elaborating on the ways in which the medical discourse, specifically obstetrics and midwifery, internalizes and reinforces heteronormative assumptions about conception, the author delineates how she had been "primed for the next clue that would reveal the impossibility" (Summers 2014, 14) of her giving birth. Illustrating how obstetrics follows the mainstream logic of exclusion in perceiving non-typical/queer pregnant bodies as abnormal, Summers depicts herself being examined "for a condition called an android pelvis" (14) which, according to medical textbooks, is "characterized by narrow hips, similar to male pelvis" (14). After the examination, the doctor informs the protagonist that her pelvis is "just as normal as can be" (14). Evidently, Teek has been examined for an

Figure 22.2: *Pregnant Butch: Nine Long Months Spent in Drag*, A. K. Summers (Soft Skull Press, 2014), 32.

android pelvis because of her queer identity. It is a uniquely queer situation, since not all straight women possess a perfect gynecoid pelvic basin and yet they are not examined for android pelvis (Gruss and Schmitt 2015). Referring to this heteronormative bias in the discourses of obstetrics and gynecology that forced her to go through unnecessary examinations, Teek laments thus: "How many ob-gyn patients cry to learn they do not possess an android pelvis?" (14).

Extending her argument, the author presents her agonizing experience at a midwifery center when Teek and Vee meet the midwife for an intake evaluation. In the first panel, the midwife asks the couple, "Did you use **artificial insemination** to become pregnant?" (Summers 2014, 33; bold in the original). Here, instead of asking about the actual pregnancy, the midwife suspects Teek's conception and pregnancy itself. Responding to the midwife's emphasis on artificial insemination, Teek visibly loses her composure at the heteronormative prejudice of the midwife's question, and retorts thus: "What do you mean by 'artificial'?" (32). In the next panel, the midwife with a grim and insensitive expression asks the couple: "Did you have intercourse?" (32). Signifying the coarseness of the midwife's inappropriate question, the speech bubble is drawn as oozing, hence repulsive. When Teek responds to the midwife's question in the negative, the midwife declares that "it was artificial insemination" (33). The midwife's questions exemplify how the discourses of obstetrics and midwifery perpetuate heteronormative social prejudices that deem pregnancy through heterosexual intercourse as "natural" as opposed to the "artificiality" of medically mediated conception. The scene also reflects the discriminatory nature of medical terms such as "artificial insemination" that are used to reinforce heterosexist assumptions about pregnancy. In the next couple of panels, Summers illustrates how Teek is asked to expose her breasts to the midwife to ascertain whether she is fit to breastfeed her child. When an infuriated Teek exposes her breast, the midwife body-shames her with the sarcastic comment: "No baby is going to have a problem finding those" (34). Teek, who is forced to prove her femininity by exposing herself before the homophobic midwife, thus bemoans: "Did she think that we perverts were marked by our inverted nipples?" (Summers 2014, 34).

Summers also portrays gender-dimorphic bias in childbirth education when narrating her distressing experience of attending the hospital's mandatory birth orientation classes. When the facilitator at the birth orientation class, an "Ina May enthusiast," informs the participants that she will be using Ina May Gaskin's[2] theories on midwifery, Teek prepares to read *Spiritual Midwifery*. Lamenting the heterosexism in Gaskin's text, Summers observes that "there are no pregnant butches in Ina May's world—only men, women and children" (2014, 61). Again, in a rather sarcastic vein, Teek ridicules Gaskin's theories thus: "[t]his sounded like the kind of pep talk you'd get in basic training or Maoist re-education camp! Not as preparation for childbirth" (60). Alluding to how Gaskin's farm perpetuated patriarchal gender roles and sexist stereotypes, Summers argues that "farm birth stories present a stark division of labor. Women have babies, take care of kids, help other women give birth, inspire their men. Men build stuff, fix shit and rub breasts" (62). Illustrating how such a patriarchal and sexist system ostracizes not only women but also queers who do not conform to gender binaries, Teek is pulled out of a workshop by a man, shouting, "Come on outta there, gal!" (62). Here, Summers launches a thorough critique of Gaskin's text, celebrated for its eroticization, exoticization, and prelapsarian spiritualization and mystification of childbirth, an otherwise normal life event. After attending the deeply heterosexist birth education classes at the hospital, Teek longs for a birth orientation class filled with queers: "I'd like to hear how others carved out their roles as 'birth givers' and 'birth partners' without the obfuscations of Ina May Gaskin. . . . In my dream class there'd be at least one other pregnant butch" (Summers 2014, 72). Thus, Summers not only criticizes the heterosexual hegemony in the discourses of midwifery/obstetrics but also appeals for an accommodating and inclusive system. She also longs to hear how queers have imagined their roles as would-be-mothers.

CODA: "I DID IT"

Dominant heteronormative conceptualizations of the maternal not only situate the institution of motherhood within a heterosexual paradigm but also imagine it as an exclusively feminine realm, discounting alternative experiences of pregnancy and mothering. Against such a backdrop, there has been a burgeoning of verbal/visual narrative representations of LGBTQ+ pregnancy, adoption, and mothering, thereby queering motherhood practices. Such discursive queering of the maternal often dismantles the heteronormative and cisnormative assumptions that support the mainstream underpinnings of motherhood. Summers's graphic memoir *Pregnant Butch: Nine Long Months Spent in Drag* is an account of the author's travails of being a pregnant butch in a society that equates motherhood with femininity. The narrative concludes on a positive note, with the protagonist emerging triumphant after delivering her child. In fact, towards the end of the narrative, readers are even given full access to her essentially different family. Through the portrayal of being butch and pregnant, the author not only exposes negative cultural attitudes towards queer motherhood but also problematizes popular culture and the discourses of obstetrics/midwifery for their insistent heterosexual bias that alienates alternative motherhood practices. In a sense, Teek embodies determination and attainment as she navigates the everyday pragmatic realities of hegemonic and heterosexual forces. Summers also appeals for an inclusive system that, rather than ostracizing queer maternal practices and labeling them as "unnatural," accommodates alternative models of motherhood in the larger sociocultural fabric. Additionally, by visualizing herself as Tintin and making visible a queer experience of pregnancy, *Pregnant Buch* deftly constructs queer maternal knowledge.

ACKNOWLEDGMENTS

The authors would like to thank the reviewers for their helpful and constructive comments that greatly contributed to improving the chapter.

Notes

1. Judith Butler (1990) theorises the heterosexual matrix as a "grid of cultural intelligibility through which bodies, genders, and desires are naturalised" (17).

2. Ina May Gaskin, the founder of the Farm Midwifery Center in Tennessee, is often described as the mother of authentic midwifery. Her work *Spiritual Midwifery* is considered a classic text on midwifery.

Works Cited

Bendix, Trish. "A. K. Summers Illustrates the Life of 'Pregnant Butch.'" March 18, 2014. https://www.afterellen.com/books/212818-a-k-summers-illustrates-the-life-of-pregnant-butch. Accessed April 4, 2019.

Butler, Judith. *Gender Trouble: Feminism and the Subversion of Identity*. Routledge, 1990.

Gibson, Margaret F. "Introduction: Queering Motherhood in Narrative, Theory, and the Everyday." In *Queering Motherhood: Narrative and Theoretical Perspectives*, edited by Margaret F. Gibson, 1–23. Demeter Press, 2014.

Grigorovich, Alisa. "'Pregnant with Meaning': An Analysis of Online Media Response to Thomas Beatie and his Pregnancy." In *Queering Motherhood: Narrative and Theoretical Perspectives*, edited by Margaret F. Gibson, 81–96. Demeter Press, 2014.

Gruss, L. T., and D. Schmitt. "The Evolution of the Human Pelvis: Changing Adaptations to Bipedalism, Obstetrics and Thermoregulation." In *Philosophical transactions of the Royal Society of London. Series B, Biological sciences* 370 (2015): 1663. doi:10.1098/rstb.2014.0063. Accessed September 10, 2019.

Holland, Sierra. "Constructing Queer Mother-Knowledge and Negotiating Medical Authority in Online Lesbian Pregnancy Journals." *Sociology of Health & Illness* 41, no. 1 (2019): 52–66.

Johnson, Jenell. "Introduction." In *Graphic Reproduction: A Comics Anthology*, edited by Jenell Johnson, 1–16. Pennsylvania State University Press, 2018.

Scott, Darieck and Ramzi Fawaz. "Introduction: Queer about Comics." *American Literature* 90, no. 2 (2018): 197–219. https://doi.org/10.1215/00029831-4564274. Accessed February 15, 2019.

Summers, A. K. *Pregnant Butch: Nine Long Months Spent in Drag*. Soft Skull Press, 2014.

Chapter 23

PIXEL FANTASIES AND FUTURES
NARRATIVE "DE-OTHERING" IN QUEER WEBCOMICS

LIN YOUNG

In an interview, Naomi Castro of the webcomic *Icarus* claims that "'Queer' has almost become synonymous with 'webcomic,'" citing popular webcomics such as *Starfighter, Check, Please!*, and *The Misadventures of Tobias and Guy* (2019). In this chapter, I explore trends and debates pertaining to plot, setting, and character conflict in the Queer webcomic. One recent trend in webcomics is a move away from storylines exploring Queerness in relation to a dominant heterosexual social system; instead, Queer webcomics often depict fantastical spaces where narrative conflict is either absent, lessened, or limited to avenues unrelated to social or heteronormative opposition to Queer lives, frequently favoring bright colors and upbeat, gentle tones. In doing so, they imagine normalized worlds either unaffected or actively resistant to heteronormative control, wherein Queerness may be depicted and explored without being necessarily oriented around or defined with regard to political oppression and its resistance. This represents a drive, I argue, for many Queer artists to confront internalized "otherness" in favor of asserting a right to futurity, hope, and uncomplicated happiness. These comics thus negotiate the inescapability, in a heteronormative social framework, of a political Queer existence by working narratively to restrict and contain the power it implies. In doing so, these webcomics constitute Queer fantasies of absent heteronormativity, fantasies that attempt to visualize the ways in which Queerness might exist and operate in idealized spaces that are largely absent of any opposition to Queerness. This chapter thus explores how Queer comic artists are experimenting with methods of "de-Othering" the Queer comic through transformative fantasies of worlds in which Queerness is normalized, made default, and is unapologetically asserted as universal. In doing so, I argue, these depictions work as latent criticism of heteronormative centricity as a means of centering Queer optimism as resistance to real-world political oppression.

WEBCOMICS AND THE CRITICAL CONTEXT

In *Cruising Utopia,* Muñoz frames Queerness as a "performative . . . doing for and towards a new and better future" (2009, 1), arguing for the concrete possibility that such a future is contained within Queerness itself. Drawing on Bloch's philosophies of hope, Muñoz describes "an expanded idea of the utopian that surpasses Thomas More's formulation of utopias based in fantasy" (2). With reference to Giorgio Agamben's concept of potentiality, he argues that the tension between the functionality and non-functionality of current social norms for the comfortable existence of minoritarian citizen-subjects can be used to mobilize the anticipatory affect of hope. To arrive at this conclusion, Muñoz argues that a performance of Queerness that contests the conditions of compulsory heterosexuality acts as an outpost of a Queer future that actually exists in the present (in that it exists concurrently with the normative present) and that this insistence surpasses the normative regulation of this temporality (which mandates that the normative present is the only present, and that this present leads inevitably and uncontestedly into a normative future). Of course, Muñoz admits that "Bloch would posit that such utopian feelings can and regularly will be disappointed," but claims that "they are nonetheless indispensable to the act of imaging transformation" (2009, 9). Ultimately, though, he argues that "Queerness is essentially about the rejection of a here and now and an insistence on potentiality or concrete possibility for another world" (1).

As Muñoz suggests, "Often we can glimpse the worlds proposed and promised by queerness in the realm of the aesthetic . . . [which] frequently contains blueprints and schemata of a forward-dawning futurity" (1). It is within the context of *Cruising Utopia*'s articulation of the political, transformative power of Queer hope and potentiality that I wish to position my discussion of Queer webcomics. One dominant theme in the discourse of the Queer webcomics community pertains to the social responsibility of providing narratives of Queer hope and optimism. In many ways, these comics imagine Queerness in much the same way as Muñoz does, as "the warm illumination of a horizon imbued with potentiality" (1). Many artists, as I will demonstrate, position their comics as stories of positive resistance to inevitable or uncontested otherness by way of narratives of hope and normalization. In attempting to provide such narratives, many comics look to destabilize the power of heteronormative social structures by decentralizing them and imagining Queer experience as the "default" experience in their respective worlds. In essence, this might be summed up as a project designed to examine and test both the possibilities and limitations of "de-othering" Queerness by drawing upon narratives of hopeful Queer potentiality.

THE SHIFTING MEANING OF "QUEER" IN THE WEBCOMICS WORLD

This chapter attempts to address a sample-size of fifteen to twenty artists as broadly, though not comprehensively, indicative of this major trend in webcomics. Interviewees were solicited in two rounds, the first as a general call for comics artists/writers who considered their webcomic "Queer," and the second asking specifically for artists of color. The respondents were selected on the basis of representing a combination of self-published webcomics and webcomics with digital and/or print publishers, as well as representing a diversity of Queer voices. Naturally, these comics and their politics are as diverse as their authors. By conducting these interviews, I sought to capture and examine a widespread debate within the Queer webcomics community that begins with the term "Queer webcomic" itself.

One trend among Queer webcomics is a preference for large ensemble casts of diverse Queer communities as opposed to stories of singular protagonists (see *Rock and Riot*, *Agents of the Realm*, *Inhibit*, etc.). Samantha Close, writing on gender in webcomics, identifies these "massive ensemble casts" as one unique feature of the webcomic itself, which, she writes, "offers multiple models of gendered identity for creator and readers to think together" (2015, 535). Of the interviews I conducted, all respondents identified their comics as having "majority" casts of Queer characters, with many identifying exclusively Queer casts; the lowest percentage of Queer characters was still set at 50 percent (*Namesake*, Hiveworks Comics) (Melançon 2019). In speaking to *Yes Homo* about *Goodbye to Halos*, Halla states, "I wanted every single character to be queer. For me, that's less about representation and more the simple fact of making it the kind of story I'd want to read" (2015). In comparison to comics like Alison Bechdel's *Dykes to Watch Out For*, however, which markets its focus on the lives of lesbian women through the title alone, the Queer webcomic has a more ambivalent relationship with respect to marketing or articulating its own Queerness beyond establishing these big, Queer-dominant casts. Rather, the trend in the Queer webcomic is often to use these Queer-focused casts to normalize Queer experience so ubiquitously as to make its labels and definitions almost invisible, while—crucially—still centering visible Queerness on the page.

Spire Eaton of the webcomic *Recoil* writes, "[t]here is a lot of pressure to make characters trumpet their own identities inside the comic in order to certify just how Queer the comic really is, and I just don't do that" (2019). *Recoil*, which tells the story of a therapy group whose participants are superpowered, depicts a world in which "[characters'] Queerness is sort of inherent and accepted by each other . . . I don't namedrop any of their identities" (Eaton 2019). Despite this lack of overt marketing, *Recoil* features an ensemble of over fifty characters, with "the majority of them" falling under the Queer umbrella. Queerness in the world of *Recoil* is thus omnipresent while simultaneously being undefined and unremarked upon. Eve Greenwood, creator of the teen superhero webcomic *Inhibit,* goes one step further by implying that the world of *Inhibit* imagines "Queer" as the unstated default: "When I haven't thought about a character's identity/orientation, they default as Queer" (2019). This is echoed by Erin Ptah of *Leif and Thorn,* who writes that her characters are "Queer-unless-otherwise-specified" (2019) by design, and by Inbar Fink of *Just a Sidekick,* who writes that she prefers stories that feature "less Heterosexual-ity-as-Default" (2019). This trend to center Queer experience as the "default" experience is one way in which this breed of Queer webcomics repositions Queer identity *as* the norm of their respective worlds, rather than something positioned in opposition to the norm.

This strategy has resulted in an ongoing debate within the community over the perceived limitations of the "Queer webcomic" label. Hari Conner, creator of the DiNKy-winning comic *Finding Home,* writes, "I don't always describe [*Finding Home*] as Queer, I think partly because it feels like a story *about* something else with Queer characters" (2019). Ptah echoes this, writing that "I tend to market [my comic] as the more precise 'webcomics with lots of LGBTQ+ characters'" (2019). Adrien Lee of the comic *White Noise* muses, similarly, on the marketing burden of the "Queer webcomic" label, and its ambiguous usage online: "I feel like people expect a story about Queerness, or at least Queer romance, when they hear the phrase 'Queer webcomic.' . . . So I stick to calling it just 'a webcomic about Queer monsters'" (2019). Similarly, in an interview with *Comics Alliance,* Valerie Halla describes her Queer fantasy webcomic *Goodbye to Halos* as "a comic whose characters, motivations and morals are deeply Queer, but whose conflict is not" (Halla 2015). This quote illustrates a conscious effort on Halla's part to differentiate between her comic's *depiction* of Queerness and what she perceives to be a general audience's impression of Queer *conflict*—specifically, narrative conflict that emerges from Queer characters experiencing social and political oppression.

Maria Izquierdo of *We Broke Up* also comments on how the "Queer" label resonates differently in the webcomics world than it might to a general audi-ence, writing that "I don't really market [my comic] like that since what I want is to be able to speak to many people, so I try to make [its marketing] the most neutral I can," but adding that it is important to her to do so "without it losing the themes" (2019). The issue with the "Queer" label, Izquierdo writes, is that "for people who are not familiar with the term, they might think that it's about gay, lesbian, or trans* people only," adding that she wishes her work to resonate with diverse audiences both within and outside the Queer com-munity, as "the experiences I'm aiming for are universal" (2019). In terms of plot, Izquierdo's comic explores the immediate aftermath of the breakup of a lesbian relationship. The very first strip depicts the protagonist celebrating Pride Day but, upon remembering her newfound singleness, then sulking; the comic goes on to alternate between explicitly Queer-coded experiences (such as celebrating Pride, or commenting on her mother's slow but ultimately flippant acceptance of her sexuality) with experiences that might equally apply to a heterosexual relationship (such as claiming that she will never shave her legs again). In this way, Izquierdo views her goal of universality as compatible with the explicitly Queer context established on page one, emphasizing that Queerness, in the context of her comic's world, is as mundane and unremarkable (and, theoretically, relatable) as unshaved legs, and—crucially—meets with as much resistance. The comic's world thus constitutes a fantasy of normalization—one in which the narrative conflict resulting from a lesbian breakup can resonate, to its readership, as simultaneously Queer *and* universal in a bid to undermine heterosexist definitions of universality or normality.

Despite this resistance to the "Queer" label, most artists recognize that Queer content is a draw for their audiences, as many imagine their readerships comprising large numbers of Queer-identifying people. Strategies to indicate Queer content without adopting the ambiguous "Queer webcomic" label can be found in hosting websites and external "digital matter." Considering the publication practices of the average webcomic—with serial, single-page updates per week being the norm, and long publication runs that leave audiences at risk of forgetting certain characters more easily—it is common practice in the webcomic world to include dramatis personae on their hosting sites for audiences' reference. These pages, though separate from the comic proper, often go into extensive detail about characters' gender and sexual identities. The cast pages for webcomics *Aspera*, *Rock and Riot*, and *This is Not Fiction*, for example, all list characters' sexual and romantic labels as part of short character surveys, as a means of assuring readers of a "Queer fabric" without necessitating the use of exact terminology in the comics themselves. Strategies such as these use digital matter to allow for diverse and individualized Queerness to be baked into the foundations of their stories without specific narrative identification or explanation. With these "digital matter" strategies, Queer webcomic artists demonstrate an interest in utilizing the malleability of the web format to allow for greater normalization of Queer identity and content in their comics, where non-normative gender identity and Queer sexualities are not imagined as things that need textual explanation in the first place.

As the normalization of Queerness is, in the real world, much more politically fraught than in the worlds presented by these webcomics, these webcomics position themselves as narratives of positive resistance. Muñoz argues that *Cruising Utopia* emerged as "a challenge to theoretical insights that have been stunted by the lull of presentness and various romances of negativity" (2009, 12). Crucially, Muñoz does not deny the potential power of the negative (he cites Virno's *Multitude: Between Innovation and Negation*, for example), but seeks instead to expand the modes through which Queer identity and expression might be understood. He writes, "The idea of hope . . . is both a critical affect and a methodology . . . from the point of view of political struggles today, such a critical optic is nothing short of necessary in order to combat the force of political pessimism" (2009, 4). These comics visualize a Muñozian aesthetic and philosophical worldview, wherein they can "dream and enact new and better pleasures, other ways of being in the world, and ultimately new worlds" (2009, 1)—or as Valerie Halla writes, "I try my hardest to represent in fiction the things I've felt and the world I want to build" by "making something as loudly and peculiarly queer as [she] want[s]" (2017). By providing hopeful narrative alternatives that center Queer experience as "default" and reject the need for definitive labels and explanations, these comics project "de-Othered" and expanded Queer worlds.

TRENDS IN TONE AND CONFLICT IN THE QUEER WEBCOMIC

Among comics that consider themselves a part of this project of Queer normalization and positive resistance, I suggest that there are two major storytelling trends to be found in the Queer webcomic:

Tonal Resistance. Stories that create positive resistance by depicting Queer-majority worlds that are sweet, light-hearted, brightly colored, and prefer more domestic, incidental, or low-stakes conflict.

Narrative Resistance. Stories that create positive resistance by reorienting narrative conflict *away* from conflicts dependant on social or political opposition to Queerness.

The first strategy of tonal resistance is perhaps best illustrated by webcomics like Katie O'Neill's *Princess Princess*, which rewrites the fairy tale trope of the princess locked in a tower as a lesbian romance between Princess Sadie and her royal rescuer, Princess Amira. In *Princess Princess*, the suggestion of two princesses falling in love is uncomplicatedly embraced, as homophobia or heteronormative expectations appear utterly absent in the world of the comic proper. The comic's print epilogue, "Ever After," concludes the story in typical fairy-tale fashion, with Sadie and Amira's marriage meeting with no political or systemic opposition, with Amira remarking that "somehow, nothing seems scary right now" (O'Neill 2016, 54). In a review of the print edition, *The Mary Sue* describes the comic as characterized by "sweetness and snark" with an "adorable art style and use of color [that] would be at home in any prose children's book," and highlighting "the importance of sweet, innocent, romantic fairy tales . . . featuring LGBTQIA characters" (Jusino 2016). Muñoz writes that Bloch makes distinctions between "abstract utopias and concrete utopias, valuing abstract utopias only insofar as they pose a critique function that fuels a critical and potentially transformative political imagination" (2009, 3). However, comics such as *Princess Princess*, which arguably function more as abstract utopias, ultimately position their very existence as an act of resistance, serving, perhaps, as a useful first step for younger audiences in imagining potential Queer futures or Queer worlds.

Other webcomics aimed at more general audiences, such as *Goodbye to Halos*, employ strategies that particularly emphasize their soft tones and "gentle" conflicts. *Goodbye to Halos* tells the story of an "entire cast of Queer characters" and their fantastical adventures in a world comprised of anthropomorphic animals. *Goodbye to Halos* explicitly markets itself as a comic that "strives to be mature while still being friendly, cute, and accessible" (Halla "About"), with Halla adding that she has "always loved the idea of alternating big silly fight scenes with tender moments and panels framed in flowers," before ultimately describing the comic as "a comic about friends and relationships and cuddling, with some incidental knife fights" (Halla 2017). This description highlights the comic's tender elements while simultaneously acknowledging and depowering, through the offhanded "incidental," the threat of more serious violence. In an interview with *Yes Homo*, Halla states that the comic was originally imagined as being more "hyperviolent" in tone during its development stages but eventually settled on a tone and setting wherein "most of the conflict ended up being emotional" (Halla 2015), such as several characters' relationships with anxiety and romantic entanglements. Halla describes her decision to feature an exclusively Queer cast as being effectively a claiming of space, writing that, "I'm bored of straight people, they have their own comics, it's gay time now" (2015). Like *Princess Princess*, in the Queer webcomics world, these more abstract utopias often resonate as political through this assertion of their own right to exist, and to center Queer experiences uncompromisingly.

Another approach to tonal resistance can be observed in *We Broke Up*. Izquierdo describes *We Broke Up* as "a slice of life comic, with a very light-hearted and comical approach" (2019). The comic, which details the aftermath of a lesbian breakup, keeps a consistently light-hearted tone despite the serious subject matter. The central conflict of the comic, according to Izquierdo, comes from "all the silly situations in which one manages to find themselves in" following a breakup (2019). As such, the comic frequently focuses less on moments of deep sadness, which are often banished from the page in favor of a joke about the protagonist's comedic coping mechanisms. The comic thus focuses more on the humor to be found in the ways in which the protagonist

manages her shifting environment and ingrained habits following the dis-
solution of the relationship, such as her lingering instinct to offer food to her
absent girlfriend or greet her in the morning. Izquierdo describes this tonal
strategy thusly: "[t]he idea was to find the nice, silly and fun in everyday life
even though one is hurting and heartbroken" (2019). In doing so, the comic
favors small, light-hearted, domestic conflicts as opposed to focusing on the
character's oppression or outsider status.

Izquierdo emphasizes this tonal strategy as a pointed and conscious narrative choice in the strip with her mother, who comments blithely at how well
she's been doing at accepting her daughter's lesbian relationship, only for the
two to break up. This strip is one of the few that actually suggests the possibility of opposition to Queerness in the comic's world, by alluding vaguely to a
past wherein the mother was less accepting than she is (or, at least, attempts
to be) now. However, by suggesting this past through a mere punchline, while
simultaneously refusing to depict it in the comic proper, Izquierdo asserts
a kind of narrative control by highlighting her awareness of—and, in fact,
experience with—opposition to Queer lives, by pointedly banishing opposition from the page. Essentially, Izquierdo limits the narrative eye of the comic
to this image of positive (if imperfect) change *after* the change has occurred
off-page, without making such a journey the focus of the comic as a whole. Just
as Muñoz writes that "queer aesthetics map future social relations" rather than
serving as an "escape from the social realm" (2009, 1), *We Broke Up* chooses
instead to emphasize the mother's positive progress and future potential, and
in doing so characterizes the relationship between mother and daughter as a
hopeful one. *We Broke Up* thus emphasizes the hopeful politics at its core by
acknowledging the potential for opposition to Queerness, while simultaneously
depowering that opposition by denying it narrative space in favor of a more
hopeful, tonally playful Queer landscape. In this way, it becomes less of an
abstract utopia—as defined by Muñoz and Bloch—and inches towards a more
concrete one, defined by Muñoz as "relational to historically situated struggles
. . . the realm of educated hope" (2009, 1).

These comics belong to a larger project in the Queer webcomics community
that adopt tone as a form of positive political resistance to narrative associations
of Queerness with struggle, opposition, or strife. *The Queer Comics Database*
reflects this trend by including an archival listing for "Tone." Significantly, the
offered tags weigh heavily towards lighter, more positive terminology: "sweet,"
"silly," "inspirational," "cheerful," "tranquil," "reflective," and "sentimental" are all
offered tags, compared to only two "negative" tags such as "bleak" and "tense"
(the *only* tags that allow the visitor to seek out darker fare). Content tags also
allow visitors to avoid comics that deal with homophobia, transphobia, or
biphobia specifically. These tags can only say so much out of context, but their

Figure 23.1. *We Broke Up*, Maria Izquierdo (2016), 9.

existence suggests something significant about how the database assumes its readership will want to engage with its sorting system. Namely, that there is an interest in creating tools that allow for readers to guide their reading according to comparative tones and levels of social opposition specifically.

On the other side of the tone debate, artist Sarah Fowlie, creator of *The Quick & Dirty Life of Fritz Fargo,* writes that "I always feel a bit awkward when I read a list of 'best Queer webcomics' and they're all super cute, nice, and uplifting" (Fowlie 2018a). She adds, "I still see people . . . bemoaning downer Queer stories for even existing. That they're sick of it, and does no good" (Fowlie 2018b). *Fritz Fargo* is a dramatic comedy about the vocalist for a band called Hot Bat; it tackles themes of abuse, addiction, and mental illness. Fowlie's comment illustrates the community's awareness of a broader trend of the "soft and hopeful" Queer comic, and she adds that "when I see fans recommend *Fritz,* they either don't mention the story at all or have a huge disclaimer about it being 'on the darker side'" (Fowlie 2018c). Ptah comments further on the widespread nature of this debate, depicting the field as a "whole spectrum" of comics, "from 'real-world issues created by dangerously homophobic/transphobic societies' to 'totally unrelated struggles in a world where Queer/trans* identities are 100% normalized.'" She laments that "people complain about either side—not just saying they don't want to read it, but claiming it's Bad Queer Representation to write it at all," adding that there is value to appreciating a wide scope of Queer experiences (Ptah 2019). Quotes such as these illustrate the active debates occurring within the Queer webcomics community with respect to the limitations of tonal resistance as a widespread project, particularly when considering Queer webcomics such as *Recoil* or *Fritz* that still wish to depict heavier themes.

The second storytelling trend in the Queer webcomic is narrative resistance. Many Queer webcomics are actively responding to perceived decades of "Queer tragedy" narratives, typified by films such as *Brokeback Mountain* or *Boys Don't Cry,* where Queer experience is inextricably linked to violence, grief, and outside resistance to one's identity. Goltz states, "[s]edimented myths of LGBT sexual predation, suicidal ideation, and misery have circulated for decades in mainstream discourses" (2013, 136), and internet projects like *It Gets Better* (IGB) speak to the pervasiveness of these narratives. As with Muñoz's description of Queer potentiality, Goltz argues that initiatives like IGB "proliferate [. . .] multiple and contradictory meanings for 'better,' extending and challenging sedimented homophobic and heteronormative discourses of time and future" and enacting "a radically Queer intervention for reclaiming and revisioning the future" (2013, 136). Queer webcomics often work to model, stylize, and heighten these "imagined" Queer futures in their experimentally normalized worlds, placing themselves in opposition to what Laura Lee calls Queer "tragedy porn" (2019). While Lee acknowledges the importance of these narratives to exist in their own right, she speculates that "when there's such little content that's been given to us which is almost exclusively tragic, it makes us weary and exhausted of anything that might tread into these territories," adding that "I want to read stories that are about Queer people with a variety of different conflicts that's not just related to our current ongoing persecution" (2019). Conner echoes this, citing the webcomic community as "the place where I've seen the most varied Queer content and stories that are unique, imaginative, joyful or just interesting combinations of genre" as opposed to other media, which they describe as being almost "exclusively gritty, tragic and brutal, or possibly rom-coms where the characters' sexualities are a huge sticking point" (2019). Ahmara Smith of *Hellbound*, which she describes as a "fantastical and light-hearted adventure romance" despite the central plot involving a rescue-mission to Hell, also describes a general dislike for Queer stories that "focus on the trauma . . . more than the positive aspects of being Queer" (2019). Halla is motivated by a similar resistance, stating that "the driving force behind all my work has always been my desire to counter those tragic stories with hope and acceptance and normalcy" (2017). It is important to note that these authors' resistance to more tragic Queer narratives is not designed as commentary on the quality or social utility of such narratives, but rather a response to the perceived oversaturation of such stories due to the comparative absence of stories of Queer optimism and hope for the majority of history, and the effect such marketplace saturation has on Queer potentiality. Rather, these comics express a desire to materialize Queer hope according to Muñoz, wherein "Queerness is a longing that propels us onward, beyond romances of the negative and toiling in the present" (2009, 1).

The principal narrative strategy for resisting "Queer tragedy" is to reorient central narrative conflicts deliberately away from those that deal with characters' struggles with their sexuality or larger social oppression to Queerness. Mad Sparrow of *Ghost Slappers*, a webcomic about a house-flipper attempting to sell a haunted house, comments that "I think it's important to have representation of strong Queer characters [whose] stories don't revolve around their sexuality or the social backlash to being Queer" (2019). In writing *Ghost Slappers*, she claims that "I wanted the focus and conflict in Jenny's story to come from her situation and not from her sexuality" (Mad Sparrow 2019). This strategy often employs a resistance to the "coming out" narrative. *Yes Homo*, one of the few websites dedicated solely to reviewing Queer webcomics, was founded on this resistance, as its "About" page laments that "if you want to see a Queer and/or trans main character, you have to settle for the 'LGBT' genre, and I don't know about you, but I've seen enough dry, depressing, artsy films about coming out" (Wisp). As Eve Greenwood writes, "The characters being Queer doesn't need to be a central conflict for the comic to be called Queer—they can just be Queer and go on a little adventure and not struggle with their identity at all and it'll still be a Queer webcomic" (2019). Mad Sparrow elaborates on a kind of "politics of being" that motivates this strategy, writing that "it's such a small part of being a Queer person and [I] would love to see more Queer characters just 'being'" (2019). In justifying this narrative preference, Sparrow adds,

> Queer characters . . . are often only seen in coming out stories or romances and [I] wanted to give my Queer readers a role model that they could relate to, one [whose] life doesn't revolve around their sexuality and who's in a relationship that's firm and solid and not the driving force of the plot. (2019)

Strategies like these abound in Queer webcomics, where Queerness is positioned not as a designation of outsider status or a source of conflict, but rather as an uncontested facet of the comic's world. In essence, these transformative strategies further imagine the hopeful possibilities of Queerness, where Queer characters can exist in fantastically idealized, normalized, and "de-Othered" spaces, without the need to recognize their own Queerness as inherently opposed to a dominant societal viewpoint.

Another narrative trend that enables this mode of positive resistance is in a widespread turn to fantastical genres and Queer-centric worldbuilding in order to destabilize social narratives of Queer "Others," and to imagine Queer-centered societies from the ground up. *Yes Homo* acknowledges this trend, writing that "scifi, fantasy, and other kinds of spec-fic webcomics abound with Queer (and, to a lesser extent, trans) characters" (Wisp "About"). In *Leif and Thorn,* Ptah works within a fantasy context to reorient the "intrinsic conflicts" of Queer experience, such as a lesbian couple working to conceive a biological child, but notes that "[n]one of the conflicts stem from homophobia or transphobia, since this is a fantasy world that doesn't have them" (2019). Conner adds that "writing in a fantasy setting is a way to imagine and explore a world with less of that struggle, or reimagine that struggle in a more abstract sense" (2019). Adrien Lee, meanwhile, describes his comic as having "fantastical themes dealt with in a realistic way" by "us[ing] a lot of the 'mechanics' of social prejudice and persecution . . . without being a 1:1 metaphor for any one group" (2019). Sooz, creator of *Patchwork and Lace*, includes fluid sexuality as a core tenet of her comic's cosmopolitan world, writing that "the story is set in a fantasy world with different ideas surrounding genders and sexualities, so many characters would . . . not think of themselves as different." Laura Lee's *Ghost Junk Sickness*, a comic about space bounty-hunters living in the wake of the near-destruction of their planet, imagines a futuristic, cosmopolitan setting that establishes pansexuality as the assumed default, and where "gender is free and fluent" (2019). In building Queerness into the foundation of the comic world's social norms and systems, Laura Lee describes the unique power of worldbuilding—particularly in fantastical genres—to consciously center Queer experience without granting narrative space to the depiction of resistance or opposition to that experience: "In a world where humans are fully integrated together with a multitude of different sentient species, we just couldn't imagine that it would be a heteronormative society." She adds, "*Ghost Junk Sickness* was created to normalize our existence as Queer people, and for us to live in a world where identities with sexuality and gender is not up for 'political debate'" (2019). In general, many of these comics assert a kind of politic of hopeful, transformative fantasy, fantasies which imagine that narratives of Queer identity can be structurally centered, normalized, and "de-Othered," and that heteronormative worldbuilding and storytelling can be rejected and depowered.

One variation on this type of worldbuilding strategy can be found in Chelsea Furedi's *Rock and Riot,* which depicts the love lives of two Queer gangs in a stylized 1950s America. The comic employs both tonal and narrative resistance strategies, featuring bright pastel colors, a goofy but heartfelt tone, and an exclusively Queer cast. Significantly, however, *Rock and Riot* presents an alternate history where openly Queer teenagers are afforded the community, vocabulary, and broader social acceptance that Queer teenagers would certainly have struggled to find in the real-world 1950s, a decade characterized by the resurgence of heteronormative, patriarchal family values, functioning—in Muñoz's words—as "a backward glance that enacts a future vision" (2009, 4). *Yes Homo* describes *Rock and Riot*'s world as one that "leaves period racism (and other forms of discrimination) out for [one] reason: fun" (Wisp, "Rock"). *Yes Homo*'s review appreciates *Rock and Riot*'s deliberately anachronistic worldbuilding with respect to its lack of any substantial threat to its Queer characters' happiness and prosperity, writing that,

> the homophobia and misogyny are still there, but in a more toothless form . . . presented more as individual prejudice than systemic oppression. . . . Neither is serious or scary: systems of oppression reduced to feeble bogeymen for the entertainment of readers affected by them in real life. In this way, *Rock and Riot* is something of a power fantasy. (Wisp, "Rock")

Indeed, only in the comic's final arc do the characters face any substantial objection to their Queer identities and romances from outside groups, when they are banned from bringing their same-sex partners to the prom. Further, after the characters "riot" through the dance hall in mischievous protest, the

Figure 23.2. *Rock and Riot*, chapter 16, Chelsey Furedi (2017), 25.

entire auditorium of heterosexual pairings is inspired to embrace same-sex dance partners, figuring the authoritarian teachers as minority outsiders whose power over the student body is easily and comically overcome by the sheer force of the Queer majority (Furedi 2015). When Connie, one of the gang leaders, comments, "They didn't let us in. We weren't accepted," her girlfriend Carla implores her to "look around." Upon observing dozens of Queer couples, the characters are forced to reorient their conceptions of acceptance to exclude heteronormative definitions altogether, and to recognize themselves as uncomplicated insiders within their own powerful communities. The comic ends on a note of overwhelming Queer majority in the face of opposition, figuring the school's resistance to Queer love as more akin to adult disapproval of teenage rebellion rather than the result of meaningfully powerful systemic oppression. In this way, the narrative keeps its conflicts light even through the suggestion of opposition, resisting any implication that the structural prejudices of its world will ever have any serious consequences for its characters. In this way, *Rock and Riot* engages more readily with Queer social histories by evoking its realities through its aesthetics and plot beats, and then making conscious choices to limit the narrative power of such social histories over its characters. *Rock and Riot*'s conscious historical revisioning thus illustrates a structurally harmonious and fantastical landscape for its Queer characters, one in which Queer identity is both normalized and centered through depictions of the universalized experiences of young love and community rather than characterized by the inherent opposition, isolation or struggle that its chosen time period would, in a work of straightforward realism, otherwise demand.

CONCLUSION

Whether these comics employ tonal or narrative resistance (or both), all of them seek to explore Queer potentiality—what Muñoz defines as "unlike a possibility, a thing that simply might happen, a potentiality is a certain mode of nonbeing that is eminent, a thing that is present but not actually existing in the present tense" (2009, 9)—in different ways by creating Queer frameworks that work to limit or make consciously invisible the assumed power of heteronormative expectation. Contrary to the uncertain state of politics in the real world, Queer webcomics participating in this project illustrate a sustained interest in exploring the politics and visualization of Queer normalization, and if such a thing is ultimately possible; idealized worlds here are positioned by the community as inherently political for their transformative and hopeful potential.

    Comics that belong to this project of normalization and "de-Othering" ultimately function as a widespread deconstruction of what constitutes, to either a general audience or a Queer audience, the inherent associations of Queer identity. In doing so, many Queer webcomics engage in a politic of transformative hope and positive resistance. This politic essentially seeks to imagine how Queer identities might themselves shift or redefine themselves in response to an (idealized) improved political climate, and how to meaningfully visualize worlds that center normalized, de-Othered Queerness. Whether or not those climates are reflective of the real world is not generally a point of interest to this group—arguably, these comics are largely motivated by the realities, for Queer people, of hostile climates and political uncertainty. In doing so, they embody many of Muñoz's philosophies on Queerness itself, and the motivations of this project reflect his position that "Queerness is a structuring and educated mode of desiring that allows us to see and feel beyond the quagmire of the present. The here and now is a prison house" (2009, 1). The work of these comics, as envisioned by their creators, is to combat this quagmire with transformative, deconstructive fantasies of hope. Naturally, the Queer webcomics community is hardly a monolith: some artists resist the turn away from "Queer Other" conflicts and the vogue for more tonally upbeat stories, while others embrace them. As a general trend, however, this widespread politic of Queer hope and positive resistance, either in tone or narrative, demonstrates a shifting mode of thought with respect to how Queer identities and experiences are defined by these communities, and how their stories are told. They largely articulate a depiction of Queerness that resists traditional narrative associations with outsiders, difference, or Otherness, or else engage with actively reworking those narratives. In doing so, the Queer webcomic asserts its political and cultural right to these pixelated fantasies in order to engage in a reclamation of joy, hope, and love.

Works Cited

Castro, Naomi. Interview by Lin Young, April 24, 2019.

Close, Samantha. "The Absent Presence of Gender in Webcomics." *Feminist Media Studies* 15, no. 3 (2015): 533–38.

Conner, Hari. Interview by Lin Young, January 5, 2019.

Eaton, Spire. Interview by Lin Young, February 26, 2019.

Fink, Inbar. Interview by Lin Young, April 15, 2019.

Fowlie, Sarah. Twitter post. January 24, 2018a, 3:31pm. https://twitter.com/whotookfowlie/status/956248059230523394.

Fowlie, Sarah. Twitter post. January 24, 2018b, 3:35pm. https://twitter.com/whotookfowlie/status/956249013992525825.

Fowlie, Sarah. Twitter post. January 24, 2018c, 3:36pm. https://twitter.com/whotookfowlie/status/956249319635636229.

Furedi, Chelsey. *Rock and Riot*, 2015, https://rockandriotcomic.com/.

Goltz, Dustin Bradley. "It Gets Better: Queer Futures, Critical Frustrations, And Radical Poten-tials." *Critical Studies in Media Communication* 30, no. 2 (2013): 135–51. *Informa UK Limited*, doi:10.1080/15295036.2012.701012.

Greenwood, Eve. Interview by Lin Young, April 10, 2019.

Halla, Valerie. "About." Goodbye to Halos. http://www.goodbyetohalos.com/about.

Halla, Valerie. "'Anxiety and Skirts' – an interview with Valerie Halla." By Wisp. *YesHomo.net,* November 22, 2015. https://yeshomo.net/anxiety-and-skirts-an-interview-with-valerie-halla/.

Halla, Valerie. "Knife Fights and Queer Smooches in Valerie Halla's 'Goodbye to Halos.'" By Jon Christianson. *Comics Alliance*, January 25, 2017, https://comicsalliance.com/valerie-halla-goodbye-to-halos-interview/

Izquierdo, Maria. Interview by Lin Young, April 20, 2019.

Izquierdo, Maria. *We Broke Up.* 2017. http://vinzul.tumblr.com/

Jusino, Teresa. "Review: *Princess Princess Ever After* Is a Sweet LGBTQIA Fairy Tale." *The Mary Sue*, 2016, https://www.themarysue.com/review-princess-princess-ever-after/.

Lee, Adrien. Interview by Lin Young, February 4, 2019.

Lee, Laura. Interview by Lin Young, February 3, 2019.

Mad Sparrow. Interview by Lin Young, February 3, 2019.

Melançon, Isabelle. Interview by Lin Young, January 12, 2019.

Muñoz, José Esteban. *Cruising Utopia: The Then and There of Queer Futurity*. New York University Press, 2009.

O'Neill, Katie. *Princess Princess Ever After*. Oni Press, 2016.

Ptah, Erin. Interview by Lin Young, February 4, 2019.

Smith, Ahmara. Interview by Lin Young, April 22, 2019.

Wisp. "About." *YesHomo.net*. https://yeshomo.net/about/

Wisp. "Rock and Riot." *YesHomo.net*. https://yeshomo.net/rock-and-riot.

ABOUT THE CONTRIBUTORS

MICHELLE ANN ABATE is professor of Literature for Children and Young Adults at the Ohio State University. She is author of six books of literary criticism. Her first book, *Tomboys: A Literary and Cultural History* (2008), was nominated for a Lambda Literary Award in the category of LGBTQ studies. With Kenneth B. Kidd, Michelle coedited the essay collection *Over the Rainbow: Queer Children's and Young Adult Literature* (2011). Michelle has also published more than thirty peer-reviewed journal articles on subjects including Alison Bechdel's *Fun Home*, lesbian pulp fiction, and the ex-gay movement to lesbian affect in Willa Cather, a queer reading of *The Sound and the Fury*, and the first lesbian character in US comics. In 2018, Michelle was a guest coeditor on a special issue of the *Journal of Lesbian Studies* dedicated to the topic of comics. Michelle's fifth book, *Funny Girls: Guffaws, Guts, and Gender in Classic American Comics*, was released in 2019. Her most recent project, *No Kids Allowed: Children's Literature for Adults*, was released in Fall 2020.

WILLIAM S. ARMOUR is an honorary senior lecturer in the School of Humanities and Languages, UNSW Sydney. He holds an MA (Applied Linguistics) and a PhD in Education. He has taught courses in Japanese language, intercultural communication, Japanese popular culture, and Asian masculinities. His research interests focus on identity, multimodal meaning making, and learning and teaching. He is the author of "Representations of the Masculine in Tagame Gengoroh's Ero SM Manga," *Asian Studies Review* 34, no. 4 (2010): 443–65.

ALISON BECHDEL is a lesbian American cartoonist and graphic novelist whose long-running, landmark comic *Dykes to Watch Out For* (1983–2008) was one of the earliest strips to feature LGBTQ+ lives, loves, and politics, focusing on a diverse group of (mostly) lesbian characters. Over the course of its twenty-five-year run, the strip appeared in the *Funny Times*, in syndicated LGBTQ+ newspapers, and online, and it spawned at least a dozen separately published collections. Published in 2006, Bechdel's graphic memoir *Fun Home: A Family Tragicomic* soon achieved tremendous commercial and critical success. Seven years in the making, it chronicles Bechdel's complex relationship with her closeted gay father through a nonlinear, recursive narrative in which her lesbian self-discovery leads her to contend with her familial past and to find sympathy for her father's abnegation. A *New York Times* bestseller and *Time* magazine's Best Book of 2006, *Fun Home* was adapted as a musical in 2013 by Lisa Kron and Jeanine Tesori. It opened on Broadway in 2015 and won five Tony Awards, including Best Musical. Bechdel's second graphic memoir, *Are You My Mother?: A Comic Drama* (2012) interweaves recollection, dreams, and psychoanalysis to understand her relationship with her mother. Bechdel's comics have appeared in the *New Yorker*, *Slate*, *McSweeney's*, the *New York Times Book Review*, and *Granta*.

JENNIFER CAMPER is a lesbian Lebanese American cartoonist and graphic artist whose work explores the intersections of gender and race, while reveling in women's sexuality. She published her first cartoon in 1980 and began contributing to the comics series, *Gay Comix*, edited by Howard Cruse. Her work has appeared in newspapers and magazines since the 1990s, as well as in exhibits in Europe and the United States. She has published two books, *Rude Girls and Dangerous Women* (a collection of her cartoons) and *SubGURLZ* (a graphic novella about three women living in abandoned subway tunnels). The editor of two *Juicy Mother* comics anthologies, Camper is an important queer community builder: among her other initiatives, she is the creator and director of the Queers & Comics conference, a biennial event that brings together established and emerging queer cartoonists from around the world.

TESLA CARIANI is a Mellon Interventions Project Public Scholarship Teaching Fellow and PhD candidate in the Department of English at Emory University, where she also holds a graduate certificate in Women's, Gender, and Sexuality Studies. Her dissertation focuses on representations of queer and trans* embodiment in comics, graphic novels, and photographs. Encompassing questions of framing, affect, and political activism, her work arises from the intersection between visual culture and literary studies. Tesla has been published in *PMLA*, and her experience working in documentary film production continues to inform her visual approach to texts.

MATTHEW CHENEY is assistant professor and director of Interdisciplinary Studies at Plymouth State University in Plymouth, New Hampshire. He is the author of *Modernist Crisis and the Pedagogy of Form: Woolf, Delany, and Coetzee at the Limits of Fiction* and *Blood: Stories*.

HILLARY CHUTE is distinguished professor of English and Art + Design at Northeastern University. She is the author or editor of six books, including *Why Comics? From Underground to Everywhere*, *Disaster Drawn: Visual Witness, Comics, and Documentary Form*, *Outside the Box: Interviews with Contemporary*

Cartoonists, and *Graphic Women: Life Narrative and Contemporary Comics*. She has written for venues including *Artforum*, *Bookforum*, the *Village Voice*, and the *New York Review of Books*. She is a comics and graphic novels columnist for the *New York Times Book Review*.

EDMOND (EDO) ERNEST DIT ALBAN is lecturer in East Asian Studies at McGill University where they teach classes in film and gender studies. Edo holds a PhD in Moving Images and Film Studies from Concordia University and a Doctorate in Communication Studies from Paris Saint-Denis University. Their dissertation, and book project, examine the overlooked participation of female and queer otaku fandoms in the emergence of Japanese Media Mix strategies through the urban history of recycled media networks in otaku sanctuaries. Edo's publications include a chapter cowritten with Marc Steinberg for Paul Booth's *A Companion to Fandom and Fan Studies*, a recently edited special number of the online journal *Synoptique*, as well as upcoming articles on the history of women's anime cultures, gay manga history and queer animation. Since 2011 Edo has been involved in the multilingual translation and global circulation of French fanzine *Dokkun*. Their collaborations include book projects, "Le bara ça n'existe pas" (2013), as well as the upcoming podcast series *Dokkun Radio*.

RAMZI FAWAZ is associate professor of English at the University of Wisconsin, Madison. He is the author of *The New Mutants: Superheroes and the Radical Imagination of American Comics*, which won the 2017 Book Prize of the Association for the Study of the Arts of the Present. His work has been published in numerous journals including *American Literature*, *GLQ*, *Feminist Studies*, *Callaloo*, and *ASAP/Journal*. With Darieck Scott, he is coeditor of an award-winning special issue of *American Literature* titled "Queer About Comics" (2018); he is also a coeditor, with Deborah E. Whaley and Shelley Streeby, of the *Keywords for Comics Studies* volume. His new book *Queer Forms* explores the influence that movements for women's and gay liberation had on American popular culture in the 1970s and after. *Queer Forms* will be published by NYU Press.

MARGARET GALVAN is assistant professor of visual rhetoric in the Department of English at the University of Florida. She is at work on a book, *In Visible Archives of the 1980s: Feminist Politics & Queer Platforms*, under contract with the University of Minnesota Press, which examines how publishing practices and archives have shaped understandings of the visual within feminist and queer activism. Her published work, which analyzes comics in social movements, can be found in journals like *American Literature*, *Archive Journal*,

Australian Feminist Studies, iNKS, Journal of Lesbian Studies, and *WSQ: Women's Studies Quarterly.* See margaretgalvan.org for more information.

JUSTIN HALL is the creator (or cocreator) of *True Travel Tales, Hard to Swallow, Glamazonia,* and *Theater of Terror: Revenge of the Queers.* He has work in such publications as the *Houghton Mifflin Best American Comics, Best Erotic Comics,* and the *SF Weekly* and edited the Eisner-nominated and Lambda Literary Award-winning *No Straight Lines: Four Decades of Queer Comics,* which he is now producing as a documentary film. He is a Fulbright Scholar, an associate professor of Comics at the California College of the Arts, a curator of multiple museum shows of LGBTQ+ comics, and the co-organizer of the Queers & Comics conference. www.justinhallawesomecomics.com.

ALISON HALSALL is associate professor in the Department of Humanities at York University, Toronto, Canada. She holds a PhD in English literature, with specialties in Victorian and Modernisms. She is at work on a book that examines world "crisis comics" for young readers and the many circuitous routes that graphic literature for young people takes in and out of discourses of nation and belonging, moving with and oftentimes against currents of power. She has published articles about *The Graveyard Book,* Nam Le's "The Boat," *Penny Dreadful, South Park,* and neo-Victorianism in contemporary graphic novels.

LARA HEDBERG is a late-stage doctoral candidate who teaches in Children's Literature and Media and Communication at Deakin University. Her research focuses on queer girls in children's literature and media cultures, alongside queer fan practices and spaces. She has published on queer young adult novels and coauthored papers on LGBTQ+ picture books and bullying in young adult literature.

SUSANNE HOCHREITER studied German studies as well as philosophy, psychology, and pedagogics at the University of Vienna and at the FU Berlin. In 2003, she received her PhD with a thesis on gender and space in Franz Kafka's novel fragments. She has been working as an assistant professor at the German department, University of Vienna since 1999. She was a visiting lecturer in Berne (Switzerland) in 2002, a visiting professor at the Wake Forest University in Winston-Salem (NC) in 2006–2007, and the Max Kade Distinguished Visiting Professor at the University of Illinois at Urbana-Champaign in 2015. From 2001 to 2016, she led a research project, "Discursive Intersections in Literature on Hermaphroditism," which was supported by the Austrian Science Fund (FWF). Her research interests include modern German and Austrian literature, comics and graphic novels, drama and performance, focusing on gender and queer studies. As equal opportunity officer she is involved in the gender equality and anti-discrimination activities at the University of Vienna.

SHEENA C. HOWARD is an award-winning author, filmmaker, and scholar. In 2014, Sheena became the first Black woman to win an Eisner Award for her first book, *Black Comics: Politics of Race and Representation* (2013). The Eisner Awards are considered the "Oscars of Comics." She is also author of several critically acclaimed books and comics books. In 2017, she published the *Encyclopedia of Black Comics*, which is the first book of its kind, profiling over 100 Black people in the comics industry. The *Encyclopedia of Black Comics* was named the 2018 American Library Association's Outstanding Reference Source. She has appeared on NPR (National Public Radio), ABC, BBC, PBS as well as other networks and documentaries as an expert on popular culture, politics, and social justice. Sheena is the subject of a 2018 Emmy-nominated episode of *State of the Arts*, which airs on NJTV and WHYY. Her website is www.sheenachoward.com.

REBECCA HUTTON is a children's and young adult literature scholar, specializing in young adult LGBTQ+ narratives. She has published articles in academic journals including *Papers: Explorations into Children's Literature* and the *Journal of Popular Culture*. She has coauthored chapters on female protagonists in film and television for young audiences (with Clare Bradford, in *The Middle Ages in Popular Culture: Medievalism and Genre*) and gender and sexuality in popular music and music videos (with Emma Whatman, in *The Routledge Companion to Media and Fairy-Tale Cultures*).

remus jackson is a genderqueer cartoonist pursuing a PhD in English at the University of Florida with a research focus on queer/trans embodiment in comics and zines, critical prison studies, and museum studies. They received their MA in English from the University of Florida. Their work exploring gender identity has appeared in the Ignatz-winning, all-trans comic anthology *We're Still Here* and *Rainbow Reflections: Body Image Comics for Queer Men*. Their self-published work includes the Prism Award-winning *See Me* (2019) and *Flux* (2017). They cohost the scholarship-driven comics podcast *Drawing a Dialogue* (2017–).

KEIKO MIYAJIMA holds a PhD from the Graduate Center, the City University of New York. She has taught Japanese, Japanese culture, film, and manga/anime at several universities including Adelphi University, Hofstra University, CUNY Queens College, and CUNY John Jay College. Among her publications are "I–Thou Relationships in Tourism: The Case of Cross-Cultural Interaction between Okinawan Locals and Japanese Tourists" (coauthored with Henning, Graham and Kawabata, Shinsuke, in *Tourism Culture & Communication*, vol. 11, 2011); "Spatializing the Self: Places of Experience in Henry James, William James, and Kitaro Nishida" (*Journal of the American Literature Society of Japan*, no. 40, Tokyo, Japan, 2004); and "Looking from the Other Side: Gaze, Gender, and *The Aspern Papers*" (*Strata* no. 16, Tokyo, Japan, 2002).

CHINMAY MURALI is assistant professor of English at Sanatana Dharma College (India). His research interests include literature and medicine, graphic narratives and visual culture, critical health humanities, and narrative medicine. His doctoral work concentrates on women's reproductive disorders and graphic medicine. His research articles have appeared in *Journal of Graphic Novels and Comics, Perspectives in Biology and Medicine, Journal of Medical Humanities, Women's Studies*, among others. He is currently working on a book, *Travails of Motherhood: Infertility Comics and Graphic Medicine*.

MARINA RAUCHENBACHER studied German studies and communication studies at the Universities of Salzburg and Vienna. She is affiliated with the University of Vienna and is a co-applicant and team member of the research project *Visualities of Gender in German-Language Comics*. In 2012, she completed her doctoral thesis on the reception of the German writer Karoline von Günderrode. She worked as a research assistant to the project *Kunst im Text* (*Art in Texts*) at the Universities of Salzburg and Vienna, as well as a university assistant at the department of German studies, University of Vienna. In 2014 and 2015, she was affiliated with the Beatrice Bain Research Group, University of California, Berkeley. Marina cofounded the *Austrian Association for the Research and Promotion of Comics* and is a board member of *aka—Arbeitskreis Kulturanalyse*. Her research and academic teaching include visual culture studies, comics, image theories, gender studies, and reception theory, as well as German-language literature of the twentieth and twenty-first century.

KATHARINA SERLES studied German studies, English studies, and art history at the University of Vienna, where she also worked as a research assistant for the projects *Art in Texts* and *"Art Quotations": Intermediality and Tradition* (both funded by the Austrian Science Fund) and as a university assistant at the department of German studies from 2009 to 2015. From 2016 to 2018, she was employed as an artistic/scientific assistant at the Art Academy Dresden/ Germany. Since 2019, she has worked as a researcher for the FWF-project, *Visualities of Gender in German-Language Comics*. Her main fields of research and teaching include comics, literature, and visual arts, as well as gender studies and image theories. She has cofounded the Austrian *Association for the Research* *and Promotion of Comics* and is a member of the *German Society for Comics Studies* (ComFor). For more information, see http://www.katharinaserles.com.

SATHYARAJ VENKATESAN is associate professor of English in the Department of Humanities and Social Sciences at the National Institute of Technology, Tiruchirappalli (India). He is author of five books and over eighty-five research publications that span African American literature, health humanities, graphic medicine, film studies, and other literary and culture studies disciplines. He is most recently coauthor of *Gender, Eating Disorders and Graphic Medicine*. He is currently completing a book project entitled *India Retold*.

JONATHAN WARREN is associate professor in and former chair of the English Department at York University, Toronto, Canada. He received his PhD in English Literature from the University of Toronto with special focus on American literature, critical theory, and modernism. Nearly twenty years ago, he launched York's wildly successful undergraduate courses on comics and cartoons, regularly filling lecture halls to capacity ever since. He has since added a graduate seminar on long-form comics and the graphic novel to a teaching roster that also includes an advanced graduate course on the theories and practices of camp. An expert in the work of Henry James, among his other publications he counts two Norton Critical Editions of James's *The Turn of the Screw*.

LIN YOUNG completed her PhD at Queen's University in Kingston, Ontario. Her dissertation, "Spectral Objecthood: Biology, Thingness, and the Ghostly Body in Eighteenth- and Nineteenth-Century Popular Fiction," situates the ghost story within evolving cultures of nineteenth-century technology, industrial production, and visual media. It examines the influence of urban industrialization and commodity cultures of the city on literary representations of ghostly bodies, spirit worlds, and experiences of objecthood. In addition to her dissertation being distinguished as Queen's "Outstanding Humanities Thesis" for 2020, her work has been awarded the 2018 Mary Eliza Root Prize from the Victorian Popular Fiction Association. Her secondary area is in the comics field, particularly the work of Queer women artists, in the new digital landscape of serialized webcomics.

INDEX

Page numbers in **bold** refer to figures.